DISCOURSES AND REPRESENTATIONS OF FRIENDSHIP IN EARLY MODERN EUROPE, 1500–1700

Réunion des Musées Nationaux/Art Resource, NY. Raphael (Raffaello Sanzio) (1483–1520), *Self-Portrait with a Friend* (1518–19). Oil on canvas, 99 × 83 cm. Photo: J. G. Berizzi. Location: Louvre, Paris, France.

Discourses and Representations of Friendship in Early Modern Europe, 1500–1700

Edited by

DANIEL T. LOCHMAN
Texas State University – San Marcos, USA

MARITERE LÓPEZ
California State University at Fresno, USA

LORNA HUTSON
University of St Andrews, UK

ASHGATE

Published by
Ashgate Publishing Limited
Wey Court East
Union Road
Farnham
Surrey, GU9 7PT
England

Ashgate Publishing Company
Suite 420
101 Cherry Street
Burlington
VT 05401-4405
USA

www.ashgate.com

British Library Cataloguing in Publication Data
Discourses and Representations of Friendship in Early Modern Europe, 1500–1700.
   1.Friendship – Europe – History. 2. Friendship in literature. 3. European literature
   – Renaissance, 1450–1600 – History and criticism. 4. European literature –
   17th century – History and criticism.
   I. Lochman, Daniel T. II. Lopez, Maritere. III. Hutson, Lorna.
   302.3'4'094'09031–dc22

Library of Congress Cataloging-in-Publication Data
Discourses and representations of friendship in early modern Europe, 1500-1700 /
   [edited by] Daniel T. Lochman, Maritere Lspez and Lorna Hutson.
      p.   cm.
   Includes index.
   1. European literature – Renaissance, 1450–1600 – History and criticism. 2. European
   literature – 17th century – History and criticism. 3. Friendship in literature.
   I. Lochman, Daniel T. II. Lspez, Maritere. III. Hutson, Lorna.
   PN721.D57 2010
   809'.93353–dc22   2010031930

ISBN   9780754669036 (hbk)

Printed and bound in Great Britain by
TJ International Ltd, Padstow, Cornwall.

Contents

PART I: CONVENTIONAL DISCOURSES REIMAGINED

PART II: ALTERNATIVE DISCOURSES: FRIENDSHIP IN THE MARGINS

PART III: FRIENDSHIP IN ETHICS AND POLITICS

List of Illustrations

Notes on Contributors

Penelope Anderson is an assistant professor of English at Indiana University, Bloomington. She is publishing an essay on women's friendships (forthcoming) in *Literature Compass* and is completing a book about Civil War women writers' appropriations of the classical discourse of friendship as a means to address the problem of conflicting political obligations.

Sheila T. Cavanagh is a professor of English at Emory University. She specializes in pedagogy and early modern literature. She has authored books on Edmund Spenser and Lady Mary Wroth, and she is now editor of the *Spenser Review* and Director of the Emory Women Writers Project, a website devoted to early modern women's literature that is supported by the National Endowment for the Humanities.

Gregory Chaplin is an assistant professor of English at Bridgewater State College in Massachusetts. He edited *The Culture of Early Modern Friendship* (2005), a special issue of *Texas Studies in Literature and Language*. With John Rumrich, he is the editor of *Seventeenth-Century British Poetry: 1603–1660, A Norton Critical Edition*. He has published articles on Ben Jonson and John Milton in *ELH, Modern Philology*, and *PMLA*, and he is completing a study of Milton and Renaissance friendship.

Constance M. Furey is an associate professor of Religious Studies at Indiana University. She is the author of *Erasmus, Contarini, and the Religious Republic of Letters* (2006). Her articles about the religious valence of friendship, utopian ideals, and invective appear in *The Journal of Medieval and Early Modern Studies, Church History*, and *Harvard Theological Review*. She is completing a book-length study about intersubjectivity in Renaissance devotional poetry and theoretic work on utopian history and religious sexuality.

Donald Gilbert-Santamaría is an associate professor at the University of Washington. He is author of *Writers on the Market: Consuming Literature in Early Seventeenth-Century Spain* (2005), which examines the influence of the marketplace on the poetics of the novel and public theatre in early modern Spain. His articles appear in *Hispanic Review, Bulletin of Hispanic Studies, Modern Language Quarterly*, and *Hispanofila*. He is completing a manuscript that examines early modern friendship in Spain in relation to the emerging distinctions between public and private life.

Thomas Heilke is a professor of Political Science and Director of Global and International Studies at the University of Kansas. He has written on a variety of topics in political philosophy, including civic friendship, political theology, the political thought of Friedrich Nietzsche, Eric Voegelin, John Howard Yoder, and Thucydides, and Anabaptist political thought. He has authored or co-authored four books and edited or co-edited six others. His articles appear in *American Political Science Review*, *Political Theory*, *Polity*, *The Review of Politics*, and *Modern Theology*. He is working on conceptions of civic friendship in the Protestant Reformation, a comparison of the political thought of John Howard Yoder and Reinhold Niebuhr, and a book on Anabaptist political thought.

Lorna Hutson is Berry Professor of Literature at the University of St Andrews, Scotland. She is the author of *Thomas Nashe in Context* (1989), *The Usurer's Daughter: Male Friendship and Fiction of Women in Sixteenth-Century England* (1994), and of *The Invention of Suspicion: Law and Mimesis in Shakespeare and Renaissance Drama* (2007). She has edited or co-edited five works, and she has recently completed essays on Ben Jonson's drama and the poetry of Katherine Philips.

Allison Johnson is at the University of Miami, where she is completing a dissertation on representations of friendship in the works of Isabella Whitney, Aemilia Lanyer, Elizabeth Cary, and Katherine Philips.

Daniel T. Lochman is a professor of English at Texas State University–San Marcos. He has published articles on pedagogy and Tudor culture and literature, including John Colet and other Tudor humanists, Elizabethan romances, Shakespeare, and the works of Milton. His work appears in the *Journal of the History of Ideas*, *Renaissance and Reformation*, the *Sixteenth Century Journal*, and *Milton Studies*. He is completing an edition and translation of Colet's comments on Dionysius's *Ecclesiastical Hierarchy* and a study of empathy and passion in literary, rhetorical, theological, and medical contexts.

Maritere López is an associate professor of History at California State University, Fresno. Her work has focused on the lives and letters of sixteenth-century courtesans as they evince the appeal and limits of definitional categories available to early modern women, particularly at the intersection of patronage and friendship. She is presently working on several essays on representations of love and sex in Italian Enlightenment conduct manuals.

Christopher Marlow is a senior lecturer in English at the University of Lincoln. He is particularly interested in representations of gender, friendship, and community in early modern drama. His work appears in *Shakespeare Studies*, *Cahiers Élisabéthains*, *The Dalhousie Review*, and *Peer English*. He is currently completing a book entitled *Masculinity in English University Drama 1537–1642*.

Wendy Olmsted is a professor in the New Collegiate Division, the Humanities Division, and affiliated with the Department of Classics (PAMW) at the University of Chicago. She is the author of *The Imperfect Friend: Rhetoric and Emotion in Sidney, Milton and Their Contexts* (2008) and *Rhetoric: An Historical Introduction* (2006). She has co-edited two volumes, *Rhetorical Invention and Religious Inquiry* and *A Companion to Rhetoric*. She has published articles in *Modern Philology*, *Exemplaria*, *Spenser Studies*, and *New Literary History*. Her interests center on ancient and Renaissance literature, rhetoric, and social history; and her current project concerns ancient and Renaissance representations of "the other" or "the stranger" as understood in relation to hospitality and civil conversation.

Marc D. Schachter is the author of *Voluntary Servitude and the Erotics of Friendship: From Classical Antiquity to Early Modern France* (2008). Other recent publications include articles on La Boétie, Montaigne, Tasso, and, with Martin Eisner, Apuleius and Boccaccio. In the 2009–10 academic year, he was the Francesco De Dombrowski Fellow at Villa I Tatti, the Harvard University Center for Italian Renaissance Studies. For the 2010–11 academic year, he is an Andrew W. Mellon Fellow at the Folger Shakespeare Library.

Hannah Chapelle Wojciehowski is an associate professor at the University of Texas at Austin, and an affiliate of the University's Program in Comparative Literature. She is the author of *Old Masters, New Subjects: Early Modern and Poststructuralist Theories of Will* (1995) and *Globalization and Group Identity in the Renaissance* (forthcoming, Cambridge University Press) as well as essays on Francis Petrarch, Veronica Franco, Thomas More, William Shakespeare, Fernão Mendes Pinto, Galileo Galilei, and others. She is currently working on a performance-oriented edition of Shakespeare's *Cymbeline* (forthcoming 2011). Her current interests include the global sixteenth century, comparative colonialisms, early modern science, technology and culture, feminist and gender studies, and psychoanalytic and cognitive approaches to literary studies.

Preface

Our frontispiece, which reproduces the painting by Raphael conventionally titled *Self-Portrait with a Friend* (c. 1518–19), fits the essays gathered here in that the figures, both the young man pointing out of the frame of the painting and the standing man behind him, disrupt conventional symmetries of friendship at the same time that they draw upon them. The soft fluidity of the seated man's glance back to the standing figure and the tender relaxation of the latter's left hand upon the other's shoulder bespeak the friendship of two men. Yet the visual presentation shows friends who are not the same. Although their garments are similar in type and color, their posture, facial expression, and animation differ markedly.

The figures' differing positions and heights skew the line of sight between them and amplify the sense of asymmetry. One may follow the visual angle from the seated man's extended hand back to the standing companion, this line not quite parallel to the diagonal one extending from the painting's upper left corner through the subjects' eyes to the fluid cornea and sclera of the seated figure. The latter, together with the extended hand, is also a focus on a vertical axis that implies a third dimension extending from the background up to or adjacent to the position of the viewer. Unlike most early modern double portraits, wherein both subjects face the viewer, here only the standing image of Raphael does so, with the seated figure mediating between him and the unseen object of attention in the foreground. Although the subjects' gestures convey an intimacy, benevolence, and affection associated with friendship, the lack of visual symmetry heightens the difference between them and, literally, points to a surrounding context, thereby offering an implicit alternative to the closed loop of mutual regard that typified Greco-Roman ideas of true friendship.

The asymmetry of Raphael's double portrait contrasts with others, such as Pontormo's well-known *Portrait of Two Friends* (c. 1522), and extends even to the identities of the subjects in that the standing figure has long been confidently identified as Raphael whereas the identity of his more animated companion, like the painting's occasion and patron, remains uncertain. Scholars cite the work for its unprecedented boldness and active presentation in that it replaces the nearly still-life presentation of most portraits in the period with animated gesture, interaction, and sensual intimacy emphasized by the contrasts of stark black and white garments. Joanna Woods-Marsden places the painting alongside Raphael's innovative "proto-baroque" paintings, such as his *Transfiguration*, due to its "complexity, movement, and extreme contrasts" (130–31).[1] Like the subjects of the essays in this volume, then,

---

[1]   For other interpretations of this painting, often titled *Raphael and His Fencing Master* until the last couple decades, see Prisco 164, Jones and Penny 171, Oberhuber 202–3, and Fischel 119.

Raphael's painting challenged preconceptions of friendship, both proclaiming the mutuality of friendship and revising its traditional representation and expression.

This volume grows out of lively discussions of early modern refigurations of friendship that followed an interdisciplinary panel at the Atlanta Sixteenth Century Studies Conference in 2005. The panelists, three of whom contribute substantially expanded essays to this volume, discovered then the intersecting lines of their interdisciplinary applications of conventions about friendship, and this discovery energized conversation and encouraged new investigations. Like Raphael's painting, the early modern friendships examined for the panel at once retained the vocabulary of friendship and disrupted its conventions, the resulting tension both illuminating the distance between early modern ideals and lived experience and ultimately raising questions about the ways we understand ourselves in relation to others. This book, then, has grown from that initial conversation, and the editors hope that it may prompt others to join our discussion, one ongoing for more than a millennium.

Many have helped to bring this project to completion, and we wish to thank all who have done so. We are particularly grateful for the encouragement and support of leaders at our respective institutions, including Ann Marie Ellis, Dean of the College of Liberal Arts, and Michael Hennessy, Chair of the English department, both of Texas State University, San Marcos; Luz Gonzalez, Dean of Social Sciences, and Michelle DenBeste, Chair of the History department, both of California State University, Fresno.

Thanks to those who have offered advice at panels and informal conversations, including especially Clifford Ronan and William Johnson—both participants on the original 2005 panel—as well as many who have encouraged friendship studies, including Mary Beth Rose and Mariko Suzuki. Thanks also to Erika Gaffney, an anonymous external reader, and staff at Ashgate Publishing for their helpful, knowledgeable advice, as well as to Márta Fodor at Art Resources.

A book on friendship must acknowledge those who have been both good friends and helpful consultants. Thanks, therefore, to the wise and friendly Edgar Laird, who provided learned references to medieval views on friendship, to Susan Morrison for her willingness to share knowledge of theory and medieval friendship practices, and to friends and colleagues, including Catherine Campbell, Lori Clune, Charles T. Lipp, Paul and Robin Cohen, Nancy Grayson, Melissa Jordine, Marilynn Olson, Arnold Preussner, Teya Rosenberg, and Steve and Nancy Wilson. Thanks also to seminar students at Texas State University who helped identify types of early modern friendship and Melissa M. Morris of California State University at Fresno, who helped develop the index.. Finally, special thanks to all contributors to this volume, who have offered valuable advice and generous assistance at key moments throughout the process leading to publication.

Daniel T. Lochman, Maritere López, and Lorna Hutson

To Alice, Michael, Matthew, and Nicholas
&
To José C. López-Alberty and María M. Rodríguez

Introduction
The Emergence of Discourses: Early Modern Friendship

Daniel T. Lochman and Maritere López

This volume offers a series of interdisciplinary reinvestigations of the varied ways in which early modern Europeans imagined, discussed, and enacted friendship. Although early moderns inherited a rich tradition of friendship, shaped by the ancients and restyled by medieval Christians, the period between 1500 and 1700 saw a flurry of works in which contemporaries flouted many commonplaces while fully embracing others. Philosophical treatises, literary works, and accounts of lived friendships reveal a preoccupation with and yearning for the inherited ideals and the wish to manipulate and/or actualize the reciprocity presupposed in classical and medieval models. As contemporaries often acknowledged, the rub was to attain such reciprocity in the context of a highly stratified, changing world in which equality, sameness, and the closeness they could engender—the *sine qua non* of traditional friendship—were as a rule merely illusory. By focusing upon artifacts such as letters, treatises, fictions, poetry, and drama, the essays in this collection bring to the fore tensions between ancient and early modern friendship discourses, while acknowledging the dominant position of traditional ideals and their ongoing cognitive and affective influences.

Each of the thirteen studies in this collection investigates from a different perspective the nature of and the difficulties posed by the divergence between the theory and praxis of friendship, as well as the varied ways in which contemporaries attempted to resolve it. By examining various discursive, gestural, and literary representations, the contributors reveal both constructed ideals and concessions to the everyday, and demonstrate how particular early modern writers reshaped friendship to fit their own experiences, as a bond on which to build a variety of interpersonal relationships, including familial coteries, confessional communities, and even citizenries. Our essays reveal that contemporaries altered friendship in surprising ways, expanding it to include not only impassioned relationships between "others" traditionally not defined as friends, but also any number of relationships with specific political, economic, or social ends. In aggregate, the essays clarify the breaking points of conventional friendship discourses and outline the patterns of emerging ones. Moreover, they lay the groundwork for a taxonomy of the transformations of friendship discourse in Western Europe and its overlap with emergent views of the relationship of the self to individuals, classes, social institutions, and the state.

The collection is distinguished, first, by its broad range of disciplines. Including essays by scholars of British, French, and Spanish literature, as well as historians, a religionist, and a political scientist, this volume reflects the very complexity and multifaceted nature of early modern friendship. Individually, the essays each offer a case study analyzing specific contexts, events, and/or lived friendships. Each chapter thus elucidates in microcosmic fashion a facet of friendship as understood and enacted in the period. Moreover, each expands our understanding of the particular author, topic, or aspect of friendship discussed. Together, the essays do more: using methods specific to their respective discipline and in conversation with the methods and sources of the other contributors, the authors present innovative theoretical and methodological approaches with which to consider anew the nature of interpersonal relations in the early modern period.

Our aims are multiple. First, we endeavor to identify and examine the various types of friendship associations and networks that emerged in early modern Europe across social and/or national boundaries. Next, by uncovering the theories that framed conventional discourses of friendship and the ways in which early moderns received, understood, and reacted to such constructions, we hope to situate emergent relationships within a unique early modern ideological and psychological framework. Finally, we aim both to suggest new directions for theoretical and methodological advances in the analysis of early modern friendship, particularly, and to contribute to conversations concerning early modern culture and its study more broadly speaking. We are especially interested in expanding the investigation of friendship and culture by proposing questions such as the following: how was friendship configured in relationships shaped by gender, the family, marriage, and utilitarian reward? how did quotidian experience in urban and courtly settings affect traditional discourses of friendship and other interpersonal relationships? how were ideas of friendship expressed in social groups such as religious communities, coteries, courts and other political groups? how did interpersonal relationships writ large receive literary, intellectual, and/or performative expression? and how did understandings of friendship relate to emerging views of the body and its functions as well as to ideas about the self and others?

This introduction outlines the varied discourses that provoke these and other questions. It intends to provide a common point of departure both by reviewing the ancient and medieval traditions early moderns received and by examining recent theoretical and methodological approaches that emerged with the flourishing of scholarship on early modern friendship in the early 1990s. Necessarily, the overview is selective; nevertheless, we hope that it will offer an overarching frame within which to situate the specific discourses employed by the writers and communities this collection examines. This overview is followed by a preview of the groups of essays and their organization according to early moderns' adaptations or renovations of received friendship discourses.

The Language of Friendship: Ancient and Medieval Contexts for Early Modern Discourse

In *The Arts of Friendship: The Idealization of Friendship in Medieval and Early Renaissance Literature* (1994), Reginald Hyatte offers a learned historical and philosophical overview of friendship in Europe, from the pre-Socratics through the fifteenth century. Hyatte outlines the historical development of friendship in Greco-Roman philosophy and literature, medieval and early Renaissance religious writings, chivalric narratives, and collections of stories. He begins with early Greek writings, such as those ascribed to Heraclitus and Empedocles, who introduced the view that friendship originated as the principle of attraction, creating order from chaos by drawing like elements to like or, in the case of Euripides, attracting opposites—views that influenced poetry in praise of rivers, such as Ausonius's *Mosella* and early modern river poems by Edmund Spenser and Samuel Daniel (Hyatte 9, Pangle 18–19). Likewise, the Pythagoreans were said to have advanced an ideal of communal friendship and to have disregarded the boundaries of gender and class in friendship that Aristotle and later writers established in the context of the political and social order of the *polis* or republican or imperial Rome. Interestingly, the communal ideal reappeared among Christian communities under the Empire as well as later monastic communities and post-Reformation writers who espoused mutuality in marriage (Hyatte 8–9, Thom 92–102).

The ancient traditions of friendship that gained most influence, however, were a pastiche of commonplaces and rules of friendship taken originally from the ethical and moral philosophy of the Greeks and Romans. The works best known to medieval and early Renaissance writers were Plato's *Lysis*, *Symposium*, and *Phaedrus*, Aristotle's two works on ethics (the *Eudemian* and *Nichomachean*), and Cicero's *De amicitia* and *De officiis*. These latter two offered later readers a series of assertions and responses broadly in agreement with Platonic and Aristotelian ideas, yet with many specific nuances and areas of disagreement as well as important shifts in emphasis.

In the *Nichomachean Ethics*, Aristotle identifies the best form of friendship as virtuous and ethical; it is most excellent when the intellect exercises its natural authority to constrain desires and passions, virtuously moderating discordant impulses but not excluding passion altogether (Pangle 148–50). In ordering the soul, virtuous friendship contributes to the formation of a coherent, unified "self" whose stable existence may be traced in time (Hyatte 17, Stern-Gillet 25–8). Perfect friendships are enduring and self-sustaining, unlike lesser ones that have as their goals utilitarian ambitions or transient pleasures and that are apt to veer away from virtuous, rationally determined moderation and toward excess and the appetites associated with vice. Among all people, Aristotle explains, the exemplary form of friendship tempers disorderly excess, quarrelsomeness, and flattery.

Although an intellectual activity, "perfect" friendship and slightly diminished forms (the latter allowing for the improbability of attaining an absolute state) have an affective dimension in that, according to Hyatte, they embody the "mutual goodwill and feeling of love or esteem that unite people." Hyatte cites Diogenes Laertius as recounting that Pythagoras and Plato had asserted before Aristotle that true friends hold goods in common due to *philia*—a Greek word for friendly love or affectionateness that is distinct from *eros* (8–9). *Eros* signified "love," "desire," or "passion" as an intense, irresistible attraction capable of transgressing reason's control; it stands apart from *philia*, which conveys "solidarity" and "friendship," because it evokes conflicted pleasure and pain of the sort Anne Carson discovers in Sappho's word *glukupikron* (3–9). David Konstan distinguishes both *eros* and *philia* from *storge*—an affection more often signifying familial love, especially the mutual love of parents and children—and *agape*, the strong personal affection that Paul employed to describe the godly love expressed by the Trinity, Christ, and Christians. Konstan usefully comments that *eros* conveys a "transitivity" evident in derived forms such as *erastes* ("lover," a masculine agent noun) and *eromene* ("beloved," a feminine passive participle). The agency implicit in *eros* is alien to *philia*, which is *intransitive* and a "single, reciprocal term" that refers to all parties (12–13, 35). One can "do" the erotic or "receive" it, but one can only "have" *philia*, friendship.

Although Aristotelian friendship is often presented as being almost exclusively abstract, *The Rhetoric* reminds us that in some circumstances at least there is a link between friendship (*philein*) and *emotion*. In applying rhetoric to political ends, Aristotle defines a friend as one who wishes to do good to another for his sake and who inclines to achieving that good as much as possible: "those who think they *feel* thus towards each other think themselves friends" (*Nic. Eth.* trans. Rackham 2, 4, 1381a; added emphasis). Within families and in civil society, Aristotle often refers to relationships with words that convey emotionality such as cordiality and concord, but his language tends more to the intellectual than the affective when he considers the "ethically excellent," "perfect," or "true" friendship (*teleia philia*), which is an activity of nobility or *areté*. The latter's most important traits— important also for later traditions of friendship—include the following:

- Perfect friendship exists between men who are the same or very similar in virtue, one drawn to the other by the principle of like-to-like. Linked to rationality and stability, masculinity is essential to Aristotelian virtue, the latter defined as the "settled disposition of the mind determining the choice of actions and emotions, consisting essentially in the observance of the mean relative to us" (Hyatte 17; cf. *Nic. Eth.*, 2, 6, 1107a).
- Friendship overlaps with but is distinct from other virtuous behaviors such as cordiality, generosity, self-love, piety, beneficence, and magnanimity; it is averse to everything opposed to these, including excessive devotion to utility, pleasure, or fame. Friends act virtuously when they wish one another so much good that each helps the other maintain and improve in goodness. Perfect friends do what is good for the friend's sake and harbor no self-interest (Pangle 43–56; *Nic. Eth.* 8, 3, 1156b).
- In contrast to Socrates' identification of friendship in Plato's *Lysis* as rooted

in the deficiency of a good, self-sufficient man, Aristotle's exemplary friendship is a positive state ideally enacted by noble, virtuous, and self-sufficient men; those lacking this perfection may sustain a mutual, progressive improvement as they grow in self-awareness and virtuous self-sufficiency and as they receive pleasure from reciprocal acts performed with respect and affection (Pangle 20–36; Stern-Gillet 132).

- Exemplary friends share love, as the word *philia* indicates, but in Aristotle and generally in ancient Greek this love is distinct from *eros* and appetitive forms of love (Stern-Gillet 64–75). Rather than being loved or desiring an other, a friend values goodness above all, expresses *philia* through a reciprocating, virtuous cycle of beneficent actions, and achieves through them great happiness, which is giving pleasure to one like oneself. A true friend is the same as or nearly the same as the self, and his growth should mirror one's own improving virtue (*Nic. Eth.* 9, 8, 1168a–1168b; 9, 9, 1170b).

- *Pleasure* (which attracts the young) and *utility/advantage* (which attracts the mature and experienced) cannot be adequate motives for exemplary friendship (*Nic. Eth.* 9, 11–12, 1171b–1172a). However, the virtuous acts required of perfect or exemplary friends necessarily yield mutual pleasure and advantage as effects.

- Due to participants' need to perform beneficent acts, friendships thrive if they involve frequent contact, a shared locale, men with agreeable natures, and ideally just two individuals (*Nic. Eth.* 9, 10, 1170b–1171a).

- One must test the character and progress of a friend over a long time to determine whether he may be exemplary in stability and equality. A friend who cannot or does not progress, who acts without regard to virtue, or who alters in the performance of virtuous acts, must be cut off. Nevertheless, those who part are to treat one another cordially to honor their former relationship (Pangle 123–41; *Nic. Eth.* 9, 3, 1165b).

- For Aristotle, intellectual contemplation (*theôria*) is the chief means to human happiness (Hyatte 20–21; *Nic. Eth.* 10, 7–8, 1177a–1178a) and transcends the moral virtues. As a consequence, *philia*, though the highest of the moral or *practical* virtues, achieves a lesser pleasure that is related to the well-being of the city-state and its citizens rather than the most complete happiness: contemplative serenity. However, as Hyatte notes, beholding one's virtue in the other is one way, if a diminished one, to contemplate universals and achieve profound happiness (21; Pangle 197–200).

In both the *Eudemian* and *Nichomachean Ethics*, Aristotle links "civic friendship" (*politike philia*) to self-interest, yet he ambiguously places it between the morally unsound and sound and sometimes identifies it as an important means of achieving social concord. Due to their interests in the advantage of the individual and/or the state, civic friendships do not rise to the level of exemplary friendships, which ought to be free of self-interest (Stern-Gillet 147–54; *Eud. Eth.* 7, 9–10, 1241b–

1243b; *Nic. Eth*. 8, 9, 1160a). Just as imperfect individuals aid one another to grow in virtue, a morally sound political community seeks the good of fellow citizens by providing good laws that foster the virtue of justice (Stern-Gillet 154–7).

Cicero's treatises concerned with friendship, *De amicitia* (or *Laelius*) and *De officiis*, disseminated Aristotelian ideas through his discussion of *amicitia*, a word that etymologically recalls erotic love (*amor*) but is distinct from it (Fiore 61; *De amicitia* trans. Falconer XXVII.100, VIII.26). Hyatte observes that, despite appropriating much from Aristotle, Cicero altered theories of friendship in important ways. Unlike Aristotle, for instance, he emphasized Roman rather than Greek examples of friendship; he altered friendship's alliance to *aretê* by linking the potential for happiness achieved through rational judgment to a Roman idea of "virtue," one which implied action performed for the "preeminence and glory" of the Republic (Donald Earl, qtd by Hyatte 27) and which implied that a principle of "reciprocity of obligation" bound members of the imperial community as "friends" in a politicized sense (Fiore 72–3). In so doing, Cicero replaced exploration of the ethical and political dimensions of friendship—these taken as givens—with a legal and social framework built up from *amicitia*'s "laws" and "contractual duties" that include fulfilling a friend's needs without request, appealing to a wavering friend's honor, and defending a friend's reputation and honor to the point of sharing disgrace (Hyatte 27).

Cicero models ideal *amicitia* through the voices of Laelius Sapiens, who seems to speak for him, and Scipio Africanus the Younger, who, recently deceased at the time of composition, was admired as an iconic patrician representing Roman intellectual, military, and political virtue. The dialogue features Ciceronian vocabulary centered on the lifelong "unanimity" or "accord" (*consensio*) that joins friends in benevolence and love as *caritas* (Pangle 106). Yet the dialogue shows that *vera amicitia* is not just a relationship between two men but a condition that involves domestic affection, social concord governed by noble lineage, the reciprocity of physical elements such as air and fire, and cosmic harmony. Against this principle Cicero sets the Roman politicians of the declining Republic, who were often moved by a concern for power and wealth that is antithetical to social concord and civic friendship (*De amicitia* XVII.64). Good friends should strive for the *summum bonum* of "perfect mutual benevolence" as the "necessary ingredient" that only incidentally accrues pleasure and advantage (Hyatte 27).

At the same time that Cicero contrasts utilitarian, pragmatic friendships with the principles of cosmic, social, and domestic harmony, he applies those ideals of concord to specific, practical cases. If over time *sworn* friends grow unequal in virtue, he points out, the superior must bear with the weaker because their commitment, being sworn, is "irrevocable." If not sworn, however, the friendship must be broken, although the split should occur "slowly and naturally" to preserve a "semblance of amity" and preclude open enmity (Hyatte 31). On the model of Laelius and Scipio, true friendship should survive death and embrace future generations. Shared accommodations, common meals, companionship in battle and travel, agreement in public affairs, and a common thirst for knowledge all advance the virtue (32). For Cicero, true friendship is not limited to the philosopher or sage but is available to military and political men of good will acting in civil society, like Laelius and Scipio. However, in a pragmatic work, *Commentariolum Petitionis*, Cicero admits that a "calculating use of [civic] friendship" may be useful "as a prop for political ambitions" and allows some value even to utilitarian political friendships since partisan supporters are necessary to advance a good candidate to office (Fiore 69–73).

Cicero's views inspired reaction and debate. Seneca generally supported Cicero's ideal of friendship's universality by emphasizing (contra Plato and Aristotle) that even the perfectly self-sufficient man needs and desires friends, and he observed that the impulse to sociability is natural, however virtuous one may be (*Epistulae morales* IX). In the *Moralia*'s "How To Tell a Flatterer from a Friend" and "On Having Many Friendships," Plutarch used the common discourse of friendship to affirm the equality, duties, and benefits of friends. Yet Plutarch specifically cautions against false friends and flatterers who employ the language of friendship to conceal utilitarian "patron–client" interests. Edward N. O'Neil observes that the split Plutarch implies between the discourse of ideal friendship and its practice becomes visible in the Roman Empire's address of client states as *amicus* and *amicita*, language that helped to sustain an illusion of friendly equality that pacified enemies and advanced Rome's domestic, commercial, and political interests (108–10).

Other traditions of friendship derived from ancient narratives rather than ethical and political discourse. The pairs Theseus and Peirithoüs, Achilles and Patroclus, Damon and Pythias, and Orestes and Pylades became commonplace emblems of friendship in ancient texts, and their inclusion in widely disseminated compilations such as Valerius Maximus's *Factorum et dictorum memorabilium libri novem* (c. 31 CE) insured their exemplary status among medieval and early modern writers. Hyatte writes that the "one ethical feature" uniting these disparate narratives was the absolute fidelity of friends willing to die for the sake of the other (34), a loyalty whose "spectacular self-confirmation" produced late medieval spin-offs in Boccaccio's tale of Titus and Gisippus, Chaucer's Palemon and Arcite, the French Ami and Amile, and other pairs of friends in chivalric romance (35). Hyatte notes that Arthurian romance merged conventions from *amor courtois* with those of *amicitia*, the *Prose Lancelot* (c. 1220) presenting the masculine friendship of Lancelot and Galehout as equal or superior to the "fatal love-sickness" of Lancelot and Guinevere. Friendship offers a positive model of "adoration, self-sacrifice, humility, the confusion of extreme joy and sorrow" that contrasts with the destructive consequences of courtly love (90). In the early modern period, humanist copyists and translators, though often spurning the medieval romance, supplemented compendia like Valerius's with vernacular translations of works such as Plutarch's *Lives of the Noble Grecians and Romans* that offered new narrative models of friendship.

Similarly, humanists revived ancient Greek romances, narratives combining the authority of late antiquity with the allure of alternatively gendered friendships.

Focusing upon Heliodorus's *Aethiopica*, Steve Mentz explains that this work appealed to Protestant writers of romance in Elizabethan England because "the redemptive ending emerges neither from the heroes' swordarms (as it would in chivalric romance) nor from their cleverness (as in a novella), but from Providential (and authorial) control" (43). In conceiving a romance plot as providentially ordered, Greek romances, like those translated in the sixteenth century such as *Clitophon and Leucippe, Daphnis and Chloe,* and Heliodorus's *Aethiopica,* not only narrativized conventional same-sex pairs of friends but also mixed-sex friends who sometimes combined conventional *philia* with *eros,* with or without the tacit approval of the gods (Konstan 14–59). Focusing upon Chariton's *Chaereas and Callirhoe,* Ronald F. Hock concludes that the title characters, a husband and wife, exemplify "the highest form of friendship," even if they represent an "equality of education and experience" that Aristotle would have found "inconceivable" (162). Together with standard motifs of shipwrecks, pirates, and confused identity, complex friendships that cut across gender and class divisions and are sometimes sexualized contributed to the appeal of these writings, together with influential early modern romances such as Ludovico Ariosto's *Orlando Furioso* (1532).

Other lines of early modern friendship discourse derive from the attempted synthesis of classical ethics with Christian theology and practice. Medieval and early modern religious writers mingled the traditions through scriptural authority, such as New Testament references to the "friend" (*philos* in Greek; *amicus* in the Vulgate), which signifies individuals like Lazarus (Jn 11:11) as members within the Christian community (for example, Acts 19:31, Jn 15:13–15) or the faithful as friends of God (for example, Jas 2:23). Alan C. Mitchell argues that the Gospel of Luke borrows principles such as reciprocity, equality of friends in virtue, and community of goods from Greco-Roman traditions; suppresses others, such as exclusivity in social class and sex; and replaces friendship's connections to the state and classical deities with emphases upon religious community and the Christian deity (225–62). Hyatte traces the development of a Christian ideal of friendship within the Christian community from Augustine's *City of God* through monastic communities such as John Cassian's (c. 365–435) (45, 58–9). Medieval theologians such as Anselm and Aquinas accepted friendship as consistent with the injunction to love one's neighbor as oneself; but, in doing so, they exposed implicit tensions between the ancient and Christian views, such as the disjunction between the classical emphasis upon self-love in friendship and the Gospels' injunction to love God above all (*Summa theol.* II, II. Q 23. 1, Pakaluk 171–3). Moreover, in violation of the Greco-Roman emphasis upon mutual unity, identity, and *consensio,* Christians are to love all—enemies as well as friends—with fraternal charity, and they are to achieve the ideal of perfected friendship in heavenly rather than civil society.

Early Christian writers explored the friendship of the individual and God in the expressions *amicus Dei* and *amicitia Dei,* but it was after Robert Grosseteste's Latin translation of the *Nichomachean Ethics* (c. 1250) and the rise of the universities that the theological discourse of Greco-Roman friendship became extensive, with emphasis placed upon both the horizontal dimension of friendship—the community of Christians or humanity in general—and the verticality implicit in *amicitia Dei*. Hyatte refers to the horizontal as "a preferential affection that joins two or a few Christian friends through the medium of God's love" (61). The vertical is most fully articulated in the *Amicitia spiritualis* (1147–67) of Aelred of Rievaulx, a work that justifies the intimate and personal love of a Christian friend as an instance of Christ's refracted love. This spiritual friendship between Christians may evolve progressively through stages of "selection, probation, admission, and near perfection," although absolute perfection is reserved for the afterlife (62–6). Aelred's work and others provided models for a discourse of friendship that could accommodate some elements of personal affection to a Christian point of view.

These and still other friendship traditions extend from the pre-Socratics to the early moderns. They offered early modern writers a rich and varied texture of words, concepts, networks, gestures, and performative acts that could be appropriated, modified, or rejected.

Recent Innovations and New Discourses of Early Modern Friendship

Modern scholarship on the friendship traditions dates at least from Laurens J. Mills's *One Soul in Bodies Twain: Friendship in Tudor Literature and Stuart Drama* (1937), a work that usefully identifies and gathers literary references to the topic. However, theoretical interest in early modern friendship surged only in the 1990s with the publication of a number of studies that explored from varied approaches and emphases the types of friendship discourse available to early modern writers. Importantly, recent studies have highlighted the constructedness of both the ancient traditions and early modern reactions to them, and they have underlined contemporary readers' limitations in deciphering both. Together, they provide a series of sometimes overlapping contexts for the essays included in this collection.

Among modern studies, five stand out as most influential to early modern friendship studies. The first, Ullrich Langer's *Perfect Friendship: Studies in Literature and Moral Philosophy from Bocaccio to Corneille* (1994) is distinctive in emphasizing the study of literary texts as the best means to comprehend the theory and practice of friendship among the Continental early modern writers he examines. This is so, he argues, since the intellectualized constructs of the Greeks and Romans, Christian theology, and early modern courtesy books all limit or disregard the practice of friendship, together with practical ethics and morality. Philosophical and theological treatises that work deductively from universals tend to produce elaborate structures that are removed from experience, whereas, according to Langer, early modern literature in its particularity becomes "more and more the ground for imaginative experimentation, for experimentation with the multiple codes and values of an expanding civilization" (28). This experimental quality differentiates early modern constructs of friendship both from the ancient tradition and from the medieval tradition of exemplary pairs of friends. Langer suggests that, despite the tendency of early modern treatises to define the utility of literature through a medieval emphasis upon exemplarity—reading about virtuous people inclines one to act virtuously—early modern literature is generally more concerned with the "trying-out of hypotheses, of situations." The impulse to write and to read depends upon a "pleasure and usefulness" that combine the affective and cognitive and make moral philosophy seem relevant to experience (28–9). Langer focuses on works that situate fictive friends in narratives whose temporality erodes the timelessness and stability of Greco-Roman exemplary friendship, and he emphasizes changes that challenged the ancient models. Medieval philosophy usually spoke of friendship in relation to Christian charity rather than Cicero's *amicitia*, and fictional representations such as Rabelais's Pantagruel and Panurge represented friends as individuated and divided. Langer similarly emphasizes Montaigne's ways of undermining friendship conventions. At one place, Montaigne writes that he wishes to abandon his essay on friendship, a product of language that inevitably masks the "inexplicability of true friendship." Elsewhere, Langer observes, Montaigne identifies the "motivation and explanation" of true friendship as a pragmatic "economic interest" alien to Aristotle: the beneficent act of a friend is reduced to interest paid to reciprocate prior actions (174). Langer calls Montaigne's critique "sublime" in that it reveals the limits of conventional friendship discourse, and he pairs Montaigne's approach with fictions that represent friends who, though "perfect" in fidelity, do not employ the discourse and gestures of friendship or who are "imperfect" in that they use conventions of friendship to conceal utilitarian ends (175–244). For Langer, literary representations offer a richer sense of friendship than does moral philosophy. Even though they present little or no theory of friendship and often fail to exemplify it, they are more "useful" to the cultural historian due to their narrativized applications (246).

Langer's book reviews early modern topoi that deviate from—and sometimes contradict—traditional friendship discourses. It builds a theory that authorizes literary representations outside of conventional discourse and that attributes their authority to playful experimentation rather than heavy-handed exemplarity. In this way, Langer shares with writers such as Lorna Hutson and Laurie Shannon an awareness of the constructedness of friendship's language and gestures, an artificiality that may be examined in historical and biographical narratives, moral treatises, and familiar letters as well as literary texts. Precisely this expanded awareness, together with its varied discourses, provides the motive for the essays that follow this introduction, and collectively they provide for the discernment of types of discourses seen from various perspectives—for example, the disciplinary, concerned with perpetuating received friendship conventions; the generic, dealing with forms of expression of friendship in various media; and the resistant, concerned with confronting conventions more or less openly, displacing them, and replacing them with new or adapted discourses.

Contemporary readings of early modern friendship receive exceptionally strong impetus from Hutson's *The Usurer's Daughter: Male Friendship and Fictions of*

Women in Sixteenth-Century England, also published in 1994. Hutson examines friendship in relation to early modern constructions of gender, particularly those in drama and literary texts, and she focuses on practices of friendship that follow the cultural transformations that result from printing and humanist education. The book offers a radically different approach to friendship by focusing on quotidian discourse seen from the vantage of cultural anthropology. Hutson pays little attention directly to traditional friendship discourse, but she critiques it through her analysis of pragmatic interests that belie the rhetoric of early modern humanists. She argues that the latter appropriated the discourse of *vera amicitia* for pragmatic ends that precluded the essentialized, unified identity—the "meeting of minds"— that tradition had ennobled.

Like Langer, Hutson argues that early modern friendship shifted away from the inherited "code," but she bases her argument on emergent social and economic structures rather than literary texts. She emphasizes that the "faithfulness" of a friend in the medieval, feudal social arrangement received its warrant by the performance of "acts of hospitality and the circulation of gifts through the family and its allies." Among humanists, however, expressions of friendship often demonstrated the "instrumental and affective relationship" of patronage, and they were validated through "emotionally persuasive communication, or the exchange of persuasive texts" rather than hospitality or gifts (2–3). Humanists' study of rhetoric and the ability to fashion the appearance of friendship and intimacy through the acts of writing and reading created illusions of "altruistic, non-instrumental friendship" while secretly advancing agendas aimed at personal advancement.

The older, codified friendship had centered on the achievement of "credit"— signifying belief and trust as well as material support—enacted through an exchange of gifts or tokens. This economy presumed a deferred obligation of reciprocation that cemented the friendship and ensured its continuance. Hutson illustrates the newer approach by means of a letter wherein Erasmus, writing to Peter Giles, attacks the idea that "material things" can symbolize friendship and appropriates the topos that excellent friends share thoughts intimately. Correspondingly, the physical separation of those called friends invites literary, not material, gifts—"persuasive" texts that ultimately accrue to the author's material advantage (4, 5). The humanist fashions illusions of friendship rhetorically for unmet patrons, and its textuality not only serves as a monument of the writer but also as a "productive" and "interest-bearing" gift that promises to make its recipient rhetorically fashionable (5–6).

Hutson calls attention to a troubling aspect of the new approach—its dislocation of the humanist's persuasive purposes and "interest" from the idea that a "good" friend acts without ulterior motives on behalf of the other. The rhetorical slant of humanist education, aimed at the separation of authorial purpose from the surface discourse, undermined conventional ideas of friendship as well as the older practice of exchanging material gifts.

Hutson introduces the issue of gender while investigating representations of early modern women as strong and therefore transgressive, a tendency seemingly contrary to the practice of humanism, which had permitted few choices even for educated women. She explains this phenomenon with reference to her preceding analysis of the emerging "economy" of friendship. Since medieval Europe viewed women as "signs of credit"—"the most precious of gifts" in a culture of gift exchange—they had strengthened bonds between male "friends" within networks such as the family and commerce. The increasing prominence of women in literature, specifically sixteenth-century English fiction and drama, coincides with the increasing instability of medieval gift-exchange. Literary voices of assertive women signal the collapse of the feudal model and the vulnerability of the emerging humanist counterpart to feigned professions of credit. After humanist persuasion displaced the woman as the pre-eminent gift, husbands in literary texts began to seek new ways to assure the credit of friends. As one indirect consequence, the dramatized wife (or potential wife) could assume a strong voice, as evident in Shakespeare's Beatrice and Rosalind. Alternatively, because women were thought vulnerable to rhetorical persuasion, theatrical representations featured dangerous women like Lady Macbeth, given to alliances with unwarrantable men (13).

Hutson's inflection of early modern friendship situates it within a network of cultural, economic, and gendered interests outside the traditional fold of ethics, and it introduces important new emphases on the social implications of friends' ritualized exchanges of gifts, "credit" in its manifold senses, and re-evaluations of the unstated purposes and practical interests of those employing humanist rhetorical strategies in their dealings with others. A similar reorientation occurs in Laurie Shannon's *Sovereign Amity: Figures of Friendship in Shakespearean Contexts* (2002), a study that begins with emphasis upon the conventional unity of friends—each friend is "another self"—but goes on to examine early modern appropriations and rewritings of this self-identity in a social and cultural network that insists upon difference. Shannon first notes the "doctrinal status" early moderns attributed to the conventions in treatises on friendship: as an extreme example, Walter Dorke's *A Tipe of Friendship* reductively listed twenty laws by which to recognize the true friend. Such books presumed a Stoic reliance upon rational self-mastery or "self-rule," linked the individual's *vera amicitia* to political rule centered upon the "sovereign," and introduced a discourse of political "friendship" that expanded Stoic self-control to domination over others (7).

The traditional model of friendship, emphasizing the participants' social, psychic, economic, and political equality, leads to an impossible construct that Shannon calls "two sovereigns"—an ideal opposed to all theories of monarchy. As seen above, *amicitia* is allied to political consensus; for Shannon, Cicero's "consent" conveys an intimate, interior likeness and agreement between citizen friends that contrasts with the differences in class and station that are central to early modern versions of polity (7). The resulting tension between traditional friendship discourse and early modern governance was reinforced by Renaissance discourses that associated "sovereign" friends with heterosocial/sexual love and with "broader political questions and metaphors of rule" (9). However, the idea that a public sovereign might have a friend seemed impossible since the role of a "peerless" monarch prohibits consensuality or mutuality. The sovereign cannot move from a "public" and therefore non-intimate relationship to a "private" one without invalidating the idea of autonomous self-sufficiency inherent in sovereignty (11). As regards one's ability to practice *amicitia*, Shannon notes, the subject "has more power than the king" (10).

Shannon examines the conflicting interpersonal, political, and gendered vectors of "sovereign" friendship in English treatises and fictional works, with a focus on the drama of Elizabeth Cary, Marlowe, and Shakespeare. As she notes in her introduction, she draws on Jacques Derrida's *Politics of Friendship* (1994, English trans. 1997) when examining the reversibility and instability of the early modern "friend" or "enemy"—one word, according to Derrida, always implying the other in both personal and political relationships. In that work, Derrida argues that the logic of traditional friendship discourse as represented in Cicero and Montaigne leads inevitably from private to public: "Reason and virtue could never be private. They cannot enter into conflict with the public. These concepts of virtue and reason are brought to bear in advance on the space of the *res publica* ... All the couples of friends which serve as examples for Cicero and Montaigne are citizen couples" (184). Yet Derrida sees in the language of Montaigne a contrary impulse that drives friendship toward the "apolitical" and the secret—"placing the law of secrecy above the laws of the city" (184). He reminds us of the manifold implications of friendship discourse, including humanity's wish to preserve the possibility of interacting with an other despite God's lack of a friend, friendship's incommensurability in time, and its many implied oppositions: friendship implies absence and its opposite (hostility); perfection implies imperfection; overt masculinity implies oppression of the feminine; cognitive theory implies the performative; and the languages of fraternity, community, and politics all invoke their opposites. In short, binaries make visible the construction of friendship in its Greco-Roman origins even as Derrida himself expresses a reluctance to deny its existence and value to humanity as an expression of love (and hate).

In *The Friend* (2003), historian Alan Bray writes that in reading Derrida's book he discovered a search parallel to his own. Derrida raises questions that seek to transcend "the ethical problems raised by friendship in a diverse world" (8)—problems that derive from the traditional discourse itself as well as its reformulation in the Enlightenment, when Immanuel Kant grounded the morality of friendship in an "undifferentiated moral benevolence" (8). Bray describes Kant's homeostatic morality as alien both to postmodern doubt and to historical *representations* of the evidence of friendship that are invisible to conventional methods of historiography. Rather than inferring the nature of friendship from material evidence such as legal rolls and census documents, Bray turns to *interpretable* forms of evidence—the design of tombs, sacramental and social rituals, statements in private correspondence, and vows of sworn brotherhood—as the bases for historical conclusions. From such evidence, he concludes that in the "traditional cultures" of the late medieval and early modern periods "friendship was ultimately inalienable from the particular loyalties in which it was begun," a conclusion that places contingency rather than theory at the forefront (8). Demurring from the ideology that shaped his previous book, *Homosexuality in Renaissance England* (1982 1996), Bray assembles evidence that illustrates specific "cultural practices" selected from many centuries rather than a theory, and from these he derives the limited conclusion that "the ethics of friendship operated persuasively only in a larger frame of reference that lay *outside* the good of the individuals for whom the friendship was made." Our comprehension of that frame of reference draws upon discrete representations of friendship framed by ritual and social constructs ranging over many centuries (6), and these shift our view to purposes other than those of the people named "friends." In this way, Bray introduces the idea of an unframed friendship that is alien to the Greco-Roman ethical tradition, which had identified the source of the individual's happiness and tranquility of soul in the exercise of virtue (as distinct from material goods or mere pleasure) *within* the self, not outside of it. Secondary benefits such as political power and wealth, as well as the reinforcement of the state or one's culture, were linked to friendship over time through the collaboration of men who espoused virtue and acted virtuously, with the happiness of virtue supplying a motive for friendship.

Bray recognized that his approach, centered upon "readings" of sculptured tombs, stained-glass windows, letters, and some documents, would be controversial, cutting against the grain of accepted practices of the selection and use of evidence. But his book has received critical comment also from some scholars who focus on early modern female friendship and lesbianism. While praising Bray's refusal to reconfirm absolute categories of gender and sexuality that moderns tend to read back into early modern texts and cultural practices, Valerie Traub faults his approach for its "strategic ambiguity" (27), the focus on practices and texts leaving conclusions too often unstated, sexual implications of male friendships possible but unargued, and female friendship largely though not entirely forgotten. Although Traub points to these interpretive and methodological defects, she also recognizes that Bray's book highlights a weakness of theoretically inflected studies of friendship that reduce the experience to a construct, to analysis of performative gestures or artifacts drained of feeling and a yearning for companionship.

Traub's essay appears in Palgrave's recently published collection, *Love, Friendship and Faith in Europe, 1300–1800*, ed. Laura Gowing, Michael Hunter, and Miri Rubin (2005), a collection of essays that, in focusing on Bray's work, is slanted toward historical approaches. As its title indicates, it has broad thematic and chronological interests beyond early modern friendship. This collection followed closely upon a 2005 special issue of *Texas Studies in Language and Literature*, edited by Gregory Chaplin, that featured essays on Petrarch and Montaigne as well as Dutch, Spanish, and English culture and literature. Another recent collection, *L'amitié*, edited by Jean-Christophe Merle and Bernard M. Schumacher (2005), offers a range of essays centered on philosophical identification of the self and its complication in theories of friendship, though only Ullrich Langer's essay focuses on the early modern period. Still more recently, Vanessa Smith and Richard Yeo have co-edited a 2009 special issue of *Parergon* on friendship in early modern philosophy and science, with essays on John Locke, Margaret Cavendish, Robert Southwell, Vicenzio Vivani, Mary Astell, and Elizabeth Montague that explore the "rhetoric of intimacy within scholarly networks," the "gendered nature of sociability," and friendship as a "conduit of cultural exchange" (1).

Recognition of the constructedness of friendship evident in traditional discourses has led also to increasing interest in early modern definitions and redefinitions of the self and human relationships in literary studies, contributing to a sense that, while recovering the language and experience of friendship among the ancients, early moderns unleashed intercultural tensions that led to social, political, sexual, and religious reassessments of humanity and human nature emerging clearly only in the modern period. Three recent monographs study the intersection in early modern English literary texts of friendship with language, performative acts, and cultural institutions. Thomas H. Luxon's *Single Imperfection: Milton, Marriage and Friendship* (2005) argues that Milton's works reveal an ongoing engagement with the humanist absorption of classical ideals of homosocial friendship to Protestant rationalizations for the institution of marriage, with the "competition" between the two "codes" leading to Milton's often unsatisfying "supersession of friendship by marriage" (7–21). Tom MacFaul's *Male Friendship in Shakespeare and His Contemporaries* (2007) looks to the ways Shakespeare and others altered ideals of friendship discourse to suit the pragmatic relationship realized in everyday life, drama, and other literary forms, and he argues that early moderns such as Shakespeare replaced the problematic idea of absolute equality, shown to be disjunct from the utilitarian interests of practical experience, with one of symbiosis rooted in sympathy and allowance for individual difference (13–29). Likewise, Wendy Olmsted's *The Imperfect Friend: Emotion and Rhetoric in Sidney, Milton and Their Contexts* (2008) explores the consequences of difference in friendship but does so by arguing that Sidney and Milton represent friends' persuasive rhetorical strategies in ways that evaluate and redefine "cultural norms" and ultimately complicate conventional binaries such as reason and emotion, men and women, solitude and companionship (16–19).

The present collection shares with these recent publications the intention of studying personal relationships in a variety of religious, sexual, and class settings, and it likewise intends to spark examination of friendship. However, it is unique in focusing on the diversity of specific cases of early modern friendship and in examining the varied applications of traditional discourses from so broad a range of disciplines and methodologies.

The Collection

The essays in this collection consider anew the manifold ways in which early modern Europeans envisioned, theorized about, and discussed friendship. Focusing primarily on early moderns' simultaneous adoption and substantial revision of classical and medieval discourses of the subject, the essays are organized according to three main types of challenge to those inherited traditions. Those collected in Part I investigate early modern examinations of and challenges to conventional friendship dicta, particularly ancient and medieval concepts of *amicitia* as viable only between pairs of virtuous and rational individuals united by their similarity. In Part II, the authors examine cases in which early moderns questioned *amicitia perfecta*'s exclusivity, principally in terms of gender and social hierarchy, and developed alternative definitions of friendship to fit their lived experience. Finally, in Part III, the essays explore instances wherein early moderns considered the question of friendship's utility and its viability as a theoretical basis and/or practical model for the polity.

Part I: Conventional Discourses Reimagined

The essays in this section each investigate one of three interconnected preoccupations characteristic of early modern reimaginings of classical and medieval theories of friendship. The first is the elucidation of who could—and who could not—in fact be a friend. In this section, the question is focused particularly on the viability of friendship between husband and wife, a possibility categorically denied by ancient and medieval theorists alike based on the hierarchical subordination of wife to husband. Crucially, early modern answers to this query were varied, often conflicting not only with ancient dicta but also with other contemporaneous explorations of the subject, a divergence which illustrates the complexity of both the topic and the intellectual context which engendered the discourse. A second key preoccupation constitutive of the early modern discourse of friendship is the feasibility of *vera amicitia* between more than two friends. At the core of this question is the loyalty requisite between friends, an exclusive fidelity made impossible, according to the ancients, by the conflicting allegiances that result when a third individual— another friend or a wife, for example—is introduced to the relationship. Inevitably, as early modern theorists highlighted, such conflicts led not only to heightened emotional tension but also to the almost compulsory selection of one relationship over the other. The third interrelated concern involves the role of the passions, particularly love, in the constitution—or obliteration—of friendship. While both the classical and medieval discourses of friendship represent *eros* as leading to the end of friendship, through the rivalry which results from the friends' love for the same woman, early modern thinkers reconsidered the potential of the passions to unite rather than separate, thus offering radically new conceptions of the nature and development of friendship to counter traditional ones.

   As Constance M. Furey illustrates in Chapter 1, early modern discourses of friendship attempted not only to delineate the nature of friendship but also to outline the characteristics which defined the friend, among which, in accordance with classical prescriptions, the "same-selfness" of the friends prevailed as the *sine qua non* of true *amicitia*. The language of "oneness," however, was not exclusive to discourses of friendship, raising the question of whether individuals sharing similitude, regardless of other constraints, can be—or necessarily are—

friends. This conundrum particularly pervaded humanist considerations of the possibility of friendship between husband and wife, since the Christian discourse of sacramental marriage also highlighted the unity of the pair based on their becoming "one." However, while friendship and marriage were thus closely linked in contemporaries' imaginations, nevertheless they were simultaneously differentiated, in that marriage prescribed a hierarchical relationship contrary to classical definitions of *amicitia perfecta*. The sameness requisite of friends in classical sources was clearly negated by the wife's subjugation in marriage, a difference that, at least in theory, should have led early moderns to echo the ancients in elevating friendship over marriage.

Instead, as Furey contends, humanists such as Juan Luis Vives and Erasmus defined marriage not as inferior to but as a superlative form of friendship, a relationship closer than that between mere friends, since husband and wife share, through sacramental union in Christ, not only one soul, as do friends, but also one body. The unity made possible by sacramental marriage, however, did not equalize the relationship between husband and wife, since the latter was still subjugated to the former's rule. Rather than creating equality, sacramental marriage, through the corporeal union of husband and wife, simultaneously overcame and affirmed difference. This seeming contradiction necessitated the humanists' reworking of the theory of likeness, which Vives equated to similarity between the pair and Erasmus to their compatibility. In both versions, while likeness entailed the wife's conformity to her husband, a certain degree of equality was deemed necessary, based on a common purpose between the pair and made possible by the complementarity needed between husband and wife for mutual recognition and, consequently, voluntary union. In its argument for sacramental union based on likeness, the humanists' vision of marital friendship thus offered an alternative to ancient discourses on the topic, one which allowed married unequals to participate in a relationship similar—but simultaneously superior—to that between ideal friends.

Hannah Chapelle Wojciehowski's re-evaluation of friendship in Thomas More's *Utopia* further investigates the complex relationship between *amicitia* and marriage as understood by early modern theorists. Although friendship is a core theme of the *Utopia*, it is in fact not directly discussed in the text; More's emphasis is exclusively on conjugal and family ties as the underpinnings of society. Challenging prior scholarship on *Utopia*, Wojciehowski argues that the explanation for this exclusion lies not in the text itself—that is, in the unspoken normalcy and universality of friendship in an island where class distinction and gender differentiation have been minimized—but rather outside of it, in the complex triangulated friendship between the author and his humanist friends, Erasmus and Peter Giles. Tracing their relationship through personal correspondences and the *Utopia*'s paratext, Wojciehowski brings to light not the exemplary *amicitia* which other scholars have made it to be, but rather a conflicted, ultimately ill-fated friendship.

As the author elucidates, More's friendship to Peter Giles and Erasmus came to fill the void left by More's physical separation from his family while he was abroad. However, upon his return to England More missed both his friends and the freedom he enjoyed while with them, feeling oppressed by the restrictions of marriage and other familial obligations not to be shirked. More's frustration with the situation, Wojciehowski argues, was exacerbated by the deep emotions engendered by his relationship to both humanists—including perhaps envy of the closeness between the other two, as well as possibly even erotic feelings towards Giles. These conflicted emotions came to shape More's understanding of friendship as a commitment not only in tension with and exclusive of others but also necessarily secondary to them. Accordingly, More disallowed amity as a feasible foundation for the polity, even in Utopia. In this, as we shall see in Part III below, More stood in sharp contrast to contemporaries who argued for *vera amicitia* as a likely model for the development of civic order.

More's rejection of the conflicting commitments and heightened emotions friendship provokes when triangulated obliquely reveals broader early modern concerns about the nature of the passions and their role in human interactions. As Daniel Lochman argues in Chapter 3, Philip Sidney's *New Arcadia* reconsiders the function of the passions particularly in producing virtuous action, in the process positing a fundamentally new understanding of friendship with which to replace both ancient and medieval discourses—as well as Sidney's own earlier representations of *vera amicitia* in *Old Arcadia*. This shift is most obvious in Sidney's radically different presentation of the interactions between two exemplary pairs of friends: the shepherds, Claius and Strephon, and the princes, Musidorus and Pyrocles. The first pair Sidney depicts as iconic "true friends" whose shared unrequited love for Urania leads to compassion for one another. Claius and Strephon serve as a foil to Musidorus and Pyrocles, who in *New Arcadia* fall short of *amicitia perfecta* because they lack the stability offered by the lateral affection exemplified by the shepherds and are unable to understand "beauty" as a prompt for chastity.

At the core of Sidney's revised depiction of friendship, Lochman argues, is the shift of friendship's principal site from the mind to the passions. Influenced by early modern medical re-evaluations of the relationship between body and mind that made indistinct the boundaries between them, in the *New Arcadia* Sidney reconsidered the relationship between love and friendship, in effect minimizing the ancient distinction between *philia* and *eros*. While in the *Old Arcadia* the passions led to disastrous consequences, in *New Arcadia* the passions work as intermediaries between mind and body, allowing friends to join in "love-fellowship," an empathy born from the lateral affection that develops when men share the knowledge and pain of the other's unrequited love for the same absent beloved. Through "love-fellowship" Claius and Strephon move one another to compassion and consequently to virtuous action, thus becoming models of a redefined perfect friendship that presupposes, rather than negates, the utility and necessity of the passions.

Part II: Alternative Discourses: Friendship in the Margins

As the essays in Part I illustrate, early moderns did not uncritically adopt the classical and medieval traditions of friendship which they inherited; rather, incorporating other discourses—both long-standing and new, writers such as More, Vives, Erasmus, and Sidney fundamentally modified *amicitia*. Remarkably, it was not only scholars and theorists who challenged traditional models of friendship. Contesting particularly the relationship's exclusivity to equals with no utilitarian need for each other, individuals debarred in theory from participating in true friendship also attempted to redefine *amicitia*. Expanding on this thread, the essays in Part II focus on discourses of friendship particularly about and by "outsiders" who did not fit the mold of classical friendship. In examining non-traditional approaches to *amicitia*, these essays shed light on early modern attempts to understand not only theoretical assumptions of friendship as based upon intersubjectivity and equality, but also the gap that existed between those assumptions and the reality of creating and maintaining interpersonal bonds in an urban and hierarchical world.

In Chapter 4, for example, Donald Gilbert-Santamaría examines Mateo Alemán's depiction of friendship between unequals in the picaresque novel *Guzmán de Alfarache*. Exploring the viability of *amicitia perfecta* in the fictional world of the picaro, Alemán's portrayal of the relationship between the characters of Guzmán de Alfarache and his companion, Sayavedra, offered a substitute for traditional understandings of friendship and highlights the fragility of associations based on that very alternative. In the picaro's world of tricksters and cheats, the main character stood alone, cut off from the intimacy possible between individuals in the larger, public world. In such isolation, de Alfarache came to experience the bitterness of knowing that his "other self," the *alter idem* extolled by the ancients, may in fact not exist. Faced with such a possibility, de Alfarache instead latched on to Sayavedra, a fellow picaro who initially tricked him but whom the protagonist refused to denounce to the authorities. Sayavedra's consequent offer of service and deference created between the two an intimate bond parallel to that between friends, but one rooted on utility and hierarchy as well as solidarity in crime rather than virtue.

The picaros in this way joined not in a classically defined friendship but in a fluid companionship that nevertheless provided a makeshift space for closeness and trust in an otherwise alienating setting. Yet, as Gilbert-Santamaría explains, for such trust to survive, the picaro had to self-identify with his companion, going so far as to remold the other's life story to reflect his own, in the case of de Alfarache, or literally to take on the other's identity, in the case of Sayavedra. Such self-identification also required the negation of any other relationships, both to individuals and to society at large. Only then could the picaro achieve equality with the other and make of him his "other self." Unity between "friends" so tenuously achieved, however, required continuous testing and was constantly at risk of dissolution, characteristics more closely aligned with modern understandings of friendship than with classical ones. Ultimately, Gilbert-Santamaría contends, the picaresque's reworking of friendship highlights not the viability of this alternative form but rather its extreme fragility and ultimate impossibility in the early modern world.

The fragility of friendship between unequals and the need continuously to bolster such relationships in real life also preoccupied individuals involved in hierarchical patronage relationships. Seemingly motivated not only by the emotive longing for an "other self" explored by Alemán, but also by pragmatic considerations such as the need for financial support and social mediation, such individuals sought to forge with their patrons bonds of amity that would sustain them both personally and socially. However, since ancient and medieval discourses of friendship alike relegated patronage relationships to the transient, because of the hierarchy and utility constitutive of such associations, clients seeking to cement more permanent relationships were constrained to reimagine *amicitia perfecta* so as to fit their actual experiences. As Maritere López argues in Chapter 5, at least two Italian courtesans, Camilla Pisana and Tullia d'Aragona, undertook such recharacterizations of *amicitia*. Unlikely friends to their respective patrons (Francesco del Nero and Benedetto Varchi) not only because of their subordination as clients but also due to their gender and venality, the courtesans could not simply adopt unchanged the classical language of friendship. Rather, Pisana and d'Aragona needed not only to redefine utilitarian friendship as perfect but also recast themselves as virtuous, and therefore worthy, friends.

This exercise of redefinition was inherently circular, in that, in order to assure their patrons' support in perpetuity, the women attempted to create cycles of continual reciprocity between themselves and their patrons based not on the imbalanced needs of patrons and clients but on the equal virtue of friends. Their respective equality to del Nero and Varchi, however, necessarily was based on a redefinition of virtue that highlighted attributes unique to each woman. Thus, Pisana offered del Nero the gift of a perfect friendship based on her honesty and prudence, traits which made her able to protect his reputation even to her own detriment, while D'Aragona offered Varchi empathy and the alleviation of his suffering or distress, emotive goods only she could offer because of the similarity of their tribulations. Regardless of what traits each woman stressed, both believed that, thus redefined, virtue equalized their standing in relation to their patrons, guaranteeing the continued benevolence and support which the ancients argued exist between perfect friends.

An analogous appropriation of the discourse of friendship, as Allison Johnson discusses in Chapter 6, was undertaken by Isabella Whitney within her collection of poems, *A Sweet Nosgay*. Deploying the rhetoric of virtue in similar fashion to that of Pisana and d'Aragona, Whitney cast herself as a virtuous friend for pragmatic ends, diffusing threats to her reputation resulting from her public role as a single woman writer. Johnson argues that Whitney spurned both domestic service and marriage as incongruous with her desire to write, and replaced the hierarchical relationships of master/servant and husband/wife with the equality of virtuous friends. At the core of Whitney's self-definition as virtuous, and therefore as protected from the pitfalls of public life, are two interconnected strategies: first, her self-identification as an active member of a caring, honorable circle of friends and kin; and, second, her appropriation of the trope of friend as a counselor whose responsibility it is to guide an other towards virtuous action and away from the dangers of love and passion, particularly.

As Johnson explains, Whitney's first stratagem is clear in the paratext of *A Sweet Nosgay*, where the poet included an epistolary dialogue with members of her family, friends, and supportive male literary figures. This conversation in letters created a framework which not only advertised her standing in a group of mainly male literary friends, thus providing countenance to her literary ambitions, but also firmly established Whitney's equal and reciprocal membership in a protective community which neutralized the dangers of her disavowed domesticity. Whitney employed her second strategy in several of the collection's poems wherein the speaker, wiser for having been forsaken by a treacherous lover, rejects the excesses of love and warns other women about its pitfalls. It is the friend's experience, as well as her consequent virtuous rejection of love and marriage, that allows her to teach both good sense and good morality, moving her audience also towards virtue. Having thus distanced herself from both love and marriage, recasting herself as a virtuous counselor in the process, Whitney simultaneously created and validated her claim to friendships cemented on virtue and equality. Whitney's representation of friendship was thus simultaneously congruent with—because it hinged on the virtuous likeness of the friends—and contrary to traditional discourses of *amicitia*—because it asserted the viability of women as virtuous friends.

The question of whether women could be true friends was similarly posed and answered by Katherine Philips some seventy years later. Examining Philips's claim of friendship between women as politically exemplary because it was possible even after betrayal among friends, Penelope Anderson bridges, in Chapter 7, Parts II and III of this collection. As Anderson argues, Philips diverged not only from traditional models of friendship, as did Whitney, but also from royalist visions of monarchy that predicated the success of the sovereign upon a policy of forgetting the past—particularly the betrayals of those who, directly or by their inaction, allowed the previous monarchy's demise. Philips challenged traditional understandings of *amicitia* primarily through her depictions of women as true friends, particularly as the inclusion of women necessitated, in Philips's vision, a complete denial of friendship as a stabilizing relationship founded on singularity and fidelity.

Philips stressed not the stability of friendship but its volatility. In poems that follow the arc of her real-life "multiplied" friendship with different women, relationships ultimately dissolved due to marriage's exclusive commitments, Philips underscored that even true friends are in reality often disloyal. Further, friendship's destabilizing potential affects not only individuals but even the state: at best, friendship forces friends to make impossible choices between conflicting obligations, such as those to family and those to friends; at worst, when pitting friends against others, the relationship may authorize conspiracy and even political rebellion. However, if understood not as exclusive but as multiple and flexible enough to accept and forgive betrayals as Philips seems to have done in her own relationships, friendship could serve as a model upon which to build a polity. Ultimately, the clemency Philips prescribed to friends seemed to her also the key to the survival of the state during the interregnum and restoration since the polity ought not forget the past but forgive while learning from past betrayals.

Part III: Friendship in Ethics and Politics

The collection's remaining essays examine two additional, interrelated strands of the early modern discourse of friendship. The first explores the problematic multiplicity of ethical friendship's categorical definitions—as virtuous and exclusive of utility, as socially efficacious while based on virtuous similitude, or as solely utilitarian, among others—and the dangers pursuant to the confusing of true friendship with false. The second, presupposing the utility of friendship to the virtuous, considers the viability of amity as a model or basis for social and political organization. Early moderns engaged this second thread of inquiry not only in theory but also in practice; while some extensively explored in literature the political efficacy of friendship, others went so far as to establish communities upon the belief that friendship is a viable foundation for the polity. The essays in this section are organized so as to highlight this variety: they begin with considerations of representations of friendship in ethics and politics, and they culminate in an investigation of a historical community that presumed individuals bound by friendship move one another to the virtuous actions requisite for the success of the state.

The first three essays in this section examine the ethics of friendship, particularly early modern inquiries into the intersection between virtue and social usefulness in friendship and into its dangers, especially when its rhetoric is unethically appropriated for self-serving purposes. In all three essays, the authors highlight early moderns' common understanding of the usefulness of friendship, whether for emotive support or for practical protection against vicissitudes faced in both the personal and political arenas. However, early moderns also recognized both its inconsistent efficacy, resulting from the imperfection of even the most "perfect" of friends, as well as the hazards which dependence on friends may entail, particularly when vice is disguised as virtue through the use of friendship's rhetoric.

As Sheila T. Cavanagh elucidates in her study of Mary Wroth's *Urania*, early moderns clearly acknowledged the centrality of reliable ties of friendship to the survival of persons, families, and countries. To the characters of the *Urania*, friendship was instrumental in providing a safe haven for the individual, preserving familial prosperity, and protecting states against enemies. These multiple levels of utility reflect the inclusivity of friendship's definition in the text, as kin, political allies, and even lovers, at one point or another, could all become friends. Crucially, Wroth situated both the viability and instrumentality of such friendships on similitude between the friends, a likeness based, most relevantly to the *Urania*'s characters, on shared attributes such as lineage and station. Notwithstanding similitude's unifying effects, however, the categorical elasticity of friendship results in its unreliability. In fact, as Cavanagh argues, Wroth's narrative draws attention to the frequency with which individuals succumb to temptations that undermine their honesty and consequently fail to fulfill their friendly obligations.

The greatest risk of depending on friendship, however, comes not from sidetracked friends but from others who unethically appropriate its rhetoric for their own selfish gain, often to the direct detriment of the individual. Simultaneously duped by false friends who use feigned similarity to gain their trust and unable to see beyond that apparent similitude, characters in the *Urania* are often undermined by the greed and self-interest of deceptive "friends." Cyclically, that gullibility reinforces the need to cultivate and retain true friends to help discern deceivers, cementing the primacy of friendship regardless of its perils. While thus upholding the supreme value of friendship, Wroth's representation of it in the *Urania* simultaneously underscores contemporary concerns about the disjuncture between idealized *amicitia* and reality, warning the reader against unquestioned reliance on likeness as a guarantor of true friendship.

As Marc D. Schachter argues in Chapter 9, early modern concerns about the limits and dangers of false *amicitia* are also at the heart of the twelfth novella of Marguerite de Navarre's *Heptaméron*. A fictionalized account of the relationship between Alessandro, Duke of Florence, and his cousin and assassin, Lorenzo de' Medici, the novella considers the deformation of friendship at the hands of those who deploy its rhetoric to disguise a relationship of utilitarian exchange utterly devoid of virtuous intent. The men in the story stand in stark contrast to the classical ideal friends, for they are similar in wickedness rather than in goodness and abet each other in vice rather than in virtuous action. The characters of Duke and Gentleman nevertheless call each other friend, pretending to love one another while exploiting the relationship: the Gentleman gained favor and political influence from the Duke, who in turn gained in the Gentleman a procurer to help fulfill his sexual voracity. Ending in the Gentleman's assassination of the Duke for asking the Gentleman to pimp his own sister—to him a slight against the family's honor rather than against the sister—the narrative reveals the fragility of friendship as a category. Easily appropriated and distorted by the wicked, the language of friendship can deceive and coerce, going so far as to disguise evil intent and, if unchecked, abet tyranny.

These interrelated themes—the ethical divergence of friendship from the pursuit of self-interest and the association's possible pitfalls when appropriated for wicked ends—also permeate Shakespeare's tragedy, *King Lear*. Considered by Wendy Olmsted in Chapter 10, one of the play's main concerns is Lear's rebuff of "plain" speech, a truthfulness contrary to the flattery he craved yet essential, according to ancient and Renaissance discourses of friendship alike, for *vera amicitia* to exist. Lear's rejection of honesty was absolute, epitomized in his exile of Kent for opposing Cordelia's own banishment. As Olmsted elucidates, Lear's tyrannical stubbornness had two crucial consequences for friendship in his realm:

first, the vacuum left at court by honest friends was filled by false ones, flatterers who employed the language of friendship to bolster their own power and who, in the process, undermined the king; and, second, true friends were forced to resort to disguise in order to pursue ethical friendship and made to develop new ways to offer counsel, highlighting the necessary art of discernment at court between true friend and false.

The king's unscrupulous older daughters, Goneril and Regan, for example, subtly use the rhetoric of friendship to wicked effect, offering Lear the "honest" praise and "sound" counsel friends should proffer, self-servingly bolstering the king with lies, only to cut him down by severing the political, social, and familial bonds that defined his identity. Lear is not yet without friends, however, since Kent, in his guise as Caius, came to his defense. Crucially, so disguised, Kent was able to help the king realize, even if to no happy end, that a subject's unquestioned agreement and flattery are not necessarily good, whereas plain speech is the sign of a true friend. Ultimately, Olmsted argues, in *King Lear* Shakespeare offers a cautionary tale of false friendship, highlighting the need for prudence in choosing one's friends. Equally important, the play stresses that in tyranny, where friends cannot speak freely, friendship cannot exist.

The categorical opposition of friendship and tyranny, as well as the more general question of whether friendship can serve as the foundation of political communities, is the strand of the early modern discourse of friendship with which the last three essays of this collection are concerned. As the authors in this section illuminate, the issue was one recurrently examined during the period, in political treatises and fictional works alike. Perhaps most importantly, early moderns did not limit themselves to the theoretical investigation of friendship's viability as a political model but went so far, in the case of the Swiss Anabaptists, as to establish communities founded on bonds of amity. Whether in imaginary settings or attempted in fact, friendly civic communities presumed the similitude of citizens (whether that similarity was of purpose, faith, or nature) and promoted an egalitarianism that resulted from that likeness, the community's free choice of membership, and the rejection of tyranny in any of its possible guises.

As Christopher Marlow explains in Chapter 11, for example, William Cartwright in his Platonic play, *The Lady-Errant*, presented a unique version of the ideal polity that challenged the tyranny that men exercised upon the women who loved them. The play's main characters are the fictional women of Cyprus, left behind while their husbands are away at war. Virtuous and rational, the Cyprian women challenge both that regime and the patriarchal system it represented, one which made them powerless and left them languishing under an ineffectual monarchy. In a revolutionary move, they attempt to overthrow the government and establish a female parliament founded on womanly equality. Based on their shared love and grief for their absent husbands, yet ultimately exclusive of those very lovers, the women's similitude binds them to a freely chosen, egalitarian community wherein social differences dissolve and in which queen and commoner alike play essential roles. The new government is, therefore, organized according to principles of friendship rather than love, contrasting the freedom and equality of female friends against the tyrannical oppression of women under their male lovers—a patriarchal subjugation both personal and civic. Although ultimately unsuccessful, the female friends' challenge of absolute monarchy marks Cartwright's play, Marlow argues, as a subtle commentary on classical and early modern theories of friendship, as it concurrently follows yet modifies tradition by insinuating that friendship between women not only is possible but can also serve as the basis for egalitarian political communities.

In Chapter 12, Gregory Chaplin examines a more radical condemnation of tyranny and espousal of friendship as the only source from which a rational political order could ensue: John Milton's discourse of friendship as expounded in both his 1649 *The Tenure of Kings and Magistrates* and his 1660 *The Ready and Easy Way to Establish a Free Commonwealth*. As Chaplin argues, Milton's treatises amount in fact to a theory of revolution that replaced Stuart tyranny with a community of self-governing male citizens who, through reason and bonds of amity, avoid anarchy. Milton based his arguments on the discourse of voluntary servitude, first introduced in the seventeenth century by Etienne de La Boétie, which maintains that each male citizen has sovereignty over his self and household, a personal dominion inherently incompatible with absolutism. Man's sovereignty was thought to stem from his natural equality to his fellows, all created in the likeness of God. According to Milton, from this parity it follows that men are naturally free and only through their own volition can be governed by a centralized state. However, man's natural rights have been eroded by custom and lack of learning, and they have been purposefully undermined by the patronage practices of corrupt monarchies—practices that lead to citizens' continued bondage to tyrants.

Yet, as Chaplin explains, Milton proposed that the citizen's absolute right to personal sovereignty, granted by the law of nature and upheld by reason, guarantees men the right to resume authority, change leaders, or substitute government types at any time, through violent means if necessary. This was, in effect, his justification for the English republic enacted after the execution of Charles I. In Milton's theory, however, neither the personal liberty given by nature nor the actions needed to protect it should lead to anarchy. Rather, good men who love freedom must consciously cultivate classical virtues such as self-knowledge, steadfastness, and, most importantly, loyalty to friends. Thus united by their natural likeness and shared fidelity, both acknowledged sources of amity, autonomous male citizens consensually create fraternal societies maintained by personal discipline and collective virtue. Clearly shaped by both classical and Renaissance commonplaces, yet revolutionary in its application, Milton's deployment of the discourse of friendship therefore allowed for the dispersion of civic authority—and the establishment of individual sovereignty—while avoiding the chaos of anarchy.

Early modern explorations of the political efficacy of friendship as the basis for orderly communities were not confined to theoretical or imaginative considerations or *ex post facto* justifications such as the ones offered by Cartwright and Milton, respectively. Rather, as Thomas Heilke discusses in Chapter 13, the Swiss Anabaptists not only theorized friendship as a viable foundation for stable communities but also established them on that premise. Early Anabaptist leaders affirmed amity's civic potential in at least two of their foundational texts: "The Schleitheim Confession" and the "Admonition" of 1533/1542. While the latter is much more explicit than the former in its linking of church practices to friendship, together these sources articulate the Anabaptists' rejection of tyrannical regimes that lacked excellent laws to train their citizens in virtue, as well as their adoption of an alternative type of community in which friends in Christ can gather to promote virtuous action.

Like other thinkers and writers discussed above, Anabaptists based their prescriptions of amity as politically effective on the similarity of the community's members. Disparate in their personal attributes, the similitude of the members is defined in the texts as a similarity of faith in Christ, of purpose—the living of a virtuous Christian life—and of practice—the observance of behavior and practices which separates the members of the community from others. Crucially, their likeness thus defined leads members to choose freely to band together in a community that is sustained and maintained by acts of mutual support. In contrast to John Milton's autonomy of the citizen discussed above, however, Anabaptist leaders envisioned a polity in which amity among members was mediated by the direction and discipline of the church, an ecclesiastical regime which concurrently defined and enforced the right practices of the community and thus set the parameters for inclusion in—and exclusion from—both the community and its foundational friendship. The Anabaptist views of friendship and its link to the polity were, as Heilke reveals, thus consistent with Aristotelian sensibilities, both in their rejection of tyrannical regimes not conducive to virtue and in their turn to an alternative community based on the likeness of its members. Anabaptist leaders nevertheless modified theories of friendship, expanding the discourse by incorporating the structured intervention of the church as essential to the success of the friendly polity.

As the full descriptions above illustrate, the thirteen essays in this collection reveal broad, trans-European refigurations of and resistance to the traditional discourses of friendship that early modern writers nonetheless appropriated, reactions marked implicitly or explicitly by tense, conflicting claims for the self and the community and building upon emerging conceptions of the passions, gender, and the individual's relation to the community, society, and state. Although there seems to have been widespread awareness of the limits and even deficiencies of theoretical structures and exemplary narratives to explain quotidian relationships in courtly and urban environments—these increasingly requiring the reservation of one's self behind expressions of courtesy, manners, and deference—early moderns nevertheless suggest through direct statement or indirectly through irony, comedy, or implication a persistent yearning for mutual companionship and affection that they express with the aid of received, if outmoded, conventions.

PART I
Conventional Discourses
Reimagined

Chapter 1

Bound by Likeness: Vives and Erasmus on Marriage and Friendship

Constance M. Furey

Friendship and marriage circled each other warily in early modern Europe. Where friendship advocated equality between members of the same sex, usually men, marriage upheld male–female hierarchy; while friendship cultivated self-possession and choice, marriage encouraged female submission and obedience. As Laurie Shannon puts it, "If friendship discourses establish a counterpoint to absolutism (monarchical or tyrannical), marriage, in contrast, operates by analogies to it in the mirroring logics of Renaissance thought" (61). And yet friendship and marriage were clearly opposed in part because they were so closely linked. The standard marriage sermon in Elizabethan England enjoined husbands and wives to live together lawfully in "perpetual friendship" (*Certaine sermons* 506), and both discourses celebrated unity and idealized the process of two people becoming one. For most scholars, however, this connection between friendship and marriage seems less interesting than the opposition; the connection, when mentioned at all, is usually attributed to friendship's influence on companionate marriage (Lipton 17, 43; Shepard 82). From the perspective of friendship studies, the reason for this disinterest seems clear enough: marriage lacks the utopian promise and richly intersubjective theory of selfhood that made friendship alluring to early modern writers and fascinating to scholars today (cf. Dolan 43–4).

There are some notable exceptions. In *The Friend*, Alan Bray argues that up until the seventeenth century friendship and marriage "turned on the same axis"; both were simultaneously social and spiritual, sanctioning exclusive allegiances while affirming a more encompassing notion of unity (214, 259). In *Politics of Friendship*, Jacques Derrida indicts male friendship's exclusion of women and love alike—the very things that differentiate friendship from marriage—even as he points out that the distinction is impossible to sustain: although male friendship discourse contemptuously associated women and love with hierarchy and bondage, love and friendship necessarily intertwine and women find ways to make their presence felt (277, 290). However, in seeking to demonstrate that some same-sex relationships were akin to marriage, Bray disregards the notable differences between marriage and friendship; and Derrida queries these differences from within a discourse that insists upon them, by relying exclusively on male-authored philosophical texts about perfect friendship. In what follows, I take a different approach by analyzing sixteenth-century marriage treatises that explicitly connect *and* differentiate friendship and marriage. Like Derrida's, my sources are all written by men. As a result, however, of what Lorna Hutson describes as the textualization of friendship, these humanist authors inscribe bonds with one another through their "mental husbandry" (the adroit handling and textual exchange of women); consequently, these male-authored marriage treatises focus as much or more on women as men and, just as importantly, attend to bodies and sex as well as reason and emotion.

The treatise that inspired this essay is Juan Luis Vives's *De institutione feminae christianae* (*Education of a Christian Woman*). Vives's influential text appeared in Latin in 1524, was translated into English in 1531, and had been published in seven languages and nearly forty editions by 1600. Desiderius Erasmus, Europe's most famous humanist, published his own long treatise about marriage, *Institutio christiani matrimonii*, just two years later, in 1526. Vives wrote *De institutione* while employed as a tutor to Henry VIII's daughter, Mary, and he and Erasmus both dedicated their works to Catherine of Aragon just a few years before a royal divorce dramatized how consequential beliefs about marital unity could be. Like all other marriage treatises in the sixteenth century, these texts adamantly endorse patriarchy, and yet the discussions of marital friendship in Vives's and Erasmus's treatises also intimate an alternative to the dichotomy of hierarchy and equality. The claims about marriage and friendship in these two texts are echoed in many sixteenth-century humanist discussions of marriage, including Erasmus's earlier *Encomium matrimonii* (Latin 1518, English trans. 1536) and Vives's later work, *Office and Duetie of an Husband* (Latin 1525, English trans. 1555), as well as related treatises by Heinrich Cornelius Agrippa and contemporary Protestants such as Heinrich Bullinger and Edmund Tilney.

In these texts, friendship and marriage do not clearly stage a contest or perform a merger; rather, they are unsettled and alternating discourses. In *De institutione,* Vives describes marriage as a superlative form of friendship, and he was neither the first nor the only author to link friendship and marriage in this way. Erasmus, who had read Vives's work before writing his own, hailed friendship as a "meeting of minds based solely on inclination of will and choice," only to conclude that husbands and wives were even closer than friends because they shared one body as well as one soul (*Institutio* 219). These claims highlight an important tension: while affirming that perfect friendship sets the standard because it is a meeting of minds, the texts also suggest that the union between friends based on will and affection is in some important way inferior to the union between husband and wife because the latter is corporeal.

Intriguingly, when studied with an eye to their spiritual valence and sacramental language in particular, the pairing of these discourses reveals not just repressive norms—though these certainly exist—but also nuanced claims about allegiances, affinity, and accord. If, as Frances Dolan persuasively argues in *Marriage and Violence: The Early Modern Legacy,* our vision of equality today remains distorted by the early modern emphasis on marital unity—"the ultimate message," she points out, "is that marriage only has room for one" (3)—we might well learn also from the ambiguities and nuances in early modern marital discourse. Specifically, I am interested in how the humanists' mobilization of the discourse of spiritualized corporality produced claims about unity as both a premise and a process, enabled through divine participation. Reflecting on how unity that is divinely granted (through sacramental grace) must also be achieved between two people who are self-evidently different (because male and female), these texts vector the relational process through God, at once affirming and overcoming difference—and thereby aiding our attempts to rethink intimacy and parity today.

The Premise of Unity: Two in One Flesh

Vives's flat assertion in *De institutione* that marriage is the best form of friendship calls attention to the importance of spiritualized corporality. Marriage not only meets but improves upon perfect friendship, for "if friendship between two souls renders them one, how much more truly and effectively must this result from marriage, which far surpasses all other friendships" (II.iii.15). Vives's conditional logic presumes sacramental assumptions about likeness and bodily unity even as it measures marriage against the standard set by friendship's vision of unity. Others might emphasize the social utility of friendship and the alliances and aid that friends provided to one another; from this perspective, friendship took over where kinship left off, establishing bonds between people unrelated by blood or family allegiances. Vives, however, invokes the more abstract notion of perfect friendship conveyed by the classical description of a pair of friends as "one soul in two bodies." As the earliest English translation of Cicero's *De amicitia* had it, a friend is "another ... the same" (Tiptoft, qtd in Shannon 3). A friend is another self. Friendship can turn two into one. How, then, could marriage be superior? Vives renders this question rhetorical by trumping the classical adage about friendship with the line from Genesis where Adam declares that Eve is "bone of my bone and flesh of my flesh" (Gen. 2:23).

The second creation story in Genesis authorized commentators such as Vives to assume a sacramental chain of association between the pair in Eden and all subsequent married couples. Vives understood this marital unity as both originary and ultimate, as he emphasizes by setting marriage at the center of an ever-narrowing circle of intimacies. Friendship is supplanted by family, which in turn is superseded by the voluntary pairing that spawns the family:

> Beginning with that association and friendship by which all men are joined together like brothers descended from God ... our special friends are dearer to us, and among these, our kinsfolk are more beloved, and of those joined by blood none is closer than the wife, whom that first progenitor of the human race, upon first seeing her, immediately proclaimed she was bone of his bone and flesh of his flesh. ("De coniugio" 245; cf. II.1)

This biblical imagery was standard fare in Christian discussions of marriage, but here Vives uses it specifically to establish that the unity accomplished through marriage exceeds the unity of friendship: marriage creates one body whereas friendship merely overcomes the fact of two ("one soul in two bodies"). Marriage is not just a form of friendship; it is the best friendship. Given these assumptions, it seems straightforward not only to conflate marriage and friendship but also to suppose that marital friendship surpasses all other forms.

A passage in Vives's *Office and Duetie of an Husband* that tacks back and forth between marriage and perfect friendship underscores that this claim about the pre-eminence of spiritualized corporality was more an assertion than an assumption—needing to be made and remade:

> Paule doeth saye, he that loveth him selfe loveth his wife, for ther was never a man that hated his owne flesh, but doth nourish and cherish it, as the lord doth cherish his church; Aristotle ... doth define a frend that he is the self same thyng with another. And god doth saye, the wife with her husband is al one thing. And Cicero to confirme and kepe amitie geveth this counsel, that the inferior shuld ascend and the superior descend, for so the thinge may be brought to equalitie. But in matrimonye this nedeth not, for it is sufficiente both for the man and the wyfe, to perceyue and understand, that they are parte eche of others bodye. (M3r–4v)

Vives emphasizes that the Christian language about marriage affirms self-sameness just like the discourse of classical friendship, but the two discourses differ nevertheless because sacramental marriage makes the goal inseparable from the premise: husband and wife are joined as one, "al one thing," *because* they are "parte eche of others bodye." Throughout Christian history, claims of marital unity stifled objections to female subjugation and bolstered the husband's claim to authority (Dolan 26–31), and Vives perpetuates this repression of women by arguing that Cicero's mandated process of alleviating inequality becomes unnecessary for a husband and wife. Instead of working toward unity, the marital couple is unified at the outset by their mutual affirmation of unity. In this Christian vision of marriage, in other words, the decision itself creates the conditions for the unity it proclaims. Sacramental marriage thus seems to be stripped of the attention to process and the interest in how parity is achieved that makes perfect friendship discourse ethically appealing. Yet even as the circularity of this premise mystifies the process, it also directs attention to the way that any intimate relationship entails an initial claim of attention. This insight is broadly applicable: some form of commitment necessarily precedes the intimacy that makes meaningful commitment possible.

The clarity of this principle notwithstanding, sacramental marriage was contested terrain within Catholicism. From the fourth century onward, there were divergent claims about whether the sacramental union was ratified by consent alone, or whether physical intercourse was also required (Elliott 137–48). Vives, Erasmus, and most other writers of marital treatises clearly conflated marriage and sex, but in doing so they equivocated about whether the physical union claimed for married couples should be understood as a state of being (an ontological premise because of the complementary creation of male and female) or an activity (achieved because and only because of active copulation). The spiritualized body of the sacramental couple encompassed both possibilities. Again and again in *De institutione*, Vives appeals to the New Testament to authenticate this claim: "Above all these considerations this is the first and perhaps only law of marriage: 'they shall be two in one flesh.' This is the hinge of marriage, the bond of a most sacred fellowship" (Vives II.i.4, citing Matt. 19:5). This "hinge" is the reason why the married pair is united in a way that friends and kin cannot claim to be:

> ... she is one person with her husband and for that reason should love him no less than herself. I have said this before, but it must be repeated often, for it is the epitome of all the virtues of a married woman. This is the meaning and lesson of matrimony, that a woman should think that her husband is everything to her and that this one name substitutes for all the other names dear to her—father, mother, brothers, sisters. This is what Adam was to Eve. ... Therefore it is said that wedlock does not make just one mind or one body of two, but one person [*unum hominem*] in every respect. (II.iii.15)

At the outset, Vives reminds his reader that his claims are based on the passage from the Gospel of Matthew he cited earlier, where Christ responds to the Pharisees' question about divorce by saying that husbands and wives cannot be separated because they have become one body. The 1531 English translation of Vives's treatise underscores this by rendering "unum hominem" as "one body" rather than "one person" (*Instruction* 93). The all-encompassing claims of oneness that frame this quotation are thereby anchored in the body. The opening emphasis on the wife who is one person (or, in the contemporary English translation, "as one body") with her husband recurs in the concluding list of unities. One man, one mind, one body, each in itself partial but contributing to the ultimate expression of a couple united as one person. By presenting this description of unity as a gloss on the biblical injunction that husband and wife should be "two in one flesh," Vives emphasizes bodily unity over the sacramental requirements of volition and mutual consent, though he invokes these latter two implicitly at the end, with his proclamation that true unity involves body and mind alike.

This sacramental vision of marriage encouraged hyperbolic descriptions in many contemporary marriage treatises of how corporal unity overcomes duality and difference. In *Commendation of Matrimony* (1545), the occult philosopher and theologian Heinrich Cornelius Agrippa elaborates the twining of mind and body that marriage would ideally achieve: "in one agreeable minde two bodies, in two bodies one minde and one consent. Only man and wife, one envieth not an other, they alone loue eche other, out of measure, in as much as either of them hole hangeth of the other ... one fleshe, one minde, one concorde" (sig.A8r). As in Vives's text, the repetitive cadence of the final list—one flesh, one mind, one concord—merges three distinct features of the human person into a single intonation. The unity is, then, both self-contained and excessive: to the degree that they each take hold of the other ("hole hangeth of the other"), their love surpasses degree, "out of measure." The literal dimension of this physical imagery is affirmed by Agrippa's final sober concession: "only death can separate them" (sig.A8v). In death, without hands to touch or skin to feel, the couple becomes unimaginable, separate rather than unified. No longer living physical beings, they are also no longer together. The exalted vision of marital unity that Agrippa's breathless rhetoric invokes is inseparable from a sacramental understanding of physicality.

From this religious vantage point, divine intervention displaces human effort, as Vives underscores in *De institutione*: "He is her alter ego as she is his. O what force in the divine word, worthy of our total adoration … . He spoke only three words [*Quod Deus coniunxit*] and gave expression to what mortals cannot explain in the longest speeches but merely labor and try to explain in their infantile stammerings" (II.i.4). Here Christ, the third party to a union between two, catalyzes a transformation that people alone cannot achieve. The lines between literal and metaphoric union blur, and the divine participant effaces the differences between male and female, human and divine:

> When he says 'one flesh' it means literally one flesh. Moreover, flesh means mankind, both male and female, according to the proper meaning of the Hebrew tongue. Therefore those who were previously two human beings become one, joined together in matrimony. This is the marvelous mystery of marriage, that it so joins and unites the two spouses that the two become one, which was true also of Christ and the Church, as the Apostle Paul teaches. No power could bring this about except it were divine. Of necessity this must be a very holy thing since God is present in it in such a special manner. (II.i.1)

Vives presents total accord, the sense of affinity that makes it possible and compelling to talk about two things becoming one, as something humans alone cannot achieve and can scarcely understand.

This language of holy mystery was used by Protestants and Catholics alike. Agrippa's *Commendation* referred to marriage as a "holy mystery," in contrast with natural family ties: whereas "father, mother, children, brethren, systerns, kynsfolke, be the friends of nature, and workes of fortune: man and wife be the mystery of God" (sig.B1r). Similarly, the popular treatise *The Christen State of Matrimonye* (English trans. 1541) by Heinrich Bullinger—Zwingli's successor in Zurich—proclaims that marriage is the "highest loue and feloshippe that may be under God" (21r) because Christ is the example and "mirroure" of marriage (56r). The pervasiveness of this sacramental assumption is demonstrated by the fact that it appears also in Edmund Tilney's widely circulated and notably secular treatise on marriage entitled *The Flower of Friendship* (1568), which describes how "the almightie instituted this holy ordinaunce of matrimonie in the blisseful place of

Paradise" and counts it a necessity not only for social order and friendship but also, above all, a source of immortality (105).

The need for a transformative holy power spurs Erasmus into uncharacteristic flights of theological eloquence in his *Institutio christiani matrimonii*. Those united by the sacrament of marriage transcend corporal confines, for they are "joined by more than the human affection engendered by the body's desires." The breath of the Holy Spirit and the "gift of heavenly love" are on a different plane altogether than the physical union (224). As he contemplates the meaning of the "visible union" of man and wife, Erasmus asserts that this relationship between physicality and spirituality should be understood as analogous to the mystery of the incarnation:

> [I]n one and the same hypostasis were joined the Son of God, a human soul, and a human body, and an indissoluble link was forged between the heavenly and the terrestrial, the eternal and the mortal, the visible and the invisible, the infinite and the finite, the created and the uncreated, the highest and the lowest. What could be more divine than this alliance? Such diverse natures come together in a single being, though their essences remain distinct. (226)

Here is unity *with* distinction, a unity of body and soul that maintains difference while signifying inseparability.

This theology does not preclude anti-feminist claims even as it envisions a unity that makes marriage comparable to friendship. Thus Erasmus states explicitly that the authoritative husband encompasses the weaker wife, for "the man represents the principles of form and action, the woman, of matter desiring form" (226), and that their capacity to unify is both caused by and modeled on unity with God—"See how duality is by some inexpressible means reduced to unity in God and man, in husband and wife; God is the first cause of both unions" (226–7). The invocation of a divine third party thus sanctions the inequality but it also leads to claims about the analogies between marriage and friendship. Erasmus consequently appeals to the indissolubility of friendship to assert the permanence of marriage: "If the man who said, 'Friendship that could end was never true friendship,' was right, it would be even more true to say, 'A marriage that could be dissolved was never a true marriage.'" Erasmus extends this analogy between marriage and friendship by insisting that marriage is defined by the quality rather than the legality of the relationship: "I call a true marriage not one that is approved by the law but one that is cemented between equals in virtue by true affection" (227). Like friendship, marriage entails equality. In this way, Erasmus uses the connections between friendship and marriage to affirm the unity he attributes to God.

In this section of Erasmus's treatise, interest in the links between friendship and marriage underscores the importance of volition in particular. Echoing Cicero, Erasmus heralds friendship as a meeting of minds, superior to all other relationships because it is freely chosen. Yet he then mutates the dictum about friendship's superiority into a celebration of marriage:

> Among the ancients, as long as there remained some vestiges of honour and dignity in human behaviour, hardly any form of kinship or relationship was held in more respect than [friendship] ... which extended to guests as well as to benefactors. I shall not delay the reader here by recalling the laws of friendship .... . But among all relationships, natural, voluntary, or both, there is none closer or more holy than marriage, because it involves the complete and perpetual intermingling of two destinies and connects, unites, and joins body to body, spirit to spirit, in such a way that it seems to make two people one. Pythagoras described friendship as "sharing a soul," but marriage goes even further and also means "sharing one body." (218–9)

The corporal unity hailed at the climax of this passage supersedes attention to volition—a topic that usually marginalized women because of the assumption that women were rationally deficient and less capable of self-governance and judicious choice. Here, as in many humanist texts, misogynistic assumptions coexisted with doctrinal teachings about the spiritual equality of men and women; in this case, Erasmus skims over this contradiction by insisting that bodies unite souls. Lacking an explanation that will reconcile the initial emphasis on volition with the subsequent assertion about the primacy of the body, Erasmus replaces rational explanation with a spiritual declaration: "there is none closer nor more holy than marriage" (219). Like Vives, Erasmus conspicuously fails to discuss the specificity of bodily claims or marital sex, or even a spiritualized eroticism of physical encounters, but he hereby equates physical unity with holiness—a holiness that both requires and replaces volition.

This humanist claim that marriage differs from other forms of friendship because of the holiness of its corporal union stages an alternative to the Christian tradition of ambivalence about marital sex—a tradition brilliantly analyzed by James Grantham Turner. Tracing the way writers from Augustine to Milton handled the collision between optimistic and pessimistic views of how sex relates to salvation, Turner finds a unique resolution in Milton's erotic dream of Paradise. In *Paradise Lost*'s vision of Adam and Eve, Milton connects the desire for God with sex, and thus develops an ideal of married love which should not, Turner concludes, "be thought of as a social drive or as a higher form of friendship, but as a private bonding of male and female suffused with erotic energy" (207). For Erasmus and Vives, and some of their contemporaries, by contrast, the sacramental act itself was a model of union as premise, forged through the mysteriousness of holiness vectored through divine participation rather than sex specifically. Linking marriage and friendship, moreover, intensified the need to integrate the language of holiness with discourses of volition, likeness, and equality.

The Process of Unity: Likeness and Holiness

The framework for all sixteenth-century discussions of marital friendship—even for Protestants who denied that marriage was a sacrament—was the sacramental teaching that marriage symbolized "the inseparable union of Christ and the church" (Aquinas 123.vii; cf. Eph. 5). The long, slow development of sacramental marriage began with Augustine of Hippo, whose (contradictory) assumptions about marital unity and male–female difference persist in sixteenth-century humanist texts. James Turner helpfully parses these enduring contradictions by showing how Augustine uneasily pairs teachings about the fundamental distinction between Adam and Eve with discussions of how they overcame disparity. In his exegesis of the second creation story in Genesis, Augustine focuses on sex because he could not imagine any other reason for the creation of woman: if companionship were the goal, it's obvious that a male friend would be preferable (Turner 99, citing *De genesi* IX.iii). In his marriage treatises and *The City of God,* however, Augustine moves beyond this procreative focus to more expansive and complex ruminations about unity. At the beginning of *De bono coniugali,* Augustine emphasizes that both relationships—male–female and human–divine—are forms of hierarchical unity, so marriage should be understood as "a true union of friendship [*amicalis quaedam et germana coniunctio*] with the one governing and the other obeying." In the same text, however, he uses *pariter* or "equally matched" (a term he uses to explain male friendship) to describe the strength of Adam and Eve's union, "for those who walk together, and together observe the direction which they are taking, are joined side by side in unity" (*De bono* I). He lauds marriage for creating a natural society between the sexes and argues that single (as opposed to polygamous) marriages "symbolically signify the unity of all of us which is to be made subject to God" (*De bono* XVIII; cf. Turner 100). Against the Pauline tradition and all previous Christian commentators, Augustine thus repudiates the idea that marriage was justified and ratified by sex; borrowing from the requirements of Roman free marriage (based solely on the consent of the couple and their families), he instead maintains that marriage is validated by voluntary affection between husband and wife (Elliott 43–9). Augustine elaborated a Christian theological framework for this Roman precedent in *The City of God*, explaining that God created Adam and Eve, two from one, to endorse "unity in plurality" and to provide a model of harmony for subsequent human relationships (*De civitate* XII.24, 28; cf. Turner 100). Augustine did not, however, move beyond his focus on the symbolism of marriage to make further claims about how the marital bond enacts unity.

Among medieval theologians, Augustine's sacramental theology of marriage gave rise to more elaborate claims about the spiritual value of marital affect, and twelfth-century popes ratified the doctrinal claim that Christian marriage consisted of mutual consent informed by marital affection (Lipton 1–4; Elliott 139). In the thirteenth century, writing in a context in which sacramental marriage had been established as the privileged model, Thomas Aquinas likened marriage to friendship, arguing that both relationships prioritized the mutual cultivation of virtue. Aquinas's argument echoed Aristotle's insistence that friendship depends less on who the friends are—on each individual's social status or family—than on what friends do for one another. Aristotle contended that this is particularly crucial because friendship might otherwise devolve into narcissism. If equality alone were enough, friendship could mean simply affirming the existence of a person like oneself. Aristotle thus argued that living together may well be the greatest benefit of friendship, because we differentiate friendship from self-love through ongoing interaction with a person different from ourselves (*Nic. Eth.* trans. Rackham VIII.5; IX.12).

Aquinas and Aristotle diverge, however, in their discussions of marital friendship. Aristotle classified marriage as a secondary form of friendship because husband and wife are bound by utility or pleasure rather than shared virtue. Aquinas notably fails to reiterate this point about the necessary inferiority of marital friendship. Instead, observing that friendship "consists in equality" and that "strong friendship is not possible in regards to many people," Aquinas concludes in an argument from inference that the rigorous requirements of friendship explain why marriage, too, is selective and limited to one man and one woman (124.iv–v). Aquinas asserts that marriage is a natural, hierarchical form of social organization, but he also stresses that it is important above all because it models the *process* of unification. He thus argues that marriage is prohibited among relatives because those who are bonded by blood "already share." The process of marriage, by contrast, "is making union out of diversity, and experiencing stronger bond because of it" (125). In other words, Aquinas shifts the focus from socially defined equality to the work of creating exclusive unity through engagement and choice. Aquinas thereby equates marriage with the process of unification, although he does not further explore how this is achieved.

Vives picks up where Aquinas leaves off. Like other humanists writing about marriage, Vives repeatedly emphasizes the relationship's social utility and "natural" necessity ("societe and to liue together is the most effectuous and surest knot to knitte and ioyne amitie and loue amonge men and all other beastes" [*Office* sig.L3r), and argues that marriage rightly synthesizes both divine and human imperatives: "both gods lawe and mans shoulde make and knyt up, as it were a knot of pietie and faythfull lovue" (*Office* sig.2Cv). But what is it about marriage that makes it holy? Why is it "the image of high and divine things?" Vives is not just echoing a conventional trope when he talks about the holiness of marriage. What the "holy mystery" signifies in his texts, as in Erasmus's *Institutio christiani matrimonii*, is the mystery of unity: "This is the summe and ende of all loue and amitie, to be so ioyned with the thing that thou dost loue that thou mayst become one thing with it" (*Office* sig.L6r). When Vives, Erasmus, and others stressed that marriage synthesized human and divine imperatives, they equated holiness with the process, rather than just the premise, of unification. When the divine appears in these texts, whether as a force of unity or active third party, it does so not simply in the mirroring function of the traditional analogy (husband–wife = Christ–church) to sanction social convention and religious tradition, but more intriguingly as the catalyst for a complex relational dynamic, one that exposes the tension between unity and difference that traditional friendship discourse handles so differently, with its emphasis on shared virtue and Stoic self-control.

Thus *De institutione,* for example, repeatedly asserts that likeness is achieved through conformity—by wives adapting themselves to their husbands—but the requirements of holy concord and love call forth more nuanced claims about likeness or similitude. The text reiterates that women should be chaste, obedient, and subservient, ready always to bend their necks and willing even to be beaten without complaint, recognizing that man is the head of woman just as God is the head of man (II.iii.39–48). And with a nod to the discrepancy between the discourses of marriage and friendship, Vives admonishes that "A husband is not to be loved as we love a friend or a twin brother, where only love is required. A great amount of respect and veneration, obedience, and compliance must be included" (II.iii.24). But the goal, the great value of marriage, is a "holy and happy concord," and that calls for an emphasis on sharing rather than simple conformity. Married life, Vives insists, "consists of talking together and sharing all fortunes." This requires a "common purpose." Citing Sallust, Vives again invokes friendship to affirm that the strength of the bond depends on shared desires: "If husband and wife love each other mutually, they will want and not want the same things, which in the last analysis is staunch friendship" (II.iv.51). This establishes a model superior to adulation or adoration, and requires the wife to love her husband "no less than" herself. As Christian theologians since Augustine had insisted, what is required cannot then be imposed or simply enforced. Vives invokes friendship as a model to make this point: "Love is not obtained by force, but elicited; and one who has been dragged somewhere by force against his will, and is there held prisoner, will never be a friend" (I.xv.161). This requirement of concord and the likeness it involves can only be achieved when marriage is understood as a union of "love, benevolence, friendship, charity, and piety." In the midst of repeated calls for female subjugation, Vives attempts to clarify what, lacking equality, likeness should entail: volition, self-regard, and love, manifest in interaction and shared aims. The common desires and aims that these emotions engender make it possible to "form one soul out of two persons, which is the natural effect of true love" (I.xv.162). Thus the premise of physical unity is intertwined with friendship's emphasis on merging souls.

In marriage, as in holiness, this joining is achieved through likeness. "One thing must be heeded," Vives insists, "that there be a certain equality, or better, similarity, between husband and wife, that unites their souls and holds them together more tenaciously than anything else. Likeness is the tightest bond of love" (I.15.139). Absent likeness, unity becomes unthinkable. One can only fully embrace someone whom one knows or recognizes, someone like oneself. Here Vives hesitates. The shift from equality to similarity in this passage seems inconsequential, a mere hiccup. The initial claim of equality was not wholehearted ("a certain equality"). And it need not have been controversial to claim that husbands and wives were equal, since *spiritual* equality was doctrinally orthodox. Vives quietly amends his terms nevertheless, because the assumption that only equals can be friends, on the one hand, and his fervent conviction that marriage requires hierarchy, on the other, create a confusing mix of religious and social claims about likeness.

Vives makes the link between likeness—a condition of friendship and marriage both—and the logic of holiness especially clear in his *Office and Duetie of an Husband,* when he observes that similarity is a premise of all amity or love. Husbands and wives are bound by "a certain secret consente and similitude of nature" (sig.F8r). As the reference to secrecy suggests, Vives does not envision this similarity primarily in terms of utility or external factors but instead as something less obvious and more difficult to explain: "For every man doth call unto him, and gredely doth retain and hold, that is most likest unto him, or els through a certayn contagiousness or some familiar conversation, he becometh like unto it." Having exhausted these metaphors and attempts at explanation, Vives ends the discussion by quoting a line from Psalms: "With the holy thou shalt be holy" (*Office* sig. F8r–8v, quoting Ps. 18:26). This biblical imperative—with the holy thou shalt be holy—reflects what had for over a millennium been a key premise of Christian soteriology, that like can only be known by like. Thus one who desires to be saved, to dwell with God, must seek to become holy like God.

Desiderius Erasmus initially approaches the issue of likeness from a different vantage point—pragmatic rather than religious—in passages in his *Institutio* that affirm complementarity over likeness or equality. He begins by amending a straightforward endorsement of equality with a warning that husbands and wives should not be too much alike. Thus, he observes, one "can understand why Pitactus' dictum 'Marry an equal' is so well known among scholars, since, as the proverb says, like attracts like, and they stick together," but "too close a resemblance is not always a good thing" (311). Caught up in musings about how the extravagant husband would benefit from a thrifty wife, Erasmus revises the force of the proverb he quoted: "The point here is less that your wife should be your equal than that she should suit you" (313). On this pragmatic note, Erasmus confidently explains why compatibility trumps likeness: "Compatibility is so important that sometimes people who are dissimilar, but right for one another, will live in greater harmony than those who are more alike, despite the very proper saying that similarity breeds good will" (315). When pragmatics prevail, when the focus turns directly to social questions about suitability and utility, Erasmus and other authors usually emphasize female subordination.

The conviction that wives are weaker and that husband is to wife as spirit is to body diminishes, however, when the language of friendship and religious union comes to the fore. Throughout *Institutio* these discourses induce Erasmus to explore the desirability of likeness and equality. Husbands and wives are friends united by equal devotion to God and shared reverence for religion, he observes, and so less by their physical union than their conversation, for there is "nothing better to maintain friendship" than conversation (343). Similarly, he asserts that the virtues of faith, hope, and love are nourished by equality and similarity; without equality, affirmed by Christ's redemption, no friendship can survive.

Biblical exegesis also demonstrates how religious views could sanction likeness even as the assumption of hierarchy affirmed complementarity instead. In *The Christen State of Matrimonye*, the Protestant Bullinger, like the Catholics Vives and Erasmus, accepts the traditional claim that marriage was instituted for three reasons: to prevent fornication and to provide offspring and companionship. And, like the others, Bullinger finds companionship the one purpose that engendered the most comment. Interpreting Genesis 2, he explains that God wanted to alleviate Adam's loneliness; after considering the animals he had already created, God recognized that none could solve the problem because Adam needed someone like himself. God consequently made woman to satisfy the requirement of likeness, and created Eve from Adam's rib to make clear that she is made of the same stuff as man. In his exegesis, Bullinger immediately modifies likeness to mean complementarity by pointing out that the wife does not share everything with her husband: "Yet was she not made of the head, for the husband is heade & master of the wyfe" (1v). He also interprets the body analogy in a compatible way: just as there is great unity and mutual love within one's body, so should there be within one's marriage. Those who meet this requirement dwell together in "frenshippe and honestye" (3v). And so Bullinger concludes that the moral of the Eve story is that Adam recognized her as like him, for it is "natural," Bullinger observes, that two people who are alike should "bear more will the one toward the other" (21r). Fond as Christian moralists have been of the idea that men and women belong together as two (different) parts of the same whole, reading Bullinger's slide from complementarity to likeness in light of Vives's hesitation about which he should emphasize highlights the importance of the latter category.

Edmund Tilney's *The Flower of Friendship* appeared in more English editions than all but three other texts on marriage (including the treatises by Heinrich Bullinger and Desiderius Erasmus) and drew on Vives and Erasmus both. Early in *The Flower,* one interlocutor asserts that there must be equality between husband and wife, or how else could there be friendship? "Equalitie is principally to be considered in this matrimoniall amitie, as well of yeares, as of the giftes of nature, and fortune. For equalnesse herein, maketh friendlynesse" (lines 286–9). Appearing at the culmination of a discussion of marital customs in other cultures, this suggests that a commitment to equality and "friendlynesse" makes Christian marriage superior. Tilney smooths over any cracks that threaten to open in his text by talking about equality as synonymous with likeness. In her critical edition of this text, Valerie Wayne argues that, in Tilney's work, the claim of parity expresses an emergent view at odds with, but not fully contained by, the dominant ideology of female subordination. The latter wins out late in the treatise, when a character named Erasmus states firmly that a husband has "absolute auchoritie, over the woman in all places" (1177). The disjunction between the two, Wayne argues, "opens the text up to reproducing some of the instabilities and contradictions within Renaissance ideologies of marriage" (4). Vives's hesitation, described above, when he asserts equality and then shifts to likeness instead, supports Wayne's argument about ideologies of marriage. But the tensions between these two positions say something also about the issue of unity more generally by underscoring that equality and subordination are not necessarily diametrically opposed. The contradictions between "absolute authority" and equality underscore that unity does not efface difference.

In their discussions of marital friendship, Vives and other male authors thus expose the complexity of likeness: likeness entails equality, but not absolutely; compatibility or complementarity are not the same as likeness, but they're close; and similarity thus glints through the cracks not simply as something that can be imposed through obedience but, more subtly, as a necessary condition for recognizability and consequently unity. These varied claims are inflected by religious assumptions: the relationship between husband and wife is like the bond between Christ and the church, and a union between two human beings is like a union with God.

Conclusion

In his study of medieval and Renaissance friendship, Alan Bray traces the way Christian thinkers writing about friendship twisted the prism to see the divine sanctioning their bond, their parity. The result was that they could imagine the relationship *both* as particular, specific, with the intensity of singularity, *and* as expansive, transcending a particular time and place, setting in motion an interplay of different loves. Bray argues that the religious significance of friendship was based on Anselmian logic, the notion that Christ's sacrifice was efficacious because through it he made those he saved kin and friends: Christ "draws the eye beyond that eternally appealing prospect of 'You and I, then, here,' beyond the individuals for whom a friendship is made, to Christ and to *his* kindred and *his* brethren" (259). But what is notable about the humanist vision of marriage I have discussed in this essay is that it presumes spiritual triangulation without forsaking the compelling simplicity of two into one.

The marital bond, like that claimed for perfect friendship, is forceful in its singularity and particularity. Spiritual triangulation thereby works in tension with this dualist–monist dynamic, rooted in carnal specificity. The coupling of bodies becomes the necessary condition of a unity which must subsequently be constructed; by the same token, the virtues the couple embody are simultaneously predetermined and contingent. The emphatic claim of spiritualized carnal unity thus grounds the discussion of marital friendship in a way that differentiates it from spiritual friendship and the humanist discourse of perfect friendship. Thus marital friendship is not just a way to expand visions of equality or to focus the discussion of how to resist tyranny with visions of shared consent and self-sovereignty, as Shannon rightly emphasizes in her discussion of Renaissance friendship. Instead, marital friendship is intriguing because the sacramental framework encouraged humanists to expand their theories of likeness beyond restrictive dichotomies. Their patriarchal prescriptions thus incongruously trace interweaving of similarity and difference, hierarchy and equality in a context that invokes utilitarian language of common possessions and common interests alongside spiritual language of transcendence.

Chapter 2

Triangulating Humanist Friendship: More, Giles, Erasmus, and the Making of the *Utopia*

Hannah Chapelle Wojciehowski

In 1515, Thomas More, Under-Sheriff of London, traveled to the Netherlands in order to conduct trade negotiations on behalf of King Henry VIII. Sometime after those negotiations were suspended in July of that year, and before being recalled to England in October, More traveled to Antwerp.[1] There he met Peter Giles, the *griffier* (town registrar) of that city.[2] Giles was also a close friend of Erasmus, who had suggested that they meet. During or after his visit, More began writing what would become Book II of *Utopia*, with Peter Giles as one of the three interlocutors. Underpinning this literary masterpiece was an intense friendship between More, Erasmus, and Giles—a friendship that energized More's composition of the work, and that helped bring his manuscript into print in 1516, and again in 1517 and 1518.

This friendship was memorialized in the paratext surrounding the *Utopia* in its various early editions—letters by More, Giles, and Erasmus celebrating their friendship, as well as letters from a supporting cast of humanist friends and well-wishers, including Guillaume Budé, Jerome Busleyden, Johannes Desmarez, Cornelius de Schrijver, and several others. Peter Allen has suggested that these letters not only functioned as endorsements, but also were intended to shape the reader's reception of the text. The paratext directs the reader "both to enjoy the fiction and to understand its basic didactic purpose" (101).

While the included letters may guide the reader to understand the text as a work of practical philosophy (Allen 104), they do not guide the reader to any clear interpretation of the place of friendship within More's text. The suppression or invisibility of individual friendships on the island of Utopia and the foregrounding of conjugal and family ties there may, in fact, indicate a tension between the frame narrative and the paratext of the work (those letters of endorsement from friends and friends of friends) on the one hand, and the imagined social structure depicted

---

[1] On the probable dating of More's trip to Antwerp and the composition of *Utopia*, see Hexter, "More's Visit to Antwerp in 1515." 573–6.

[2] Giles (or Gilles) is the English version of Pieter Gillis, also known in Latin as Petrus Aegidius.

in Book II of *Utopia* on the other. As David Wootton has astutely observed, "the real puzzle of *Utopia* lies ... in More's decision to conceal its original subject, which is friendship" (257). Why, we must ask, does friendship seemingly have no place in the ideal commonwealth, given that it played such an important role in the life of its author and in the production of his most famous work?

A further element of that puzzle is a representational question. Not only the *Utopia* itself, but also the humanists' letters surrounding it, need not be interpreted as transparent or straightforward declarations of the authors' personal sentiments, as scholars such as Lisa Jardine and Thomas I. White have noted. Arguing against the tendency to read Erasmus's letters as "neutral 'documents' offering true insights into the great man of letters," Jardine emphasizes Erasmus's "active and conscious construction" of his own history and image via the print medium (153, 155). In a related vein, White highlights the conventional element of declarations of friendship within the writings of Renaissance humanists, which self-consciously imitate "a theme and literary conventions from classical moral philosophy" (493).[3] Jardine and White underscore an interpretive dilemma: how may a modern reader differentiate between carefully crafted print representations of sixteenth-century humanists and their relationships and the possible sentiments behind those representations? For the most part, Jardine confines her analysis to textual representations (a method which nevertheless raises complicated questions of intentionality), while setting aside the preferred biographical approach of numerous earlier scholars; White, meanwhile, weighs representation against biography, ultimately suggesting how, in the case of More and Erasmus, they seem to be at odds.[4] While it is not possible to determine with certainty the historical realities behind the Renaissance conventions of friendship foregrounded in the letters exchanged by More, Erasmus, and Giles, it is more with White's approach and view that the present essay aligns.

In a 1519 letter to Ulrich von Hutten, Erasmus famously offered a verbal portrait of his friend Thomas More. There he declared that More seemed to have been born and made for friendship: "no one is more open-hearted in making friends or more tenacious in keeping them. ... In a word, whoever desires a perfect example of true friendship, will seek it nowhere to better purpose than in More" (999, *Correspondence* 7: 18).[5] Erasmus's portrayal of his friend, which describes at some length More's appearance, mannerisms, habits, and virtues, attests not only to More's openness to others but also to the deep and longstanding bond between the English humanist and his mentor and friend Erasmus—a friendship

---

[3]   These classical conventions and their Erasmian adaptations have been richly analyzed by Eden in her essay "Between Friends All Is Common."

[4]   White concludes, "For a variety of reasons, the relationship between More and Erasmus is more complicated and a shade darker than its traditional picture" (504).

[5]   For all references to Erasmus's correspondence, the first number indicates Allen's Latin numeration; the second, the corresponding English translation in Mynor and Thompson.

begun some twenty years earlier.[6] Erasmus's role in the publication and reception
of *Utopia* would be pivotal, and his endorsement letter addressed to the publisher,
Johann Froben, which appeared in the third and fourth editions in 1518, served,
in Allen's view, "as the final step in identifying *Utopia* to any sixteenth-century
reader as an important humanist book and, to the humanist reader, as a book which
could not be ignored" (99). Erasmus was an important friend to More in many
senses—one who encouraged and supported his younger colleague's intellectual
and creative aspirations, and one who, as the pre-eminent humanist of Europe, was
in an excellent position to promote such aspirations to a larger audience (White
496). Wootton has argued that Erasmus's writings—specifically his *Adages* on
friendship, equality, and communal ownership—exerted a profound influence
on More's conception of his masterwork (255–61). John Freeman suggests that
Erasmus not only extensively edited *Utopia,* but also may have written portions
of it (16, 30–31).

Equally if not more important to the initial publishing of *Utopia* were the
interventions of Peter Giles, who may have helped to conceive the book, who
in all likelihood handled the printing arrangements of the first edition, and who
invented a Utopian alphabet and a quatrain in Utopian for that edition. Moreover,
Giles may have suggested the pun "eu-topia," or "good place," as E. F. Bleiler
has argued (306; 316–7). Giles's pivotal role is described by More in the story's
frame narrative, in More's dedicatory letter to Giles, included as paratext, and in a
second letter from More to Giles included in the 1517 edition only. In the opening
pages of the *Utopia*, More mentions that the friendship and hospitality of Peter
Giles helped to mitigate More's homesickness while abroad. More describes Peter
Giles rather as Erasmus would later describe More to von Hutten—namely, as the
perfect friend:

> Apart from being cultured, virtuous and courteous to all, with his intimates he is
> so open-hearted, affectionate, loyal and sincere that you would be hard-pressed
> to find another man anywhere whom you would think comparable to him in all
> the points of friendship. No one is more modest or more frank; no one better
> combines simplicity with wisdom. Besides, his conversation is so pleasant,
> and so witty without malice, that the ardent desire I felt to see again my native
> country, my home, my wife and my children (from whom I had been separated
> more than four months) was much eased by his most agreeable company and
> delightful talk. (*Utopia* 43)

In Antwerp, More missed his family intensely. Nevertheless, it was in the absence
of his wife, children, servants, and usual home life that More was able to begin
the greatest intellectual and creative adventure of his life, an adventure seemingly
inspired, at least in part, by his feelings of friendship, admiration, and kinship for

---

[6]   On the friendship between More and Erasmus, see Routh 14–21 et passim; Basset;
Marius, 79–97; Jardine 27–53; and White 489–504.

the young *griffier* of Antwerp. In some sense, all of these feelings serve as the emotional scaffolding for the story More relays to his readers—a story told to him by Raphael Hythloday, fictional voyager to the island of Utopia.

As soon as he was back in London, More intensely missed his new friend, as well as the creative freedom he had enjoyed abroad. In the letter to Peter Giles prefacing the *Utopia*, More writes of his difficulty in completing the work he had begun in Antwerp:

> [A]lmost all day I'm out dealing with other people, and the rest of the day I give over to my family and household; and then for myself—that is, my studies— there's nothing left.

> For when I get home, I have to talk with my wife, chatter with my children, and consult with the servants. All these matters I consider part of my business, since they have to be done unless a man wants to be a stranger in his own house. Besides, you are bound to bear yourself as agreeably as you can towards those whom nature or chance or your own choice has made the companions of your life. (*Utopia* 33)

Even when construed as humor, these comments seem to belie More's sense of frustration. In memory, Antwerp has become More's Utopia, and it is now Giles whom he misses. Writing with deep affection, enthusiasm, and possibly eros, he states in his closing to the prefatory letter, "Good-by, my sweetest friend, with your excellent wife. Love me as you have ever done, for I love you even more than I have ever done."[7]

Let us pose the perilous intention question: what did More intend to teach or to endorse—if anything—through his fantasy of Utopia, particularly on the subject of friendship? Wootton, arguing that *Utopia* is, in fact, a book *about* friendship—an interpretation I take to be correct—attempts to account for its concealment in the text. According to Wootton, More penned a narrative that took to heart Erasmus's celebration of the adages "Between friends all is common" and "Friendship is equality. A friend is another self" (258–60). However, on an island without class distinctions and comparatively minimal gender divisions, Wootton contends, "love and friendship themselves become invisible because, instead of being exceptional and exclusive, they are normal and universal." Hence, "*Utopia* may have begun

---

[7]   Here I depart from the Cambridge edition of *Utopia* and revert to the earlier Yale translation, in this instance the more literal one. The Latin text reads: "Vale, dulcissime Petre Aegidi cum optima coniuge, ac me ut soles ama, quando ego te amo etiam plus quam soleo" (eds Surtz and Hexter, 44–5). The Cambridge translation neutralizes the warmth of More's closing and also ignores the parallelism of the construction: "Farewell, my very dear Peter Giles; my regards to your excellent wife. Love me as you always have; I am more fond of you than I have ever been" (*Utopia* 38–9).

as an account of true friendship, but it took shape as a discussion of communism, equality, and labor, not friendship" (266).

Since More does go to some lengths to represent other relationships—notably marriage—while excluding friendship entirely, Wootton's solution to the puzzle of friendship's concealment in *Utopia* is not entirely persuasive. In Utopia, the tight ordering of culture around the social unit of the nuclear family, the extremely strict punishment of adultery, the infrequently exercised option of divorce only when agreed upon by both parties *and* by the Senators and their wives—all of these restrictions and many more—leave little space, literally and figuratively, for the pursuit of any other human relationships, including friendships.

Yet, while the restrictive construction of marriage in Utopia, which seemingly excludes extramarital relationships of most every kind, may have been a representation of More's personal beliefs up to a point, that construction may simultaneously represent More's frustration or struggle with such restrictions, including those operating in his own life—a frustration he described in his prefatory letter to Giles. As George M. Logan has suggested in his introduction to the *Utopia*, "the personality and views of More's two main characters [Raphael Hythloday and the character called Thomas More] project his [the author's] own persistent dividedness of mind" (*Utopia* xxiv). This dividedness, which might also be called ambivalence, may explain many or all of the conflicting points of view within the work, and may shed light upon the marriage/friendship question.

The locus of emotional intensity in More's life during the years surrounding the writing and publication of what would become his greatest work seems to have been his friendships—especially those with Erasmus and Giles—more than his marriage. As Wootton writes, "For More, and for the men of his day, it was a friend, not a wife, who was 'another self'" (271). In the remainder of this essay, I shall analyze certain of the letters exchanged between these three men from 1515 to 1522, in order to contextualize the split between family and friends represented by and in the *Utopia*—the paratext and frame narrative standing for friendship and Book II standing for family. These two affective poles, I shall argue, represented for More conflicting and sometimes mutually exclusive commitments, an internal conflict not easily resolved. Though I cannot do justice to the letters here, I will suggest that the conflict between friendship and family is, in a psychoanalytic sense, the unconscious content of *Utopia*, or part of it. Yet friendships provided their own conflicts, as we shall see.

As I have suggested, friendship appears in *Utopia's* paratext and frame narrative as the idealized "outside" of marriage and family, institutions rigorously regulated on the island of Utopia. Yet friendship, like marriage, was not uncomplicated for More; indeed, the highly complex, sometimes conflictual relationship between the three renowned humanists also merits further discussion. I shall show how some of these complexities may be traced through their correspondence, despite the fact that conflicts between these friends have been little remarked upon by More's biographers; instead, the three-way friendship has almost invariably been idealized. Richard Marius, for example, states that the friendship between More and Erasmus "was one of the jewels of the Renaissance," and that Giles was "destined to be a dear and lifelong friend to both [More and Erasmus]" (79, 152).[8] My discussion of this triangulated relationship will move toward an analysis of the double portraits of Erasmus and Giles, painted by Quentin Matsys and given as a gift by the two friends to the third, More, in 1517. I suggest that this famous gift may mark the winding-down of that celebrated triadic friendship, rather than its culmination, as previous scholars have generally argued. It was not only in relation to the institution of marriage that friendship provoked ambivalence in More, I suggest, but also friendship itself, which was fraught with complicated emotions and entanglements for all involved. Let us now turn to their correspondence—that portion still preserved, largely by Erasmus—for information and possible clues to the friendship puzzle described above.

London, 3 September 1516: Thomas More writes to Erasmus a letter accompanying his recently finished book manuscript of the *Utopia.* "Greeting," he writes, "I send you my book on Nowhere, and you will find it is nowhere well written; it has a preface addressed to my friend Pieter. Well, you must do what you can for it. I know from experience that you need no urging" (461; *Correspondence* 4: 66).[9] In this self-deprecating letter, More does and does not ask Erasmus for the favor of editing and publishing his book, for which his friend "need[s] no urging"—save for the prompting provided by More's missive and by the manuscript itself. More will write again to Erasmus on 20 September, reminding his friend that he had sent the manuscript "some time ago," and that he longs to see it published soon, "and well furnished too with glowing testimonials" (467, *Correspondence* 4: 79).

Antwerp, 2 October 1516: Erasmus writes to More, also asking for favors. He complains of his financial problems, regarding which he would like More to intervene. Toward the end of the letter he states matter-of-factly, "As for your Island, and all the other things, they shall be taken care of." In the final lines, he adds, "Pieter Gillis [Peter Giles] is devoted to you. You are constantly present with us. He is delighted with your *Nowhere,* and greets you most warmly, you and all yours" (474; *Correspondence* 4: 93). Despite Erasmus's slighly dismissive tone

---

[8]   Marius does, however, explore the ways in which the friendship between More and Erasmus would, by the fall of 1517, be tested on both sides. The controversy concerning Erasmus's *Novum Instrumentum*, Erasmus's faint praise for the *Utopia,* expressed in his prefatory letter in the 1518 Froben edition, and More's quarrel with the French poet Brixius were three issues that created strain in their friendship. See 244 ff. Marius' discussion of the sometime tensions within the friendship between More and Erasmus has been heavy-handedly characterized by R. J. Schoeck as the "non-friendship thesis" (11).

[9]   Allen notes that "Nusquama" (Nowhere) was at that point the working title of More's text (*Epistolae Erasmi* 2: 339).

toward More's manuscript, Edward Surtz asserts that there is "nothing really odd about this exchange," since Erasmus in all likelihood had read the manuscript while visiting More's home in England in early August, and had already agreed to help publish his friend's text (Yale *Utopia* xvi).

Brussels, 17 October 1516: Erasmus writes to Peter Giles, asking him to send publication materials for More's *Utopia*: "I am getting the Nowhere ready; mind you send me a preface, but addressed to someone other than me, Busleyden for choice. In everything else I will act as a friend should" (477; *Correspondence* 4: 98). Erasmus and Giles are heavily involved in bringing More's project to fruition. Erasmus, more experienced in the publishing industry, tells Giles how to proceed. Why, we must wonder, does he ask Giles to dedicate his prefatory letter to Busleyden, rather than to himself? More's biographer Richard Marius speculates on Erasmus's comment regarding the publication of the *Utopia*: "It is a strange remark, perhaps susceptible of various interpretations, but it looks as if Erasmus meant that he would be a friend to More by getting the work in print but would not go so far as to endorse it" (240). One possibility, Marius further suggests, is that Erasmus was ashamed of the book, with what he considered its uneven Latin style;[10] another is that Erasmus was not fully pleased with More's response to Martin van Dorp, a vocal critic of Erasmus's *Praise of Folly* (240).

London, 31 October 1516: Responding to an earlier letter from Erasmus, More talks about controversial word choices in Erasmus's translation of the New Testament that aroused the wrath of certain critics. He warns Erasmus to proceed slowly with the work. Switching gears, he writes near the end of the letter:

> I am delighted to hear that Pieter approved of my *Nusquama;* if men such as he like it, I shall begin to like it myself. I should like to know whether Tunstall approves, and Busleyden, and your chancellor [Jean le Savage]; that it should win their approval is more than I dared hope ... I expect therefore that they will like my book, and very much hope they will. But if the opposite way of thinking is deeply implanted in them by their own success, your vote will be more than enough for my judgment. We are 'together, you and I, a crowd'; that is my feeling, and I think I could live happily with you in any wilderness.

> Farewell, dearest Erasmus, dear as the apple of my eye. (481; *Correspondence* 4: 114–7)

The tone of this letter is warmer than those of the previous month. More acknowledges his debt to Erasmus in getting *Utopia* to press, as well as his longing for approval from both Erasmus and Giles.

---

[10] White also supports this view, arguing that Erasmus and/or More concocted the role of Peter Giles as the facilitator of *Utopia's* publication, precisely because the senior scholar did not want to be too closely associated with that project (501–2).

Brussels, 18 November 1516: Erasmus writes a short letter to Giles. He mentions in passing that *Utopia* is in the printer's hands (491; *Correspondence* 4: 131). *Utopia* was most likely published in December of that year in Louvain (*Utopia* 271).

London, c. 4 December 1516: More writes humorously and excitedly to Erasmus of Tunstall's positive reaction to *Utopia*. More offers the following fantasy to Erasmus: the Utopians are planning to confer upon More "the perpetual office of prince." "In fact," he writes, "I see myself already crowned with that distinguished diadem of corn-ears, a splendid sight in my Franciscan robe, bearing that venerable scepter consisting of a sheaf of corn, and accompanied by a distinguished company of citizens of Amaurote" (499, *Correspondence* 4: 163–4). More promises not to forget Erasmus after he has assumed his exalted new position, and offers to receive Erasmus with hospitality should his friend one day visit him on the island of Utopia. This is a joyful letter in which More takes pleasure in his own accomplishments and feels comfortable sharing his exuberance with his friend Erasmus. More seems to understand or to intuit that his book would change his life and define his career, as indeed it did. In December and the spring of 1517, several other letters would pass between the humanists.[11]

Antwerp, 30 May 1517: Erasmus has important news to report to More, some of it good, some of it bad:

> Pieter Gillis and I are being painted on the same panel, which we shall soon send you as a present. But it so happened, very inconveniently, that on my return I found Pieter seriously ill, even dangerously, from some sickness I know not what, from which even now he has not properly recovered. I myself was in capital health, but somehow the physician took it into his head to tell me to take some pills to purge my bile, and the advice he foolishly gave me I was fool enough to take. My portrait has already started; but after taking the medicine, when I went back to the painter, he said it was not the same face, and so the painting was put off for several days, until I look more cheerful. (584; *Correspondence* 4: 368)

---

[11]   499, More to Erasmus (London, c. 4 December 1516), 4: 162–4; 502, More to Erasmus (London, 15 December 1516), 4: 169–72; 543, Erasmus to More (Antwerp, 1 March 1517), 4: 270–73; 545, Erasmus to More (Antwerp, 8 March 1517), 4: 274–5. One other extant letter possibly dating from this period is More's second letter to Giles, included in the 1517 edition of the *Utopia* (see n. 14, 20). This edition, printed by Gilles de Gourmont, most likely appeared at the end of September 1517 or shortly thereafter (see notes 14 and 20, below). More's second letter to Giles, then, was composed no later than the book's publication date, but most likely earlier that same year, after the first edition of *Utopia* had begun to circulate. The Latin text of the letter and English translation appear in *Utopia* 266–9.

This letter describes the Quentin Matsys double portrait of Erasmus and Giles (Figures 2.1 and 2.2), which the two men sent to their friend upon completion.[12] Erasmus also mentions the mysterious illness afflicting Peter. And finally he, Erasmus, is also sick, not from an illness but from medicine for an illness he does not have. Crucially, the gift of the portraits is linked from the beginning to the illness of More's friends. As I shall argue, Giles's illness and its possible causes would become something of a preoccupation for More.

Louvain, 10 July 1517: Erasmus writes to More:

> Pieter Gillis is not really fit even now; he suffers frequent relapses and is afraid of something—I know not what, but I can guess. I very much hope it will not happen. His wife had a miscarriage about the time I returned from England, from anxiety, I suppose, at the danger to her husband. (597; *Correspondence* 5: 9)

London, 16 July 1517: More responds to Erasmus:

> You have made me anxious, dearest Erasmus, by your latest letters (for I have had two), which give me to understand that our friend Pieter is not yet really restored to health and has something else hanging over him as well. What sort of thing this is you guess rather than know, and I could wish that whatever it is that you guess you had given me a few oracular hints, for even guesswork is beyond me, and affection being full of fears, I am driven to be afraid of many things which may be worse than the truth. (601; *Correspondence* 5: 16–17)

What was this mysterious illness of Giles, which creates so much anxiety in Erasmus and in More? Why could it not be named? More feared things "which may be worse than the truth" concerning this illness of Giles. Why, we might also ask, did Erasmus write to More about it, dropping broad hints? Perhaps because in the late summer of 1517 illness was on everyone's mind. A devastating epidemic called sweating sickness was sweeping across England and parts of Europe. Sweating sickness could kill in a matter of hours. More was terrified for himself and for his family, and depressed by the death of Andrea Ammonio, a member of their circle of humanist friends. More was also anxious about his upcoming diplomatic mission to Calais,[13] where the sickness was also raging, and Erasmus was afraid for him, as he states in a letter to Giles. Yet there may have been other reasons why More and Erasmus were concerned for Giles and fearful of his sickness, as I shall discuss below.

---

12   On the fate of the diptych after More returned to England and its subsequent history, see Campbell et al.

13   More would remain abroad until December. Ackroyd 188–91.

Late summer or autumn, 1517 (?): More writes a letter to Giles that would be published in the Paris edition of the *Utopia*, which appeared sometime that fall.[14] In this letter, More addresses criticisms of his book leveled by an unnamed reader, possibly invented by More himself. This critic is not certain whether the book is fact or fiction, but, either way, More's book has numerous problems. If More's letter was written tongue-in-cheek, it seems nevertheless defensive in its response to the anonymous critic. The letter is cooler toward Giles as well—compared, that is, to More's prefatory letter to Giles in the first edition, which appeared in this and later editions as well. "Farewell to you, my dear Peter, to your charming wife and clever little daughter," More closes; "to all, my wife sends her very best wishes" (*Utopia* 269). More's wife, about whom he complained floridly in his earlier published letter to Giles, here becomes a kind of emissary. This closing, in contrast to that of the prefatory letter to the first edition, seems to subordinate their friendship to their marriages.

Antwerp, 8 September 1517: Erasmus writes to More in Calais:

> I send you the pictures, so that you may still have our company after a fashion, if some chance removes us from the scene. Pieter contributed one half and I the other—not that either of us would not gladly have paid the whole, but we wanted it to be a present from us both. Pieter Gillis is still confined by that sickness of his. I am living in Louvain, all among the reverend doctors, and am in my usual health. I am sorry for you, tied to Calais as you are. If nothing else is possible, do at least write often, even a few words. Farewell, my dear More, whom I love best of mortal men. (654; *Correspondence* 5: 106)

The gift of the double portrait, delivered with this letter or perhaps soon after, was rendered in a complex way, tied as it was to Giles's threatening illness, which would never be named in writing. The threat of the epidemic was also hanging over all of them.

This gift, together with the letters that Erasmus wrote with it and those More wrote back to his two friends, has been frequently interpreted—and celebrated—as the apogee of their three-way friendship.[15] This portrait also adds to the mythology and mystique of the Renaissance humanist friendship tradition. Erasmus is depicted in the middle of scholarly activity, for he is shown writing out his paraphrase of Romans. On the shelf behind him are many books, including an edition of Lucian's epigrams (published jointly by Erasmus and More in 1506), Erasmus's own translation of the New Testament, his *Moriae encomium* (*The Praise of Folly*), and a copy of St Jerome's Vulgate. Giles, too, is posed in a humanist setting. Behind him are printed editions of Plutarch, Seneca, Suetonius, and others. He holds in his left hand a letter bearing Thomas More's signature, reproduced with striking realism. On it one may read the words "Vir Literatisimo

---

[14]   On the possible dating of the second edition, see *Utopia* 270–72.

[15]   See, for example, Jardine 29. See, too, n. 21.

Petro / Egidio Amico charisimo / Antwerpiae" ["To the most lettered Peter Giles of Antwerp, my dearest friend"].[16] Underneath Giles's right hand there lies an ornate book, variously identified as Erasmus's *Querela pacis*, his *Antibarbari*, or, as Lisa Jardine has argued, a newly published copy of More's *Utopia*—"a symbol indeed of the three men's *amicitia*" (38).

Underscoring the iconography of humanist friendship conveyed in the Matsys double portrait, Jardine explains of the painting and correspondence about it:

> The exchange of letters between intellectual friends 'frames' the diptych, which is itself a tribute to, and token of, that friendship. The letters provide a setting, an occasion, and a collection of harmonizing sentiments which give the graphic representations additional meaning. They contrive an atmosphere of vivid excitement; they dramatize a flurry of delighted exchanges which supposedly attended the transportation from Antwerp to London (via Calais) of the double portrait. (29)

In her analysis of the two paintings, Jardine notes that "the Gilles panel is indeed laden with visual 'clues' which link him much more securely with Erasmus than More" (37). But the friendship between the two men opens out to a third member, More, "the recipient of the individual, equal gifts, whose cost they insist is shared equally between them" (37). Jardine seems to suggest two interpretations at once—the combined gift announces the friendship between Erasmus and Giles, yet also includes More in a triadic friendship commemorated in the panels. In support of that second interpretation, Jardine links the diptych to the publication of *Utopia* that same year. She also foregrounds the "harmonizing sentiments" behind the paintings. However, possible dissonant notes can be detected, as well—notes of ambivalence in his letters to both friends that underlie More's expressions of enthusiasm and gratitude for the unique gift. These suggest that the triangulated friendship was more complicated than previous scholarship has held.

Calais, 7 October 1517: More, still on his diplomatic mission abroad, writes a thank-you letter to Erasmus, which he includes in a letter to Giles. More praises the painting, then declares his love for Erasmus:

> You would hardly believe, my most lovable Erasmus, how my affection for you, which I was convinced would admit of no addition, has been increased by this desire of yours to bind me still closer to you, and how forcibly I exult in the glory of being so highly valued by you; for in this remarkable document you put it on record that there is no one else whose affection you rate so highly. For such is my own interpretation at any rate—conceited it may be, but thus it is: you have sent me this present to remind me of you not merely every day but every hour. (683, *Correspondence* 5: 147)

---

[16]   These words appear in Fig. 2.2, presumed to be Matsys's original portrait of Giles (Gerló 14)

More expresses delight at receiving the portrait of Erasmus. This warm and loving letter of thanks acknowledges the gift of the painting, cherished by More. Significantly, More projects his friendship with Erasmus into the remote future. "[D]istant posterity will remember me for my friendship with Erasmus," he writes. This prediction has proven true, since to this day their bond of friendship continues to be celebrated and mythologized as the archetypal humanist friendship.

Calais, 6 and 7 October 1517: More pens a letter to Giles that is less effusive than the accompanying letter to Erasmus, and also more labyrinthine.[17] More opens with an expression of sympathy over Giles's illness:

> My dearest Pieter, greeting! I want passionately to hear whether you are getting strong again, which matters no less to me than any of my own concerns; and so I make careful enquiries and diligently pick up all I can from everybody. A certain number of people have given me a more cheerful account, either (as I hope) because they know it for a fact, or just to give me what they knew I wanted.

He mentions that he has included a letter to Erasmus, which is unsealed, "for there is no reason why anything addressed to him need be sealed when it comes to you." Then More announces that he has included some verses on the painting, and sends a copy to Giles. "If you think them worth it, pass them on to Erasmus; otherwise put them on the fire" (684; *Correspondence* 5: 149).

More offers the poem (quoted below in prose translation) primarily to Giles (who may share it with Erasmus, if he wishes, or simply destroy it). He opens by focusing on the friendship between Giles and Erasmus:

The Picture Speaks

> I show Erasmus and Giles, friends as dear to each other as were Castor and Pollux of old. More grieves to be absent from them in space, since in affection he is united with them [*coniunctus amore*] so closely that a man could scarcely be closer to himself. They arranged to satisfy their absent friend's longing for them: a loving letter represents their minds, I their bodies [*Reddat amans animum littera, ego corpus*]. (684; *Poems* 3.2: 298–9)[18]

---

[17]   The differing rhetoric and tone of these two letters has been noted by Bek, who finds the letter to Erasmus more substantial and personal than the other, and concludes that More "was consciously tuning the two letters to suit the diverse personalities of his two friends" (477). Gerló, in contrast, finds the letter to Giles "moins solennelle et pompeuse" (12–13).

[18]   Here I switch to the prose translation in More's *Latin Poems* (eds Miller et al.) rather than the versified translation in Erasmus's *Correspondence,* which is not literal enough.

Castor and Pollux are twin sons of Leda (in some versions of the myth, one is mortal, the other immortal), as well as friends. More's reference to the twins may also be a means of describing the diptych itself, as well as the close friendship of Erasmus and Giles. More is separated from that pairing by geographical distance, and implicitly by degree of relation, yet he states that he feels closely joined to them (*coniunctus amore*) nonetheless. There is much speculation about the meaning of *littera* at the end of this passage, which some have taken to refer to a lost letter from Thomas More, or, Wootton suggests, to the *Utopia* itself.[19] Jardine also proposes an identification: the *amans littera* may refer to the letter from More to Giles that appeared in the 1517 French edition of the *Utopia* (40–41).[20]

Later in the poem More himself speaks, at one point addressing the painter, Quentin Matsys. He asks:

> Quentin, reviver of an ancient art, not less an artist than great Apelles, marvelously gifted to lend life by a mixture of colors to lifeless shapes, alas, why were you satisfied to paint on perishable wood [*fragile ... ligno*] portraits so painstakingly, so beautifully, done ... .These portraits you have done ought to have been entrusted to a more enduring medium [*materiae fideliori*] which could preserve through the years what it had received. O, if you could only have looked out for your own fame and the desires of posterity; for if future ages preserve any love of the fine arts and if savage warfare does not obliterate the arts, then what a price posterity would pay for this picture! (*Poems* 3.2: 300–301)

A tension between decay ("perishable wood") and preservation ("a more enduring medium") may represent in a different register the paradoxical relation of Castor and Pollux, of mortality and immortality. These paired letters that More penned to Erasmus and Giles themselves bear out this theme of unequal twinship. While the letter to Erasmus closes with a positive image of "distant posterity" remembering More's friendship with the great humanist, the poem contained in the letter to Giles points out the vulnerability of wood and the possible destruction of the

---

[19] "What is the *amans littera*?" Wootton asks. "A *littera* (the word is rare in the singular, more common in the plural) can be a carved letter (as on a tombstone), handwriting (as in a signature), a letter (for posting), a text, or a book. The general assumption has been that More is referring to some letter that has not survived. This seems to me to miss the convention of the poem, which is explaining how we should read the picture. The *amans littera,* I suggest, is *Utopia* itself, the volume which Giles is portrayed presenting to More" (269).

[20] Following Allen, Jardine contends that More himself may have authorized that edition (cp. n. 11 and 14, *sup.*). If this is true, then it is not clear why More would demand that letter back, unless we take at face value his desire to keep the letter on hand to compare with the painted version. On the significance of More's second letter, to Giles, which addresses the concerns of an unknown critic of the *Utopia,* see Surtz, 319–24, and McCutcheon, 55–8.

painting. In an oblique way, More may also be alluding, perhaps unconsciously, to Giles' mysterious illness. Lastly, the underlying fantasy of the destruction of Giles's portrait may reflect jealousy or rivalry on the part of More, who may have felt excluded from the close friendship between Erasmus and Giles.

At the end of his letter, More asks for one of his letters back—specifically, the letter that appears in the painting of Giles. "My dear Pieter," More writes, "marvelously as our Quentin has represented everything, what a wonderful forger above all else it looks as though he might have been! He has imitated the address on my letter to you so well that I do not believe I could repeat it myself." "[D]o please let me have the letter back," he asks, "it will double the effect if it is kept handy alongside the picture. If it has been lost or you have a use for it, I will see whether I in my turn can imitate the man who imitates my hand so well. Farewell, you and your charming wife" (684, *Correspondence* 5: 151). The tone of urgency or insistence in this portion of the letter is striking. Why might More have wanted his letter back—whichever letter it may have been—and why does he fantasize about the possible destruction of the painting in this letter to Giles, while in the companion letter to Erasmus he imagines that the painting will attest to their friendship in the far distant future? Scholars have typically taken More at his word. It may be, however, that More requested his letter back because he was in some way retracting its sentiments as well.

Louvain, c. October 1517: Erasmus writes to Giles a chastising letter.

> I wish you could overcome your hot temper; it is very bad for your health and contributes so little to the dispatch of business that it is actually a great hindrance. Why need you let it be known that you were angry with the physician? ... Take my word for it, unless you abstain from two things, disorder of the mind and unseasonable sexual relations, I would rather not confess what I fear for you, my most dear Pieter. So I beg you most urgently, put your health in all respects first. (687; *Correspondence* 5: 156)

Here Erasmus connects Giles's illness, his temperament, and his "unseasonable sexual relations." The possible connections between these three things are not clear from the letter, though a later one suggests an answer, as we shall see. The specific reasons for Giles's anger are also not known, though the scolding from Erasmus may not have been particularly welcome. Erasmus also mentions that he will not be visiting at Christmas because of his work.

Louvain, 3 November 1517: Erasmus writes to Giles urging him to hold steady in the face of life's challenges. He seems to allude to Giles's illness, as well as that of Giles's father: "I have great hopes of your father's life," Erasmus states, "but yet, if anything should happen, see to it that I do not lose two friends at once." A few lines later he adds:

> Farewell, my best of friends, and quit you like a man—or rather, remember that man is but mortal and play out your part on the stage of this life. My best wishes

to you and yours, and specially to your excellent father. (702; *Correspondence* 5: 182–3)

Calais, 5 November 1517: More, still working abroad on the King's business, writes to Erasmus about several matters. He concludes with a further discussion of the epigram he had composed on the Matsys diptych. More relates that "a certain friar" criticized the reference to Castor and Pollux: "He said you [Erasmus and Giles] should have been compared to Theseus and Pirithous or Pylades and Orestes, who were friends, as you are, and not brothers." Declaring his annoyance with this friar, More sends to Erasmus a second epigram:

> Quoth I, of two great friends in brief
> The affection to declare,
> 'Such friends they are as once of old
> Castor and Pollux were.'
> An owlish brother takes me up,
> Of those who wear the cowl:
> 'Who friends and brothers thus confounds,
> Sure, he must be an owl!'
> 'How so? What can more friendly be
> Than brother is to brother?'
> He laughed at one who did not know
> What's known to every other:
> 'A large and crowded house is ours,
> Brothers ten score may be;
> In those ten score (my life upon't)
> Two friends you will not see.' (706; *Correspondence* 5: 190)

The target of this satirical epigram appears to be the intrusive friar, a 'brother' who lives in a house with ten score others, and in a brotherhood no way conducive to friendship. "What can more friendly [*amicior*] be / Than brother is to brother?" More asks the friar naively, only to get the humorous response that More places in the friar's mouth. But satire often cuts in multiple directions at once, as it may in fact be doing here. The relationship between Erasmus and Giles, twin-like in More's earlier comparison, is here compared ironically to the *non*-friendship of brothers (in this case, religious brothers). Alternatively, the riddle "What can more friendly be / Than brother is to brother?" could be taken to suggest an emotional or erotic intimacy that exceeds the bond of brotherhood. With this ambivalent and aggressive joke, which allows for at least two quite different interpretations, More now stands outside of the pairing, no longer *coniunctus amore* with his two friends.

Louvain, 10 November 1517: Erasmus consoles Giles, who is on the verge of losing his father:

> I wish whatever is best to your excellent father. I do beg you most urgently, dearest Pieter, bear with reason what cannot be altered, and do not let yourself be overcome with grief which will destroy you, and be a painful burden to your family and very painful to More and myself.

In order not to add to Giles's burdens, Erasmus is sending his man Jacobus to "fetch away what you have of mine," though he encourages Giles to keep whatever he would like. "I would have come myself," he writes, "but I am afraid of the phlegm and entirely occupied in revising the New Testament" (708; *Correspondence* 5: 192).

Louvain, 15 November 1517: Erasmus writes a letter of sympathy to Giles, whose father has just died. At the same time, he is pleased to hear that Giles himself has begun to recover from his illness. Erasmus also writes about their mutual friend:

> More is still at Calais, which he finds, it appears, both tedious and expensive, and the business of a most disagreeable kind. This is how kings make their friends happy; such a thing it is to be popular with cardinals. (712; *Correspondence* 5: 202)

The chattiness of portions of this letter seem at odds with the seriousness of the occasion, though a day or so later, Erasmus will compose a more formal letter of condolence to his friend celebrating the life of Nicolaas Gillis (715).

Antwerp, 22 February 1518: Erasmus writes to Johannes Sixtinus, another friend: "About Pieter Gillis' health I spread no rumours, but I did complain in a letter to More; and I only wish the report was untrue. My dear friend, there is only too much truth in it, and at the sight of the danger he is in, I fear piteously for myself" (775; *Correpondence* 5: 300). Erasmus admits to having told Thomas More about this illness, information that Giles did not want spread about as rumor. Giles had contracted a shameful disease that could not be named or discussed openly, which Erasmus had earlier linked to Giles's sexual excesses. What could this mysterious malady have been? Charles Clay Doyle has suggested that Giles may have been suffering from syphilis, which seems a plausible conclusion. This was not the treatable illness we know today, but a more virulent form with no reliable cure; the disease carried with it a strong moral stigma, as well.

Erasmus and Giles continued to exchange letters thereafter, as did Erasmus and More. Judging from the lack of extant correspondence, the relation between More and Giles remains much less clear. Many years later More mentions Giles as his "good friend" in a letter to Conrad Goclenius, written in November of 1522 (*SL* 153). Nevertheless, there is little evidence to suggest the survival of the intense and exuberant friendship that helped bring More's great piece of creative writing into being.

Despite the many "friends forever" commentaries on the Matsys portrait as gift to Thomas More, the relationship between the three men was probably more complicated than idealizing biographers and critics have suggested.[21] I have suggested that More's *Utopia* expresses the tension he felt between marriage and family life on the one hand, and the social, intellectual, professional, and emotional bonds he enjoyed with his friends on the other. The affective intensity of *Utopia's* paratext and frame narrative, as well as the letters exchanged in the years before and after its publication, suggest that these friendship attachments were not only conventional expressions of allegiances between humanists, but perhaps emotionally and/or erotically charged bonds as well. Previous scholarship has not, to my knowledge, allowed for the possible flow of eros between these three friends, nor for negative emotions that frequently accompany intense attachments, whatever their precise nature, or their mode or degree of realization. Acknowledging that possibility, however, may clarify one aspect of More's *Utopia* and its composition.

As noted at the beginning of this essay, More chose not to integrate friendship and its bonds into his representation of Utopian life; the competing demands of family life and friendship represent one form of triangulation that offered no easy resolution, either in real life or in More's fiction. A second form of triangulation, equally challenging, was the celebrated More–Erasmus–Giles friendship, shaped not only by the conventions of humanist friendship but also by the shifting emotional currents of affection, dependencies, desire, ambition, fear, and suspicion, and even jealousy or rivalry. Intriguingly, Erasmus, who had introduced his two friends to each other, may have undermined that friendship, either accidentally or on purpose, through his enigmatic letters to More about Giles's illness.

Paradoxically, then, the gift of the double portrait celebrated a unique and powerful triangular—and triangulated—friendship that had already become charged with a range of complicated emotions and rivalries. The clue to More's affective distancing from Giles—and possibly from Erasmus, as well—at least for a time—I take to be More's rather insistent request to have his letter back. Like Poe's purloined letter, it is hidden in plain sight. Its enigmatic contents are folded up. We cannot read them. What we may read, if we so choose, in More's ever so polite retraction of his letter to Giles is the possible cooling of the remarkable triadic friendship that had enabled the dream of Utopia, yet that had also been confined to its margins.

---

21 See, for example, Bridgett 108–11; Routh 81–8; McCutcheon 15–16; Mann-Phillips 30–31; Freeman 25. Marius and Ackroyd mention More's request for the letter, yet construe that request as a sign of affection.

Figure 2.1   Quentin Matsys, *Portrait of Desiderius Erasmus*. Oil on oak panel, 50.3 cm × 45 cm. The Royal Collection © 2010 Her Majesty Queen Elizabeth II. Hampton Court, England.

Figure 2.2   Quentin Matsys, *Portrait of Pieter Giles*. Oil on oak panel, 74.6 cm. × 52.2 cm. Photographic Survey, The Courtauld Institute of Art, London. Private Collection

Chapter 3

Friendship's Passion: Love-Fellowship in Sidney's *New Arcadia*

Daniel T. Lochman

The traditional discourse of psychic virtue and stability in relationships between males, drawn from Greco-Roman and medieval conventions of friendship, left its mark on Elizabethan culture generally and upon the era's literary romances particularly, including Philip Sidney's *Arcadia,* in both its original and revised forms. Yet Sidney's narratives—the *Old Arcadia* thought to have been completed before 1580 and the *New Arcadia* produced by Fulke Greville in 1590—do more than reclothe the old language of friendship in early modern dress. More or less completely and successfully, they replace ancient and medieval conceptions of friendship and supply radically new ones. In her study of friendship in the *Arcadias*, Wendy Olmsted shows that both versions of Sidney's romance revised the ancient discourse of friendship. She links shifts in the rhetoric of friendship to ideas of hospitality and emerging interests in civility as well as to heightened awareness of differences that preclude Greco-Roman ideas of the sameness of "perfect" friends and an enlarged scope for rhetorical affect due to Protestant distrust of lapsed reason (20–53, 76–105). In place of the stern deliberative or judicial rhetoric that Aristotle and Cicero advocated to bring a lapsed friend to temperance and virtue, Sidney offers what Olmsted calls a "gentle" rhetoric. In describing this new approach for aiding "imperfect" friends, Olmsted refers to the correcting friend as a moral physician and healer rather than judge (15–17, 30–33), a changed role she illustrates by examining the "new begun friendship" that emerges at the close of Book 1 in both versions of Sidney's narrative. There, Musidorus ends a friendship-threatening correction of Pyrocles—cross-dressed to gain access to his beloved Philoclea—by replacing harsh rhetoric with emotional support and love that redefine friendship "as companionship in vulnerability to fortune" (Olmsted 42; *OA* 23; *NA* 139–40).[1]

I propose to build on Olmsted's argument by setting rhetorical change within an early modern context of the body, including its faculties, members, humors, and passions. Doing so, I will argue, discloses a radical alteration in the figuration of friendship, with Sidney seemingly devising in the revision a new yet

---

[1] Throughout, I refer to the edition of the *Old Arcadia* (*OA*) edited by Katherine Duncan-Jones and to the section of the *New Arcadia* (*NA*) published in *The Countess of Pembroke's Arcadia*, edited by Maurice Evans.

incompletely realized trajectory for the passions expressed as "love-fellowship." This latter replaces the Greco-Roman noetic discourse of friendship, conventional representations of chivalric friendship and the consequent violence it evokes through triangulated love of the courtly lady, and even the masculine bonds strengthened by the imposition of strict justice in the concluding book of the *Old Arcadia*. The revised *Arcadia* instead introduces "true" friendship through the unlikely, refurbished characters Claius and Strephon, whose impassioned, multidirectional love is far from the conventions of Aristotelian *philia,* Stoic *amicitia*, and chivalric friendship (Stern-Gillet 37–77; Pangle 43–7; Hyatte 87–91). In part, I suggest, this unique friendship is a consequence of popularized Galenic medical theories that tended to blur rigid divisions between mind and body. Between the appearance of Galen's texts in England through Latin translations such as Thomas Linacre's (beginning in 1517) and Descartes's writing in the 1640s that the body is an "earthen machine," Galenism flourished in England, though often in incomplete or inaccurate translations, adaptations, and extracts more or less carefully related to the Greek originals (Schoenfeldt 2–8; Descartes 2). Eve Keller writes that during the early modern period texts published in England gradually disseminated a view of the self as "a distributed entity, a pattern that arises from the functioning in concert of the body's manifold parts." This view may allow the rational soul to govern the self, but it does not presume with Descartes that reason is the "exclusive locus of cognition" or "the single locus of personhood" (43; see Paster, Rowe, and Floyd-Wilson 16; Siraisi 190–93).

The emerging Galenic model of the body merged with early modern political theories that presumed a corporate unity comprised of discrete members. Like early modern medical writers, Sidney in the *Apology* granted provisional sovereignty to reason as the governor over a healthy body's members, yet in his argument he allowed the "erected wit" little sway over the lapsed and "infected" will (66). In principle, Euarchus and Basilius in the *Old Arcadia* are sovereign in the countries they rule, yet for each an excessive zeal for justice or a foolish wish to outdo the gods provokes the threat or reality of popular dissent and rebellion. Akin to Sidney's distinction between poetry that is *eikastic* or *phantastic* (figuring "good things" or infecting the fancy with "unworthy objects"), bodies natural and politic are subject to good or ill rule. For both, disease constitutes the just or unjust rebellion of one or more members or faculties against sovereign reason. This view takes form in the *Old Arcadia* when, at the close of Book 5, the Arcadians object to Euarchus's "insupportable" tyranny of "obstinate-hearted," "pitiless" justice (*OA* 358; Stillman 1308–13). Philisides's Ister bank fable of beasts and man, a tale learned from "old Languet," likewise recounts a rebellion (though of beasts) against the human tyrant built from their best parts, whose unwarranted pride subverts the "jump concord" that should harmonize "wit and will" (*OA* 222–5). In the *Apology*, Sidney cites Menenius Agrippa's use of a tale of the body's revolt from the belly to convince the people of the value of each civic member (85–6). Writers of medical texts used the very same *exemplum* to emphasize the value to the whole of the distributed parts of the Galenic body. In *The Touchstone of*

Complexions, for instance, Levinus Lemnius employs the *exemplum* of Agrippa to describe the value of the lowly "belly" to good health (f 12r). Although early moderns erected firm boundaries to separate mind and body as well as sovereign and subject, the differences sometimes seem malleable and fluid, expressing a soft liminality the Galenic model facilitated by placing the passions, humors, and spirits as mediaries between mind and body. Rather than merely impeding or obstructing friendship as the Aristotelian and Stoic discourse presumed, the passions could, in the Galenic model, contribute to the unity of body and mind.

Similarly mediated conceptions of body and mind appear in Elizabethan romances, especially those newly translated from Greek. Steven Mentz refers to a "Heliodoran movement in English prose fiction" beginning in the 1580s, when Robert Greene borrowed from *Aethiopica* and other Greek romances narratives wherein male and female characters undertook adventures guided by ethics and love moderated by constancy rather than desire (Mentz 47–71). In contrast to the Greco-Roman emphasis upon reason and temperance and the Petrarchan emphasis upon the pain of unrelieved desire, Greek romance elevated the passions because they were thought to join body to mind. Greek romance also initiated what David Konstan calls "sexual symmetry," a mutuality of male–female pairs that replaced rigid division of masculine reason and feminine passion and opened the way to more fluid renderings of gendered faculties; it sanctioned the masculine expression of passion; and it opened the way to representations of friendship between men and women (Konstan, *Sexual Symmetry* 14–59; Stanivukovic 173–88). Darlene C. Greenhalgh observes that ancient romance narratives would have been of particular interest to Protestants, who sought to replace sacramental marriage with a domestic economy of "reciprocal chastity" and fidelity (like that in the *Aethiopica*), "female virginity and honor in love" (as in *Leucippe and Clitophon*), and "sexual innocence and purity" in a pastoral world (as in Longus's *Daphnis and Chloe*) (19–37). Early modern translations and adaptations of the Greek romances brought the body and the erotic into dialogue with the Catholic ideal of chastity, and their publication in England overlapped with that of Galenic texts that provided a technical vocabulary of passion. Despite Galen's deep "ambivalence" toward the passions, Keller attributes to his works "an ontology of the organism in which, practically speaking, psyche and soma are mutually determining, each in some regard, or at some time, potentially dependent on the other" (39). For the early modern reader, Greek romances and their contemporary adaptations gave this physiological interdependence of mind and body literary form.

In his *Apology*, Sidney seems to have reconsidered the usefulness of the passions to the poet. In the *Old Arcadia*, the passions had led to the disastrous consequences evident in Basilius's foolish efforts to seduce Cleophila and the nearly deadly consequences of the princes' sexual advances toward the princesses. The *Apology* affirms, however, that a skilled and virtuous poet should move the passions in order to lead an audience to act virtuously (122, 68–71). Through art, the "right" poet overtops the "credit" of an orator, even though the latter may be capable of winning "popular ears," as Zelmane demonstrates when pacifying the rebellious Arcadians at the end of Book 2 (*OA* 121–2; *NA* 382–7). According to the *Apology*, the right poet forcefully imitates to move passions to "right" action and overcome the weakness of the mind's "inward light" after the fall (Miller, "Passion Signified" 407–13; Eckerle, "With a tale" 52–6). The passions become the surest means to move an audience to "virtuous action," the "ending end of all earthly learning" (82–3, 71). More than its predecessor, the revised *Arcadia* presents love—that most powerful passion—as crucial to the friendships of two exemplary male pairs: Claius/Strephon and Musidorus/Pyrocles. Though both pairs represent a new discourse of friendship, the pastoral "love-fellowship" of Strephon and Claius serves as an iconic as well as ironic model and as a measure for the evolving friendship of the princes, Musidorus and Pyrocles.[2] Both friendships mingle the distancing effect of comedy with delightful conveniency, and both elicit impassioned action—or empathetic "com-passion"—and therefore, according to Sidney's *Apology*, should produce virtuous action.

The 1590 *Arcadia* opens with the shepherds Claius and Strephon, in contrast to the *Old Arcadia*, where they do not appear until the Fourth Eclogues when the narrator describes them as "gentlemen" who have forsaken their patrimony in order to pursue the shepherdess Urania, "like two true runners both employing their best speed, but one not hindering the other" (*OA* 285). For their efforts, both earn Urania's "hate." Petrarchan lovers as well as gentry in shepherds' clothing, they conventionally displace sexual frustration through song, as in the Eclogues' double sestina "Ye goat-herd gods" and the dizain "I joy in grief," both poems alternating speakers in stanzas whose interlocking repetitions emphasize the friends' parallel erotic frustration. In the *New Arcadia*, however, Claius and Strephon are genuine shepherds, and they are elevated, not degraded, by their shared admiration for a still distant yet now responsive Urania.

During the opening conversation and subsequent rescue of Musidorus, the pair acquire a significance that exceeds their space in the narrative. The narrator identifies them as "true friends" after they empathize with Musidorus, who, despite a brush with drowning, grieves for his own lost friend, Pyrocles (*NA* 68). As an icon of *vera amicitia*, the pair present what at first may seem a conventional narrative of friends divided by a shared love-interest, the triangulated relationship of chivalric romances that presupposes the objectification of the beloved and often produces violence (Olmsted 87–8; Greenhalgh 18–19). Yet Sidney undermines the anticipated narrative by presenting a pair of men whose mutual, intimate memories of the absent female confirm a "love-fellowship" centered on Urania,

---

[2]   In "Friendship in Sidney's *Arcadias*," Tom MacFaul argues that in both versions friendship frames the whole action and is "redemptive," and he calls the princes' "mutual sympathy" at the opening of Book Three of the *Old Arcadia* "pivotal" as an instance of the redefinition of their friendship (20–21). Significantly, this scene is omitted in the *New Arcadia*. Although MacFaul sees the latter version as generally promoting the "greater dignity" of the princes relative to the earlier version (24), the princes' dignity may seem in question when the text breaks off.

an imagined presence who becomes indirectly tangible when her letter addressed to both friends arrives at Kalendar's house and sends them scurrying to meet her. In the revision, Urania is no longer the Petrarchan object of masculine pursuers whom she hates (though this is a role she reprises, oddly, in the "Barley-break" poem added to the First Eclogues in the Countess of Pembroke's 1593 version [197–212]). Though bodily distant, she is inwardly present to the shepherds due to visceral, imprinted memories of her natural "cheerfulness," "sweet words," and compassion—memories that inspire a chaste, friendly, and impassioned *ménage à trois*. Strephon recreates for Claius the place where, departing, "she laid her hand over thine eyes, when she saw the tears springing in them, as if she would conceal them from others and yet herself feel some of thy sorrow" (62). Although Strephon initially laments her absence, memory turns his complaint to rapt apostrophe of her imagined form—"O Urania, blessed be thou, Urania, the sweetest fairness and fairest sweetness!" (62)—and produces in Claius a climax of joy that displaces pain: "let us think with consideration, and consider with acknowledging, and acknowledge with admiration, and admire with love, and love with joy in the midst of all woes" (63). Benjamin Scott Grossberg identifies the motive of this friendship as repressed heteroeroticism projected as mutual affection and a displacement that, according to Grossberg, mirrors the social repression of the homoerotic in the masculine culture of Elizabeth's courtiers (64). His psychosocial reading anticipates what Daniel Juan Gil capaciously describes as Elizabethan England's emerging "social imaginary" of "shared humanity"— "a powerful new way of envisioning social relationships and the social world." From this perspective, Sidney's shepherds' passion for one another and Urania instantiates an Arcadian imaginary of fellowship set against the comparatively deficient behavior of friends in the narrative universe known to Musidorus and Pyrocles and the material world recognized by Sidney's reading audience. Claius and Strephon inhabit the pastoral stability that precedes the tumult of the ensuing romance narrative with its episodic ambition, violence, warfare, eroticism, and self-aggrandizing actions—what Gil might call the "spectacular violations" that inevitably undermine belief in a "shared human core identity" (5).

For the aristocrat Kalendar, the transformation of Claius and Strephon from average Arcadians to exemplary friends seems easy to explain. After Musidorus praises their precocity, Kalendar theorizes that their elevation results from adding "learning" to nature. They seem to participate in humanist self-improvement that replaces lost material "wealth"—the profits of sheep-rearing—with learning: an exchange that Kalendar understands but does not praise. Linking the value of the shepherds' learning to the Arcadian economy, the hierarchy-minded Kalendar disallows any elevated social status to education (*NA* 83). When informing Musidorus that "it is a sport to hear how they impute [their superiority] to love, which hath indued their thoughts, *say they*, with … strength" (84, my emphasis), Kalendar implies that the shepherds' belief in the transformative power of love inadequately explains their improvement, if they have improved at all. In contrast, when Prince Musidorus admires the shepherds, he does so because his experience of their rhetorical finesse, compassion, and empathetic concern reminds him of "such shepherds as Homer speaks of, that be governors of peoples, [rather] than such senators who hold their council in sheep-cotes" (83). While Kalendar tamps down and objectifies the shepherds' achievement, Musidorus magnifies it and empathizes with them. Sidney's audience may be inclined to share this latter point of view—admiring and delighting in the opening scene's paradox of pastoral sophistication. The narrator lavishes attention upon what Paul Alpers has described as the "convening" at the heart of pastoral, together with its related "displacement of action to utterance" and consequent promotion of creative energies such as the imaginative recreation of Urania's absent beauty (Alpers 79–86; Duncan-Jones 261).

Much as the vestigial memory of Urania, once revivified, shapes the shepherds' feelings and actions, Sidney's revised opening seems designed to imprint readers' minds with an experience of impassioned friendship. Readers are encouraged to share the point of view of Claius when he interrogates the power of beauty and love:

> [W]ho can better witness that [measure of her beauty] than we, whose experience is grounded upon feeling? Hath not the only love of her made us, being silly ignorant shepherds, raise up our thoughts above the ordinary level of the world, so as great clerks do not disdain our conference? Hath not the desire to seem worthy in her eyes made us, when others were running at Base, to run over learned writings, when others to mark their sheep, we to mark ourselves? … Hath in any but in her, love-fellowship maintained friendship between rivals, and beauty taught the beholders chastity? (*NA* 63–4)

Claius's rhetorical emphasis upon the friends' shared "feeling," "love," and "desire to seem worthy," though at odds with Kalendar's economy of commerce and education, seems reasonable to those who provisionally accept the shepherds' fictive world, with its *vera amicitia*—the result of the "love-fellowship" that joins passion to passivity before the chastity-inducing effects of Urania's beauty. As friends, Claius and Strephon occupy a middle ground—neither intellectually disengaged nor aggressive, but passive in the sense of both the Middle French *passif* ("being acted upon, objectified") and the Latin *passivus* (being "capable of feeling"). Due to their perception and love of Urania as an icon of beauty, they experience something like a "radical decentering" that, Elaine Scarry writes, is key both to the perception of beauty and its response. Scarry links this decentering to a "nonself-interestedness" that seems to evoke "the other the same" (*alter idem*) of noetic friendship discourse but that she identifies with sensual perception and pleasurable affect. Moreover, Scarry theorizes that the lack of self-interest caused by beauty has a lateralizing effect that promotes viewers' perception of "fair"ness and justice in other exemplars (111–5). In *Arcadia*, a similar "lateral" dimension explains the shepherds' "love-fellowship," which is inspired by their shared perception of Urania's beauty and realization of what is "fair." From beauty, they derive an ethic of empathetic respect—a social imaginary of shared humanity, one might say—manifest in compassion to one another or to the washed-ashore Musidorus and in their suppression of sexual appetite in the service of constancy.

Seeing the shepherds in the revised text as an iconic segue to the ensuing narrative must allow, however, for the comic element that pervades the new opening. The sophistication of their pastoral conversation easily slips toward the ludicrous. It is impossible to take seriously Claius's comparison of Urania's eyelids to "two white kids climbing up a fair tree and browsing on its tenderest branches" (*NA* 63). Yet the comic mingles with what Sidney in the *Apology* had called the "conveniency" of delight (117–8). Just as the revised opening permits pastoral to open directly into the romance—rather than being segregated in the "pastorals" of the older version—so it seems to aim for a hybrid tone that mingles comedy with delight, that simultaneously objectifies the shepherds and opens them to empathy. The hybrid is evident in Sidney's language as well: the revision's first paragraph is saturated with words combining *philia* and *eros,* their ancient binary collapsing in a mingling of friendship, love, and desire. While Earth prepares for the advance of night and the "approach of her lover," the "hopeless shepherd Strephon" faces Cithera, Venus's isle and the new residence of chaste Urania. Overcome by Urania's absence, Strephon calls on his "friendly rival," Claius, to voice for him the "heavy kind of delight" evoked by Urania's departure (61). As the discourses of *eros* and *philia* brush against one another, a vestige of one adheres to the other, producing a whole whose common element is the passion that unites friends and lovers. The friends' "love-fellowship" glances at the homoerotic, as Grossberg suggests, at the same time that it bends to include the friends' lateral "compassion," this latter extended to yet another, the naked "young man of so goodly shape and well-pleasing favour that one would think that death had in him a lovely countenance" (64). The narrator shares the shepherds' visual attention to Musidorus's naked beauty and fleetingly echoes the homoerotic triad of friends suggested in Sidney's "Two Pastoralls," involving the mutual love of Sidney, Edward Denny, and Fulke Greville (Duncan-Jones 240–41). In *Arcadia*, however, the homoerotic receives lateral expression, and the consequent sense of shared humanity yields compassion. Alan Bray wisely suggested that we should avoid reducing friendship *only* to the erotic (6–7). If, to use Lisa Hopkins' phrase, we may observe that the revised *Arcadia* presents a "comprehensive definition and anatomy of love and desire" (62–74), Claius and Strephon may be said to embrace love in all its dimensions.

Granting that Sidney rethinks the relationship of the passions to poetry when drafting the *Apology*, why would he so emphasize their power in the revised *Arcadia*? For an explanation, one might look to the cultural reorganization that results from a female sovereign, to the development of the Elizabethan court, or, as Gil does, to the formation of an idea of intimacy. But an important element of an Elizabethan idea of shared humanity centers on the body and its processes. Viewing the passions as a physiological means of joining sense to intellect gives point to Sidney's representation of *vera amicitia* in Claius and Strephon.

The editors of *Reading the Early Modern Passions* have proposed that some early modern writers rejected or modified the conventional emphasis upon reason as the sovereign arbiter and governor of the passions, the latter still viewed potentially as "perturbations, or perilous forces that acted on the suffering body" but now attributed with more positive effects as well (Paster, Rowe, and Floyd-Wilson 12). Early modern medical texts reveal that a revaluation of the passions was far from consistent. Even though medical writers preceding Sidney allowed in some places that passions *could* be consistent with Christian acts of compassion, they often favored Galen's Stoic advice to achieve health through a regimen of moral and temperate behavior (*Passions and Errors* III, 31–2). Writers inclined to Calvinism emphasized the passions' proneness to incontinence (*akrasia*) and opposition to reason, the defining and superior faculty (Olmsted 60–61). In *The Touchstone of Complexions*, Lemnius figured the mind and its faculties as the "high Magistrates and Peeres of the Realme" who dispense laws and ordinances for the "poore Comminalitie" of the body, whose "lewd affections, and unbridled motions" require obedience (f 11r–v). Published more than a decade after Sidney's death, Thomas Wright's *The Passions of the Minde in Generall* (2nd ed., 1604) degrades the passions through a domestic analogy: passions are the "naughtie servants" of reason in that they are "drowned in corporall organs and instruments, as well as sense" (8). Elsewhere, however, both Lemnius and Wright mitigate the authority of reason by acknowledging that compassion, righteous anger, and charity are essential to acting well. Galen had classified the passions as "non-naturals," things external to the body and distinct from both the "naturals" (all the body's limbs and organs) and the "unnaturals" or "contra-naturals" (diseases and accidents that harm health) (Floyd-Wilson 133–4). Like other "non-naturals"—air, food and drink, sleep and wakefulness, repletion and evacuation—what Lemnius terms the "passions of the mind" may lead to health or disease (f 46r). In *The Castel of Helthe* (1539) Thomas Elyot similarly identified the "affects of the mynde" as non-naturals but emphasized their proclivity to intemperance and illnesses requiring therapies not only of "phisyke corporall" but also of "morall philosophye" to repair the damage done to "man's estimation," reason, and relation to "almighty god" at the Fall (54r–v). Writing in the 1570s, Lemnius emphasized the passions' own therapeutic value when, following Galen, he theorized that bodily "spirits"— that is, vapors derived from concoctions in the body—ascend by secret channels to the brain and mind and there act as "provokers and prickers forwarde *both* to vices & virtues" (my emphasis). As a consequence of their potential influence for health, Lemnius advises, physicians must give passions "carefull consideracion and heede, attende & loke to conserue and gouerne them orderly" (f 14v).

Like Elyot and Sidney in the *Apology*, Lemnius concedes that original sin corrupted the passions along with "imaginations and thoughts of man … onely euill and prone to wickedness." Yet, he asserts, Christ's redemption, the power of grace, and meditation upon Scripture make it possible to think that passions can promote virtue (f 14v). Wright justifies his book on the passions by pointing to Christ's actions in *the* Passion and by asserting the beneficent effects of the passions upon the "motions of our willes" so long as they are regulated by prudence and God's laws (16). He notes that the Bible attributes to God love, hate, ire, and zeal and that God reproduced the same passions in his creatures. As a consequence, human passions such as mercy, compassion, ire, shamefastness, honor, fear, sadness, and delight are, he writes, "not wholly to be extinguished (as the Stoicks seemed to affirme) but sometimes to be moved, and stirred up for the service of virtue" (16– 17). Decades earlier, Juan Luis Vives had written that the best effect possible from the passions is for one simply to overwhelm another, driving "out a nail with the help of another nail" (qtd in Noreña 217)—making the bad less bad. In contrast, Lemnius and Wright assign the passions positive therapeutic and even sanctifying functions.

Though he writes after Sidney's death, Wright describes the passions as motivating the inward activity of body and mind, much as Sidney's shepherds believed their stimulated passions inspired inward, elevated thought and feeling. Wright defined the passions or "affections" as "certaine *internall* actes or operations of the soule, bordering vpon reason and sense, prosecuting some good thing, or flying from an ill thing, causing therewithall some alteration in the body" (8, my emphasis), and he gives them priority as a site of medical treatment. Galen, in contrast, divided the observable effects of a symptom from knowledge of the internal operations that produced it; a physician could diagnose internal illnesses of the soul and the passions only by observing external actions (for example, walking, running, looking, digesting). Consequently, the physician could treat unnatural causes of disease only from a view external to a diseased patient's disturbed psychic activity (*energeia*) or internal complexion (*Passions and Errors* 46–73; *On the Natural Faculties* 1.2.6; Siraisi 124–6). Commenting on Plato's *Philebus* (1496), Marsilio Ficino paved the way to interiorizing diagnosis and treatment of the passions by emphasizing, against Plato, the metaphysical contingency of the divine and human, similar to the unity and contingency of the healthy soul and body. Ficino situated the mind's inner activity or *energeia*—derived in part from the passions—in a boundary-less *act* of mediation between body and intellect (31.298, 31.300) that anticipated Wright's definition of the passions as *internal* acts or operations mediating between the material body and the mind and susceptible to medical intervention. By acting directly upon the passions as a site of medical intervention, then, Sidney's poet could initiate a therapy of, as it were, "internal" medicine wherein the sensate experience, image, or memory of love-fellowship— the "true" friendship of Claius and Strephon—could serve as a pathway to what Wright calls the "passions of the minde," these being "immateriall, spirituall," "independent of any corporall subject," and "bred and borne in the highest part of the soule" (57–9). Michael C. Schoenfeldt writes that "the Galenic regime of the humoral self" supplied early moderns with a "vocabulary of inwardness" that led to an "invasion of social and psychological realms by biological and environmental processes" (8).

In the *Apology*, Sidney uses Galenic language to describe the force by which the passions compel internal effects in an audience. Conceding the defects of

English lyric poets who stray by substituting *eros* for the "immortal beauty" and "immortal goodness" of God, Sidney, imagining himself the beloved, goes on to critique their poor craftsmanship:

> If I were a mistress, [such poets] would never persuade me they were in love, so coldly they apply fiery speeches, as men that had rather read lovers' writings, and so caught up in certain swelling phrases, which hang together like a man that once told me that wind was at northwest by south because he would be sure to name winds enough, than that in truth they feel those passions, which easily, as I think, may be bewrayed by that same forcibleness, or *energia*, as the Greeks call it of the writer. (119)

Peter C. Herman glosses this passage by referring to Aristotle's *Rhetoric*, which advises orators to use "graphic" metaphors that encourage visualization and to prefer "expressions that represent things as in a state of activity [*energeia*]" (1411b)—principles that underlie Sidney's idea of a "speaking picture." Allied with this representational function is another wherein, as Olmsted shows, the classically trained orator was thought to express passions compellingly only when conveying felt emotions by means of rhetorically effective language (65–9). In both senses, emotional effect relies upon the impassioned orator's ability to stimulate empathy and the internal motions that precede observable activity. Therapeutic intervention results from linguistic coercion of the internal physiological processes that compel behavior. For Sidney, the right poet has the advantage of activating these internal processes by representing images—speaking pictures literally imprinted in memory—that predictably stimulate sensation, passion, and other faculties that in turn affect both mind and body. In Galenic terms, passions affect the mind via spirits that arise from concoctions produced first through digestion and then, in purer form, through fire and air in the heart. Able to stimulate passions in the "tenderest subjects," Sidney's poet and physician employs a "medicine of cherries" that is not simply metaphoric. As a moral physician, he disguises the harshness of his "physic" to win "the mind from wickedness to virtue," a result the "inward light" of reason alone cannot achieve (84–5). What the poet requires is not merely skill in rhetoric but, more importantly, the ability to convey through passion images capable of coercing physiological (and therefore psychic) effects. Sidney concedes that in principle philosophers' "words of art" may overpower wayward passions with reason, but this triumph is pyrrhic in that rhetoric cannot transmit the poet's physically impassioned *energeia* that entices us "to be moved to do that which we know" (83).

Claius and Strephon's (but not Kalendar's) version of the experience of love is similarly "grounded upon feeling" and involves the healthy operation of the passions and other parts of the body. It yields activities or an *energeia* manifest in their being moved to learn, to think elevated thoughts, to express sophisticated ideas in conversation and poetry, and to act with compassion. Erotic desire, though—or perhaps because—unfulfilled, becomes through lateralizing "love-fellowship" more a cause of delight and consolation than pain and complaint. It produces passivity and cooperation rather than aggression, violence, and competition, and it displaces narrative action with pastoral conversation. This "true" friendship glances at the heteroerotic and the homoerotic without condemning or condoning either; it is inspired by the sensation or memory of the beauty of a beloved, who bestows affection and reciprocity in place of Petrarchan disdain; and it produces a wish for chastity rather than sexual possession. Through iconic shepherds, Sidney advances an ideal of humble nobility that is not found in the *Old Arcadia* and that contrasts with the crude ambitions of Arcadians such as Basilius's grotesque rustics—Dametas, Miso, and Mopsa. Even the work's protagonists—the prince-turned-shepherd Musidorus and his boyhood friend and cousin, the prince-turned-Amazon Pyrocles—seem unstably noble when compared to Claius and Strephon.

In the revised *Arcadia*, Musidorus and Pyrocles as friends and lovers are works in progress. The princes' disguises—donned in Book 1 in order to win favor with the princesses—have the unintended yet predictable effect of transforming both. In the partially revised Book 3, Musidorus (as Dorus) and Pyrocles (as Zelmane) become marginalized as the central narrative shifts to the princesses, their treatment at the hands of Cecropia and Amphialus, and the warfare between Basilians and Cecropians. In place of the princes' sexual strategizing and predation upon Philoclea and Pamela that occupies much of Book 3 in the *Old Arcadia*, Sidney introduces emasculating failures: Zelmane is humiliatingly captured along with the princesses by twenty men in Cecropia's service (*NA* 441–3), and Musidorus fails to defeat Amphialus in single combat and sustains wounds that require his withdrawing from battle (*NA* 542–4). Shortly before the revision ends, Musidorus, formerly the "forsaken knight," may reappear as the unidentified "Black Knight," who leads "forces, by force to deliver his lady" from Cecropia's castle (581, cf. 535–6). But his restoration remains unfinished due to Sidney's broken narrative. Similar irresolution surrounds Zelmane's efforts to defeat Anaxius and win Philoclea's freedom. Disguised as Zelmane, moreover, Pyrocles is ignominiously forced to witness the seeming deaths of Pamela and Philoclea. Abandoned, alone, and awaiting rescue, he shamefully fails to fulfill his masculine obligation to his beloved. Throughout Book 3, moreover, the suffering princes remain physically separated, eliminating the comfort of shared experience and raising questions about the status of their friendship during this tragic phase of the narrative.

The separation that prevents their narrative interaction in Book 3 does not, however, subvert the work's concern with *vera amicitia*. Rather, their separation seems to prepare a trajectory of reunion wherein each prince seems likely to undergo a re-education in *amicitia* that allows for differences in opposition to Cicero's principle of *alter idem*, "the other the same" (*De amicitia* trans. Falconer 1.6–7; Shannon 40–41), that admits passion, and that balances the aggressiveness of the romance hero with empathy and compassion like that of Claius and Strephon. Raised together by Euarchus's sister, mother to Musidorus, and having received the same humanist education, the princes initially embodied a friendship reminiscent of the Greco-Roman tradition: as youths, they experienced a "memorable friendship" that "made them more like than the likeness of all other virtues, and made them more near one to the other than the nearness of their blood could aspire unto" (*NA* 259). Following their departure from Musidorus's home, they test the "conceits" they learned in their humanist education and soon experience a version of chivalric friendship in Phrygia, where they cooperate to prevent one another's execution (*NA* 266–8). Yet both these types of friendship dissolve during the princes' cumulative experiences in the romance world and, especially, during their debate in Book 1.

In both versions of *Arcadia*, the princes' debate concerns the propriety of Pyrocles's devotion to love, willingness to abandon the mutual effort to test their learning in experience, and enthusiasm for dressing as a woman in order to be near Philoclea. And in both versions the debate ends in an effusion of passion. In the *New Arcadia*, the debate concludes with Musidorus's pledge to support "these flowers of new begun friendship" by helping Pyrocles attain his "desires," language that recalls the shepherds' true friendship, and it culminates with intimate expressions of "loving" (*amare*) and "loving back" (*redamare*) characteristic of Ciceronian friendship: Pyrocles begs Musidorus to love him with "more affection than judgement," and Musidorus questioningly replies, "how can my heart be separated from the true embrace of [loving you] without it burst by being too full of it?" (*NA* 139; *De amicitia* 13.49). The episode recalls the revised opening's language of passion—friend to friend and friend to lover—and the outcome of the debate affirms that impassioned friendship is true friendship, in contrast to the Greco-Roman discourse that Musidorus had fruitlessly invoked in order to shame his friend.

The revised *Arcadia* delicately contrasts masculine love in friendship with the homoerotic anxiety that had provoked the ferocity of Musidorus's verbal assault upon Pyrocles, love, and women. In the *Old Arcadia*, Musidorus actively participated in Pyrocles's scheme to cross-dress as Cleophila (*OA* 23–5), providing a brief glance at homoeroticism when he jestingly professed that in dressing his friend he "were like enough … to become a young Pygmalion," in love with his creation (25). But Musidorus always knows Cleophila is a disguised man. Although MacFaul sees the omission of this "splendid comedy" as working to promote the greater dignity of the princes in the *New Arcadia*, Pyrocles, seen as Zelmane, appears before the equally unwitting Musidorus and reader while the narrator strives without much dignity to entice both through an eroticized blazon (MacFaul, "Friendship" 23; *NA* 130). Unlike the earlier *Arcadia*, wherein Musidorus colludes in the project of clothing Cleophila, in the *New Arcadia* he is "moved" to follow Zelmane into a private arbor where "lovingly interlaced" branches heighten erotic suggestiveness. His suspicions of the identity of the "beautiful" singer of the ditty "Transform'd in show" precede those of the reader only briefly, since he recognizes Pyrocles's voice only after "her goodliness" has deceived his eyes (*NA* 131–2; *OA* 24–5). In the revised version, Musidorus's apparent sexual attraction to his friend precedes rather than follows his verbal assault on Pyrocles's manliness, leaving the impression that his anger is fueled as much by fear of his own homoerotic impulses as Pyrocles's cross-dressing. In the revision, Sidney deliberately confuses marks of gender and sex—with detailed attention to Pyrocles's naked ankles, the "small of *her* leg" (my emphasis), and buskins cut to reveal the "fairness of the skin"—to bring to the surface the sensual appeal of Pyrocles to Musidorus. Yet, in contrast to the love-fellowship of Claius and Strephon, Musidorus's attraction gives rise to anger and misogynist commonplaces familiar to masculine Greco-Roman friendships. Only when Musidorus verbalizes his anger, anxiety, and affection does the pair initiate a "new begun" friendship marked by passion, masculine tears, and mutual professions of love. If at this moment the princes seem on the threshold of realizing the multidimensional *energeia* of the shepherds' love-fellowship, each still lacks the ongoing stability of reciprocal, lateral affection inspired by a beloved female, and each is far from appreciating "beauty" as a prompt for chastity (*NA* 64). Although the trajectory of the princes' friendship may eventually have approximated that of Claius and Strephon, it remains unrealized when Book 3 abruptly ends. The friends are separated physically and under duress psychologically. Having implemented separate strategies to win the princesses, they have had no narrative opportunity to reconfirm their affections for one another, and both have incompletely altered their reified views of women. When this version ends, the princes have yet to engage the mutuality and symmetry figured in Greek romances and the revision's opening vignette.

As the revised opening suggests, a reformation of masculine friendship as love-fellowship presupposes a reformation of masculine relations to the feminine. Urania, who awakens passion through beauty and moves her beholders to chaste love, is a source of the shepherds' alliance. The *New Arcadia* reverses the progressive diminishment of female agency in the later books of the *Old Arcadia* in that the "new" Pyrocles is made the passive student of an increasingly assertive tutor—Philoclea, after her seeming resurrection from Cecropia's staged beheading. Although critics' attention to the Arcadian princesses in the revised Book 3 gravitates toward Pamela, who displays "majesty" by deploying language and reason against the advances of Amphialus and metaphysics of Cecropia, Philoclea not only spurns Amphialus's and Cecropia's appeals to pleasure but also takes a dominant role in educating and healing Pyrocles/Zelmane. By Book 3, the relationship between Philoclea and the disguised Pyrocles has so many layers of pretense that even sharp-eyed Cecropia fails to discern the erotic entanglement concealed by their presumed female friendship. When the old woman unwittingly arranges a private meeting between them in hopes that Zelmane might persuade Philoclea to yield to Amphialus, Pyrocles at first proves simply helpless before the beauty of his beloved. In contrast to the "lateralness" of eloquent Claius and Strephon, he is so "confused withal" due to a "conceit" "darkened with a mist of desire" (*NA* 560) that he is reduced to solipsistic, fragmented speech completely at odds with the masterful oratory displayed in Book 2 when he subdued the Arcadian rebels. In Book 3, Pyrocles' rhetorical collapse is remedied by Philoclea, who is "quickened" rather than silenced by the sight of her beloved, one whom she now aggressively takes possession of as "*my* Pyrocles" (*NA* 561, my emphasis). Philoclea's action and initiative as spiritual physician coincide with her emerging dominance in the relationship, especially when she acquires greater freedom after Amphialus demands that Cecropia end the torture of the princesses. When Philoclea visits the cell of Pyrocles, who grieves due to her apparent death and at first fails to discern her shadowed figure, she poses two reasonable, consolatory propositions that should preclude the need for mourning: (1) if dead, Philoclea has, she says, "in one act both preserved her honour and left the miseries of this world" and (2) if he grieves, he grieves for himself who has "lost a friend" and not for her, who if dead would be in a happier place (*NA* 567). Surprisingly, Pyrocles replies with a misogynist outburst at odds with the charitable defense of women he had marshaled in the debate with Musidorus in Book 1: "O woman's philosophy, childish folly," he rants, "as though if I do bemoan myself, I have not reason to do so, having lost more than any monarchy, nay than my life can be worth unto me" (567). The apostrophe reveals Pyrocles's residual self-obsession, easy degradation of women, and objectification of Philoclea. These deep flaws— each outside the bounds of Claius and Strephon's love-fellowship—are healed incompletely, although, after Philoclea reveals herself to him, she brings his intemperately passionate complexion into better balance by combining reason with passion. Following Pyrocles's alteration, the pair briefly share a symmetry of reason and passion evident in mutual "sweetness in tears" and "lightsome colours of affection" until Philoclea takes the passionately chaste initiative: "content to receive a kiss, and but a kiss [... she] sealed up [Pyrocles'] moving lips and closed them up in comfort; and [went] to her sister" (*NA* 571). Although Pyrocles soon thereafter regains his liberty and at the break in the revised narrative aggressively battles Amphialus's ally, Anaxius, his masculinity seems marked indelibly due to his imprisonment, disclosed emotional weakness, and subjection to the therapeutic voice and passion of Philoclea. These evoke in him a glimmer of "com-passion" for the feminine quite opposite to the triumph that defined his sexual "bliss" with Philoclea in Book 3 of the *Old Arcadia* and that culminated in the narrative's efforts to rekindle the princes' masculine friendship during the trial in Book 5 (*OA* 211, 357–9).

When the revised *Arcadia* breaks off, the old relationship between Musidorus and Pyrocles from Book 1 has long since exploded, but what will follow is incompletely developed. The evidence of the "new begun" friendship at the end of Book 1 and the alterations in Book 3 of the relationship between Philoclea and Pyrocles suggest that Sidney works toward a quadratic fellowship among the royals that would mirror the triangulated love-fellowship stimulated by Urania's beauty. It suggests an affection extended laterally in empassioned acts of justice that would override the legalistic justice of the Arcadian state in Book 5 of the *Old Arcadia*. The *New Arcadia*, with its opening representing the masculine love and humane elevation that can result from erotic desire, replaces the fruitless friendship discourse Musidorus abandons in Book 1 with an entirely new vocabulary. It resituates friendship by locating its principal site in the passions rather than the mind, allowing for the subsequent reassessment of the right poet's role in creating fictions whose effects physiologically motivate temperate behavior. And it implies a reconception of the gendered self and humanity that, like the Greek romances, redraws the boundaries of masculine and feminine and blurs the roles attributed to each, replacing the antique idea of the friend as *alter idem* with a compassionate friendship that yields a lateral awareness of shared humanity and, with passion as its agent, bonds the body and mind.

PART II
Alternative Discourses: Friendship in the Margins

Chapter 4

Guzmán de Alfarache's "Other Self": The Limits of Friendship in Spanish Picaresque Fiction

Donald Gilbert-Santamaría

Just before jumping to his death in a fit of madness late in the second part of Mateo Alemán's picaresque novel, Guzmán de Alfarache's companion Sayavedra calls out in his delirium: "¡Yo soy la sombra de Guzmán de Alfarache! Su sombra soy, que voy por el mundo" [I am the shadow of Guzmán de Alfarache! I am his shadow that travels through the world] (307). Critics of the *Guzmán de Alfarache* tend to identify the figure of Sayavedra with Juan Martí, the author of an apocryphal second part to Alemán's highly successful narrative who wrote under the pseudonym Mateo Luján de Sayavedra.[1] As Edward Friedman notes, the "killing off" of Sayavedra constitutes an "ingenious, calculated, and effectively—hyperbolically—vindictive" response to Martí's plagiarism (106). Benito Brancaforte even suggests that the death of Sayavedra is a prerequisite for the novel's continuation (97).[2] Considering the enormous popularity of Martí's sequel—with more published copies than the author's own second part—one can perhaps forgive Alemán the small consolation of this symbolic destruction of his rival (Friedman 100).

This traditional reading of Sayavedra as the plagiarist's alter ego does not, however, exhaust the interpretative potential of this important episode in the narrative. In particular, while this interpretation illuminates the significant external forces at work in Alemán's text, it completely overlooks the internal context for Sayavedra's emergence into the narrative: the entire episode is framed as a meditation on the nature of friendship in the picaresque, first through an extensive theoretical discussion of the topic, and then, with the appearance of Sayavedra himself, through a kind of practical case study. From this other perspective, Sayavedra's identification with Guzmán at the moment of his death constitutes

---

[1]   Luján, or Martí, penned his apocryphal continuation of the first part of *Guzmán de Alfarache* in 1602, that is, two years before the publication of Alemán's own second part in 1604.

[2]   The connection between Sayavedra and the author of the spurious second part of *Guzmán de Alfarache* has also been made by Donald McGrady (122–4) and Eric J. Kartchner.

a symbolic deformation of the Aristotelian ideal of the friend as "another self" as well as the narrative's final verdict on the possibility of friendship in the picaresque.[3] In killing off Sayavedra, the narrative dramatically terminates the text's one significant experiment with this highest order of friendship.

The groundwork for this other interpretation is prepared by Guzmán himself in his extensive musings on friendship immediately prior to Sayavedra's introduction into the narrative. The influence of classical models is evident from the outset, as Guzmán argues that true friends are like quicksilver and gold that when mixed into a single substance may only be separated by the "fire" of death: "tal [es] el verdadero amigo, hecho ya otro él, [que] nada pueda ser parte para que aquella unión se deshaga, sino con solo el fuego de la muerte sola" [such is the true friend, made already another self, that nothing can undo that union but only the fire of death alone] (155). Even here, however, the pressures of the picaresque quickly rise up to the surface and Guzmán's exaltation of true friendship soon gives way to a lament on the practical difficulties of finding such relationships: "En todos cuantos traté, fueron pocos los que hallé que no caminasen al norte de su interese proprio y al paso de su gusto, con deseo de engañar, sin amistad que lo fuese, sin caridad sin verdad ni vergüenza … Siempre me dejaron el corazón amargo" [Among all those that I met, there were few whom I found who did not follow their own self-interest and pleasure, with a desire to deceive, without true friendship, without charity, without truth or shame … They always left me with a bitter heart] (157). Reflecting the "soledad" that José Antonio Maravall defines as a core principle of picaresque existence, Guzmán's contemplation of his own experiences leads to the pessimistic recognition of the difficulties of this kind of friendship in a world populated by tricksters, thieves, and charlatans.[4] More to the point here, these

---

[3]   On the ideal of the friend as "another self," Aristotle writes in Book Nine of the *Nicomachean Ethics*: "The decent person, then, has each of these features, and is related to his friend as he is to himself, since the friend is *another himself*" (trans. Irwin 246; my emphasis). Cicero continues this Aristotelian tradition in his own treatise on friendship *Laelius de amicitia:* "Ipse enim se quisque diligit, non ut aliquam a se ipse mercedem exigat caritatis suae, sed quod per se quisque sibi carus est; quod nisi idem in amicitiam transferetur, verus amicus numquam reperietur: est enim is qui est tamquam *alter idem*" [For everyone loves himself, not with a view of acquiring some profit for himself for his self-love, but because he is dear to himself on his own account; and unless this same feeling were transferred to friendship, the real friend would never be found; for he is, as it were, *another self*] (188; my italics).

[4]   Concerning the isolation of the picaro, Maravall writes, "se mantienen en el fondo de su existencia singular apartados, no «a solas» reflexivamente, para dar lugar a una meditación sobre sí mismos y su entorno, sino en una radical soledad, algo así, diría como existencialmente «solos». La soledad es el lugar moral de su emplazamiento" [at the bottom of their singular existence, they maintain themselves apart, not "alone" reflexively, in order to create space for a meditation about themselves and their environment, but in a radical solitude, so that one might describe them as existentially "alone." Solitude is the moral condition of their placement in the world.] (309). Given Maravall's insistence on this

comments at the beginning help set the expectations for what will follow, namely, a tale of friendship that ultimately goes bad.

Guzmán's grudging acknowledgment of self-interest as the only basis for interpersonal relations in the picaresque implies a radical reordering of the classical schema for friendship in which utilitarianism is the mark of an inferior form of companionship.[5] While a practical necessity at times, these inferior relationships are tolerable because they do not impede the final goal of a higher, selfless form of perfect friendship. Guzmán's "bitter heart," the result of his own personal disappointment with friendship, on the other hand, signals an emotional capitulation before the collapse of the ideal. Gone is the classical optimism that might allow one to suffer false friendships born of necessity, here replaced with despair in the face of the realization that one's "other self" may not, in fact, exist.

With the introduction of Sayavedra in the subsequent chapters, however, the narrative moves beyond the abject pessimism of Guzmán's abstract musing and provides the reader with a dramatic representation of a new model for picaresque friendship based on shared stories, common experiences, and, above all, self-identification. The narrative basis of Guzmán's one significant attempt at friendship reflects a break with the hierarchy of Aristotelian categories and, more importantly, an evolution beyond earlier classical and even Renaissance representations of this peculiar mode of human interaction. Certainly, Laelius's reminiscences on his relationship with Scipio in Cicero's *De amicitia* offer what might be described as personal insight into the relationship between the two men: "For I am indeed moved by the loss of a friend such, I believe, as I shall never have again, and—as I can assert on positive knowledge—a friend such as no other man ever was to me" (119). Showing even greater development along these lines, Boccaccio's story of Titus and Gisippus offers a narrative representation of extraordinary self-sacrifice between friends, providing an early Renaissance instance of "the tale of two friends" paradigm that would remain popular throughout the early modern period.[6] At the same time, however, both Cicero and Boccaccio never seriously question the overarching Aristotelian framework of ideal friendship. In Cicero, the emotional significance of the bond between Laelius and Scipio is hardly more than a pretext for his more extensive philosophical meditations on the nature of friendship, while

---

point, it is perhaps not surprising that he completely ignores the significance of Guzmán's friendship with Sayavedra in his extensive study of the picaresque narrative.

[5] This hierarchy is most clearly articulated in the *Nicomachean Ethics*, where Aristotle argues that friendships may be broken down into three categories based on utility, pleasure, and goodness. For a discussion of these three kinds of friendship, see Pangle 377–56. Cicero, in contrast, argues that relationships based solely on utility are excluded altogether from the realm of true friendship, which he argues can only be founded upon virtue. See in particular Cicero's discussion of utility in friendship in Book X of *De amicitia*.

[6] The story of Titus and Gisippus may be found in the eighth story recounted on the tenth day in *The Decameron* (745–64). For a discussion of "tale of two friends" tradition, see Juan Bautista Avalle-Arce, 163–235.

in Boccaccio the friendship between Titus and Gisippus is already established by the time the main action of the story takes place. In both instances, idealized friendship is taken for granted as the starting point for either theoretical meditation or narrative representation. In the case of Boccaccio—perhaps the more interesting example for our purposes here—the imitative poetics that would take the friend as an "alter idem," although challenged by external pressures, both sexual and social, nonetheless remains untouched by any internal self-doubt. Reflecting the lingering prestige of the Aristotelian model, Boccaccio's two friends remained locked in the categorical paradigm of the highest, most selfless mode of friendship.

In contrast to these earlier texts, Alemán allows the reader to witness the narrative process through which Guzmán's one true friendship comes into being. Whereas the underlying friendship in these other texts is never called into question, the more purely discursive model for personal intimacy on display in the *Guzmán* gives new life to the Aristotelian notion of the friend as "another self," replacing the categorical ideal with a dynamic, inherently modern vision of friendship as a complex emotional relationship subject to continuous renegotiation and at constant risk of dissolution. Understood in this way, Sayavedra's untimely end comes to reflect less the impossibility of picaresque friendship than its inherent fragility. Perhaps more than in any other genre of the period, the ruthless deceptiveness of life in the public sphere relentlessly threatens to undermine the benevolent impulses that make stories of private friendship possible.

***

Throughout the chapters that describe Guzmán's relationship with Sayavedra, the novel never strays far from the central problem of friendship in a fictional world populated by compulsive liars. This relationship begins auspiciously enough after Sayavedra intervenes to defend the outnumbered Guzmán in a street brawl. At this point, however, the narrative displays little interest in the interpersonal dimension of this new friendship. Sayavedra eventually informs Guzmán of the most superficial details of his own background, and then provides the impetus for the latter's departure from Rome, suggesting that in this way he might escape his present difficulties. Acceding to Sayavedra's advice, Guzmán sends most of his possessions ahead of him to Florence. Shortly thereafter, however, Sayavedra inexplicably disappears and a few pages later the reader learns that Guzmán's new acquaintance, acting in league with a criminal gang, has in fact conspired to steal all of his belongings.[7]

Contrary to what one might expect, this initial act of betrayal quickly gives way to a reconciliation between the two picaros. When Sayavedra is detained by the authorities for his presumed involvement in the plot, Guzmán refuses to denounce him, and, in a later chapter, when the two meet again by chance, he even expresses

---

[7]   Consistent with the reading of Sayavedra as a stand-in for Juan Martí, Friedman interprets the theft of Guzmán's possessions as a reference to Martí's plagiarism (106).

compassion for his companion's predicament in one of the most emotional scenes of the entire novel:

> No me bastó el ánimo, en conociéndolo, a dejar de compadecerme dél y saludarlo, poniendo los ojos, no en el mal que me hizo, sino en el daño de que alguna vez me libró, conociendo por de más precio el bien que allí entonces dél recibí, que pudo importar lo que me llevó … No pude resistirme sin hablarle con amor ni él de recebirme con lágrimas, que vertiéndolas por todo el rostro se vino a mis pies, abrazándose con el estribo y pidiéndome perdón de su yerro, dándome gracias de que nunca, estando preso, lo quise acusar y satisfacciones de no haberme visitado luego que salió de la cárcel.

> [Upon recognizing him, I didn't have the heart not to feel for him and greet him, focusing my gaze not on the evil he did to me, but on the injury from which at one point he had liberated me, considering more valuable the good he did then than that which he stole from me … I couldn't help talking to him with love, nor he from receiving me with tears, and with these flowing all over his face he came to my feet, and embracing my stirrups and asking for forgiveness for his error, and thanking me for never having denounced him when he was detained, he explained to my satisfaction why he didn't visit me upon his release from prison.] (159–60)

Significantly, this first account of the two picaros' reunion is completely at odds with the general spirit of Guzmán's narrative. Completely ignoring his apparent self-interest, Guzmán's active participation in this spontaneous show of emotion transcends the hardened utilitarianism that characterizes nearly everything else he does in the novel. Clearly moved by his companion's tears, Guzmán's behavior in this scene arguably reveals a desire for interpersonal commiseration that is more typically repressed by the social alienation of the picaro's existence.

Beyond such unexpected displays of emotion, however, the narrative's more pessimistic worldview is never far from the surface. Despite the emotional intensity evoked in the passage above, Guzmán's relationship with Sayavedra quickly falls back into compliance with the rhetorical norms of the picaresque, as Sayavedra's pleading for forgiveness gives way to abject submissiveness: "empero que para en cuenta y parte de pago de su deuda quería como un esclavo servirme toda su vida" [but, in order to pay the bill of his debt he wanted to serve me all his life like a slave] (160). Remarkably, Guzmán fails to register the troubling nature of Sayavedra's pledge and instead responds to his new companion according to the instrumentalist logic that is far more typical of the genre: "Parecióme que, si de alguno quisiera servirme, habiendo pocos mozos buenos, que aqueste sería menos malo … pues dél sabía ya ser necesario guardarme, y con otro, pareciéndome fiel, me pudiera descuidar y dejarme en la luna" [It seemed to me that if someone wanted to serve me, there being so few good young men, that this one would be the least bad ... for I already knew that I needed to protect myself from him, and with someone else, seeming to be faithful, I might not take care, and leave myself on the moon] (160). From a classical point of view, Guzmán's characterization of his relationship with Sayavedra at this point already recognizes the futility of the higher forms of friendship in the picaresque world; in place of the ideal friend as "another self," Guzmán settles for the lesser evil of a friend who might be useful if only because—and here the cynicism of the passage reaches its full crescendo— his potential for betrayal has already been exposed.

The reassertion of utilitarianism in Guzmán's final explanation of his reconciliation with Sayavedra highlights the conflicted nature of their relationship. After the emotional intensity of their original reunion, the cold calculating logic of Guzmán's decision to accept Sayavedra into his service sounds forced, highlighting a dissonance in the protagonist's attitude toward his companion that his remarks do little to dissipate. On a formal level, the relationship between the two picaros is indeed extremely hierarchical throughout the rest of their time together. Sayavedra consistently maintains a pronounced formality in his conversations with his new master, and while he does not shy from offering advice, he always defers to Guzmán in the end. At the same time, however, underneath such formalities, the complicity of the two in the subsequent chapters creates a powerful bond that finds expression in Guzmán's ever-growing confidence in his servant. Through their constant companionship and collusion in all manner of schemes, the two develop a relationship that defies the static categories of classical models for friendship in favor of a fluid, evolving partnership that creates a provisional space of intimacy and trust in a world otherwise defined by trickery and deception.

The conflicted nature of the relationship between Guzmán and Sayavedra is augmented by the narrative's repeated recourse to the classical ideal of the friend as another self—this despite Guzmán's earlier despair of ever finding such a friend. "Soy un pobre mozo como tú," [I am a poor boy like you] insists Sayavedra before launching into an extensive account of his own life story. The story that he tells does indeed mirror in important ways the sordid tale of Guzmán's own frustrated ambitions, but, more importantly, the very act of narration itself redefines the relationship between the two picaros, as dramatized in Guzmán's response to his companion's story:

> Decía entre mí: «Si a este Sayavedra, como dice, lo dejó tan rico su padre, ¿cómo ha dado en ser ladrón y huelga más de andar afrentado que vivir tenido y respetado?» ... Luego revolvía sobre mí en su disculpa, diciendo: «Saldríase huyendo muchacho, como yo.» Representáronseme con su relación mis proprios pasos; mas volvía, diciendo: «Ya que todo eso así es, ¿por qué no volvió la hoja, cuando tuvo uso de razón y llegó a ser hombre, haciéndose soldado?» También me respondía en su favor: «¿Y por qué no lo soy yo? Veo la paja en el ojo y no la viga en el mío ...»

[I said to myself: "If this Sayavedra, as he says, was left so rich by his father, why has he become a thief, and why does it please him to live offending others rather than to be held in respect?" … Then I turned my thoughts to his defense, saying: "He must have been fleeing as a boy, like me." With his story he portrayed my own steps; but I turned my mind again, saying: "And if all of this is as he says, why didn't he turn the page and use his head, and become a man, enlisting as a soldier?" And again, I responded to myself in his favor: "And why am I not one? I see the speck in his eye and not the plank in my own …"] (228–9)

The dramatization of Guzmán's ambivalence in this passage underscores the inherent barriers to commiseration in the picaresque world. Accustomed as he is to distrust the motives of everyone he meets, Guzmán's clear desire to sympathize with his companion's narrative runs up against the practical experience of picaresque deceit and deception, both in his previous dealings with Sayavedra and as a defining characteristic of the genre. From this perspective, the reference to Matthew 7:3–4 with which the passage ends provides a powerful biblical inflection to Guzmán's earlier lament over the lack of true friends in this case, through a version of the same mirroring process that defines the classical idea of the friend as "another self." Jesus' admonition in the Sermon on the Mount serves to underscore the key moral problem of compassion that is at the heart of the modern practice of private friendship.

Despite such difficulties, however, the overall tone of the passage is, in fact, optimistic, suggesting the possibility of sympathetic commiseration even in the corrupt world of the picaresque. Echoing Sayavedra's own claim that "I am a poor boy like you," Guzmán returns repeatedly to contemplate the parallels between their two lives, leading him at one point to efface completely the differences between them: "With his story he portrayed my own steps." Here, the unrealistic expectations of the idealized classical model of the friend as "another self," arguably the source of Guzmán's own bitter heart, finds compensation in the possibility of a different mode of identification between friends based on a shared personal narrative. Guzmán's equivocations in the passage above effectively dramatize the process through which his companion's life story is made to fit his own. Unlike the static ideal of classical friendship, Guzmán's identification with his companion's predicament involves an active molding of his self-image to the requirements of a sympathetic reading of Sayavedra's narrative. The ideal of the friend as "another self" is thus reanimated as an act of goodwill between two very imperfect individuals.

The efficacy of this new model for friendship reflects a more general desire for recognition that might compensate Guzmán's abject social marginalization and the accompanying tendency to obscure any sense of his concrete, individual identity. In this sense, this emphasis on mutual recognition in the passage above suggests an important evolution beyond the view of Alemán's protagonist as either purely "protean" (Cros)—that is, marked by a never-ending series of mutations—or as the reified object of "a process of typification" (Dunn). Guzmán's ability to identify with his new friend underscores the potential of private friendship as a bulwark against the crushing anonymity of public life in the picaresque.[8] Constructed in direct opposition to the larger social context, Guzmán's new friendship with Sayavedra provides him "with the opportunity as well as the necessity to demonstrate his own uniqueness" (Johnson, *Inside Guzmán* 39).

Finally, the tension between private friendship and public anonymity that emerges in Guzmán's one true friendship also intersects with the poetic structure of the picaresque and its peculiar response to Renaissance *imitatio*. I have argued elsewhere that the poetics of the picaresque, with its emphasis on the deceptiveness of experience, involves an essential inversion of the Renaissance principle of imitation (Gilbert-Santamaría 108–12). In place of the Renaissance ideal of an aesthetics that attempts to emulate its models—whether taken from "real" life or from other works of art—the picaresque presents a physical and moral universe in which things are never what they seem. Guzmán's "bitter heart" in the face of false friendships may be understood as one aspect of this fundamental principle of the picaresque. In effect, the failings of Guzmán's friends provide a moral analogue to what is, in the first instance, a problem of poetics. From this perspective, Guzmán's role as sympathetic listener may be taken to involve a reassertion of the optimistic potential inherent in any imitative poetics. In Guzmán's attempt to read his own life story into Sayavedra's autobiography—to literally self-identify with his companion—the narrative implicitly aligns private friendship with a mode of imitation that embraces the ideal of representational transparency based on what is essentially an act of goodwill on the part of both characters. Or, to put this same idea in other terms, it holds out the possibility that Guzmán and Sayavedra may come to truly know each other.

The strong correlation here between the poetics of *imitatio* and the rise of private friendship as an alternative to the abject loneliness of life in the picaresque also throws light onto the underlying structure of modern friendship. Unlike the classical ideal, the notion of the friend as "another self" that emerges in Guzmán's relationship with Sayavedra is grounded in an imitative representational procedure that eschews the very possibility of an idealized teleology such as may be discovered in Cicero and Boccaccio. This is already evident in Guzmán's struggle to come to terms with Sayavedra's story. The product of a self-conscious act of goodwill, the identification between the two picaros that provides the foundation for their friendship can never be taken for granted but must be constantly reaffirmed in a discursive process whose end marks, as I will show in the discussion that follows, the end of friendship.

***

---

[8]   The distinction between private and public life that I use throughout this essay was first inspired by the work of Phillipe Ariès and Georges Duby, and in particular their encyclopedic *A History of Private Life.*

In the sordid world of picaresque fiction, friendship is subject to pressures unknown in the classical discourse on the topic. Where the classical ideal realizes its highest expression in a process of mutual purification involving a rejection of the corrupting influences of everyday life, Guzmán's friendship with Sayavedra cannot escape the pressures of an impoverished material existence on the margins of society. In particular, while Sayavedra does show himself to be Guzmán de Alfarche's one true friend, the proof of his devotion is invariably cast in terms of morally dubious propositions and outright criminal schemes that provide a stark manifestation of what Michel Cavillac describes as "el irreductible divorcio entre la verdad subjetiva del hombre y su experiencia del individuo degradado por la realidad objetiva de las relaciones sociales" [the irreducible divorce between man's subjective truth and his experience as an individual degraded by the objective reality of social relations] (16). Despite the questionable moral foundation of their relationship, however, Sayavedra shows himself to be intensely loyal to his new master, leading Guzmán to ever greater displays of familiarity, from his first casual use of the epithet "amigo" to his final acknowledgement of Sayavedra as his "otro yo" (274). In the inverted logic of the picaresque, solidarity in crime becomes, or so it would seem, the ultimate measure of friendship.

At the same time, the bond that grows between Guzmán and Sayavedra through their various criminal plans helps to delineate a clear barrier between their "private" relationship and society at large. Unlike Guzmán's abstract musings on friendship in an earlier chapter, this division between private and public life emerges through a series of encounters with other characters who collectively provide the foil against which Guzmán's new friendship comes to claim its privileged status. Three of these minor personages stand out in particular for their representative value: a greedy Milanese merchant, Guzmán's malevolent Genovese uncle, and another would-be friend whose protestations of loyalty are seemingly as sincere as those of Sayavedra himself. Each of these three men helps to delineate the external world against which Guzmán's relationship with Sayavedra is defined. Thus, Guzmán's ruthless scheme to swindle his uncle as payback for earlier mistreatment creates a sharp contrast between the breakdown of the ostensibly natural bonds of family life and the solidarity of his constructed criminal association with Sayavedra. Similarly, Guzmán's collaboration with Sayavedra in an elaborate plan to frame the Milanese merchant may be read synecdochically to represent the clear distinction between their very unique friendship and the irremediable deceptiveness of the larger society. Finally, the appearance in the narrative of the merchant captain and would-be friend, Favelo, exposes the arbitrary nature of friendship in the picaresque and in the process calls into question the very possibility of amicable sincerity. Taken together, these three examples underscore the stunted nature of private life in the picaresque so that Guzmán's special relationship with Sayavedra is finally revealed as the truly unusual case, the exception that confirms the more general rule of cruelty and marginalization that is far more typical of the genre.

In helping to solidify the relationship between Guzmán and his companion, the first encounter with the greedy Milanese merchant plays a formative role in establishing the boundaries between the ruthless competitiveness of public life and the growing solidarity of loyal friendship. Significantly, the episode begins with a scene that quashes the last vestige of Guzmán's former distrust of his friend. Having recently arrived in Milan, Guzmán spies Sayavedra deep in conversation with someone he has never seen before. Later, when they reunite for a meal and Sayavedra fails to mention his secret meeting, Guzmán can hardly control his consternation: "Que la sospecha es terrible gusano del corazón" [For suspicion is a terrible worm in the heart] (233). No longer able to contain himself, Guzmán finally confronts Sayavedra about the meeting. In the exchange that follows, Sayavedra's innocence becomes quickly apparent as the unknown man is revealed to be an old friend who seeks Sayavedra's—and later Guzmán's—help in a plot to swindle his master, that is, the greedy merchant who shortly thereafter becomes the central interest of the narrative. While Guzmán does not explicitly acknowledge it, the revelation of Sayavedra's innocence marks a watershed moment in their relationship. From this point on, Guzmán displays nothing but absolute confidence in the loyalty of his friend.

In contrast to the growing bond between Guzmán and Sayavedra, the plan to rob the greedy merchant is represented from the very outset as a contest of wits in which the two parties attempt to outmaneuver each other. As Guzmán himself puts it concisely, "Conformidad teníamos ambos en engañar" [We were both intent on deception] (245). Here, the synecdochal value of the episode comes into view as Guzmán's encounter with the greedy merchant provides a personified condensation of the picaresque social dynamic, a reading of the scene that is only accentuated by the narrative's explicit reference to the merchant's dodgy reputation:

> Eran en mi favor la voz común, las evidencias y experiencias vistas y su mala fama, que concluía, y decían todos: No es nuevo en el bellaco logrero robar haciendas ajenas.

> [In my favor were the common voice, the evidence and witnessed experiences, and his bad reputation, which concluded the affair, and everyone said: "There's nothing new about this greedy scoundrel trying to steal other people's property."] (253)

The tension in this passage between the merchant's local reputation and the fact that he is never mentioned by name transforms him into a social stereotype; his particular identity matters much less than what he represents to the "voz común," that is, to a public all too familiar with the picaresque discourse of deceit and deception. He embodies, in this sense, the purest expression of the Bakhtinian notion of the character as "ideologue," a "socially significant" representation of an ideologically determined "language" whose particular destiny is of secondary interest (333).⁹ Furthermore, the anonymity of both public opinion and the avaricious merchant provides a powerful contrast with the discursive process through which Guzmán comes to identify Sayavedra's personal narrative with his own. Where the anonymity of social relations in the public sphere reflects an irredeemable condition of "otherness," the personal friendship between Guzmán and Sayavedra depends on a process of active self-identification. Where the "voz común" speaks out in loud condemnation, Guzmán listens with quiet sympathy.

The significance of this final distinction becomes palpably clear at the end of the two friends' stay in Milan. Announcing to Sayavedra his plan to travel to Genoa to avenge the cruel treatment he had formerly received from his family there, Guzmán indicates that he and Sayavedra should exchange clothing in order to "desmentir espías" [throw off spies] (258). Sayavedra's hearty embrace of this idea, which goes far beyond the practical requirements of a ruse, underscores the intrinsic force of self-identification in the relationship between the two picaros:

> —Paréceme muy bien—dijo Sayavedra—y digo que quiero heredar el tuyo verdadero, con que poderte imitar y servir. Desde hoy me llamo Guzmán de Alfarache.

> ["This seems very good to me," said Sayavedra, "and I declare that I want to inherit your true name, with which I can imitate and serve you. From today, I will be named Guzmán de Alfarache."] (258)

Moving beyond the more practical considerations that motivate Guzmán's original proposal, Sayavedra parlays a simple picaresque trick into a more authentic sign of his self-identification with his companion. As a response to the anonymity of public social relations—so aptly captured in the previous episode of the Milanese merchant—Sayavedra's claim to Guzmán's name calls attention to the idiosyncratic nature of personal intimacy, while his expressed desire to imitate his companion reminds the reader of the underlying poetic structure of modern friendship. Once again, public deception provides the foundation for private solidarity between these two partners in crime.

The narrative extends this meditation on the underlying poetic structure of personal relationships in Guzmán's fateful reunion with his Genoese uncle. Guzmán's own drive for revenge in this episode provides the ostensible motivation for this reunion, and recalls his earlier mistreatment by this same family member in

---

⁹ Bakhtin's emphasis on the character in the novel as "an *ideologue*, and his words" as "*ideologemes*" highlights the incompatibility of his key concept of *heteroglossia* for an analysis of friendship in the picaresque, and, arguably, Alemán's novel in general. Where Bakhtin's analysis focuses on the ideological foundation of novelistic discourse, the concept of private friendship that I propose here depends by definition on the individuality of particular personal narratives that may or may not have a larger social significance.

Part One. For my purposes here, however, the most striking moment in the episode arises with the uncle's complete misrecognition of their previous encounter:

—Sabed, sobrino, que habrá como siete años, poco más o menos, que aquí llegó un mozuelo picarillo, al parecer ladrón o su ayudante ... diciendo ser ... mi sobrino. Tal venía y tal sospechamos dél, que afrentados de su infamia, lo procuramos aventar de la ciudad. ... De la vuelta que le hice dar me acuerdo que se dejó la cama toda llena de cera de trigo: ella fue tal como buena, para que con el miedo de otra peor huyese y nos dejase. Y pues, quería engañarnos, me huelgo de lo hecho. Ni a él se le olvidará en su vida el hospedaje, ni a mí me queda otro dolor que haberme pesado de lo poco.

["Nephew, you should know that about seven years ago, more or less, a young picaro came here, looking like a thief or a thief's apprentice and saying that he was my nephew. Such was his appearance and such were our suspicions about him that, affronted by his infamy, we worked to throw him out of the city. ... Of the turn we gave him, I recall that he left his bed full of excrement: that was a good one, and for fear of another worse we hoped he would flee and leave us. In effect, he wanted to deceive us [*engañarnos*], and I'm happy about what was done. Nor will he in all the days of his life forget the lodging he received, nor will I have any other pain than that he suffered so little."] (277)

The uncle here aligns his earlier abuse of Guzmán with his nephew's impoverished outward material appearances: that Guzmán at that time looked "like a thief or a thief's apprentice" provides his uncle with sufficient cause to inflict all manner of suffering in an attempt to drive away an uninvited rogue. Unwilling to verify the claims of his visitor, the uncle presupposes Guzmán's "true" identity in the trappings of his poverty and, in the process, misrecognizes his own flesh and blood.

Despite the uncle's clear misrecognition of his nephew on a personal level, his assessment of what might be described as Guzmán's public condition is, in fact, quite accurate: Guzmán was and continues to be both a thief and an apprentice of thieves. Viewed from this perspective, the problem of recognition may be said to evince a certain indeterminacy that follows the same public/private divide that was observed previously in Guzmán's encounter with the Milanese merchant. Where his uncle sees only the synecdochal criminal—that is, the personification of the social phenomenon of picaresque criminality—Guzmán recognizes in his uncle's words an excerpt from his own life story: "Yo pobre, como fui quien lo había padecido ..." [As I was the poor boy who had suffered ...] (277). In effect, the uncle unwittingly repeats back to Guzmán a version of his own personal narrative in a manner that reveals the complete lack of communication between the two men. Despite their family ties, his uncle is incapable of relating to Guzmán in the language of sympathetic commiseration that characterizes friendship in private life. Unable to see beyond the social type of the generic picaro, the uncle's view comes to embody instead the same anonymous public opinion that, according to Johnson, consistently imposes its will on Alemán's protagonist throughout the novel ("Defining the Picaresque" 168–9).

As the previous example demonstrates, the discursive nature of private life, as well as its close association with a poetics of imitation, leads to inevitable conflicts with the dominant representational principles of the picaresque novel. In such a context, the "naturalized" category of family, as George Mariscal has observed for early modern society in general, provides a wholly inadequate measure of private life.[10] Such relationships are, to borrow a term from Timothy Reiss, wholly "embedded" in a larger social fabric that, in the case of the picaresque, embodies a kind of collective alienation with little room for meaningful self-expression (3).[11] In effect, family relationships as depicted in the genre are so closely integrated into the larger framework of picaresque social norms that they are unable to supply a meaningful escape from the oppressive isolation of picaresque existence. Friendship, on the other hand, precisely because it arises out of a self-conscious resistance to the genre's social and poetic norms, establishes a new framework for human interactions that offers at least the hope of individual self-expression as an antidote to the marginalization and misrecognition that characterizes Guzmán's autobiography up to this point.

Yet even friendship can never fully escape the pressures of the genre's representational logic, a fact that the narrative finally makes clear through the last character I will examine, a sea captain named Favelo whose enthusiastic but ultimately frustrated attempt to forge a friendship with Guzmán is repeatedly compared to Sayavedra's more perfect bond with the novel's protagonist. On first glance, the contrast between Favelo and Sayavedra would appear, once again, to reinforce the special quality of Guzmán's one "true" friendship, a point that Guzmán himself emphasizes shortly after meeting his new would-be friend:

> Siempre lo procuré conservar y obligar. Llevábame a su galera, traíame festejando por la marina, cultivándose tanto nuestro trato y amistad, que si la mía fuera en seguimiento de la virtud, allí había hallado puerto; mas todo yo era embeleco. ...

---

[10]   "The idea of the family as an isolated group of nurturing individuals set in opposition to society, which seems to us both natural and historically constant, was in fact relatively alien to early modern culture" (Mariscal 67).

[11]   Reiss's concept here is drawn from his larger argument against modern notions of independent "subjectivity" and, by extension, against the conventional dichotomy between public and private life throughout this entire period. In light of this background, his passing reference to Montaigne's view of friendship in the following passage is particularly noteworthy: "for him [i.e. Montaigne], in an atypical anti-Ciceronian (and anti-Aristotelian) move, friendship was a strictly *private* affair" (468, original italics). At the very least, that Reiss would make such a statement highlights an important distinction between private friendship and modern subjectivity. The first does not necessarily imply the second.

Comunicábamonos muy particulares casos y secretos; empero que de la camisa no pasasen adentro, porque los del alma solo Sayavedra era dueño dellos.

[I also tried to preserve our friendship and win him over. He took me to his ship, and showed me around the fleet, cultivating our friendship so well that if mine had followed virtue, I would have found a harbor there; but I was nothing but deception. … We communicated particular cases and secrets; but they never entered beyond my shirt, because only Sayavedra was possessed of the secrets of my soul.] (274)

Having offered both here and elsewhere a highly favorable account of Favelo's person, Guzmán nonetheless rejects the possibility of a deeper relationship. On its face, the hierarchy that relegates Favelo to an inferior kind of friendship appears quite arbitrary. Indeed, from an objective point of view, Favelo is arguably the better candidate for friendship: Unlike Sayavedra, he has no history of deception and his comportment throughout their relatively brief relationship is absolutely above reproach. This perhaps accounts for the slightly self-incriminating tone of the passage above—"But I was nothing but deception." With these words, Guzmán not only accepts responsibility for his unwillingness to engage this new friend, he also implicitly acknowledges the ascendancy of utilitarian values in his treatment of Favelo. As the reader soon learns, Guzmán cultivates this new friendship only so that Favelo might provide him passage to Spain once his plan to dupe his Genoese family has come to fruition.

Guzmán himself explains his disinterest in pursuing a "true" friendship with Favelo in a passage that, once again, highlights the moral ambiguity of picaresque private life: "Que no los amigos todos lo han de saber todo. Los llamados han de ser muchos; los escogidos pocos, y un solo el otro yo" [Not all friends have to know all things. Those who are called are many; the chosen few, and only one the "other self"] (274). While ostensibly invoked to lend moral authority to his friendship with Sayavedra, Guzmán's reference to the biblical parable of the wedding feast, in fact, highlights the moral relativism at work in their relationship. More specifically, the exclusivity of their communion reflects not the exemplary "goodness" of their characters—as in the case of the classical ideal—but rather a practical accommodation to the picaresque's social and poetic reality; in a world where "all is deception," Guzmán can be true to Sayavedra only to the extent that he is free to deceive everyone else.

If Favelo's appearance in the narrative underscores the moral ambiguity of picaresque friendship, the end of Guzmán's relationship with Sayavedra calls into question the very viability of such associations. Shortly after making their escape from Genoa on board Favelo's ship, Sayavedra is struck with a fever, leading him, in a fit of madness, to call out the lines with which I opened this discussion: "I am the shadow of Guzmán de Alfarache! I am his shadow, that travels through the world." The play on the classical notion of the friend as "another self" thus comes full circle as Sayavedra's earlier self-conscious assertion of his desire to "inherit" Guzmán's "true name" in order to "imitate" him is symbolically transformed into a madman's caprice. As Guzmán himself explains:

> Con que me hacía reír y le temí muchas veces. Mas, aunque algo decía, ya lo vían estar loco y lo dejaban para tal. Pero no las llevaba conmigo todas, porque iba repitiendo mi vida, lo que della yo le había contado ... Guisábame de mil maneras y lo más galano—aunque con lástima de verlo de aquella manera—de lo que más yo gustaba era que todo lo decía de sí mismo, como si realmente lo hubiese pasado.

> [With these words he made me laugh, but also fear him on many occasions. But, although he was saying something, [the shipmates] saw him as crazy and left him as such. But he didn't convince me completely, because he kept repeating my life and all that I had told him ... He cooked me up a thousand different ways, and made me look so gallant—even though it made me sad to see him that way—but what pleased me most was that he said it all about himself, as if he had really experienced it all.] (307–8)

The palpable ambiguity that runs throughout this paragraph reflects the fragile foundation of Guzmán's friendship. He laughs at Sayavedra's mad ravings, but then, realizing that he is retelling Guzmán's own life story, fears the public disclosure of his shady dealings. An ironic fulfillment of his earlier promise to imitate Guzmán's life, Sayavedra's behavior in this final scene of his life makes a sad mockery of the sympathetic storytelling that provided the original basis for their relationship. With Sayavedra's delusional mimicry of the stories that he has heard, the imitative poetics that previously offered the promise of a mode of private friendship that might resist the corrupting influence of picaresque *engaño* falls into disrepair.

The breakdown of the poetic and emotional framework of Guzmán's friendship presages the demise of his friend and the final triumph of the picaresque poetics. The passage above is immediately followed by a cursory account of Sayavedra's death and Guzmán's reaction to his one true friend's tragic end. Still suffering from his mad delusions, Sayavedra rises in the middle of the night and, as I mentioned in my introduction, throws himself to a watery death. The entire scene is portrayed in three sentences and culminates with the account of Guzmán's response to his shipmates' offer of condolences: "y así se quedó el pobre sepultado, no con pequeña lástima de todos, que harto hacían en consolarme. Signifiqué sentirlo, mas sabe Dios la verdad" [and thus, the poor man was entombed, with no small amount of sadness to everyone, who overwhelmed me with their offers of consolation. I showed that I felt it, but God knows the truth] (308). Confronted with the death of his "other self," Guzmán retreats into the picaro's habit of deception while simultaneously negating to his reader any trace of his former friendship. After a couple more explicit statements confirming Guzmán's absolute indifference to Sayavedra's fate, the narrative quickly moves on to other matters, as if to underline the utter failure of this single picaresque experiment with friendship.

The close alignment between Guzmán's denial of any emotional attachment to his former friend and the reassertion of the discursive norm of *engaño* reflects, once again, the implicit poetic structure of the picaresque engagement with the emerging early modern split between public and private life. Perhaps more than any other literary mode of the period, the picaresque affirms the essential deceptiveness of public life against which any expression of sincere personal intimacy must constantly struggle to gain even merely transient recognition. In this sense, Guzmán's friendship with Sayavedra is doomed from the very beginning not because of any inherent personality defect in either picaro, but rather as an aesthetic requirement of the genre. Arguably the first comprehensive literary engagement with the new urban reality of the late sixteenth century, the picaresque novel's unforgiving portrayal of public life sheds a harsh light on the difficulties of friendship in the modern world.

Chapter 5

The Courtesan's Gift: Reciprocity and Friendship in the Letters of Camilla Pisana and Tullia D'Aragona[1]

Maritere López

Mando a vostra signoria la mia sfera materiale di legno … gli mando ancora un paro di colombi che sono eccelenti i quali non possono stare tre giorni a fare l'uova … quell[i] non accetti … in dono, ma le godi per memoria degli obblighi ch' gli tengo finchè mi sia concesso il pagarne qualcuno.

[I'm sending to your lordship my wooden orb … I'm also sending you a pair of doves, which are excellent and cannot be more than three days away from laying eggs … don't accept these [things] as gifts, but enjoy them in memory of the obligations I have towards you, so that I may repay some of my debt.] (Palatini 13)

So wrote Tullia d'Aragona (1510–56), one of Florence's most famous courtesans, to her patron, Benedetto Varchi (1502–65), head of the Florentine Academy and part of Duke Cosimo I's intellectual circle. D'Aragona's concern—her desire to prove her value as client by proving her ability to reciprocate Varchi's patronage through gifts of her own—is echoed in all her extant letters to him, underlining the need continually to court the patronage of one whose esteem and protection was crucial to her very livelihood. Though recognized by some contemporaries as one of Italy's leading female poets, d'Aragona was nevertheless a courtesan, reviled and attacked as a corruptor of social mores because of the sexually venal nature of her profession. Not only vituperated in pornographic poems, but also brought before the courts in 1547 for failing to wear a yellow veil required of prostitutes in Florence, d'Aragona needed to deny her venality and prove instead, with the aid of literary friends and patrons, her active involvement as poet and, thereby, her virtue (Bausi 61; López 105–33). Varchi was central to this undertaking, helping d'Aragona create and dedicate to Cosimo I's duchess, Eleonora of Toledo, the collection of sonnets that gained her an exemption from wearing the dreaded veil.

[1]   I would like to thank Charles Lipp, Lori Clune, Anna Vallis, Dan Lochman, and Lorna Hutson for their insightful comments and editing. All remaining errors are, of course, my own.

Faced with such a debt, how could this woman, so clearly Varchi's social inferior, assure his support against future slander and attacks?

D'Aragona was not the only courtesan to face this conundrum. Some thirty years earlier, Camilla Pisana (writing in 1516–17) sought to protect her reputation and network of patronage by arguing, in what can be termed an epistolary campaign, her ultimate worth. Pisana wrote most of her surviving letters to Francesco del Nero (1487–1563), an intimate member of the Medici circle in Florence, banker to the pope, and right-hand man of Pisana's lover, Filippo Strozzi (1489–1538). Although it was this role that first brought del Nero into Pisana's life, he became her patron in his own right, someone to whom she could turn for support, financial or otherwise. Del Nero not only paid for many of her expenses and sent her a myriad of gifts, but also used his influence within the city to her advantage. Perhaps most significantly, del Nero offered Pisana protection from the derision of his acquaintances, even that of Strozzi himself, who requested that Pisana share herself sexually with others as proof of her love for him. For Pisana, as for d'Aragona, the issue remained one of constantly proving her worth, maintaining her patron's protection, and thus influencing the way society at large—and particularly del Nero's own *padrone*—perceived and behaved toward her.

The basic challenge faced by these women, therefore, was that their relationships with their respective primary patrons were characterized by a complex and uneasy balance. Although clearly active in the men's respective milieu, both women were cognizant not only of their full dependence on their patrons' continued support but also of the social inferiority that cemented that need. Beautiful, highly educated, and trained in the arts, these women nevertheless were fundamentally prostitutes even if, as courtesans, they did more than sell their body. Both offered a rarified experience involving both body and mind. Combining wit and intellect with luxurious sensuality, courtesans catered to individual members of the male elite, men rich or famous enough to win their favor (Lawner 9). Their refinement and erudition not only gained courtesans direct access to patrician circles, but actually made them an immensely sought-after sign of their patrons' own wealth, power, and intellectual prowess. As Guido Ruggiero has argued, the courtesan "made the man, her lovers marked out as true aristocrats merely by being accepted into her company" (281). Crucially, the courtesan also stood apart because of her exclusivity, as her body was "hers to dispose of as she wished, not the common property of all men, as was regularly claimed for 'common' prostitutes" (Ruggiero 281). However, their education and exclusivity notwithstanding, courtesans were not only legally undistinguishable from ordinary prostitutes but, more importantly, considered by many as nothing but common whores (Robin 38; Casagrande 87), inferior both personally and socially, to be used and discarded accordingly.

Indeed, courtesans were often castigated or virulently attacked by contemporaries. Highlighting the women's supposed contagious moral degeneracy and predatory venality, the attacks stressed that the courtesan's trade was iniquitous, regardless of her beauty and education. First, detractors argued that her sexual excess made her a likely carrier of syphilis and a promoter of sinful debauchery (Cohen

201). Second, contemporaries were afraid not only that she would contaminate them physically and spiritually, but also that her "siren's call" would lead men to economic and social ruin (Ruggiero 284). Finally, a courtesan's ability to infiltrate elite circles and participate in the intellectual life of the city might also imperil men's livelihoods because the woman's success in this arena made her a viable competitor for patronage (Rosenthal, *Honest* 49–53). Strikes against courtesans' claims to exclusivity were particularly common, since this assertion seemed the foundation of their high status and resulting wealth. For example, writings such as the *Dialogo dello Zoppino* (c. 1539) and the *Tariffa delle puttane di Vinegia* (1535) coarsely maligned courtesans—including Tullia d'Aragona herself—undermining their reputation for intellectual prowess and depicting them as little more than gross body parts rented by many for sexual release (Pesuit 51–3). Other defamatory works, such as Lorenzo Veniero's *Il trentuno della Zaffetta* (1531) against Angela Zaffetta and Maffio Veniero's series of poems against Veronica Franco (1546–91), targeted specific courtesans who had, in the authors' minds, overstepped their place. The former work made public Zaffetta's gang-rape, an attack orchestrated by Veniero himself when he found he was not her only lover (Pesuit 25–9); the latter described Franco as a blighted whore, ridiculing her claim to a place within the highest echelons of Venetian society (Rosenthal, *Honest* 52–3). Whatever the specific case, attacks against courtesans aimed to undermine their exclusivity and resulting prestige, thus forcing them to act in accordance both with their gender and lower-class status (Pesuit 24).

Reacting to such assaults, courtesans attempted to challenge specific offenses and safeguard themselves against future threats. Most famously, the Venetian Veronica Franco engaged in an exercise of redefinition whereby, through poems and published letters alike, she recast herself as a writer, replacing the image of the debased courtesan with that of the virtuous poet. Crucial to Franco's exercise was her claim to membership in a literary world wherein she collaborated with men in the creation of culture. Her redefinition was thus not only made publicly but had a public end—her continued acceptance in male literary circles and its resultant honors—which intrinsically challenged both gender ideologies and practices (Rosenthal, *Honest* 8). Similarly driven, as we shall see, Tullia d'Aragona also undertook a public exercise of redefinition, highlighting her literary accomplishments and continued participation in the rarefied milieu of academics such as Varchi (Bausi 61). D'Aragona's public redefinition was ultimately successful, if only temporarily, as proven by Cosimo I's pardon in the yellow veil incident: "fasseli gratia per poetessa" [grant her grace, as a poet] (qtd in Bongi 90).

D'Aragona's defense, however, was also mounted on a second front: the private arena of her relationship to Varchi. As Pisana did to del Nero, d'Aragona wrote a series of personal letters to her patron, arguing her worth to the man whose favor could influence both the views and the actions of others. In their respective correspondence, Pisana and d'Aragona highlighted above all the attributes they believed made them viable clients—and thus assets in the broadest terms. Most intriguingly, beyond minor offerings such as the wooden orb and doves mentioned in the epigraph above, both women highlighted as their greatest asset the ability and willingness to be friends to their patron. Promising reciprocity through future beneficent acts, constant love, prudent action, and emotive empathy—all reimagined attributes of the perfect friend—each courtesan proffered true friendship as the ultimate gift. Crucially, in both cases the offer was an oblique one: rather than formally proposing a new friendship, the women highlighted a relationship already in place, an invaluable present that, both argued, had already been proven true both by sentiment and through actions. This tested friendship, they stressed, was founded on love and equality and should therefore be understood as an irrevocable commitment. Different from patronage relationships—defined as ordinary friendships based solely on utility and therefore ultimately inferior because inevitably temporary—the women argued instead for relationships of mutual responsibility in perpetuity.[2]

While facilitating the women's claim for continual reciprocity, however, their appropriation of the classical definition of friendship presented them with a seemingly insurmountable obstacle because, as both Aristotle and Cicero stressed, perfect friends are each other's "other self," equal in stature, wealth, and virtue (Aristotle, *Nic. Eth.* trans. Rackham 1156b; Cicero, *De amicitia* trans. Copley 1.6–7). This claim was clearly difficult for either woman to make in view of not only her social and economic inferiority but also the "immoral" venality of her trade. To circumvent these obstacles, Pisana and d'Aragona both undertook a complex exercise of redefinition, simultaneously recharacterizing perfect friendship as based on both virtue *and* utility, while recasting themselves as virtuous friends by proposing new and unique conceptions of virtue. Each woman's undertaking is therefore significant, for it not only echoed contemporary concerns about the nature of friendship, but also illustrates some of the methods by which early moderns, in this case social inferiors, confronted and attempted to bridge the chasm between classical theories of friendship and early modern lived experience. While equally illuminating, the paucity of sources upon which to recreate Tullia d'Aragona's private relationship to Varchi—as only eight of her letters to him survive—constrains me here to focus primarily on Pisana's redefinition of friendship, which she developed in twenty-seven surviving letters addressed to del Nero. I then turn my attention to d'Aragona's case, which in its recasting of virtue as the foundation of *vera amicitia* simultaneously echoes and expands upon Pisana's.

---

[2]   The question of whether early moderns recognized a fundamental difference between friendship and patronage continues to be contested. For example, Dale Kent argues that contemporaries generally did not differentiate between the two (7). In contrast, cases like that of the Florentine notary Lapo Mazzei and his relationship with the merchant Francesco Datini—most famously analyzed by Richard Trexler—highlight at least one crucial difference: for early moderns, the utility and social hierarchy upon which patronage was based inevitably led to the inferior party's loss of honor.

Prudence and the Safety of the Friend: Camilla Pisana's New Definition of Virtue

Not much is known about Camilla Pisana's life before or after her short-lived affair with Strozzi.[3] However, the few available documents, particularly her letters to del Nero, offer a crucial window into her relationship to both men. Most likely in her late teens at the time, in 1516 Pisana—along with three other girls—was established by Strozzi in a house outside Florence's Porta San Gallo, in the neighborhood of Pio.[4] There Pisana took on the role of *doyenne*, responsible for the house's provisioning, the entertainment of visitors, and the fulfilling of Strozzi's desires—sexual or otherwise. As mentioned, in these undertakings Pisana was aided by her main correspondent, Strozzi's right-hand man (*braccio*) and friend, Francesco del Nero. Perhaps best known as Niccolò Machiavelli's brother-in-law and as banker to Pope Clement VII (Cellini 113), del Nero rose to prominence after meeting Strozzi in 1514; as Strozzi's *cosa*, or creation, del Nero enjoyed many of the favors and financial contracts Strozzi reaped from his connection to his in-laws, the Medici (Bullard 89 n. 91). Most crucial to Pisana, del Nero's role as Filippo Strozzi's *braccio* required of him more than the supervision of Strozzi's business dealings. As confidant, he acted in his friend's stead in all matters, including affairs related to Strozzi's family and to the house at Pio.

While it was this facet of his association with Strozzi that first brought del Nero to Pisana's life, he soon became to her a patron in his own right, someone to whom she could turn for financial or other support. Besides paying for many of her expenses and sending her various presents, del Nero used his access to and influence with important people within the city to her advantage. His mobilization of other clients on her behalf ranged from convincing one of the best doctors in the city to come to Pio to take care of one of Pisana's housemates (50–51, XI) to politically substantial favors, such as arranging through the court system the collection of a debt owed to her (51, XI). Further, del Nero's patronage also served to heighten Pisana's social standing, partly by helping her to forge greater fame as hostess, partly by allowing her to become a patron in turn. His support included again the trivial and the critical, from helping her procure the best produce for her dinner parties (see, for example, 29, II) to the hiring of one of the city's best-known artists to redecorate her house (38, VII). These benefits were crucial to Pisana, whose fame, and thus financial stability, depended not only on her own charms but also on the sumptuousness of her surroundings and her excellence as

---

[3] Only four other contemporary sources mention Pisana. First, she was listed in the 1527 Roman census (Lee 65–6; 3126 and 3214). Twenty-two years later Pisana appeared in the *Dialogo dello Zoppino* mentioned above, which listed her as one of the "stale and rancid whores of Rome" (Flosi 143 n. 49). This portrayal was countered by Pietro Aretino, who visited her Roman home at least once (*Letters* 2: 646), and who raved about her *La Cortigiana* (II. xi).

[4] On the dating of Pisana's relationship to Strozzi, see López 13 n. 25.

hostess, reflections of the courtesan's personal refinement. As Pisana recognized, del Nero's patronage brought more than just material benefits for which to be grateful: "in vero non è persona al mondo dove io sia piú obrigata, e da chi abbi ricevuto piú ben utile e honore" [in truth there is no one else in the world to whom I owe more, or from whom I have received more useful things and [greater] honor] (49, XI). Pisana referred to the fact that del Nero's support also improved her standing within Florentine society, enabling her patronage of neighbors and family members such as her brother, who, thanks to her, benefitted from del Nero's beneficence (see, for example, 87, XXVI). The connection to del Nero thus earned Pisana a degree of influence and honor that otherwise she would not have enjoyed. Consequently, even del Nero's seemingly trivial benefits ultimately increased Pisana's ability to care for herself.

The material and social benefits del Nero offered Pisana paled, however, in comparison to his intervention on her behalf in her affair with Strozzi, which was rapidly waning by 1517. Moving on to new lovers, and therefore in her judgment being "unfaithful" to her (25–6; I), Strozzi not only stopped visiting the house in Pio almost completely, but also tried to have Pisana give herself sexually to others supposedly as proof of her love for him:

> [I]l mio Macedonico, con certe sue persuasione ingannese e false, voria che io come semprice, anzi poco amatrice di esso, fussi del mio proprio ad altri domatrice e conducitrice … mostrandomi con alcune sue auttorità, non mai é udite né viste, che non si può dire che una veramente ami se negli amplessi del suo amato qualche numero di giovane non conduce.

> [My Macedonian [Filippo], with his deceitful and false persuasions, would like that I, like a simpleton, was of my own self a donor and guide to others, even if I little liked it … showing me with his authoritative words, never before heard or seen, that one cannot say that she truly loves unless she also includes in her lover's embrace a number of young men.] (76, XXI)

Affronted by what she understood not only as an insult to her love for Strozzi or an outrage to her dignity, but also as an explicit threat to her exclusivity and the security it provided, Pisana in most of her letters entreated del Nero to become involved, either directly by pleading her case to Strozzi or indirectly simply by understanding—and agreeing with—her side of the story.

It was in fact this last benefit which drove Pisana in her relentless campaign to prove her worth to del Nero, who, as a true friend—and therefore as a perfect mediator (Hyatte 177)—she hoped would change Strozzi's view of and actions toward her. Primary in her undertaking was the clear delineation of the things she could offer in exchange for del Nero's support. She started from the assumption that material things would not do. As she saw it, to reciprocate del Nero's many benefits "no gold, silver, or treasure in the world … could satisfy in the least" [non oro, non argento, non tesoro ha lo universo ... potria in minima parte satisfare] (39, VII). Her most obvious asset—her body—was also out of the question, a sensible exclusion considering the context of their respective links to Strozzi. This omission she broached openly, playing on the double meaning of the fact that he had, as she states, "never received pleasure from me" [mai a nessun tempo ricevuto piacer da me] (86, XXVI).[5] Instead, Pisana outlined several alternatives that, arguably, only she could offer in exchange.[6] Most salient among those was a perfect friendship pragmatically redefined to fit both her personal attributes and the nature of her relationship to del Nero. Pisana's recasting of *amicitia perfecta* in many ways followed the traditional model of true friendship. However, as we shall see, she could only adopt without modification what can be termed secondary attributes of the relationship. The primary traits of true friendship—the absence of utility as the relationship's motive and the virtuous equality of the friends—she was constrained to modify.

To begin, Pisana was able to embrace unchanged three attributes of *amicitia perfecta*: the steadfastness of true friends, the willingness that perfect friendship be tested and proven, and the belief that the foundation of friendship is love for the friend. Conflating the first two into one intertwined principle, Pisana argued to del Nero that "not all of those who call themselves 'friends' can be understood to embody perfect friendship, but only those who ... in every arduous test have been unmovable and constant" [... non tutti quegli che si chiamano amici si posson tenere d'amicizia perfetta, ma quegli dico che a ogni arduo cimento stanno immobili e costanti] (63, XV). The implication, of course, was that she has been such a proven and tested friend. Throughout the letters, Pisana not only repeatedly recounted for del Nero the many ways in which she has been steadfast to him, but continually encouraged him to put her to the test: "... e se non credi alle parole mie, fa quella esperienzia che ti piace, e vedrai quanto io son tua" [... if you don't believe my words, make any experiment you please, and you will see how much I am yours] (62, XV). Her focus on tested rather than simply avowed constancy is telling, for it highlights that her offer of friendship, as she understood it, did not carry with it the disadvantages of untried acquaintances. Already tested, her friendship to del Nero was a present given repetitively and faithfully, the benefits of which he could reap into the future. In this way, she assumed, her gift was of significant value and thus worthy of further reciprocal benefits.

Pisana's words that "not all of those who call themselves 'friends' can be understood to embody perfect friendship" are doubly significant, for with them she did not just offer del Nero true friendship; rather, she simultaneously set herself apart—and above—others of del Nero's "friends." In many of her letters Pisana

---

[5]   Pisana's ruling out of sex as capital in her relationship with del Nero may also reflect the medieval differentiation between friendship and sexual desire, in which the former serves as a foil for the latter (Stretter, "Rewriting" 240–42).

[6]   Three of these—remembrance, fidelity, and deference—I have discussed elsewhere, stressing their typicality as capital in the patron–client exchange (López 169–74).

called attention to the several ways in which del Nero's current friends failed to meet the standards of true friendship. She explicitly stressed that his so-called friends did not love him as she did: "So bene che non vi manca de l'altre amicizie piú grate e d'altra sorte non siamo noi, *tamen* non si potranno mai adequar a l'amor nostro ..." [I know well that you don't lack other, more pleasant friendships, and [with friends] of different status than ours [Pisana and her housemates]. But they will never measure up [in terms of] our love] (57, XIII). Consequently, his other friends, regardless of their higher social status, deserved neither his love nor to be placed above her in his affections.

Pisana's concern with the nature of del Nero's other friendships and the likely attributes of his other friends highlights the fact that, notwithstanding her espousal of the classical model, she could not literally offer del Nero a "perfect" friendship as defined by the ancients. Most obviously, the sexual nature of her profession—not to mention its venality—and her social inferiority precluded two crucial primary attributes of Greco-Roman perfect friendship: the absence of utility as the relationship's motive and the equality of the friends. The first of these attributes differentiated perfect friendship from two other types of lesser friendships—the pleasurable and the useful—each motivated respectively not by love for the friend but by the pursuit of pleasure or useful goods from the friend. These friendships were seen as ultimately inferior because, stemming not from love of the friend "for what he is" but from love of the goods one friend can get from the other, they develop accidentally and last only as long as the goods last (Aristotle, *Nic. Eth.* 1156a). Pisana's critical need for del Nero's continued support, for both material and emotive "goods" coming from him, skewed their relationship towards the utilitarian, theoretically dooming it to end when one of the friends—most likely she—stopped being useful to the other. The second problematic attribute of perfect friendship in this context is its restriction to men identical in all aspects, particularly stature, wealth, and virtue. Best encapsulated by Cicero's idea of friends as each other's *alter idem*, or "other self," such equality was clearly the opposite of Pisana's standing vis-à-vis del Nero.[7]

Pisana was not alone in recognizing the near impossibility of attaining such an ideal relationship in the real world and therefore the need to modify it. The ancients themselves seemed to have realized the divergence between the theory and praxis of *amicitia perfecta*, a fact highlighted by the conspicuous absence in their works of examples of model friendships between actual people. As Reginald Hyatte highlights, even Cicero's depiction of the historical bond between Laelius and Scipio is an idealized one, making his representation of these friends a myth of *vera*

---

[7]   Intriguingly, neither Pisana nor d'Aragona broaches in her private letters the subject of gender as relevant to her treatment of friendship. Remaining silent about conventional denials of the possibility of true friendship between the sexes, the courtesans concentrated instead on their assumed inequality in social and moral terms. In this I disagree with Fiora Bassanese's analysis of D'Aragona's letters, the deferent language of which she takes to reflect not only social inferiority but also gender difference (74–5).

amicitia rather than a verification of "the social reality of perfect friendship" (32). Motivated to bridge this theoretical gap by defining ways in which true friendship could be both applicable and viable in real life, early Renaissance writers such as Leon Battista Alberti (1404–72) developed alternative theories of friendship. While fundamentally rooted in the ancient tradition, their versions crucially offered "updated measures of perfection" based on new concerns such as patriotism and family honor, and they stressed the centrality of utility in true friendship (Hyatte 1). In the fourth book of *Della Famiglia*, Alberti offered not only a new basis upon which to assess the perfection of friendship but also a new set of attributes to define the perfect friend. Alberti never rejected the classical model; after all, two of his interlocutors, Adovardo and Lionardo, embrace wholesale the maxims to be learned from the ancients—whose authority Lionardo endorses in an understated way as "by no means to be ignored or disdained" (269). Nevertheless, through the character of Piero Alberti the author expands upon acceptable and authoritative models of friendship. A "man of the world," Piero's practical experience serves as a foil to the theories presented by the other two. Pragmatic in his understanding of friendship as fundamentally utilitarian, Piero highlights not a virtuous character as the most desirable trait of the perfect friend but rather diligence and prudence, coupled with perseverance and worldly wisdom (Hyatte 180–81).

Pisana's own handling of the seemingly insurmountable dichotomies between the theory and reality of friendship mirrored the exercise of redefinition undertaken by Renaissance theorists such as Alberti. While similarly offering alternative measures of perfection, but ultimately intending to guarantee the continuation of del Nero's favors, she recast perfect friendship as fundamentally and ideally utilitarian. Nevertheless, to differentiate it from lesser forms of friendship, this newly imagined perfect relationship was still to be based on the virtuous equality of the friends. For such a redefinition to work, Pisana also recast virtue, basing it specifically on prudence and the protection of the other as the pivotal attributes of the perfect friend. She defined prudence not as Alberti did, namely as perseverance and worldly/political wisdom, but as the discernment to know what it could—and actually did—cost del Nero to be her friend. More importantly, she stressed the active nature of prudence: it is not enough to know the cost of friendship, but one must act according to that knowledge, minimizing the cost to the friend whenever possible.

To show prudence at work, Pisana highlighted repeatedly how she endeavored to protect del Nero's position from any injury, economic or social, which his acquaintance to her might cause.[8] Pisana subscribed to the belief that gossip

---

[8]   As Alexandra Shepard has convincingly argued, the early modern gendered standard which clearly made a woman's "honesty" the ultimate measure of her worth also constrained, if to a lesser degree, a man's sexual conduct by tying it to his economic and professional integrity (156). Sexual dissipation, real or imagined, could be seen as reflecting an intemperance detrimental to business, thus leading to the man's loss of currency—social and financial (160).

about their relationship could lead to the view that he was sexually dissipated, a charge that could damage del Nero's respectability and be directly detrimental to his social status. Therefore, Pisana went to extremes, particularly in terms of her subterfuge in sending her letters to him, for even those could be damaging to his reputation. For example, Pisana never once signed her letters in full, limiting herself to initialing most of them at the end. She also made sure not to write when doing so would "cause scandal," and she took care that the letters were personally delivered to del Nero by third parties trusted by both (see, for example, 35–6, V). The ultimate proof of her prudence, moreover, was her willingness to end their friendship because she understood its cost to him:

> ... conosco tutto quel che fate non è per obrigo, ma per propria vostra gentilezza, onde bisogna pure aver qualche discrezione, e pensar che avete de l'altre spese al mondo, senza avere a metter ogni cosa in noi. Forse che ... doverr[ò] terminar questa cosa ...

> [I recognize that everything you do is not out of duty but out of courtesy, therefore I need to be discreet, and remember that you have other troubles in this world, without investing everything in us [Pisana and her housemates]. So that maybe ... [I should] put an end to this relationship ...] (51, XI)

This, of course, was not Pisana's desired end. Yet, her willingness to protect him, even to her own detriment, only served to reinforce her claim to virtue.

Pisana not only recurrently stressed the lengths to which she would go to protect her friend, but she also argued repeatedly that in her desire for his safety, as in her love for him, she surpassed his other friends. Her ability to protect him she linked to her directness and lack of hypocrisy, even if these attributes sometimes made her seem intemperate: "Credo ormai che tu conosca la mia condizione; io son súbita, non so simulare, se niente me va pel capo, lo dico aperto" [I believe that by now you know my nature: I'm spontaneous, I don't know how to pretend, and if anything comes to mind, I say it openly] (42, VIII). Her candor, however, was not to be misunderstood. Her inability to pretend meant that he could always trust her implicitly, as he could not his other acquaintances, whose shiftiness and unspecified intrigues Pisana implicitly denounced in all the letters. In this, Pisana's protection of the friend harked back to the classical idea that honesty, as the core of *amicitia perfecta*, guarantees that neither friend will ever harm the other (Hyatte 30; Stretter, "Cicero" 357; Aristotle *Nic. Eth* 1157b). Pisana's offer of friendship thus hinged primarily on her unique ability to protect his wealth, honor, and reputation. This safety only she could offer, Pisana implied, once again highlighting the unique value of her gift.

Of course, in order for her claim of virtue to work, Pisana had first to deny, to whatever degree possible, the venality and immorality of her profession. As she could not literally erase her past, or the fact that she was indeed a courtesan, she based her refutation on contemporary nuances of *castità* (chastity) that, as Julia Hairston has argued, made it synonymous with *fedeltà* (faithfulness): she countered her lack of purity with an assertion of fidelity to del Nero as friend (475–6). Her claim included two elements: a claim of eternal and selfless love for him, partly discussed above, and a consequent rejection of all other admirers and friends. Pisana reiterated time and again her love for del Nero, which she went so far to describe as the adoration of a mortal for a god (82, XXIII). Interestingly, this love she did not see as conflicting with her feelings for her lover, but rather as further linking her to del Nero through his own love for Strozzi, his other friend. Therefore, she paradoxically presented their friendship not as shared among the three, but rather as exclusively between herself and del Nero. Indeed, Pisana explicitly claimed to have chosen del Nero as her one and only friend, even if this was patently not true, Strozzi being the obvious exception. Still, she persisted in rejecting friends other than him, even if he should encourage her to make them: "Voi siate la mia corona, la mia gloria, e un vero paradiso non finto. ... Non mi dire adunque, favorito mio caro, ch'io abbi altri amici. ... E chi vuo' ch'io ami fuor de voi?" [You are my crown, my glory, and a true paradise. ... So don't tell me that I [must] have other friends. ... [W]hom do you want me to love other than you?] (58–9, XIV). As we shall see, she implied that this single-minded and exclusive fidelity deserved to be reciprocated in kind.

Pisana's refutation of her lack of worth and her consequent redefinition of virtue allowed her to claim explicitly a level of equality to del Nero that would have been absurd if proposed under the assumptions of classical true friendship. To achieve her desired goal—his protection from all, even from Strozzi—Pisana emphasized their equality in fidelity, ability to love, and trustworthiness. As regards fidelity, Pisana played upon not only her loyalty as friend to del Nero but also her faithfulness to Strozzi. These three become conflated, all intimating a virtuousness mirrored in del Nero's own loyalty to Pisana and Strozzi. However, it was the Pisana–del Nero fidelity that she stressed, in a sense making Strozzi an outsider to the friendship and thus less worthy of del Nero's allegiance. The implication was simple: del Nero and Pisana were alike, morally equivalent, and thus naturally inclined to side with one another against those who were not. Thus, she set the stage for her diatribes against Strozzi's demands and del Nero's support of them, which otherwise would have been unacceptable and implausible, respectively.

The most important of their shared virtues, as she defined them, were their prudence and trustworthiness; in fact, it was these virtues that persuaded Pisana to complain to del Nero. If his honor, thoughts, and secrets were safe with her, then Pisana's own could be no less so with him. Her turning to him for empathy was propelled by her belief in that safety and by her confidence in del Nero's allegiance, even in the face of his own friendship to Strozzi. As she stated:

Io non ho possuto fare non mi lamenti con voi, dove sempre ripongo ogni secreto mio, per essalare la mia passione, e poi son certa che, benché mostriate forse con llui di riderne, avete tanta discrezione in voi che conoscete quel che è mal fatto, ma portandogli reverenzia e onore per l'altre parte che sono in lui, non biasimeresti le opera sue.

[I haven't been able not to complain to you, to whom I always trust my secrets, to vent my anger, and besides I'm certain that, although perhaps you pretend to laugh about it with him, you have enough discernment in you to know that which is badly done. [But I also know that because] you honor him for the worthy attributes he possesses, you won't belittle his accomplishments.] (54, XII)

Thus, although cognizant of his duties to Strozzi, Pisana felt sure that del Nero's friendship to her, buttressed by the discernment between right and wrong that he clearly shared with her, would allow him not to be unduly influenced by Strozzi.

This was particularly important in relation to Strozzi's desire to give her to others. Therefore, Pisana beseeched del Nero: "... dammi la tua resoluzione e fa che l'amicizia e la sua lunga conversazione non ti facci contaminar la verità" [... give me your verdict and make sure that his [Strozzi's] friendship or his long conversation do not contaminate the truth] (77, XXI). She was sure that del Nero would not allow this to happen, and hence felt comfortable enough to put her fate into his hands: "Aspetto la tua graziosa risposta e non preferirò di mettere a essecuzione quanto mi dirai, nonostante che io ben conoscessi operare il mio danno" [I await your gracious response, and will execute everything you tell me, even if I knew well that it would be to my detriment] (77–8, XXI). The implication was evidently that such a negative outcome was impossible, for true friends defend, support, and stand up for each other regardless of other social and personal obligations they might have to bear. This scenario could only be plausible, however, within the framework of Pisana's redefined version of friendship. Pivoting as it did on shared prudence, defined as the selfless protection of the other, her offer of friendship to del Nero was designed to bring her real benefits, especially protection against direct threats. Although in this way utilitarian, for Pisana such friendship was perfect.

Empathy and the Alleviation of the Friend's Pain: Tullia d'Aragona's New Friendship

Pisana's redefinition of friendship was echoed by another famous courtesan. Born in Rome in 1510, Tullia d'Aragona became a courtesan while still in her early teens, most likely trained and educated by her mother, also a courtesan (Biagi 678). Her vivacity and desire to learn marked her as one of the favorites of Rome's elite: her circle of admirers even included Filippo Strozzi, who roughly 15 years after his affair with Camilla Pisana served as papal treasurer and whose taste in courtesans evidently remained highly discriminating. By 1535, d'Aragona was living in Venice, where she met many of the leading intellectuals of the age, most importantly Sperone Speroni, who in 1542 made d'Aragona the central character of his *Dialogue on Love*. His characterization of d'Aragona as a learned and eloquent interlocutor in matters of love propelled her fame above other courtesans and women writers. Consequently acclaimed as an intellectual prodigy and welcomed into top literary circles around Italy, d'Aragona achieved her highest success in Florence between 1546 and 1548, during which period she published both her *Rime della Signora Tullia d'Aragona et di diversi a lei* [*Poems of the Lady Tullia d'Aragona and from various men to her*] and her *Dialogo della Infinità di Amore* [*Dialogue on the Infinity of Love*]. It was also during these years that she faced the greatest threats to her standing, being not only publicly vituperated in pornographic works, as we have seen, but also indicted for not wearing the yellow veil required of her as prostitute. Such accusations of iniquity were unthinkable to her. They were a real threat to her livelihood since they could lead to her being forced to leave Florence in shame and forsaken by her supporters (Palatini 14).

To counter accusations of her immorality and escape punishment for her sumptuary crime, d'Aragona publicly refuted her venality, presenting herself instead as a poetess whose continued literary accomplishments and personal virtue gained faithful admirers through whose patronage she earned a living. Central to the staging of this personal recharacterization was the mobilization of her most prominent admirers, whose verification of d'Aragona's "rare knowledge of poetry and philosophy" [rara scientia di peosia e filosophia] (qtd in Jones, *Currency* 104) moved Duke Cosimo I to grant her an exemption from the law. Both in gratitude and as a means to cement a relationship with the ducal house, d'Aragona compiled and dedicated to Duchess Eleonora of Toledo a collection of sonnets both by her and many of the best known humanist poets of the era. In essence what Ann Rosalind Jones calls a "group portrait" (*Currency* 103), the collection categorically linked d'Aragona both to exclusive academic circles and to patrons whose support could guarantee protection against future threats.

Primary among these patrons was the recipient of her surviving private correspondence, Benedetto Varchi, perhaps the most prominent literary figure in 1540s Florence. A favorite of Cosimo I, Varchi headed Florence's academy for the arts and letters, the Accademia Fiorentina, a position of favor and honor from which he wielded significant influence throughout the city. Fortunately for d'Aragona, he often exerted his influence to her benefit, granting her numerous favors that, as had those from Francesco del Nero to Camilla Pisana, ranged from the trivial to the critical, from mere fruit to moral support and heightened honor. Never giving her direct monetary support, Varchi's material offerings to d'Aragona, as far as can be ascertained from her letters, were instead small gifts and tokens of affection such as plums and turtledoves (see, for example, Palatini 11). To d'Aragona, most significant were instead two other favors Varchi granted her, the benefits of which indebted her to him forever: first, he continually corrected her poems and other works, saving her from literary embarrassment; second, he eased her troubles by interceding with his own patrons and other clients on her behalf.

Early in their acquaintance, Varchi became d'Aragona's scholarly mentor, a role he continued to play for much of her literary career. The primary attribute of Varchi's mentorship was his continual editing of her works, a fact to which d'Aragona refers in almost all her letters. For example, with her first extant letter she enclosed the draft of a sonnet she composed, expecting that he would correct it promptly: "gli mando una bozza de un sonetto, e la prego per quella sua verso di me solita cortesia, mi faci gratia dargli quella perfettione che gli manca, e più presto ch' potrà, mandarmelo" [I am sending you the draft of a sonnet. I pray you, as by your usual courtesy towards me, that you do me the favor of giving it the perfection it lacks, and return it to me as soon as you can] (Palatini 10). D'Aragona recognized Varchi's editorial intervention as a special favor, a "gift" deriving from his loving nature. More importantly, his help, without which she would "blush" over the imperfection of her work, was vital both to her continued acclaim as poet and to the protection such categorization offered her (Palatini 17). Crucial to d'Aragona's continued welfare was also Varchi's use of his influence and his mobilization of his network of patronage on her behalf. This vital favor and its benefits were most clearly illustrated by Varchi's intervention in the yellow veil incident, throughout which he vouched for her literary standing, ultimately facilitating her pardon. Varchi not only wrote seven poems to be included in d'Aragona's *Rime*, but he also—and more significantly—wrote the letter of introduction to the Duchess that originally accompanied the poems (Bausi 69). In fact, d'Aragona requested Varchi to write the missive, recognizing his greater suitability for the task: "questa supplica … a vostra signoria sarà facile no' altrimenti che se ragionasi familiarmente" [this plea will be as easy for your lordship as if you were talking among friends] (Palatini 14). His familiarity with and comfort in ducal circles were thus crucial assets which d'Aragona not only recognized but also hoped—expected, even—to enjoy continually.

Notwithstanding her willingness to make use of Varchi's literary expertise and of his social connections, she recognized the degree to which his favors indebted her to him and was distressed that she could not reciprocate them. In fact shamed by such inequality, she complained to him about her inability to repay him equitably: "me agrava quanto mi conosco non bastevole condegno guidardone rendergli se non integro cambio, almeno quasi uguale" [I am bothered by the knowledge that I'm unable to give you, if not full, at least comparable exchange] (Palatini 12).[9] So shamed, she prayed: "Così me concedessi la fortuna ch'io un giorno potessi in qual parte pagare gli grande oblighi ch'ho co vostra signoria però in cosa che utile e di uso contento fussi …" [Were that one day fortune would grant that I become able to repay, in any part and in a useful and satisfying way, the great obligation I have towards your lordship] (Palatini 13). Not satisfied to wish away her debt, however, and hoping to guarantee Varchi's future support, d'Aragona sought to balance the account, as it were: "ma già che più di quello ch'io a suoi meriti ubbligata sono non mi posso ubbligare gli renderò del presente quelli maggiori

---

[9]   On the shame produced by the inability to reciprocate, see Lytle 56.

gratie che per me si puote e devono ..." [since I cannot be more obligated to your merits than I already am, I will repay for now the greatest favors, as I should and can] (Palatini 12).

Since by January 1547 d'Aragona was no longer Varchi's lover, as her letters obliquely reveal, the courtesan could not offer her body in exchange. Therefore, as did Pisana before her, d'Aragona proposed alternative gifts she could offer Varchi to secure his continued benefaction. Starting with the trivial, d'Aragona sent him token material goods, such as the wooden orb and the doves mentioned in this essay's epigraph, to recompense similar objects Varchi had given her. To reciprocate in kind one of his more substantial favors, d'Aragona offered him editorial help with his own works. Repeatedly, she enjoined him to send her his work, for she was willing to complete for him both menial tasks such as having his sonnets copied and more essential ones such as constructively criticizing his poems (see, for example, Palatini 13). This editorial exchange allowed d'Aragona comfortably to assume further reciprocity on his part: "[S]olamente pregherò ... che ogni volta ch'io gli mandaro qualche cosa mia al solito della sua bontà come mio maestro, e il mio da me, si degni corregerla e ornarlla" [I will only ask that ... every time I send you one of my compositions, you deign to correct and embellish it, as is usual of your kindness as my teacher and of me towards your own [work]] (Palatini 13). Capitalizing on her literary status and offering her professional help in exchange, d'Aragona hoped to sustain in perpetuity a relationship with Varchi, one from whom she could continually benefit without losing honor.

However, d'Aragona's literary aptitude was clearly not equal to Varchi's, making her offer to edit his works uncertain to yield the desired result. Therefore, d'Aragona offered a last, incomparable gift to Varchi: a newly defined perfect friendship, based not on prudence or safety, as Pisana's had primarily been, but rather on three different key virtues of the true friend: constancy, trustworthiness, and an empathy leading to the alleviation of the other's unhappiness or suffering. D'Aragona portrayed these virtues, which simultaneously embraced and expanded upon classical theories of friendship, as epitomized by her relationship with Varchi, recast not as a temporary patronage association but as a permanent commitment to one another. D'Aragona presented the first virtue—constancy—in a way reminiscent of Camilla Pisana's own avowals of faithfulness to Francesco del Nero. Having selected him as her only protector and counselor (Palatini 12, 14), d'Aragona repeatedly offered to love Varchi exclusively and forever, making herself "remember and love, serve and honor [his lordship] with all my might" [ricordarmi di lei [Vostra Signoria] ed amarlla, servirlla ed honorarlla a tutto mio potere] (Palatini 10). Crucially, she presented the perpetual nature of her love for him as almost compulsory, stemming from his kindness, perfect judgment, and virtue—all traits she implicitly claimed to possess as well and which could not but lead him to love her in return. Finally, D'Aragona exhorted her friend to test her love for him, allowing her to "prove to you with actions what I have ... many times told you and write to you about" [mustrargli con effetti quello che ... piu volte gli ho ditto, e scrivo] (Palatini 13). Like Pisana, d'Aragona believed proven constancy to be not only of greater value than an untested, new relationship but also more likely to lead to further reciprocation from her friend.

While proven constancy was to d'Aragona a highly desirable trait of perfect friends, more valuable still was the friend's trustworthiness. D'Aragona clearly subscribed to Cicero's maxim that friends should be able to trust one another, free "to share ... without reservation, all their concerns" (*De amicitia* 17, 61). Without such trust, Cicero concluded, friendship cannot endure. Not just embracing the equality implied in this classical ideal, but also stressing the relief to be found in sharing one's concerns with someone who cares, d'Aragona divulged to Varchi her distress about not only major predicaments such as her sumptuary difficulties but also personal issues such as her mother's undiagnosed sickness (Palatini 11). The considerable space occupied in d'Aragona's short letters by this last topic— one which could be inappropriate in the context of a conventional patron–client relationship—reflects d'Aragona's understanding of her association with Varchi. As not just her benefactor but her true friend, Varchi would naturally not be bothered by her complaints:

> Se io non fussi havezza ogni giorno rilevare delle bastonate dalla mia cativa ed inimica sorte non ha dubbio ch'io tanto con voi mi dorrei havendo poco risguardo al dispiacere che io vi causerei, essendo voi l'anima mia.

> [If it were not that I'm made every day to take notice of the blows that fortune, evil and inimical, strikes against me, there is no doubt that I would not complain so much to you. [But I do so,] paying little heed to the displeasure I could cause you, because you are my soul.] (Palatini 11)

D'Aragona's conviction that she could trust her innermost feelings and anxieties to him was also an invitation. Based on their equality in virtue and trustworthiness, measured soul to soul (Palatini 16), d'Aragona encouraged Varchi to share his own troubles with her, which she would regard with the same care with which he attended to her own concerns.

D'Aragona's trust in Varchi was further driven by the belief that he would not only listen to her but also, more importantly, understand her anxieties and ease her troubles. This conviction reflects the most important attribute of d'Aragona's redefined friendship: empathy for, and the alleviation of, the friend's pain. Once again seemingly influenced directly by the ancients, d'Aragona embraced the ideal of unanimity among true friends, who completely sympathize with each other in all matters of importance (Cicero, *De amicitia* 6, 20; Aristotle, *Nic. Eth.* 1166a). D'Aragona hinted that her empathy for Varchi rested on their similarity, for they confronted tribulations the nature and consequences of which no one else could truly understand. While d'Aragona faced the iniquity and real threat of sumptuary laws designating her as a prostitute, Varchi faced accusations of sexual misconduct, particularly the corruption of one of his male pupils and the rape of a young girl. In the spring of 1545 Varchi was arrested and imprisoned for this last act, discharged only after he publicly accepted culpability.[10] Although soon after he became head of the Accademia Fiorentina, accusations against him continued to plague Varchi: relentless in their persecution, and aiming at his fall from ducal favor and the loss of his influence, his enemies continually accused him of eschewing public morality. Varchi's troubles were thus of a similar nature to d'Aragona's, stemming from the use of sexual and moral codes as weapons against their reputations and very livelihoods. Based on this comparison, d'Aragona implies that, of his reputed friends, only she could truly empathize with him, highlighting a cycle of reciprocal sympathy in which the understanding and comfort Varchi had selflessly given her he must then accept in return.

D'Aragona took classical sympathy further, stipulating not just understanding of but also the active mitigation of the friend's troubles by whatever means possible. Thus, for example, she asked that Varchi forsake other responsibilities in order to visit and comfort her when her mother worsened (Palatini 11). As we have seen, she also requested that he help compile the poems to be included in, and write the letter of introduction to be sent with, her *Rime* (Palatini 15). Whether in relation to private or public concerns, therefore, d'Aragona required more than just Varchi's empathy; she called as well for his active intervention in ameliorating her problems. Intriguingly, echoing Camilla Pisana's own conviction that del Nero would side with her against her lover's design to give her to others, D'Aragona seemed to expect Varchi's acquiescence. As her *vero amico*, she implied, he could do no other. Nevertheless, d'Aragona's anticipation of both emotive and useful benefits from Varchi she did not mean to be one-sided. The true friendship she offered was to be mutual: "sopra ogni cosa ... mi comandi con quella ferma fede che v.s. ha in questo ch'io ne miei bisogni sono ricorsa alla bontà, e amorevolezza sua" [above else, I pray you always turn to me ... firm in the conviction ... that I turn to your kindness and loving nature whenever I'm in need] (Palatini 13). Thus reciprocated, her gift would, in theory, continue to benefit both friends always.

Conclusion

The courtesans' conviction that their offer of redefined friendship would lead to relationships of reciprocal utility, furnishing both tangible benefits and protection against threats in perpetuity, proved misguided. Although both did receive from their respective correspondent further assistance, neither of their friendships proved as long-lived as the women had hoped. Tullia d'Aragona did benefit from Varchi's intervention, being recognized by Duke Cosimo I as a poet and thus exempted from having to wear the yellow veil. However, she died in relative poverty and virtual obscurity, clearly no longer assisted by any of her old patrons

---

[10]   For the accusations against Varchi as a pedophile and rapist, see Pirotti 12–16 and 26–7.

and friends. Camilla Pisana's failure was equally injurious but more abrupt: within a few months of her letters to del Nero, she was living in Rome, reduced by 1520 to court the patronage of Francesco degli Albizzi, a man whom she seems to have disliked intensely (Graf 221–2). Later, she too died in obscurity. Perhaps worse in her immediate context, Pisana's offer of perfect friendship did not garner her the unquestioned support she expected. As del Nero's letters to Pisana's housemate make clear, he had serious misgivings about Pisana's charges against his friend Strozzi. While ready to describe her as "wonderful and rare" [mirabile e rara], and therefore being "willing to pretend to believe her in this way abused" [voglio fingere di crederla a questo modo ingiurata], he still thought her to be "rather a liar" [alquanto buggiardetta] (223r). Pisana's redefinition of herself as prudent and honest, and thus the perfect friend, obviously fell on deaf ears.

While ultimately unsuccessful, Pisana's and d'Aragona's attempts to redefine perfect friendship remain nevertheless crucial to understanding early modern discourses and experiences of friendship. First, the courtesans' exercise reveals early modern perceptions of the problematic and uncomfortable disjuncture between the theory of *vera amicitia* as defined by the ancients and contemporary lived reality. Tackling in their recasting of friendship the uneasy balance between profit and honor in patronage relationships, the women dealt simultaneously with classical proscriptions of utility as an acceptable basis for perfect friendship and the prescription for perfect equality between true friends. Requiring specific benefits from their correspondents, particularly sustained protection against ongoing threats to their social standing and livelihoods, Pisana and d'Aragona recast utilitarian friendship as perfect by creating a cycle of continual reciprocity based not on the disproportionate needs of patrons and clients but on the equal virtue of friends. Their respective equality to del Nero and Varchi, however, necessarily was based on a redefinition of virtue that highlighted attributes unique to each woman. Thus, Pisana offered del Nero the gift of a perfect friendship based on her honesty and prudence, traits which made her able to protect his reputation even if to her own detriment, whereas D'Aragona offered Varchi empathy and the alleviation of his suffering or distress, emotive goods only she could offer because of the similarity of their tribulations. Regardless of what traits each woman stressed, both believed virtue thus redefined equalized their standing vis-à-vis their correspondents, guaranteeing the continued benevolence and support which the ancients argued exist between perfect friends. The courtesans' practical yet imaginative reworking of the classical model of friendship suggests one further characteristic of early moderns' reception of friendship conventions: while embracing the Greco-Roman model as authoritative, they still believed it malleable, some of its attributes able to be amended so as to make it applicable to everyday life. Perhaps surprisingly, not only theorists and literary figures like Alberti—or others in this collection such as More, Sidney, and Shakespeare—tried their hand at such revision. Even women marginalized and attacked as immoral attempted it.

Chapter 6

The "Single Lyfe" of Isabella Whitney: Love, Friendship, and the Single Woman Writer

Allison Johnson

Isabella Whitney begins her collection of poetry, *A Sweet Nosgay,* by evoking personal failure, sickness, and isolation, as many critical studies have observed.[1] Whitney's misfortunes—the loss of her position as a domestic maidservant, her poor health, and her loneliness—lead her to read Hugh Plat's *The Floures of Philosophie*, which in turn inspires her to versify and organize his adages. Her hardships thus authorize her poetic project. While it is certainly true that Whitney strategically employs the tropes of illness and disenfranchisement, she mitigates these claims of isolation with representations of connection and friendship. Whitney does make her way to Plat's Plot "all sole alone," but only after speaking to (and ignoring the advice of) a friend; moreover, she includes in the *Nosgay* an epistolary dialogue composed of letters to and from relatives, friends, and fellow writers, thus framing her collection of poetry with depictions not of total isolation but rather of friendship (A6r). Whitney uses these portrayals of friendship to shore up her self-representation as a virtuous woman writer: her poetic exchanges with male writers demonstrate her ability to participate actively in the masculine world of literary production, while her correspondence with her siblings and other family members illustrates her enduring connection to a supportive family circle, even as she moves beyond the confines of the domestic sphere.

Of course, moving beyond that sphere to claim a public position as an author was no easy feat for an early modern woman who was expected to confine herself and her speech to the home and family. Therefore, even as Whitney highlights her family connections, she distances herself from love and marriage, both of which would pose a threat to her independence (or, in the case of love, her chastity and reputation) and effectively place her back in the home. However, her condition

---

[1]   Lynette McGrath claims that the *Nosgay* "opens and closes with the speaker essentially isolated from those possibly 'spightful' inner circles of London marked by privileged class and financial security" (144), and Laurie Ellinghausen argues that Whitney's "writing is predicated on her isolation from service, family, and textual communities" (1). I suggest that Whitney mitigates this isolation with her depictions of friendship and her inclusion of letters to and from friends and kin.

as a single woman and her decision to publish her poetry could also damage her reputation; as Patricia Phillippy has demonstrated, single urban women were often associated with "loose living" (446), and, as Ann Rosalind Jones claims, the association of "female eloquence with promiscuity" made publication a fraught enterprise for any early modern woman, but especially a woman who did not enjoy the protection of an authorizing husband or aristocratic status ("Writing to Live" 1). I argue that Whitney defuses these threats by emphasizing her own chastity and virtue and by fashioning herself as an active and equal member of a caring community of friends and kin. Friendship, including friendships among siblings and other family members, allows Whitney to depict virtuous relationships with others that—unlike the traditional marital and domestic roles to which early modern women were usually relegated—are based on equality. Adopting the trope of the friend as counselor and equal, Whitney dispenses advice to her friends, relatives, and readers, thus illustrating that, while this single woman writer may inhabit a public role, she is protected both by her own morality and by a virtuous support system of family and friends.

Unlike marriage, friendship is—ideally, at least—a relationship between equals. The contemporary discourse of friendship that would have been available to Whitney celebrated the absolute equality of friendship; for example, Cicero's oft-quoted formulation of the friend as an "another self" demonstrates the appeal that the equalizing potential of friendship held for early modern humanists (*De amicitia* trans. Falconer 21. 80).[2] Therefore, when Whitney distances herself from love and marriage and instead describes her relationships with men in terms of friendship, she replaces these hierarchical relationships with one that is predicated on equality. This equality allows her to depict relationships with men without being bound to their authority.

In the author's introduction to the *Nosgay,* Whitney recounts an experience that illustrates how the equality of friendship, as well as her choice to write poetry, subverts masculine oppression: she wanders outside only to have a male friend immediately order her back to her domestic space, commanding, "yf you regard your health: / out of this Lane you get. / And shift you to some better aire, / for feare to be infect" (A6). Behind the friendly concern of these words lies an inherent threat, for, as Wendy Wall notes, "the author's introduction links infection to circulation 'abroade,' a word that was commonly used to describe publication, travel and harlotry" (48). By using the word "infect," the friend implies that it is Whitney's sexual virtue and not necessarily her physical health that is truly endangered by her foray into the public realm. Even though Whitney's friend's advice is couched in terms of concern—he reminds her how "wofull" he and her other friends will be if she dies—he nevertheless tries to restrict her freedom to wander about, a trope Whitney frequently uses to illustrate her mental and literary freedom (A6).

---

[2]   Laurie Shannon suggests that this trope provided "a way of envisioning a secular enfranchisement of a preliberal sort for the 'private' subject" (22).

Whitney initially seems willing to comply with this friend's warning, but as she makes her way back to the safety of domesticity, she ends up not at home but in Plat's Plot (A6). Her solitary freedom allows her to wander there as she chooses to "be bolde, / to come when as I wyll: / Yea and to chuse of all his Flowers, / which may my fancy fill" (A7). This boldness results in the creation of the *Nosgay*, which Whitney claims has prophylactic powers: "A slip I tooke to smelle unto, / which might be my defence. / In stynking streetes, or lothsome Lanes / which els might mee infect" (A6v). This extended allegory of wandering may be interpreted in this way: Whitney may expose her work to public view without fear of infection, sexual or otherwise, because she is protected by the type of morality espoused in Plat's adages. Her male friend's implied warning about the connection between public space and female sexual immorality proves unfounded, and since friendship gives neither friend absolute authority over the other, Whitney has the ability to simply ignore his bad advice. This friend may voice his concerns about the dangers Whitney faces as she wanders outside the domestic sphere, but he does not have the authority to place her back in that sphere.

Indeed, only because Whitney has been exiled from domestic service in the first place does she have the freedom and boldness to wander into Plat's garden and write this therapeutic poetry. However, she does not reject marriage and domesticity explicitly. As Theodora Jankowski has pointed out, early modern English culture "saw virginity as a temporary premarital condition necessary for ensuring a woman a future as wife and mother" (3). Women who prolonged this temporary condition indefinitely were therefore viewed as transgressive because they removed themselves from the patriarchal economy of marriage and reproduction. Whitney attempts to neutralize this threat by presenting herself as an unfortunate woman who has unwillingly left domestic life and would gladly return if only she could. She complains that she has been dismissed from the service of "a vertuous Ladye" and is now "Harvestlesse, and servicelesse also" (C6v, A5v). She thus occupies an independent position because, as she claims, she has no choice. Bewailing her bad luck, Whitney warns her younger sisters who are still serving in London against following her example: "The rolling stone doth get no mosse / your selves have hard full oft" (C8v). A self-acknowledged "rolling stone," Whitney is disconnected from the domestic realm because she is unmarried and unemployed, and she is disconnected from the world at large because she is sick. Yet, even as Whitney uses her own experience as a negative example, her dismissal from the domestic sphere allows her to take on the role of the virtuous counselor. She is in a position to advise her sisters in writing precisely because she no longer shares their domestic position. Thus, Whitney's string of misfortunes places her in a uniquely independent position, and this independence, which she couches in terms of hardship, is what gives her the freedom to write. Whitney's authority as a writer and counselor therefore depends both on her moral virtue, which she is often at pains to prove, and on her independence from domestic service.

Of course, marriage—the expected destiny for a middle-class woman of the sixteenth century—could potentially put an end to this independence. Although married women often could (and did) write and publish their own works in early modern England, Whitney herself imagines that marriage would curtail her literary activities. In the published letter to her married sister, Anne Barron, Whitney writes, "I know you to huswyfery intend, though I to writing fall" (D1v). Here, she contrasts her livelihood as an author to her sister's more conventional role of housewife, but the verb "fall" is what particularly resonates when we consider that women who exposed themselves and their writings to public scrutiny could be compared to prostitutes, or "fallen" women (Wall 35–62). By employing this double-edged verb, Whitney demonstrates her awareness of the threat that publication poses to her reputation.

However, the following lines serve as a reminder that this publishing author is, in fact, a virtuous woman who only writes because she is not *yet* married: "Had I a Husband, or a house, / and all that longes therto / My selfe could frame about to rouse, / as other women doo: / But til some household cares me tye, / My bookes and Pen I wyll apply (D1v). On the surface, Whitney conforms to the expectations of sixteenth-century English society: if and when she has a husband and a house, she will stop writing and perform her domestic duties just as other women do. She realistically accepts that marriage and the unrestricted use of her "bookes and Pen" are probably mutually exclusive. Significantly, Anne offers no published reply; as Lynette McGrath claims, Whitney's sister "has disappeared into a domestic space" (145). Anne likely received the same education as Whitney, but her intellectual energies seem to be directed toward the education of her "prety Boyes," whom Whitney hopes will "march amongst the best, / Of them which learning have possest" (D2). Since the "humanist theory was that learned women were more companionable wives and more intelligent mothers than unlearned women," many early modern women such as Whitney and her sisters received humanist educations but were then expected to confine their intellectual lives to the home and family (Beilin 250). Although Whitney's blessing for her nephews' education is a positive one, the scholarly aspirations of the young men in the family clearly gain priority over any their mother may possess.

Yet, what happens when an educated woman is not a wife or mother? This is Whitney's situation, and even as she shrewdly praises Anne's motherhood, she also manages to defend and quietly celebrate her own vocation. Whitney, who has no husband or children, is free to pursue her own intellectual needs, and the final couplet of the verse letter to her sister indicates that the acquisition of a husband and family is not necessarily preferable to her own single state. In marriage, Whitney imagines herself at the mercy of a household that will "tye" and confine her, in contrast to her present freedom to actively "apply" her writing implements.[3] Thus,

---

[3]   Beilin notes the "ironically contrasting verbs *tye* and *apply*" (249). I extend Beilin's analysis of Whitney's relationship to domesticity by exploring exactly *how* Whitney writes herself out of domestic space. Whitney's rejection of love and marriage and her positive depiction of an extended network of friends and family help her to neutralize the threat posed by the publication of her work.

when Whitney writes that she "wyll apply" her books and pen, she is also claiming her freedom as a single woman to apply her will—a will that she imagines would be subjugated to the demands of a husband and children if she were married.

Whitney had also opposed marriage to authorship in her earlier publication, "The Copy of a Letter, lately written in meeter, by a yonge Gentilwoman: to her unconstant Lover." In this poem, Whitney writes in the tradition of Ovid's *Heroides*, a collection of letters in which women who have been forsaken by their lovers lament their fate. Whitney takes the position of a woman who has recently discovered that her betrothed plans to marry another. However, instead of "reproducing the pleading of Ovid's abandoned mistresses (and providing pleasure to male readers by representing men's power over such women)," Whitney represents her speaker as a confident woman who, although disappointed in her lover's moral inconsistency, will survive the loss (Jones, "Writing to Live" 47). She begins the poem with a direct confrontation that highlights the betrothed's deception: "As close as you your weding kept / yet now the trueth I here: / Which you (yer now) might me have told / what nede you nay to swere?" (A2). This accusatory stance immediately gives power not to the inconstant lover but to the female speaker who can confront him because she is on the side of right.

The abandoned speaker emphasizes her own virtue by describing her eligibility for marriage: she claims to possess all of the wifely virtues of "chastnes," "constancy," and "trueth" (A4v). Even though it appears that she is attempting to win her lover back by this listing of her qualifications, in the next stanza Whitney writes, "These words I do not spek, thinking from thy new Love to turne thee" (A5). The very fickleness of the betrothed is, in fact, what authorizes Whitney's poetry, since possession of the lover would effectively silence the poet: if the man had married the speaker, there would be no reason to write the poem. Moreover, since her errant lover has acted dishonestly, Whitney can publicize his wrongs while still maintaining both the virtue of her fictional alter ego and her own virtue as the female author of a poem on love. The erotic nature of most love poetry made it a dangerous genre for any early modern woman writer to attempt. As Sasha Roberts has observed, early modern conduct books discouraged women from reading Ovid's erotic poetry. The fears that male-authored tracts express about women reading amatory literature, she claims, "tell a compelling story of the anxiety and fascination that the figure of the eroticized woman reader evoked; a story which speaks of an assumption—and fear—of women's independence in the early modern literary marketplace" (22). Whitney both challenges this patriarchal anxiety—she has clearly read Ovid and apparently remained virtuous—and defuses it by deferring sexuality into a future—marriage—that will not be fulfilled. As in the published letter to her sister, Whitney must claim the virtues of a wife, but the fact that she is not a wife gives her both reason and authority to confront this wayward lover in writing.

Because Whitney's speaker takes the moral high ground instead of pleading with her lover to return, she gains the detached authority to judge his wrongdoing. Whitney uses a number of mythological examples to illustrate her position, but, unlike Ovid, she concentrates on the deception of the man instead of the misery of the abandoned woman. For instance, the "two Ladies" whom Jason deceives are only briefly mentioned, but Whitney devotes six stanzas to his perfidy. She even imagines a proper revenge, musing that if Jason's deeds had been known to the gods, "They would have rent ye ship as soone / as he had gon from shore" (A3). The speaker's abandonment gives her the authority to pass judgment on her inconstant lover and on all the ancient heroes who loved and then betrayed women: "For they, for their unfaithfulnes, / did get perpetuall Fame: / Fame? wherfore dyd I terme it so? / I should have cald it shame" (A3v). Here, Whitney literally rewrites history (or mythology), converting the "Fame" of these heroes into "shame" by the power of her pen. The speaker's authority to expose her lover's shame in writing and to rewrite her classical sources comes directly, in the concept of the poem, from her betrayal at his hands. Just as Whitney presents her independence from the domestic realm in terms of misfortune and sickness in the *Nosgay*, so her speaker gains the authorial power to write about her lover's wrongs by claiming to be his innocent victim.

Whitney extends this authority into the following poem, "The admonition by the Auctor, to all yong Gentilwomen: And to al other Maids being in Love." In this poem, Whitney casts herself as a friendly advisor to other women, cautioning them against sharing her own unfortunate experiences. Young women who are inexperienced in love, Whitney asserts, can particularly benefit from her honest guidance: "To you I speake: for you be they, / that good aduice do lacke: / Oh if I could good counsell geue / my tongue should not be slacke" (A6v). Like a modern-day advice columnist, she warns, "Trust not a man at the fyrst sight, / but trye him well before," using the authority of one "who was deceived late" to move from the potentially disempowered position of forsaken woman to the authoritative position of the friendly counselor (A6v, A8v). Her speaker has been hurt by a false man but, as a result, has gained the experience and authority to dispense honest and helpful advice to other women. The story of the broken engagement creates the ideal space for an early modern woman poet such as Whitney: as an innocent victim, her speaker remains virtuous, but she also claims the experience necessary to proffer helpful counsel to other young women.

In the advice-giving "Admonition," Whitney applies this authority from experience and counsels women to be wary of love. For proof, she offers story after story of male deception and abandonment. She does posit the existence of honest men, such as Leander, who was accurately judged by Hero. However, this tale does not provide an example of a lasting love relationship since Leander drowns in his attempt to reach Hero. Avoidance of love altogether, Whitney indicates, is the best policy for women, and she backs this point with an allegory about a little fish that is happiest before being hooked. This story also illustrates the value of experience, for, like the speaker of the "Letter," the fish "such pretty shift did make: / That he from Fishers hook did sprint / before he could him take" (A8v). Due to this close call with death, tellingly associated with love in Whitney's allegory, the little fish learns from experience and "pries on every baite, / suspecting styll that pricke" (A8v). Beyond the humor of this double entendre is a very real claim to the value of experience, and beyond this the humanist belief that experience can be transferred textually. Unlike the male friend in the *Nosgay* who seems to believe that women must remain at home to avoid sexual "infection," Whitney implies that women can live actively in the world and still maintain their virtue as long as they enjoy the benefit of friendly advice such as hers.

By asserting that women can avoid heartbreak if they are sufficiently warned by one who has already experienced betrayal, Whitney develops a contrast between the virtuous advice that she bestows upon her female readers and the deceptive tricks that Ovid teaches to his male readers. Even as she adapts the concept of Ovid's *Heroides*, Whitney attacks erotic Ovidian literature, which "doth teach [male lovers] this same knacke / To wet their hand a touch their eies: / so oft as teares they lacke" (A6). Whitney indicates that her poetry, the poetry of a woman who has been injured by the deceptive Ovidian lover, serves a very different purpose; like the adages of the *Nosgay*, this poetry teaches good sense and good morality backed by experience. Whitney's good sense dictates that love (which, in her poetry, inevitably goes hand in hand with constraint, deception, and heartbreak) is avoidable, but even if women do fall in love and are forsaken, they can recover and become better and wiser, just as Whitney's speaker did. In her later poem to Dido, Whitney tells the forsaken queen that lost love is not the worst fate on earth, for Aeneas's "absence might well salve the sore, / that earst his presence wrought" (D3v). Whitney again rewrites her classical source by replacing Ovid's suicidal Dido with a woman who will eventually recover from Aeneas's infidelity. The speaker of the poem recasts the role of abandoned woman not only by asserting that heartbreak is both avoidable and curable but also by claiming the authority to write from her own unfortunate experience with love. She thus presents her poetry as an ethical counterpoint to that of classical male poets, claiming in the persona of the friendly and experienced counselor that a woman may gain a position of empowerment and authority by rejecting, avoiding, or simply recovering from love.

Whitney asserts that women are in need of such cautionary advice because men behave in treacherous ways when they are in thrall to sexual desire. Her skepticism about love is evident in the "Admonition" when she warns against men who use "fayre and painted talke" or "the teares of Crocodies" to deceive women, and her doubts about the integrity of male lovers reappear in the adages of the *Nosgay* (A6). Jones notes that Whitney "adds pro-woman modifications to Plat's proverbs on gender relations" by generalizing the pronouns to "include both sexes" ("Writing to Live" 42). While many of the adages about love are general enough to apply to both men and women, when Whitney does use specific pronouns in the adages on love, they are almost always masculine. This use of masculine pronouns emphasizes the sexual folly of men rather than women and represents a significant deviation from Whitney's source text, for Plat tends to focus on the danger that women pose to men. He warns, "Fayre women be daugerous marks for yong mens eyes to shoote at," and cautions his male audience to "Trust not a wonton eye in a woman, for it hath most commonly a whorish hart annexed with it" (19, 35). In her earlier poems, Whitney alters the literary tradition of Ovid's *Heroides* in order to focus on the treachery of men rather than the helplessness of women. In her revision of Plat, she again modifies her source to portray men rather than women as foolish, deceptive, or even dangerous when they are in love.

For instance, in "Flower 65," Whitney criticizes men for following their sexual desires instead of their reason: "Ech lover knoweth what he lykes / and what he doth desire, / But seld, or never doth he know, / what thing he should require" (B8). In a lighter vein, she pokes fun at the foolish behavior of male lovers in "Flower 76": "Affection fond deceaves the wise / and love ma[ke]se men such noddyes / That to their selues they seeme as dead / yet live in other boddies" (C1v). Death may be a euphemism for orgasm, and these love-dazed men "live in other boddies" in the act of sexual intercourse. Although it may seem risky for a woman writer such as Whitney to include sexual puns in her writing, her moral tone and the fact that she admonishes men and not women for their sexual appetites give her a certain amount of license. Although she often claims authority from experience, it is always negative experience, such as the lack of a permanent home or the lack of a husband, which gives her the authority to write. In Whitney's early poems, the speaker's rejection at the hands of her inconstant lover gives her the authority to condemn him and by extension all male lovers in her verse. In the adages, Whitney extends this moral authority by condemning love and dissociating herself from romantic relations entirely. Since she distances herself from both love and marriage (and, therefore, sex), Whitney claims the virtuous authority to pass judgment on—and sometimes make fun of—those who have not.

Whitney's criticisms of men in love do not, however, extend to men in general, who are apparently quite satisfactory as friends. The counsel-giving function of friendship coincides nicely with the advisory nature of the adages, and, indeed, Whitney's collection of adages begins with friendship rather than with love. The first adage provides an affirmative view of friendship: "Such freendes as have ben absent long / more joyful be at meeting / Then those which ever present are / and dayly have their greetyng" (B2). In the adages, Whitney demonstrates some familiarity with the early modern discourse of ideal friendship, even if she does sometimes turn a witty eye to the failure of friendship to live up to the exalted humanist ideal. For instance, when she asserts in "Flower 59" that "Al things with frends in comon are," she is repeating a common proverb about friendship. To this, however, she adds the ironic caveat: "at least it should be so," indicating that such ideals are not always realized in practice (B8). Even more cynically, in "Flower 28" she declares that "None in adversitie hath help, / except they prospered have / And by ye menes have purchast frends / of whom they ayde may crave" (B4v). However, this cynical viewpoint is borne out in neither the familiar letters of the *Nosgay* nor the rest of the adages, and Whitney immediately softens the jaded perspective of "Flower 28" with the claim that while "Prosperitie wyll get thee friends," poverty will demonstrate which friends are truly "faythfull" (B5). Faithful friendship may be rare, she implies, but it is possible.

Ultimately, Whitney's view of friendship is positive but also realistic; her poetic persona is that of a woman who lives in the real world and has little patience for the ideals of either love or friendship. However, while her adages on love are uniformly pessimistic, Whitney balances her more cynical statements about friendship with positive accounts of friendship's benefits. And one of the greatest benefits of friendship, according to Whitney, is good counsel. In "Flower 14," she advises, "Thy Friends admonysh secretly, / of crimes to which they swarve: / But prayse them openly, if so be, / their deeds do prayse desarve" (B3v). A good friend is above all a counselor who will privately encourage his or her friend to follow the path of virtue. This statement, consistent with the moral and advice-giving tone Whitney cultivates throughout her poetry, echoes Cicero's advice to "let the influence of friends who are wise counselors be paramount, and let that influence be employed in advising, not only with frankness, but, if the occasion demands, even with sternness" (*De amicitia* 13.44). According to Cicero, friends must encourage virtue in each other because friendship itself depends upon the virtue of the participants. "Without virtue," he insists, "friendship cannot exist at all" (6.20). Of course, the type of virtue to which Cicero refers in *De amicitia* is gendered masculine; it is a specifically civic virtue that helps to support the state. However, the persona of the virtuous counselor and friend must have appealed to a woman writer such as Whitney, for this role allows her to emphasize her own virtue and, at least textually, form non-hierarchical bonds with others. For ideal friendship, unlike love, is primarily a relationship between virtuous *equals*. Whitney signals the equality of friendship in "Flower 16" when she offers advice on how to accept correction from a friend: "Admonisht be with willingnesse, / and paciently abyde / A reprehension, for such faults, / as friends in thee have spide" (B3v). The friend who takes on the role of virtuous advisor must also be willing to listen to and, if appropriate, abide by the advice of a friend.

Whitney also draws an explicit connection between friendship and kinship in the adages, counseling: "A friendly mind, accoumpt it for / the neerest of thy kyn: / When al shal fayle, it sticks to thee, / what ever chaunce hath byn" (B6). Indeed, in the sixteenth century, the word "friend" had by no means lost its earlier meaning of family member. As a woman writer who, by her own account, has suffered the vicissitudes of fortune, endured slander, and is perhaps now risking censure by publishing her poetry, Whitney indicates that both her friends and "kyn" will remain faithful and supportive through these trials. The verse epistles positioned at the end of Whitney's adages provide evidence for this belief. Here, Whitney mingles letters to and from her brothers, sisters, cousins, friends, and fellow writers, thus fashioning herself as a valued member of a textual community of family and friends. This community of "friendly minds" provides a type of support system for Whitney, indicating that this publishing woman writer still maintains her connection to the home even as she moves outside of its boundaries. For example, in the verse epistle to her brother Geoffrey, Whitney expresses her belief that family ties may, in the case of physical separation, be sustained through correspondence. If she cannot see her brother in person, she asks that she "may have knowledge wheare / A messenger to harke unto, / that I to you may wryte: / And eke of him your answers have / which would my hart delight" (C6v). This humanist belief in the ability of textual circulation to maintain familial and friendly ties across distance echoes "Flower 3," which declares that "The presence of the mynd must be / preferd, if we do well: / Above the bodyes presence; for / it farre doth it excell" (B2). Whitney's textual community of family and friends mitigates the anxieties associated with the publication of her poetry, her removal from the domestic sphere, and her single status; this circle of friends and family, who are present in "mynd" but not in "bodye," signals to the reader that Whitney is not dangerously unattached to traditional family structures. The familiar letters of the *Nosgay* thus illustrate Whitney's enduring connection to the domestic realm without actually threatening her independence from its confines.

These letters not only attempt to neutralize any threat that Whitney's removal from the domestic sphere may pose, but also advertise her standing in a group of primarily male literary friends. Within these letters, we find Whitney aligning herself with the traditionally masculine world of literary achievement rather than the domestic world to which women such as her sisters conventionally belonged. Even though Whitney positions herself as a friend to other young women in her early poems and criticizes the behavior of male lovers, it would be misleading to call her poetry an indictment of gender inequality. Indeed, it seems reasonable to assume that she published her correspondence with male writers along with her poetry because of the validation doing so lent her writing. Whitney's printed correspondence with male poets such as Thomas Berry provided what Francis Bacon termed "countenance," which is, as Alan Bray explains, "the appearance of friendship in the public eye that was itself a kind of currency" (Bacon, "Of Followers and Friends" 83; Bray, *The Friend* 54).[4] Thus, even as she warns other women against misfortune by using her own example, Whitney claims a place for herself that is more closely allied to the masculine realm of literary production and publication than the feminine realm of domesticity and service. She seems to be, in other words, an exception to the rule. For instance, for all of the love and concern Whitney expresses in her letter to her younger sisters serving in London, she still titles it "An order prescribed" and takes on the didactic, authoritative tone of an older sister whose words should be heeded (C7v). In this letter, Whitney instructs her sisters to "Peruse these lines, observe the rules / which in the same I tell," and warns them, "I hope you give no cause, / wherby I should suspect: / But this I know too many live, / that would you soone infect" (C7v, C8). Ironically,

---

[4]   Lorna Hutson notes that the appearance of friendship within a printed text could also work as a form of credit to advertise the author's worthiness and virtue to new "friends"— specifically, potential supporters and patrons: "Offering a scent of the printed nosegay in the first of her printed familiar epistles, Whitney draws attention to the function of both … as ambassadors of her merits to the 'vertuous ladye' for whom, lacking a referent, the reader is irresistibly compelled to construct a hypothetical existence which in turn reflects back on, or 'advertises' Whitney's readiness to serve in some virtuous employment" (126).

this prescription echoes the advice that Whitney receives from her friend in the introduction to the *Nosgay*: like him, she uses the sexually connotative word "infect," and she advises her sisters to safeguard their domestic positions just as her friend warned her against wandering away from home.

Of course, Whitney's "rules" for her younger sisters are essentially protective; as Phillippy claims, the letter details "the appropriate place of the maidservant within the order of social and familial relations much as a conduct book would, but it does so as a matter of self-preservation for women dependent upon the household for their livelihood and their honor" (453). Yet, even as Whitney warns her sisters against conduct that would endanger their place within the domestic realm, she herself claims the freedom to move outside of that realm. Her letters to and from male writers illustrate—and validate—her membership in an active literary community, and in these letters she abandons the stance of superior wisdom that she takes in the letter to her sisters and instead depicts relationships based on equality. I would suggest that Whitney's strategic distancing from domestic and sexual roles enables this depiction of equality between writers of different genders. Because Whitney portrays herself as a virtuous woman writer who is neither a wife nor lover, she can describe her relationships with male writers in terms of friendly equality.

Most of Whitney's letters to and from male friends take the form of complaints: Whitney writes to a friend "bewaylynge her mishappes," and the friend responds by claiming his misfortunes to be even worse or by offering advice and condolences (D5v). Laurie Ellinghausen argues that the format of the complaint only reveals the inadequacies of Whitney's textual friendships and claims that the letters leave "the impression that the medium of exchange ultimately cannot mitigate Whitney's situation" (10). However, the complaint allows Whitney to demonstrate friendship's reciprocity, for while instruction goes only one way in her letter to her sisters, in Whitney's letters to and from male friends she both dispenses counsel and requests it, thus representing herself as an active and valued participant in a lively literary exchange. The complaint as a literary form may, in other words, be the medium through which friendship and support are expressed rather than an unmitigated expression of hardship. In these exchanges, Whitney celebrates the advice-giving function of friendship as well as her own ability to amply fulfill that function.

Whitney attempts to place these exchanges on a footing of equality by avoiding references to her own gender. For instance, in her letter to her friend C.B., she hints that she has been the victim of slander and asks for his counsel, writing, "two wittes may compasse more than one, you must confesse" (D6). Here, Whitney asks for guidance not by virtue of her gender but because "two wittes," even if equal, are always better than one. She concludes the letter by humbly commending herself "to the conducting of my Friende," and while we may read this as an example of a woman meekly submitting to male authority, the surrounding letters work against such an interpretation (D6). Indeed, Whitney proffers advice as much as she requests it. As Hutson observes, the verse epistles "build up an image of the reliability and soundness of Whitney's own judgment as a counselor to relatives and friends" (125). In the letter titled "To my Friend Master T.L. whose good nature: I see abusde," Whitney warns the recipient against those false friends who, unlike her, only surround him for his wealth. In fact, she seems somewhat indignant that her previous advice has not been heeded: "Yf warnings styll you do reject, / to late your selfe shal rew: / Do as you lyst, I wish you well, / and so I say adewe" (D8v). Whitney thus depicts herself as an equal member in a group of friends who help and advise each other in times of trouble. As she affirms in her letter to C.B., "that burthen dothe not deare, / whiche frende wyll somtyme helpe to beare" (D6).

Whitney's printed letters therefore both signify her enduring connection to a supportive family and depict her as a respected equal in a circle of friends. They also shore up her self-representation as a morally upright and chaste woman—a representation that could be threatened by her authorial activities and her avoidance of marriage—for her friends' responses uniformly express their faith in her virtue. Her cousin G.W.'s epistle declares that Whitney's woes do not arise from any fault of her own but are rather the result of the "tirant Godesse" Fortune's whims (E1). Likewise, C.B. expresses his belief in Whitney's merit when he responds, "yf evell words and other wants, / have brought thee to this woe: / Remember how that Christ him selfe, / on earth was even so: / Thy Friends that have thee knowne of long, / Wil not regard thy enemies tong" (D7). Here, C.B. encourages Whitney to be consoled by Christ's example, for they are both the innocent victims of false reports and "evell words." Whitney's fears of slander correspond to the very real possibility that she will face censure or ridicule by publishing her poetry and refusing to confine herself and her words to the domestic realm. By demonstrating that her friends will not regard her "enemies tong," Whitney attempts to neutralize this threat and control her readers' responses to her foray into print. When C.B. testifies to the "vertue that hath ever beene, / within thy tender brest: / Which I from yeare to yeare, have seene, / in all thy deedes exprest," he is also voicing his belief that female virtue and a public role are not mutually exclusive (D7). If Whitney's friends can believe in the virtue of a publishing woman writer, so too, she implies, can her readers.

As in her earlier poems and the adages, Whitney must maintain this virtue by characterizing herself as an honorable and chaste woman and by distancing herself from sexual roles. Indeed, Whitney's strategic self-distancing from sexuality and domesticity allows her to form relationships with male writers that are based on equality. Yet, given early modern cultural constructs that associated female silence with chastity and publication with prostitution, Whitney's relationship to poetic discourses such as Petrarchism is necessarily more troubled and more complicated than that of her male correspondents. For instance, while Thomas Berry's verse epistle, included toward the end of the familiar letters, utilizes standard Petrarchan tropes, Whitney shuns such Petrarchan language in her reply. Rather than respond in kind, she changes the focus of the poetic conversation by advising Berry to renounce love and embrace friendship instead. This focus on friendship rather than love allows Whitney to circumvent the sexually charged nature of the Petrarchan complaint. [5]

Berry's letter is in fact a response to Whitney's address to Dido, in which she contrasts her woes, which are caused by poor health and Fortune's spite, to Dido's troubles with love. Love, Whitney indicates in this poem, is nothing compared to the misfortunes that she is currently facing. As in her earlier poetry, Whitney downplays the power of love and focuses instead on poverty and illness, woes caused not by a cruel beloved but by an abstract Fortune. Berry titles his letter "An answer to comfort her, by shwyng his haps to be harder," and attempts to demonstrate that love is, in fact, the greater calamity. Using Petrarchan language, he claims to "pine as WAX, before the fire wastes," "freece to YCE," and "heate with perching SON" for an unnamed mistress (D4). In her response, Whitney dispenses with such Petrarchisms and, instead of assigning blame to the mistress, holds Fortune responsible for Berry's troubles. Moreover, she compares Fortune not to a cold female beloved but to an unfaithful friend, declaring that Fortune "rightly be co[m]par[e]d with those / whose painted spech, professeth frindship stil / but time bewrayes the meaning to be yll," thus changing the focus of the conversation from love to friendship (D5). Whitney concludes by declaring that once Berry's fit of love has passed, he "shall hoysed be to happye state agayne / Delighting oft among his friends & Kin, / To tell what danger earst his lyfe was in" (D5r, D5v). Friends and kin thus provide a safe alternative to the life-threatening—albeit transitory—dangers of love.

In the end of her epistle to Berry, Whitney draws a direct connection between her friendship for him and her poetic abilities by declaring, "thy Fame, for ever florish shall, / If IS. her Pen, may promise ought at all" (D5v). In other words, Whitney claims the ability to immortalize her friend through her verse. This is what poets tell their patrons and lovers tell their female beloveds, but Berry is neither patron nor beloved. Whitney's poetry repeatedly declares the superiority of friendship over love; thus, she will use her poetic abilities to confer fame on a friend. Whitney's participation in a circle of friends and family demonstrates that, despite her removal from the domestic realm, she is not an isolated and thus threatening single woman. She is not a wife, mother, or lover, but a virtuous equal in a supportive community of family, acquaintances, and fellow poets: she is a friend.

---

[5]   Whitney's "Wyll and Testament" engages more thoroughly with Petrarchism by personifying the city of London as a stingy lover. An extended reading of the "Wyll and Testament" is outside of the scope of this chapter, but it is worth noting that Whitney qualifies the speaker's poverty and alienation from her surroundings by setting the poem in the realm of the imaginary—she only "fayneth as she would die"—and by asserting that she is leaving the city "upon her Friendes procurement" (E2).

Chapter 7

"Friendship Multiplyed": Royalist and Republican Friendship in Katherine Philips's Coterie

Penelope Anderson

In many ways, Katherine Philips's poetry exemplifies the most extravagant claims of early modern friendship. In her poem "A Friend," for example, Philips lays out an abstract account of friendship that encompasses its major tropes in the Renaissance tradition: voluntary choice, likeness, fidelity, and virtue.[1] Philips also puts particular stress on the obligation to be useful to one's friend, an emphasis that aligns her with the Roman, especially the Ciceronian and Senecan, civic dimension of friendship: her friends are participants in public life, educated in civic virtue and rhetorical skill through their alliances. This is a bold claim for a woman poet to make, and in order to support it she foregrounds certain features of *amicitia* that masculine writers on friendship tend to suppress. Thus, she diverges from the usual model of *amicitia perfecta*—in some ways that critics have often noted, in others that they have tended to ignore.

Her most obvious difference from the traditional classical and Renaissance perfect friend is, of course, her gender. Discussions of friendship consistently reserve its goods to men, as Michel de Montaigne indelibly articulates: since "the ordinary sufficiency of women, cannot answer this conference and communication, the nurse of this sacred bond: nor seeme their mindes strong enough to endure the pulling of a knot so hard, so fast, and durable," "this sex could never yet by any example attain unto it, and is by ancient schools rejected thence" (McCarthy ed. 199). Philips dismisses this sexism as "a design injurious and rude" ("A Friend," Poem 64 line 21). But Philips does not only seek to include women within a pre-existing friendship model. Instead, her articulation of women's friendship reshapes royalist theories of monarchy in surprising ways.

Many critics have noted that Philips's friendship lyrics cement political alliances in a royalist coterie. This is remarkable, in part, because Philips's royalism stands in stark contrast to her husband's support of Parliament and Oliver Cromwell's Protectorate and to her natal family, which was consistently Parliamentarian in

---

[1] "A Friend," Poem 64 in Thomas. All citations to Philips's poems come from Patrick Thomas's Stump Cross edition and will be identified by his poem numbers.

politics and initially Puritan, then Presbyterian, in religion.[2] Still more surprisingly, Philips, without family connections or high social status to assist her, corresponded with prominent royalists and Anglicans. These correspondents not only read her poems as exemplary instances of friendship but also put those friendships into action, assisting her and her husband James and accepting their help in turn. Her biography thus exemplifies the conflicting loyalties experienced by most individuals and families in the years of the English Civil Wars and restoration, while demonstrating an unusual facility for turning those potential conflicts into literary and practical resources.

Philips's most perceptive critics, such as Carol Barash and Hero Chalmers, have seen friendship's political meaning as that of stability and coherence against the upheavals of the interregnum.[3] For these critics, women's friendship models an ideally faithful political world, with betrayal emerging from the conflict between marriage and friendship. As Barash argues:

> Women's friendship provided a model of political loyalty (friendship could, in this sense, transcend marriage). At the same time, if we take its political implications seriously—imagining it as a figure, let's say, in the hands of those who are not royalists—women's friendship also poses explicit threats both to heterosexual marriage and to the very myth of political stability it initially figures. (56)

For Barash, friendship becomes unstable when outside the context of the coterie, when unsympathetic readers appropriate it. During the interregnum, the referent of the absent king helps to guard against what will later become a danger for women's friendship: its construction of an emotional tie to rival heterosexual marriage. Within the royalist coterie eagerly awaiting the restoration of monarchy, however, friendship offers an idealized solidity in an uncertain world (Barash 55–100).

This narrative of friendship signifying stable royalist identity fails to account for several crucial features of Philips's *oeuvre*. First, she writes many poems excoriating her friends for betraying their friendships: thus the dominant version of friendship that emerges is not one of stability but of dissolution. This is often read biographically, as disappointment in her friends' susceptibility to the heterosexual privileges of matrimony. Kate Lilley, one of the subtlest readers of Philips's intertwined erotics and politics, writes:

---

[2]   For Philips's biography, see Aubrey; Chernaik; Limbert; Souers; and Thomas, "Introduction."

[3]   "The ideas of Philips, Finch, and Taylor intersect specifically in the conception of friendship, identified with royalism, as representative of religious cohesion and also of social stability" (Chalmers 65).

> Orinda is able to defend her own singularity and fidelity by charging her apostates
> with multiplicity and infidelity. Even as she seems to insist on the difference of
> each attachment and each woman, Philips relies on the disturbing reiteration of
> the superlative rhetoric of exclusive and incomparable friendship. There is often
> little more than a name or date to differentiate between "Rosania" and "Lucasia"
> or the fate which "Orinda" will suffer at their hands. (171)

Lilley captures the contradiction in Philips charging others with infidelity when
she herself has multiple friends. This is the second problem with reading Philips's
poems as figuring fidelity: in violation of *amicitia*'s rhetoric of twinned souls,
Philips writes effusive friendship lyrics to more than one woman. Classical and
Renaissance commentators dismiss this as a lesser form of friendship: thus, in the
Nicomachean Ethics, Aristotle writes that "Friendships between comrades only
include a few people, and the famous examples of poetry are pairs of friends"
(trans. Rackham IX.x.6). Philips's friendships aspire to be "famous examples of
poetry," but she seemingly undermines this by depicting multiple friendships. This
suggests that the model of singularity and unwavering fidelity that Lilley takes as
Philips's ideal demands modification.

The language with which Philips excoriates her unfaithful friends indeed seems
excessive: "And you appear so much on ruin bent, / Your own destruction gives
you now content: / For our twin-spirits did so long agree, / You must undoe your
self to ruine me" ("Injuria amici," Poem 38 lines 17–20). Her language of betrayal
is precisely as excessive as the language in which Philips initially describes the
union of friendship: "… never had Orinda found / A Soule till she found thine; /
Which now inspires, cures and supply's, / And guides my darken'd brest:" ("To My
excellent Lucasia, on our friendship. 17th. July 1651," Poem 36 lines 11–14). This
continuity points not toward a conflict between marriage and friendship unique
to Philips, but to a problem within the structure of *amicitia* itself. By figuring
friendship as the commitment that trumps all others, classical and Renaissance
writers construct a political threat: the conflict between loyalty to the friend and
loyalty to the state. While the goals of humanist friendship—education in virtue and
practical advantage, both enabled by rhetorical force—support and coincide with
those of the state, in practice absolute loyalty to a friend can authorize conspiracy
and rebellion. Thus, in one of the most influential and widely read books of policy,
Cicero assures us that "an upright man will never for a friend's sake do anything
in violation of his country's interests or his oath or his sacred honour," but he lists
numerous examples of insurrections orchestrated by friends (*De officiis* III.x.43).

Philips consciously takes up this conflict between friendship and the state as
the most accurate representation of her historical circumstances. Friendship, and
in particular the women's friendship Philips constructs, demonstrably comes under
threat in her historical moment. With the conflicting demands of God, country, king,
family, and friends, the interregnum and restoration provoke impossible choices.
Friendship's utility, which is central to the Roman tradition of civic friendship and

on which Philips insists, both answers this dilemma, by providing material aid, and augments it, by rendering visible conflicting obligations.

In many ways, the obvious move for a committed royalist would have been to valorize infidelity to the current political power in Parliament. Philips does not do this in any straightforward manner. Instead, her anatomy of the causes and consequences of betrayal between friends refigures the basis of monarchic power. I use the word "refigures" advisedly, for it is figures—literary tropes and allusions—that provide the means and material of Philips's political imagination. In particular, she uses the republican elements of the friendship tradition to challenge a patriarchalist explanation of monarchy, thus providing a civic role for those excluded from power: not only women, but also other royalists. Catharine Gray writes persuasively that "Philips's very exclusion from homosocial public institutions marks her as a key figure for heterosocial counterpublic activity" (*Women Writers* 116). I want to argue that Philips's reshaping of *amicitia* through gender also provides a means to reconsider the theoretical basis of monarchic power. The centrality of betrayal to Philips's friendship poems thus demonstrates that *amicitia perfecta* provides political models in addition to the idealized equality Laurie Shannon eloquently explores in *Sovereign Amity*.

Philips's emphasis on failed and multiple friendships consequently helps us to see the cultural work of friendship in the early modern period, especially in the years of the English Civil Wars and restoration, in a new way. I argue that the extravagant rhetoric of *amicitia perfecta*, coupled with realities of friendship's failures, does not give the lie to friendship, as Tom MacFaul suggests it does in a recent book on early modern friendship: "When such [ideal] friendship is taken seriously, however, it can cause an excessive sense of obligation which is often stifling, sometimes absurd" (*Male Friendship* 65). Philips's poems challenge the idea that other, more "natural" obligations—such as romantic love, or family— trump friendship. Consequently, her poems suggest that early modern friendship poses more interesting questions: what uses could this excessive rhetoric have served? how can the language of exclusivity produce a community? and why, at least in Philips's case, are the failed obligations of friendship not a shameful secret but instead the much admired subject of her poems?

In what follows, I first consider Philips's explicit discussions of multiple friendships. In the rhetoric of *amicitia perfecta*, multiple friendships ought not to exist, or at least cannot attain the status of the highest friendships between a perfectly matched pair. Consequently, the poems of multiple friendships foreground the problem of multiple obligations to different, equally compelling sources. They also, potentially, provide an answer to the question of whether the equality and civic engagement of *amicitia perfecta* can offer a model of political obligation for the commonwealth as a whole. This issue of whether friendship can be generalized lies at the heart of the problem of friendship's civic efficacy. From a consideration of Philips's poems, I then turn to their antecedent, Sir Philip Sidney's *Arcadia*, which gives Philips a revised monarchy through republican and aristocratic allusions. Finally, I discuss later responses to Philips's political imagination, particularly that of James Tyrrell, whose own writings challenge patriarchalism.

"Friendship Multiplyed"

In the classical friendship tradition and its Renaissance applications, the question of multiple friendships both dramatizes the depth of the friends' commitments to one another and raises the problem of conflicting demands. On a practical level, having multiple friends exacerbates the difficulty of meeting their expectations, as they may ask incompatible things at the same time. As Plutarch writes in "On Having Many Friends," one friend may call upon us "to join him on a voyage to foreign parts, another to help him in defending a suit, another to sit with him as judge, another to help him in managing his buying and selling, another to help him celebrate his wedding, another to mourn with him at a funeral" (*Moralia* 95.6). As Plutarch suggests, the conflicting tasks concern both utility—advocacy and judgment—and affect—joy and grief. This question of transference is also a figurative one: given friendship's emphasis on exclusivity, can its lessons of commitment translate to a larger community? Or does the very thing that gives friendship its force—the absolute commitment to a single other person—undermine its utility on a larger scale?

Rather than try to obscure the conflict between her rhetoric of exclusivity and the multiplicity of her society, Philips confronts it directly, both in poems which chronicle the shift of affections from Rosania to Lucasia and in poems on the theme of multiple friendships.[4] By maintaining consistent images (such as flames and rivers) across her poems and creating personae through the use of coterie names, moreover, Philips places the effusive lyrics of friendship in conversation with their poetic sources and her other writings. Rather than vacating the metaphorical tropes of friendship, that is, she follows them through the consequences of their dissolution. In so doing, she offers a narrative of political commitment that recognizes the inevitability of conflicting allegiances.

The poem that addresses the problems of multiplicity most directly is, unsurprisingly, "A Dialogue of Friendship Multiplyed" (Poem 97). In this poem, Philips's own persona Orinda and the male interlocutor Musidorus debate whether friendship can extend to more than two people. Musidorus argues that it can; Orinda denies it. The poem traverses the standard tropes of friendship in Philips's poetry, with a juxtaposition of images so rapid that it becomes comical. When Orinda asserts that "Friendship (like Rivers) as it multiplies / In many streams, grows weaker still and dies" (13–14), Musidorus answers:

---

[4]   Philips's coterie addressed one another by pastoral names, usually derived from royalist texts. Philips's own name was Orinda; she writes most frequently to two friends, Mary Aubrey Montagu (Rosania) and Anne Owen, later Viscountess Dungannon (Lucasia).

> Rivers indeed may lose their force,
> When they divide or break their course;
> For they may want some hidden Spring,
> Which to their streams recruits may bring:
> But Friendship's made of purest fire,
> Which burns and keeps its stock entire. (Poem 97 lines 15–20)

Musidorus uses the divided rivers to critique the failings of those who cannot sustain multiple friendships. He switches to a different—and utterly incompatible—image, that of friendship as a flame. The flame is also a central trope in Philips's other poems, but the move from one to the other, with no transition, highlights their disjointedness and thus fails to solve Orinda's objection. The divided rivers douse friendship's flame, as it were.

But the image of divided rivers does more work than that in Philips's poems. The version Orinda uses here, of rivers weakening and dying by multiplication, closely follows the form in Plutarch's essay "On Having Many Friends": "It follows, then, that a strong mutual friendship with many persons is impossible, but, just as rivers whose waters are divided among many branches and channels flow weak and thin, so affection, naturally strong in a soul, if portioned out among many persons becomes utterly enfeebled" (*Moralia* 93.2). The Plutarch parallel makes this process seem natural. Philips complicates this naturalization in one of her most famous poems on the dissolution of a friendship, "To Rosania (now Mrs Mountague) being with her, 25th September. 1652" (Poem 42):

> *Devided Rivers loose their name*;
> And so our too unequall flame
> Parted, will passion be in me,
> And an indifference in thee. (emphasis in original; 29–32)

The disparity of emotion challenges the definition of friendship. The conjunction of plural—"their"—and singular—"name"—emphasizes this paradox, which reverses the usual concern over losing one's self in another. Friends lose their identity not by union but by division. The trope of renaming gains further point from the fact that this is a poem about the dissolution of friendship after marriage, the wife's loss of her name recorded in the title's "To Rosania (*now* Mrs Mountague)." Thus, from the naturalized sense of limited affection in "A Dialogue of Friendship Multiplyed," with its source in Plutarch, the poem to Rosania describes a rupture brought about by divided loyalties based in linguistic definitions and the gender hierarchy of marriage.

The image of divided rivers can effectively evoke the breakdown of friendship here because it elsewhere depicts exemplary women's friendship. Francis Finch, a member of Philips's coterie, writes in his 1654 discourse *Friendship*: "For Burthens, like Rivers, divided loose their Name" (33). Finch uses the simile of divided rivers to describe an idealized friendship, in which the sharing of troubles lessens them. In addressing this discourse to the hyphenated "D[ear]. Noble Lucasia-Orinda," he seemingly replicates the poems' replacement of Rosania by Lucasia. However, Rosania—and the poem "To Rosania (now Mrs Mountague)"—remains in Philips's coterie. The memorial volume of poems presented to Mary Aubrey Montagu (the Rosania of the poems) on Philips's death has this as its first Rosania poem. Thus part of the meaning of these poems derives from their material form: from their order in manuscripts and printed editions, from the coterie who read and responded to them. The persistence of friends in the coterie—contrary to the repeated literary valedictions—requires an explanation of friendship that accounts not only for its successes but also for its failures. The lyrics of dissolution, through coterie circulation, strengthen and commemorate alliances.

In "A Dialogue of Friendship Multiplyed," Orinda draws on the exemplary friendship depicted elsewhere to claim the final word in the argument. Unsurprisingly, she comes down on the side of exclusive friendship, and one friend in particular: "Then though I honour every worthy guest, / Yet my *Lucasia* only rules my breast" (29–30). The name of the friend, the insistence on the authority of personal commitment, concludes the poem. Orinda seems to have won her argument, through the deployment of mixed metaphors and assertion.

The posthumous edition of Philips's poems, published in 1667, has a punchline, however. The poem that follows "A Dialogue of Friendship Multiplyed" is "Rosania to Lucasia on her Letters," and in it Rosania implores Lucasia to write with all the vehemence that Orinda deploys elsewhere:

> Ah! strike outright, or else forbear;
> Be more kind, or more severe;
> For in this chequer'd mixture I
> Cannot live, and would not die,
> And must I neither? tell me why? (Poem 98 lines 1–5)

The excess of the language speaks for itself. But it also speaks for Orinda, as, for example, in "Injuria amici," where she uses the same language of kindness and killing: "Thy least of crimes is to be Cruell Still; / For of thy smiles I should yet more complain, / If I should live to be betray'd again" (Poem 38 lines 34–6). Given Orinda's rejection of multiple friendships, how can Orinda describe passion between Rosania and Lucasia in the very same language as her own passion for first Rosania and then Lucasia?

The Politics of Literary Allusion

The complicated calculus of literary allusion in "A Dialogue of Friendship Multiplyed" provides an answer that begins to map the fraught interrelations of gender and political form in Philips's appropriation of *amicitia* for women. For in naming the male interlocutor who argues for multiple friendships "Musidorus,"

Philips alludes to Sir Philip Sidney's *Arcadia*, thus commenting upon the conjunction of pastoral and romance, the conflict between friendship and love, and the difficulties of right governance.[5] In the *Arcadia*, Musidorus, the elder of two princely cousins, dresses as a shepherd to further his suit for Pamela, elder daughter to King Basilius and heiress of Arcadia. Captured in the company of the princesses and accused of murdering Basilius, Musidorus and Pyrocles find themselves on trial before Euarchus, king of Macedonia, who has been asked to serve as magistrate in the absence of another political authority in Arcadia. Arguing that only the king of the realm can dispense equity, Euarchus follows a strict interpretation of the law to condemn Musidorus and Pyrocles to death for their trespasses against the princesses' sexual honor. Even the revelation that the disguised Musidorus and Pyrocles are in fact his nephew and his son, respectively, does not change Euarchus's judgment, though it moves him to unwilling tears. Musidorus condemns his rigor as tyranny: "'Enjoy thy bloody conquest, tyrannical Euarchus,' said he, 'for neither is convenient the title of a king to a murderer, nor the remembrance of kindred to a destroyer of his kindred'" (Sidney 843). Musidorus refuses to acknowledge the legitimacy of Euarchus's judgment, naming him a tyrant.

Musidorus's challenge to Euarchaus's authority seems to receive additional support when Musidorus and Pyrocles both compete for the chance to die on the other's behalf: "With that [Musidorus] fell again to entreat for Pyrocles, and Pyrocles as fast for Musidorus, each employing his wit to show himself most worthy to die …" (Sidney 845). The strand of the classical friendship tradition aligned with republicanism offers numerous instances in which virtuous friends' willingness to sacrifice themselves converts a tyrant to justice. Sir Thomas Elyot, in *The Boke Named the Governour*, offers the examples of Orestes and Pylades and of Damon and Pythias (1531 ed., Chapter Eleven, 164–6). In each case, a tyrant has unjustly condemned one of the friends to die; the other's willingness to die for his friend makes the tyrant realize his injustice, and he spares the friends while asking to be included in their friendship. The ruler's ability to be a friend shows that he is a tyrant no longer, as Cicero explains in *De officiis*, the source of the Damon and Pythias story: citizens have the right to kill a tyrant because "we have no ties of fellowship with a tyrant, but rather the bitterest feud" (III.vi.32). The widespread dissemination of this story in the Renaissance, through frequent printings of *De officiis* and *The Boke Named the Governour*, among other sources, means that the friends' resistance to tyranny dominates Renaissance accounts of friendship.

The precedent of the virtuous friends contending before the tyrant offers one version of monarchy, republicanism, and justice in the *Arcadia*: the two princes

---

[5]   Philips would have known the composite *Arcadia*, which begins with the Countess of Pembroke's *Arcadia* and continues with the *Old Arcadia* where the unfinished revision breaks off. Therefore, I simply refer to this composite text as the *Arcadia*, except where the distinction between the two versions becomes relevant later in the essay.

exemplify republican virtue, while the monarch Euarchus appears as an absolutist tyrant. In her reading of the *Old Arcadia*, however, Debora Shuger locates different republican antecedents to Sidney's romance in Livy's *History of Rome*. In Livy, Tarquin's brutal rape of Lucretia and her subsequent suicide lead Brutus to declare Rome a republic; then, in a final rejection of aristocratic privilege, Brutus condemns his own sons to death for their attempt to return the Tarquins to power (Shuger 526–8). The first crime parallels Musidorus's near-rape of Pamela (halted by a marauding mob) and Pyrocles and Philoclea's consensual sex; the second incident recalls Euarchus's unswayable sentence in the trial of Musidorus and Pyrocles. If Sidney had simply used Livy without modification, then the princes' misdeeds would have served as the impetus for the founding of a republic. However, as Shuger points out, Sidney rewrites Livy significantly: "First, because Euarchus is a king, his insistence upon the rule of law loses any republican coloration; the opposition between monarchic and republican government—the whole point of the traditional story—disappears from the *Arcadia*. Second, Sidney's princes, despite their sexual and political transgressions, remain the heroes of the story" (531). Shuger reads the *Arcadia* as tending instead toward what she names a "princely" theory of "personal rule," which "unlike absolutist theories … is not obsessed with legitimating kingship, whether on the basis of divine right, natural law, or paternal authority" (538).

Shuger's account of princely power compellingly places Sidney within his historical and intellectual contexts, but it omits some of the republican elements of the Euarchus episode. In his insistence that Euarchus is no tyrant, Sidney dismisses the reader's sympathies for Musidorus and Pyrocles by showing us the misguided populace:

> examining the matter by their own passions, [the people] thought Euarchus (as often extraordinary excellencies, not being rightly conceived, do rather offend than please) an obstinate-hearted man, and such a one who being pitiless, his dominion must needs be insupportable. But Euarchus (that felt his own misery more than they and yet loved goodness more within himself), with such a sad assured behaviour as Cato killed himself withal, when he had heard the uttermost of that their speech tended unto, he commanded again that they should be carried away … (Sidney 845)

The critique of the people's failed understanding supports Shuger's claim that Sidney advocates an aristocratic model. But Sidney also alludes to Cato, whom Plutarch depicts as the model of incorruptible integrity, a man whose republican convictions were so strong that he killed himself rather than submit to Caesar. In paralleling Euarchus to a republican, Sidney brings back the ghost of Livy, but in aligning that precedent with the failed republic, Sidney shows Euarchus's self-sacrifice in condemning his own family to be futile in preserving the rule of law. Like Cato and unlike Orestes and Pylades or Damon and Pythias, Euarchus's self-sacrifice does not ensure the political model he prizes.

Though many readers respond positively to Euarchus's sense of universally applicable justice, other critics have pointed to problems in his judgment. In a recent study of friendship, Wendy Olmsted argues that Euarchus's judgment demonstrates a failure to respond appropriately to the emotional rhetoric of Musidorus and Pyrocles (27). Olmsted describes an Euarchus riven by conflicting obligations to his family and his office; he chooses, unambiguously, his impartial role as magistrate (28–9). For Olmsted, equitable judgment requires a specifically patriarchal monarch: "The conflict between justice and mercy can only be resolved by a monarch, who combines in his person princely honour and benevolent fatherhood with political authority" (29). Unlike Shuger's argument for Sidney's aristocratic model, then, Olmsted sees the final resolution of the *Arcadia* as supporting a monarchy based in patriarchalism. Basilius can be that just and equitable monarch, Olmsted insists, because his own failings have taught him mercy. I want to suggest, however, that the mixed monarchic and republican allusions of Sidney's *Arcadia* demonstrate the fallibility of patriarchalism, while offering a more inclusive basis for civic participation than aristocratic status. Further, I want to argue that this is what makes Katherine Philips turn to the *Arcadia* for the story behind her multiple friendships.

Early in the trial scene, before he realizes that he is judging his own son and nephew, Euarchus makes a statement about the applicability of law to princes:

> whatsoever they be or be not, here they be no princes, since betwixt prince and subject there is as necessary a relation as between father and son; and as there is no man a father but to his child, so is not a prince a prince but to his own subjects. Therefore is not this place to acknowledge in them any principality, without it should at the same time by a secret consent confess subjection. (Sidney 834–5)

Far from naturalizing the princes' rule, the parallel between father and king places monarchic power in a specific jurisdictional relation, and, more importantly, in the subjects of that jurisdiction. Euarchus also suggests a competing model: that of social contract theory. The Arcadians' consent to be ruled would make Musidorus and Pyrocles monarchs in Arcadia, whereas the paternal analogy bars them from that rule. Euarchus, Musidorus, and Pyrocles alike are all royalty in exile, and thus specifically excluded from patriarchally based kingship.

The figures of a murdered king and an heir in exile have particular relevance for the royalist Philips in the 1650s. Despite the Christological iconography used by the supporters of the executed Charles I, he cannot enjoy the miraculous resurrection of the fictional Basilius. If Euarchus, as the monarch in exile, cannot bestow clemency, and Philips's Basilius, Charles I, cannot return from the grave, then Philips needs another way to preserve both friendship and the state, especially given the network of conflicting obligations that tears Euarchus apart—that makes him, like Cato, liable to self-destruction through the denial of his own passions. From the story of the *Arcadia*, Philips takes two elements that help define this problem. First, patriarchal authority cannot legitimate the king in exile: this model, as Euarchus states, devolves into legitimation on the basis of the people's consent. Second, the exiled monarch cannot exercise clemency, leading to the agonizing choice of one obligation over another, as in Euarchus's decision to set the law above his kindred. In her poems addressing the question of multiple friendships and conflicting obligations, Philips finds another answer. By locating political virtue in friendship rather than in patriarchalism, Philips establishes a network of alliances that is both consensual and natural, both made and found. She also sustains multiple conflicting obligations, chronicled in the poems of friendship's failures as well as in her own life, as a royalist woman married to a supporter of Parliament and Cromwell. The continuance of friendships beyond—and by means of—the poems of friendship's failures demonstrates clemency, a virtue traditionally reserved to kings (as Andrew Shifflett describes) but transferred, in the absence of a single monarch, to the royalist group of friends.

Philips's depiction of friendship between women foregrounds, rather than obfuscates, the potential for conflicting obligations that the extravagant rhetoric of friendship always tries to contain. The narratives of multiple friendships in Philips's poems raise a question of civic order: how to retain the structures of political obligation even after betrayal. In taking up this question again and again, Philips's poems enact the opposite of the official Act of Indemnity and Oblivion under Charles II: they commemorate, rather than obliterate, the history of changing allegiances. Philips overtly argues for singularity and exclusivity in friendship, a strategy that evokes absolute sovereignty. The logic of her poems' order and ventriloquization of multiple friends, however, suggest that her poems can transfer the lessons of exemplary friendship to other readers. Reading Philips's poems of friendship's dissolution as her coterie read them—as central to her project of claiming women's friendship as politically exemplary—thus drastically alters our sense of Philips's politics. Rather than a nostalgic idealization of stability, Philips struggles to produce a new version of political faithfulness that does not disavow past betrayals. The restoration's official emphasis on forgetting makes her more complicated royalism uncomfortable, and eventually unreadable.

Natural Sociability, Social Contract, and the Afterlife of Philips's Poems

The impact of Philips's poems on later thinkers demonstrates both the extent of her innovation in friendship discourse and political thought and the difficulties that the official policy of forgetfulness after the restoration of the king raises for her model. The authorized 1667 edition of Philips's poems, published after her death from smallpox, contains a commendatory poem by political theorist James Tyrrell. Though his first publication of 1661 was pro-monarchic, Tyrrell became a prominent Whig theorist and one of the leading exponents, with John Locke and

Algernon Sidney, of anti-patriarchalist theory.[6] Both personally and theoretically, Tyrrell was especially close to Locke.

In contrast to Philips's forthright acknowledgement of friendship's betrayals and conflicting obligations, Tyrrell's commendatory poem seems to want to protect both Orinda's body and her poems from dangerous influences:

> And thou impartial, powerful Grave,
> These Reliques (like her deathless Poems save)
> Ev'n from devouring Time secure,
> May they still rest from other mixture pure:
> Unless some dying Monarch shall to trye
> Whether Orinda, though her self could dye,
> Can still give others immortality;
> Think, if but laid in her miraculous Tomb,
> As from the Prophets touch, new life from hers may come. ("To the memory" E1ᵛ)

Tyrrell initially wants to keep Philips's body inviolable, locked within the grave. However, Tyrrell is more like Philips than he first seems to be, for he relinquishes the fantasy of purity for the reality of usefulness. In a play on the ceremony of touching for the king's evil, Tyrrell suggests that Philips herself can offer the monarch a cure. Her cure answers forgetfulness rather than disease: she "give[s] others immortality" not through the relics of her body but through her poems. Tyrrell thus praises Philips as a court poet while reminding the king that the dangers of forgetfulness apply to him as well. In allowing for the possible resurrection of Orinda's poetic powers, Tyrrell, like Philips, links her royalism to the remaking of friendship even after betrayal, and rejects the official policy of oblivion.

Tyrrell's poem to Philips illuminates the intersection of her thought with two central seventeenth-century discourses: *amicitia*'s relation to natural sociability and the analogy between the marital contract and the political contract. Although Tyrell writes on these topics well after Philips's death, his commendatory poem's selective response to her legacy shows the ways in which her poems diverge from his early thinking.

In many ways, *amicitia* would seem to be like natural sociability in its emphasis on affection and likeness between the friends. Tyrrell demonstrates some of the differences between the two. In his refutation of Thomas Hobbes, Tyrrell asserts a "natural sociableness among men, which we look upon as most necessary and agreeable to the nature of man" (*Brief* 262). Tyrrell depicts a "stricter League of Amity, called Civil Society," arising out of natural benevolence, in order to curb the selfishness of the few men who do not take others' interests into consideration (*Brief* 263). Only then might fear and coercion arise:

---

[6]   On Tyrrell, see Goldie, Rudolph, and Tully. Tyrrell may have drawn Philips's poetry to Locke's attention; Locke's commonplace book contains three of Philips's restoration panegyrics on the coronation (Bodleian Library, Oxford, MS Locke e. 17 fols. 93–7).

So that this Common Amity or Benevolence, cannot be omitted to be first supposed, even in the very constitution of Commonwealths: Since those who founded them, must have been before united, either by some natural relation; and a mutual confidence in, or benevolence toward each other; although perhaps, others might afterwards, out of fear of their Power, or a liking of their Government, be compelled or allured, to joyn or associate themselves with them. (*Brief* 263)

In contrast to Hobbes's fearful state of nature or Philips's exclusive *amicitia perfecta*, Tyrrell posits "Common Amity."

The reason why Philips's friendship does not simply move into this larger "stricter League of Amity, called Civil Society" becomes clear, again, through an allusion: Tyrrell, at Oxford and in a later exchange of letters with Locke, went by the pastoral name "Musidore." This suggests that "A Dialogue of Friendship Mutiplyed," Musidorus and Orinda's debate about multiple friendships, specifically answers Tyrrell's conception of "Common Amity."[7] In "A Dialogue of Friendship Mutiplyed," Orinda scores a rhetorical triumph for exclusive friendship over Musidorus, who advocates for multiple friendships, only to have that victory undermined by the next poem, which recreates her extravagant, exclusive friendship rhetoric for two other friends. In the conjunction of those two poems and the allusion to the composite *Arcadia*, I have argued, Philips commemorates the history of changing allegiances out of which her poems emerge and from which they gain their rhetorical force. The evidence of those poems demonstrates the conjunction of artifice and nature in *amicitia*: the remaking of friendships that are both made and found shows that political community depends on rhetoric and the circulation of texts not only for its dissemination but also for its origin.

I have also suggested that Philips's allusion to Sidney relates to her rejection of a patriarchally based monarchy for one founded on the consent of a group. This consensual basis suggests the second model, that of social contract theory. In the years of the English Civil Wars, both royalists and republicans use the analogy between the marital contract and the political contract to their own ends.[8] Royalists find in it a contract that is both consensual and irrevocable, thus arguing that citizens cannot legitimately overthrow their ruler. Republicans end up arguing that the revocability of the political contract extends to the marriage contract— thus John Milton argues for divorce. Contract theory is unlike *amicitia* in that it

---

[7]   Tyrrell was at Oxford from 1657 to 1663; he went to the Inner Temple after Oxford, and thus would have been in London during Philips's final residence and illness there. A letter of Philips's to Sir Charles Cotterell dated 8 April 1663 mentions sending printed editions of her play *Pompey* to London by means of Lady Elizabeth Tyrrell, James's mother (Letter XXVI, Thomas 77). "A Dialogue of Friendship Multiplyed" appears for the first time in the 1667 printed edition of Philips's works, so the probable composition time of the poem and Philips's acquaintance with the Tyrrells coincide.

[8]   See Shanley and Pateman.

insists upon a single absolute commitment, in contrast to friendship's totalizing, yet changeable, commitment. Tyrell's stance on patriarchalism in marriage is a conflicted one: where his *Patriarcha non monarcha* (1681) aims to refute Robert Filmer's *Patriarcha* (1680) by insisting on consent as the basis of subjection, he also asserts that the husband, as naturally wiser and stronger, should rule his wife.[9] In *Bibliotheca politica* (1691/2), he extends this basis in nature still further by arguing that women's subjection to men preceded the fall (11).

Tyrell's thinking illuminates his response to Philips: he allows for the royalist intervention of her poems, but not for the advocacy of women's autonomy that demonstrates the centrality of conflicting allegiances within that royalism. Tyrrell's initial refusal of "mixture" in Philips's grave is a way of limiting the transference of her political model, as a counterfactual earlier in his poem imagines it:

> Had she [Nature] such Souls plac'd in all Woman-kind,
> Giv'n 'um like wit, not with like goodness join'd,
> Our vassal Sex to hers had homage pay'd;
> Woman had rul'd the World, and weaker Man obey'd. ("To the memory" E1)

But, Tyrrell insists, this is not the case, and he ensures that it is not the case by leaving out the instances of those with wit like Philips's: her friends.

The case in which Tyrrell does allow the political valence of Philips's poems to take hold is in the revision of monarchy: her poems' "mixture" can cure the king by teaching him to remember. What Tyrrell wants the king to remember is not only the events of the Civil Wars but also the history of his coming to power. That is, Tyrrell wants the king to understand monarchic power *as historical*, constructed through an instance of consent rather than existing since time immemorial through divine right. What he cannot see—what his investment in gender hierarchy blinds him to—is that Philips's appropriation of *amicitia*'s textual generativity for women disproves patriarchalism more thoroughly because it enables the reforming of bonds after their rupture, constructing political power as process.

Backstories

In my account of Philips's use of Sidney's *Arcadia*, I stressed the second half of Livy's legacy: the trial in which Brutus condemns his own sons to death. Philips takes up this story, I argued, to demonstrate that patriarchal power does not provide a stable basis for monarchy and to indicate that clemency should not be reserved to the king alone. Tyrrell's response to Philips shows the importance of this model, I suggested, because it shares Philips's concern with a narrative of monarchic power

---

[9]   See *Patriarcha non monarcha*: "the woman, as the weaker vessel, is to be subject to the Man, as the stronger, stouter, and commonly the wiser creature" (14). See Shanley 85–7 for a discussion of Tyrrell and the marital contract.

as historical rather than natural, though Tyrrell does not go as far as Philips in imagining a continuing history of bonds undone and remade.

I did not discuss the first part of Livy's story, however, and it is to this backstory that I want to turn in conclusion. As Shuger discusses, Brutus expels the Tarquins and founds the republic because of the brutal rape of Lucretia. Thus the origin myth of the republic relies upon a rejection of violence against women, while monarchy and aristocracy seem to license that violence. The republican story is not an uncomplicated triumph for women, however, given that the depth of Brutus's outrage depends upon Lucretia killing herself for shame. Retribution for violence done against women thus only occurs in the context of a woman's violence against herself. She impels the founding of the republic, but only by rendering herself unable to participate in it.

In the textual history of the *Arcadia,* things become somewhat more complicated. Musidorus's near-rape of Pamela and Pyrocles's consensual sex with Philoclea occur only in the *Old Arcadia.* In the composite *Arcadia,* published after Philip Sidney's death, Mary Sidney, Countess of Pembroke and Philip's sister, excises both these troubling passages. Thus, the version that Katherine Philips would have read does not contain these instances of violence against women. The shadow of these sexual violations remains in the unaltered trial scene, but the charges against the princes consequently appear unjustified. In the composite version, Euarchus punishes the princes for the abduction of the princesses—abductions to which the princesses explicitly consent, in letters that the prosecutor refuses to read aloud before the assembled. Those letters offer two different versions of the grounds for clemency: Philoclea makes her plea "but a private petition;" Pamela makes a claim for sovereignty, while acknowledging its conditional status with "if I be your princess" (Sidney 827; 828). The harshness of Euarchus's judgment thus depends on the suppression of women's explicit verbal consent and a refusal of clemency on both private and public grounds.

Philips brings women's consent back to the forefront of political discourse through friendship, using the specifically textual materials of allusions and poems to offer a revised vision of monarchy. She demonstrates the theoretical insufficiency of a patriarchally based monarchy in the circumstances of the interregnum and restoration, and advocates for a clemency not reserved to the monarch but actively practiced, as a benefit of friendship. Friendship, in Philips's model, results both from explicit consent and from natural affinity: it is both made and found. More importantly, as the poems of multiplicity and betrayal show, it is remade, again and again, out of the materials of its own dissolution. Philips's poems demonstrate that acknowledging friendship's conflicting obligations does not undermine its utility as a political model, but instead allows the rhetoric of monarchy to incorporate a wider, mixed-gender community. The inclusion of women as civic subjects facilitates what, in either version of the *Arcadia,* could only occur through a miraculous resurrection: a community that forgives the past without forgetting it.

PART III
Friendship in Ethics and Politics

Chapter 8

"My foule, faulce brest": Friendship and Betrayal in Lady Mary Wroth's *Urania*

Sheila T. Cavanagh

Friendship is at the heart of social and political structures in Lady Mary Wroth's *Countess of Montgomery's Urania* (1621; c. 1626). An interconnected network of friends, relatives, political allies, and love interests populates the lengthy romance. Individuals often slide between these positions, with many figures, therefore, serving as potential friends. The characters are not always adept, however, at determining who fits best within which category, whether "friendship" simply includes anyone who is not an obvious enemy, or whether it should carry stricter qualifications. Lovers, former suitors, and relatives can all be friends, but they also regularly betray each other. "Friendship," therefore, is an important but unreliable concept. As Aristotle's widely read *Nichomachean Ethics* observes, "how can prosperity be guarded and preserved without friends?" (Ross ed. 406). This question confronts the *Urania*'s coteries continuously. Many of the central figures in the *Urania* are monarchs or others with high political status; accordingly, they are in constant need of allies against the persistent enemies of their realms. As highly social beings, these characters crave continual interaction except when overwrought by despair. Regardless of the attendant pitfalls, therefore, a range of friends remain critical in these domestic and political realms, despite the diminishment of the importance of the economy of friendship in the broader culture of the time, which Lorna Hutson notes: "by this time it was generally conceded that trust in friendship was no longer the surest form of capital investment; the newly powerful agency of money had taken its place" (53–4). In the *Urania*, however, friends—whether relatives, lovers, or social acquaintances—retain their primacy, even as they reveal their potential inconstancy. These configurations resemble the friendship/ kinship patterns that Harriette Andreadis describes for Katherine Philips whereby friendship becomes "a web of chosen kinship with all the intimate obligations and commitments that might imply" (535). In addition, just as close relatives and social contacts were important in Wroth's own life, friends are key in her romance. As Josephine Roberts indicates, many of Wroth's friends shared similar personal circumstances: "Wroth also belonged to a circle of women writers of her own generation, many of them related by kinship" (I:xxxvii). Furthermore, as Melissa

Sanchez details, Wroth was "a member of a circle of courtiers who both depended on royal favor and challenged royal policy" (449). Marion Wynne-Davies remarks upon the importance of Wroth's large, interdependent family in nurturing her art: "the social standing, wealth and cultural position of the [Sidney/Herbert] family combine with the beautiful, gracious, and protected houses, simultaneously propagating a discourse which enabled both male and female creativity" (165). Like her characters, therefore, Wroth sought personal and creative sustenance through the friendship of persons resembling herself in significant ways, both through bloodlines and political allegiances. While conventional friendship treatises may not always include lovers, relatives, and others who serve as close friends, in the *Urania*, Wroth's fictive world reflected what Andreadis describes as friendship's "multiple and layered bonds: social, political, [and] familial" (535). Friends in the *Urania* share lineage, social status, and common lifestyles; notably, women share equal access to these kinds of friendship, even though they receive less consideration than men in conventional discourses on friendship.

The emphasis upon similarity among friends links the *Urania* to numerous contemporary texts and to Aristotle, who had entertained the view that "some define [friendship] as a kind of likeness and say like people are friends" (*Nic. Eth.* 406). Wroth problematizes these parallels in ways that will be discussed below. Still, the similitude that friends in the *Urania* demonstrate corresponds generally with the early modern theories of friendship that Laurie Shannon describes: "The radical likeness of sex and station that friendship doctrines require singly enables a vision of parity. A virtual civic parity that is not modeled elsewhere in contemporary social structures" (2). Wroth includes pairings of friends that do not quite fit this model; nevertheless, parity of sex, station, politics, or lineage remains predominant. Veralinda's history, for instance, closely parallels Urania's, as Sarah Wall-Randell relates: "As Veralinda's story unfolds—her birth as a princess, her infant kidnapping, her captor's flight by sea, her adoption by a kind shepherd, and the shepherd's dispatching her to her true identity when the time comes—we see that it closely parallels Urania's" (114). The *Urania* often exposes the limitations of reliance on similitude, however, as this essay will demonstrate. Concurring with Aristotle's cautions about the transience of such likeness (407), Wroth simultaneously promotes and undermines the importance of sameness in personal and political relationships, using her trademark blend of fiction and verisimilitude to illustrate and dissect contemporary conceptualizations of friendship. While Cicero famously states that "the greatest of all things is Friendship" (*Letters* 44), the Urania demonstrates that it can also be fraught with peril.

Given the centrality of friendship within this domain, for example, it is significant that friends are not always reliable, even with those they most love or admire. Deceit runs rampant through this community, so that "friendship" often falters. Nevertheless, many of the central figures remain impervious to this threat of betrayal, possibly reflecting a belief in Thomas Elyot's contention (following Tully) that "friendship cannot be without virtue, nor but in good men only ... which so bear themselves and in such wise do live, that their faith, surety, equality, and liberality be sufficiently proved" (132). According to conventional discourse of the friendship tradition, such as Elyot's, friends are good people who can be trusted; Wroth's characters, moreover, continually seek friends who will prove to be trustworthy. Nevertheless, many of the *Urania*'s characters choose lies or betrayal when their lives become uncomfortably complicated, so that the tenets of friendship are often compromised, with long-term and widespread consequences. This kind of dishonesty, moreover, resembles the early modern concept of ingratitude, which intensifies the immorality evinced thereby. In Elyot's terms: "the most damnable vice and most against justice, in mine opinion, is ingratitude, commonly called unkindness ... he is unkind that dissimuleth" (152). This linking of dissimulation with ingratitude underscores the severity of the transgressions these characters commit. As E. Catherine Dunn notes, "The Renaissance commonplace books are rather freely strewn with references to the Persian view of ingratitude as the source of all evil. This concept of ingratitude was that of a fundamental and basic malice which disposed a man to evil of any kind, however great" (3). Still, however important trust may be within these communities, central characters regularly leave integrity behind, lapsing instead into the kind of unkindness or ingratitude noted above. Like Parselius, who abandons Urania early in the romance in order to marry Dalinea, then denies that marriage and its offspring, friends and relatives in this text often lie, bringing into question the efficacy of similitude as a reliable foundational principle for this grouping of cousins. Their varying degrees of integrity undermine the kind of similitude Dunn cites as critical in friendships of this time: "Friendship differs also in degree as well as in kind; its degree depends upon the number of things which friends have in common" (24). Dishonesty, however, regularly trumps congruity in friendship, as many of these characters learn.

This essay considers the varied communities established in this environment and discusses how friendship and unpredictable trustworthiness both fulfill and undermine critical personal and political functions. Understanding how these clusters of relationships thrive or decline remains a key component in reading Wroth's work. Families and countries cannot survive without reliable ties of friendship, whether the friends are relatives, lovers, or others. When these links are damaged, the consequences are severe. Not surprisingly, however, as Tom MacFaul notes, belief in idealized friendship often defies reality in early modern texts: "much of the writing of the period [is] shaped by the Humanist ideal of true friendship, even when they are aware that it is a will o' the wisp" (*Male Friendship* 1). While MacFaul's comments primarily address Shakespearean drama, the ways that these seemingly contradictory qualities of true friendship and "reality" intersect and collide lie at the center of Wroth's romance. Despite friendship's instability, however, the *Urania* does not encourage independent existence. Friendly allegiances remain crucial, no matter how fragile and uncertain they might be, for all but the most dedicated pilgrim, solitary griever, or intrepid man at arms. Wroth appears to recognize the important aspects of friendship noted by Shannon: "friendship discourses take up a key place not only in the vocabularies of self-fashioning, but also in political mythography. Under friendship's colors, self-determination is embodied; bonds without subordination and (doubled) selves without bounds take shape" (23). Known and potential threats flourish in these domains. Accordingly, characters need friends and military allies to help guard against a host of dangers, despite the imperfections this system of protection continually demonstrates.

While recognizing its flaws, the *Urania* often implies that consanguinity offers the most reliable bond in this uncertain environment. Familial associations regularly provide the kind of similitude that leads to friendship in the narrative, possibly since political rank and stature feature so prominently in its dominant hierarchical structures. Several groups of royal cousins make up the majority of those at the center of the main narrative lines, along with their lovers, spouses, children, and an occasional parent. These close family ties stand in opposition to a pattern MacFaul finds in the period: "With the destruction of other modes of allegiance, the family became an increasingly monolithic commitment for the individual—and friendship, the one remaining alternative mode of allegiance, therefore came to be presented in stark opposition to family" (*Male Friendship* 5). In contrast to this view, Wroth's groups of cousins remain tightly connected. Despite the sometimes daunting geographical distances that separate the countries over which they rule, these cousins spend considerable time together and remain in close, albeit improbable, contact when they are apart. The members of the group communicate openly with each other, despite the fact that one of them—Urania— was kidnapped by pirates soon after birth and did not learn her identity or meet her family until adulthood. As Kathryn Pratt suggests, this lengthy estrangement could have left Urania bereft of her most important ties in this society: "Urania ponders her place in society, and specifies that her lack of knowledge as to her estate (social condition linked to rights of material possession) is the greatest misery (emotional condition) that can befall women" (49). This potentially catastrophic separation is soon forgotten, however. In addition, while the *Urania*'s characters travel incessantly, they still create the kind of safe environment Wynne-Davies finds in the Sidney home at Penshurst, which "functioned as a place where noble women could find pleasure in one another's company without the darker and more dangerous intrigues of the early seventeenth-century court" (170). In typical romance fashion, however, reality often takes a back seat to narrative convenience. As will be discussed below, however, Wroth includes realistic representations of social situations, including friendship, at other key moments in the text, as she uses the *Urania* to experiment with generic forms. In fact, Wroth's juxtaposition of fiction and verisimilitude parallels the fraught relationship between similitude and dissimulation in the friendships portrayed. Both linguistically and conceptually, therefore, questions about authentic and feigned similarities permeate both the content and the narrative form of the *Urania*.

Although family relationships help cement the bonds of friendship linking the various groups of cousins, their alliance emanates from congruent status as well as from consanguinity. As noted, each cousin bears royal blood. While they behave graciously and appropriately with those of lesser stature, they seem most relaxed, informal, and intimate with those of their own station. This pattern is replicated in the next generation where the legitimate children of these cousins congregate together, while illegitimate sons travel communally and share quests. Both monarchs and knights can typically be found with those holding similar positions in life, presumably since this is where friendship is most likely to flourish. While Shannon suggests that "friendship discourses themselves depend on such likenesses being rare, even anomalous and bizarre" (21), the *Urania*'s cousins continually seek and find likeness around them and build friendships based upon those similarities. They presume potential friendship when they encounter new people of similar status, therefore, whether or not they share bloodlines. As Laura Gowing and her co-editors remark, "'Friend' had copious and special meanings for early modern people. It brought economic obligations: friends helped the young make marriages, carrying an interest in their future" (4). Each of the disparate groupings of friends in the *Urania* appear to recognize this interdependence. Friends, whether relatives or social equals, support and sustain those coping with the challenges of this chaotic environment, often, in Julie Eckerle's construction, forming "collectively imagined alternatives for shared problems" ("Urania's Example" 39). Friends, in other words, helped ameliorate life's difficulties.

The most prominent of these pairs of friends among the male figures are Amphilanthus and Ollorandus, while Pamphilia and Urania exemplify the pattern most strikingly for the females. In the former instance, the duo are not related, but both pairs share reasonably comparable positions and purposes in life, although the "never enough admired" Amphilanthus cannot rightly be called "equal" to any of his companions. As MacFaul suggests, "friends have to be equal, kings can never have true friends" (*Male Friendship* 121). In this case, even two kings are not equal. Nevertheless, the pair model a close relationship that illustrates the importance, both personally and professionally, of having confidants and allies with similar backgrounds and positions in life. In addition, as Aristotle comments, "perfect friendship is the friendship of men who are good, and alike in virtue" (*Nic. Eth.* 408). Fitting this profile, Ollorandus and Amphilanthus share triumphs and setbacks in the romantic realm and on the battlefield as they remain steadfast in their devotion to each other and to both the overlapping and distinct destinies of their kingdoms. These kings, in other words, demonstrate what Bacon believes is the centrality of monarchical friendships: "It is a Strange Thing to observe, how high a Rate, Great Kings and Monarchs, do set upon this *Fruit* of *Friendship*, wherof we speake: So great, as they purchase it, many times, at the hazard of their owne Safety and Greatnesse" (81). In this instance, the pair's faith is warranted. As Aristotle cautions, however, "such friendships should be infrequent; for such men are rare" (408).

This partnership reflects the characteristics MacFaul finds in Humanist ideologies of friendship: "People seek to discover themselves in their friends, and the central mirage of friendship affects the shape of all other relationships" (*Male Friendship* 1). Even when they are in disguise, and therefore unknown to each other—early in their relationship, for example—the duo pledge everlasting fealty to each other and do what they can to attend to each other's emotional needs. When Ollorandus realizes that Amphilanthus cannot sleep, for instance, he offers his friendship as a consolation:

> 'My onely friend,' said he, 'your last nights ill rest made mine unpleasing to me, and most, because mine ignorance hinders me from being able to serve you. I cannot be yet so bold to demand the cause, since what proofe have you of me, that I should thinke you might esteeme me worthy of such a favour? Yet this you may be confident of, that death should ceaze me, before I refuse to venter life to obtaine your desires; and lose it rather then reveale any secret you shall impart to me.' (1: 77)

Amphilanthus immediately replies in kind: "Amphilanthus answer'd, that he saw unexpected good happen to him in al things (especially in this blessed friendship) but in that which he most sought for" (1: 77). From this point onward, until the death of Ollorandus, the pair remain fast friends, who support each other through a myriad of personal and political embroilments. They talk at great length about the complications of their love lives and vow to confide in each other openly, with Amphilanthus proclaiming: "I will be as free with you, as you have been with me" (1: 81). As the narrative continues, this camaraderie remains strong, illustrating types of friendship Shannon notes as increasingly familiar to readers: "with sovereign, private selves who exercise virtually utopian powers of autonomy; with counselors whose liberty of speech is enshrined; and with kings who listen to that speech and also heed the examples that the 'figures of perfet amitie' provide" (53).

The knights' female counterparts, Urania and Pamphilia, have similar functions politically, although Urania seems less involved in affairs of state, presumably because her husband, Steriamus, King of Albania, is meant to be at the helm, while Queen Pamphilia rules the country of Pamphilia on her own, even after her marriage to Rodomandro, King of Tartaria. The pair also engage in disparate romantic lives after the initial sections of the romance, when Urania is involved in, then extricated from, an ill-fated love affair with Pamphilia's brother Parselius. Soon after being ritually cleansed from her love for Parselius, Urania marries Steriamus (who had earlier been in love with Pamphilia), with whom she shares a long, apparently serene marriage and produces a number of children. Pamphilia, on the other hand, languishes throughout the lengthy text in a continually thwarted relationship with Amphilanthus. Although she appears to marry him at one point in a *de praesenti* ceremony (2: 45–6), they both go on to wed other people. Their mutual passion never dissipates, however, although Amphilanthus gets romantically entangled with a series of other women—despite the guilt and despair that always overcomes him when he betrays Pamphilia.

These dissimilar fates in love do not diminish the bonds of Urania's and Pamphilia's friendship, although Urania most often takes the role of sage advisor, possibly due to her less complicated adult existence. As Geraldine Wagner reports, friendship helps "these women bravely confront the disparity between the lived experience of their bodies and its disfiguring by romantic discourse" (586). The pair represent idealized yet realistic friendship, since they treat each other with frank but loving care and never balk from taking the other's part despite their many fraught adventures. As Mary Trull indicates concerning the story of Dorolina, this kind of response frequently arises from female empathy with romantic woes: "Wroth reduces the private space of lament to a public sign indicating love, which draws as an audience of lovers who have known similar losses" (476). Urania, moreover, is always ready to offer pointed advice in such circumstances, however sensitive her intervention might be, fitting the Ciceronian view of friendship described by Shannon: "Only a tyrant fears or prohibits 'friendly' communications of a difference in views; only a tyrant fails to see the virtue of a counselor speaking the sharp language of a healthy truth in an exercise of liberty of speech" (52). Bacon agrees with the importance of good counsel, but warns that it is hard to find: "For it is a rare Thing, except it be from a perfect and entire Frend, to have Counsell given, but such as shall be bowed and crooked to some ends" (*Essays* 85). Not surprisingly, as Jacqueline Miller notes, the pair do not always agree, with Pamphilia occasionally remaining "unconvinced of the appropriateness of Urania's advice" ("Ladies" 467). Still this female pair form one of many friendships used here to provide a private place for secure counsel. Fortuitously, the two most prominent advisors in the text, Urania and Melissea, act in the best interests of their friends. As Bacon predicts, however, their reliability is frequently not replicated by others.

These representative pairs of friends form integral parts of much larger groups linked by blood, affection, and status. In the second part of the narrative, for instance, most of the central figures' legitimate children are traveling together to stay with their grandmother, the Queen of Naples, when they are caught in the enchantment that imprisons them for most of the manuscript *Urania*. Once the plan to send the children away is conceived, the group grows ever larger, until most of the cousins are involved:

> Soone after to remove at Corinth for the better shiping the infants. For Parselius sent his daughter called Candida; Rosindy onely a daughter, which was his oldest, butt this tow sonnes showld soone follow if hee might have leave also for them, which was soone graunted by the excellent Queene, who sayd her age would bee very well comforted with such rare company, she ever loving children extreamly; and tow came likewise from Leonius and his sweet Veralinda … In short time they were come altogether, and the Court att Corinthe never soe furnisht with beauties in infancie though ther had binn faire ones ther, yet never soe many att one time. (2: 22–3)

Although this journey leads to a lengthy enchantment, it initially is a trip that nearly all the cousins wish to join. It seems likely, moreover, that being enchanted together is preferable to separation.

While illegitimate offspring are not included in this adventure, they band together as knights in search of these enchanted children in order to establish their reputations. As Andromarko explains to Amphilanthus:

> all the knights gone (of youth, worth, or vallor) in this search, soe, as least wee showld be unknowne, and unheard condemnd for want of love, ore vallor, wee tooke our way in the same search, and have mett many relations of the knights passages and many hasardus attempts bravely parformed by them. (2: 145)

Among this group of knights is the Knight of the Faire Designe, a figure said to be destined for greatness, but whose parentage and specific identity is unknown:

> I ame a poore unknowne youth as yett, butt ordain'd (as I am tolde) to bee your [Amphilanthus's] servant. I knowe noe parents, nor have I a name more then the unknowne. I have a sipher on my hart, which is sayd to bee her name whom I must by many hard adventures att last gaine, and knowe her by having a sipher likewise, which shall discover my name, and then I shalbee knowne. (2: 297)

The text implies, but never verifies, that he is the son of Amphilanthus. The narrative is also silent, but fuels speculation, on the possibility that his mother is Pamphilia. Despite the ambiguity surrounding this apparent hero who will follow in Amphilanthus's stead, however, he groups together with other illegitimate children in a manner resembling the other clusters of friends. The narrative devotes less time to the personal interactions of this younger group than it does to those of their parents' generation, but it still indicates that these youth seek and value the same kind of associations that their predecessors enjoy.

The bonds cementing the friendships of either generation do not always hold firm, however. As in life, the integrity needed to keep such communities and their members strong cannot be taken for granted in the *Urania*. Like the deceptive "friends" in other romances, characters in Wroth's narrative do not always fulfill their implied and stated commitments. Sometimes characters who are basically good at heart succumb to temptations that undermine their honesty; at other times, figures of weak or malevolent temperament wreak havoc on the lives of those around them. With few exceptions, moreover, characters do not typically suspect the motives of those they encounter, whether or not they have credible reason to trust them. Unless those they meet are clearly enemies, such as the knight Drudeldoro, who openly proclaims hatred for Parselius (2: 343), characters generally believe what they are told; when those lying to them are friends, of similar status, or attractive females, this level of gullibility rises even higher. Given the number of writings from this period warning against this kind of trust, this credulity is particularly striking. As Shannon notes: "false friends and flatterers may be ubiquitous ... but they are not obvious and entire treatises engage in supplying some method, short of more convenient 'moral aversion' for detecting them" (47). Despite being less allegorical than characters in the *Urania*'s precursor texts such as *The Faerie Queene*, the kings and queens in Wroth's text tend to face similar difficulties in discerning virtue and general veracity. Although some figures, such as Amphilanthus, pride themselves on their perspicacity in assessing the character of others (2: 297) and although Urania places great faith in the honorableness of those with mystical powers (1: 230), Wroth uses such trust and pride in one's own abilities to underscore the flaws in her characters' self-awareness. The narrative is not consistent in this regard, however; sometimes those who are trusted deserve to be. Other times, they practice deceit with considerable negative consequences for those who believe them. As Jennifer Carrell comments, however, "Both men and women conspire to entwine fact and fiction in order to change the facts" (84). Neither gender nor status, therefore, can be reliable markers of trustworthiness.

Many of those who successfully deceive those around them use feigned familiarity or other models of similitude to cultivate unwarranted, and ultimately dangerous, confidence in the supposedly astute main characters. As Shannon notes, "mere simulation can look a lot like the similitude friendship celebrates" (47). Amphilanthus, for instance, is nearly killed by the widow of someone who fell to his sword because she successfully convinces him that she is a grieving woman needing protection from a dangerous, importunate suitor:

> I am a poore Lady dwelling here, not farre hence, in yonder old Abbey, Lady thereof by the death of my Husband, since which time a young Lord hath been an earnest suitor to me; but my love and fortune dying with my husband, or but living to his memory, I refused him, as many other that have sought me, whereupon he vowed to have me by force, since no other meanes would prevaile … here I hope I am secure, and shall assure myself of it, if it might please you, to take me into your protection. (1: 284–5)

Correctly surmising that Amphilanthus would believe this cover story and let down his guard, the widow comes close to avenging the death of her actual husband, Terichillus, who was killed by Amphilanthus. Like many other crafty women in the *Urania*, this angry widow relies upon Amphilanthus's weakness for female wiles and his presumption of friendship barring conflicting evidence. Although he often falls victim to such maneuvers, he never learns to be more wary. In this instance, moreover, he is doubly vulnerable because while he is under attack, Ollorandus "was held with discourse by a like deceiver" (1: 285) and only barely manages to arrive in time to save Amphilanthus from the "devilish causer of all this" (2: 286). The pair eventually survive this dangerous encounter, but their fate lies in the balance for some time.

Pamphilia's brother Selarinus similarly falls victim to a wily, mysterious woman who preys upon his gullibility and healthy libido, while choosing a disguise that suggests she is part of the inner circle from which most reliable friends are chosen. Presenting herself as the daughter of the King of Tartaria, she captivates him with her beauty and exotic presentation: "I ame daughter to the King of Tartaria; my mother was a Persian" (2: 9). The consequences of succumbing to this masquerade are quite severe, moreover, and Selarinus spends several years under the sexual enchantment of this seducer, with whom he sires several children. Like the widow of Terichillus, who correctly predicts Amphilanthus's likely response to a woman ostensibly in need, the fraudulent Tartarian princess knows how to lure the susceptible Selarinus. By presenting herself as a "friend," through her supposed place in Rodomandro's immediate family, she diverts him from asking the questions that might have arisen with a woman of less enticing pedigree. Despite the mysteries and incongruities associated with her story, therefore, Selarinus succumbs to this "deadly Hellhound" (2: 305) as soon as she is freed from her captivity in Melissea's sister's house (2: 305). Although the narrative describes Selarinus as "most excellent" (2: 305), he cannot protect himself from this "delicate Lady" (2: 303), who lures him to bed and keeps him there.

Men with a soft spot for women are not the only characters who fail to penetrate false tales and disguises, however. A figure known as the "False Amphilanthus" successfully confuses several people through his achievement of behavioral and physical similitude with the famous monarch. Most characters in the romance are not prepared to question this kind of similarity. Ironically, the fraudulent man's story is revealed when the "real" Amphilanthus is told of the feigned Amphilanthus's mistreatment of a beautiful princess:

> Amphilanthus, whose fame had won more in her, though in person never to her seene, then all they [other suitors] with their continuall petition. At last this Prince came, whose name had so soveraignis'd, as she stood not to behold, or examine what causes might in him moove her affection, but as Amphilanthus, she lov'd him. He subtill above all men, and as any, false, flatter'd her, and so much wrought with her, as he gain'd what he desir'd and what he most esteem'd; for had she given him lesse, she had, as she believed wronged her fervent love. (1: 297)

Exemplifying Wroth's humor at the expense of her characters, the major offense levied against this imposter is that he too closely imitates his doppelganger by deceiving a woman in love. Furthermore, when the true Amphilanthus protests that Amphilanthus is a worthy man, his interlocutor counters with a description that slyly inverts the praise generally attached to the exalted leader:

> hee is a faire false man, a treacherous well shap'd man, not tall, though high in mischievous ill nature, slender, but full in wickednes, curld haire, and thicke; yet bauld in vertue, and this is Amphilanthus, as he cald himselfe. (2: 299)

By calling him the "falsest, ficklest, waveringst, and unworthiest man" (2: 298), moreover, she reminds the reader of the hyperbole that often describes Amphilanthus, as well as his fickle heart in love. Neither the true nor the false Amphilanthus, in other words, may be considered as trustworthy in love or friendship.

Princess Emilina, whom the False Amphilanthus betrays in the preceding instance, is not the only character to fall victim to the false knight, however. As Dolorindus confesses to Amphilanthus, he lacked the ability to see through the disguises of those dressed as Ollorandus and his royal friend: "Antissius more in sense then I, knew they had taken your names upon them, and were not your selves; he undertooke the named Ollorandus, I the other, whose name had that power" (2: 394). Once again, with the exception of Antissius, the characters fail to look past apparent similitude. Here, the feigned countenance of an esteemed figure easily tricks those he meets. Despite such frequent misidentifications, characters fail to suspect what they think they see. When trust follows too quickly from real or pretend friendship or kinship ties, these lapses in caution have significant ramifications. Although Cicero, among others, warns that people are often "utterly careless in selecting friends" and advises readers to "test friends' characters by a kind of tentative friendship" (*Letters* 30), the main characters and their cohort repeatedly assign friendship when it is not appropriate.

The inadvisability of the unwarranted trust evinced above amplifies the text's continual diminution of the accolades so often accorded to its exalted figures. As Josephine Roberts notes, Wroth infuses her narrative with a quiet wryness that pokes gentle, but pointed, fun at her characters:

> Wroth's sudden shift from Lamb of God to lamb chops reveals a rupture
> between the world of high idealism and that of hard, pragmatic circumstance.
> This satirical method, so typical of Cervantes, is central to the treatment of the
> adventures and enchantments found throughout *Urania*. (1: xxiii)

At the same time, Wroth undergirds the optimism of the text with an infrastructure relying on pessimism and despair, so that a wide spectrum of emotions is included. Contributing to the *Urania*'s emotional verisimilitude, a range of human foibles keeps the narrative moving forward. In addition, tracking characters through several decades enables the text to construct layers of emotional history. Wroth experiments with irony, repetition, and both emotional verisimilitude and exaggeration. Her blending of fiction with realism and concurrent interweaving of a sense of possibility with a patina of hopelessness enables her to present characters who model human realities simultaneously through their credibility and their absurdity. Wroth's characters are not "real," but neither are they allegorical or symbolic. Her repeated considerations of the joys and pitfalls of close personal relationships, such as friendships, round out her representation of the vagaries of human life.

Tensions between friendship and untrustworthiness further exemplify the *Urania*'s use of character and emotion in this experimental literary style, while highlighting how greed and self-interest undermine those believing too readily in the goodness of those sharing their community, their status, and/or their Christianity. Possibly reflecting cynicism generated in Wroth's own life through her conflicted relationship with William Herbert (1: lxxxvi–lxxxix), the text's implicit caution against undue faith in others regularly competes with less suspicious perspectives. Skepticism tends to prevail, however, for the narrator and readers, if not always for the characters. Despite the importance of alliances in this environment, the selfish aspects of human nature intervene frequently enough to keep optimism at bay. Characters strive to believe in others, but they are regularly impeded. As E. Catherine Dunn notes, citing a contemporary commonplace book, deception linked with ingratitude constituted a particularly grave offense: "Ingratitude is that which maketh men impudent, so that they dare ioyne to hurt those which haue been their best friends, and them to whom they are bounde, both by blood, nature, and benefits" (4). Deceptive friends, in other words, are the worst sort of people.

In addition, the text alerts readers to the frequency with which characters are complicit in their own deception. Pamphilia, for instance, is kept from marrying Amphilanthus in a legally binding marriage due to the dual intervention of the Queen of Candia and Forsandurus, the emperor's former tutor and supposed friend. For little reason other than the jealous desire to wreak havoc, this pair target Pamphilia: "Pamphilia (the Easterne starr) must bee butt the meane anvile on whom ther threacherous Villanies must knocke and bee beaten to ther ruin" (2: 132). They mislead Amphilanthus into believing that Pamphilia has betrayed him: "his deere freindlike servant [Forsandurus] sware that, to his knowledge, Pamphilia was beethrothed to the King of Tartaria" (2: 133). Although Pamphilia will indeed eventually marry this king, here she remains faithfully devoted to Amphilanthus. She cannot defend her reputation, however, since she is busy fighting a war as these unfounded rumors fly. Amphilanthus fairly inexplicably places his faith in the deceptive duo, rather than trust his beloved, who has been nothing but stable in her commitment to the promiscuous emperor. Nevertheless, the Queen's royal position and Forsandurus's "friendlike" status combine to overcome Amphilanthus's trust. Accordingly, he marries the Princess of Slavonia, thereby precipitating long-term grief and remorse for himself, Pamphilia, and presumably for the unfortunate bride, who endures an absentee marriage until her parents intervene and insist that Amphilanthus fulfill his previously neglected marital obligations: "[Amphilanthus] received somm Embasadores from his unfortunate wives Father and Mother, who desired the consummation of the marriage" (2: 323).

The emperor's decision not to verify his tutor's tale, no matter how preposterous it appears to the *Urania*'s readers, propels much of the remaining action in the romance. Overcome with sorrow, guilt, and despair over this hasty leap into matrimony, neither Amphilanthus nor Pamphilia ever recover from the choices they make here. While their romantic lives are never placid, they become even more painful after Amphilanthus wrongly chooses where to place his trust. As noted, however, beneath the continual praise that the romance showers upon the emperor there is a barely disguised narrative recognition that Amphilanthus has erred through his own poor judgment. While the text never actively contradicts the accolades its characters and narrative voice bestow upon the emperor, it continually highlights the fragility of the compliments accorded this purportedly incomparable figure.

The irony underlying this story of Amphilanthus's trust in false friendship continues when the deception is finally revealed, although this time the narrative singles out Pamphilia for criticism. While facing imminent death, Forsandurus decides to admit that he tricked Amphilanthus:

> Hee seeing his end approached, and his guilty consience so glutted with wicked mischiefnes, and the act unpardonable dunn without recall ore ever being redrest, that molested him most, nay, made him feele the unquenchable fire burning his Very hart roote (for thether itt was then come), and such flames scorching, and with renuing fires burning him as to dy in rest hee cowld nott. (2: 386)

The tutor-turned-magician leaves little time for hesitation if Pamphilia is going to learn the truth, but the betrayed monarch nearly ruins this opportunity. Recently injured in a hawking incident, the Queen is feeling sorry for herself when Forsandurus's message arrives. She initially refuses to see the tutor, preferring to remain in testy isolation: "She replyde that they all Very well knew now nott tenn days beefor she had a hawking hurt her leg soe much as she had nott ever since binn able to stand upon itt, nor goe much less" (2: 386). Such humorous deflation of central characters is common in the *Urania*, possibly since Wroth bases so many of the figures on people she knew, including herself. Jeopardizing a key revelation because the main character is in a bad mood illustrates Wroth's efforts at incorporating realistic human frailties into the texture of her narrative. However often Pamphilia may be termed "never enough admired," therefore, the romance makes it clear that such hyperbole is not to be accepted uncritically. No matter how exalted Pamphilia and Amphilanthus may be portrayed, moreover, the narrative reminds readers that inflated rhetoric should not be mistaken for accurate reporting. Readers are warned to be more circumspect than the characters tend to be. The narrative offers cautionary tales about the consequences resulting from the human foibles that the *Urania*'s characters display, despite their apparent heroism, power, and beauty. Such qualities, the text reminds us, are no deterrent against mistaken judgment.

The intermittent gullibility of these characters, however, reinforces their need to cultivate and retain close friends. Trustworthy friends and allies help sustain those who are emotionally injured or otherwise harmed by deceit. Urania, for instance, acting as wise friend, intervenes when Amphilanthus decides that suicide is the best way to solve the problems he has created:

> Can my death save these heavenly creatures? Sure itt may; the sea wilbee passified when she hat desertles, hatefull mee to bee a sacrifice to her fury. Then take mee and glutt thy hunger with my unworthy self, and save these images of true worthe and rarest perfectnes. (2: 172)

She similarly counsels Pamphilia during emotionally tumultuous times, even when Pamphilia hesitates to reveal the cause of her despair:

> Urania then came to her when shee seemed to cease her complaints, but shee
> found her sorrowes, and strove to advise her. She still put it off, and would not
> (unto her) confes, but dissembled; Urania would many times give occasion, as
> then she did, to discover her melancholy. (1: 458)

Although the characters also turn for aid and advice to conventional iconic figures, such as the seer Melissea, the text insists on the supreme value of peer relationships. As these incidents suggest, reliable friendships equate with a successful life in this realm; its corruption, therefore, remains particularly deadly.

Given this premium placed upon friendship, it is notable that unexplained estrangements develop late in the text. These fissures are particularly striking, given common tenets of early modern friendship treatises, such as those described by MacFaul: "The crucial fictions of friendship in Humanist text were of equality and permanence, fictions which obviously impact on the individual's sense of selfhood: the fiction of equality enables a belief in the validity of social aspiration; that of permanence bolsters the individual's sense of his own integrity" (*Male Friendship* 2). Nevertheless, close friendships erode toward the end of Wroth's text, demonstrating the accuracy of Scipio's dictum in Cicero's writings on friendship that "the most difficult thing in the world was for a friendship to remaine unimpaired to the end of life" (*Letters* 20). Amphilanthus, for instance, distances himself from Parselius, although their separation is only minimally explained after Pamphilia's brother dies:

> Amphilanthus was in a heaven of hapines all this while in Pamphilias company,
> and with her favour too, butt in as great a hell of griefe for the loss of his deerest
> Parselius, who intimately hee had ever loved, though of latter times estranged
> from him. And why, his owne soule could nott tell, butt love and idle wantones
> had binn a great cause of itt. Yett now since Dalineas death, all was repented,
> and assuredly had binn, with the great glory in the world, amended. Thos small,
> mistlike faults cowld nott have mad[e] him a perfect love, and a during one, to
> an everlasting beeloved friend. (2: 404)

Parselius faces numerous challenges late in his life, many stemming from his early betrayal of both Dalinea and Urania, and he dies before his proposed marriage to Ollorandus's widow Melasinda might have restored his better fortune. It is unclear, however, how these youthful transgressions interfere with his relationship with the emperor so many years later. Given how voluble the narrative can be, such reticence is striking, particularly since the severing or damaging of a friendship among peers and relatives seriously undermines the social fabric of the romance.

A vaguely articulated estrangement similarly undermines Pamphilia's marriage quite late in the narrative, which calls into question Rodomandro's usual place in the romance's central friendships:

Then hee [Rodomandro] cowld call his deerest love to minde, and his neglect towards here, which hee now sought by all meanes to have power and safe passage to her to express. Now was hee wholly him self againe, having been mislead. ... . Now hee thinkes on not thing butt his journey to her, his asking pardon, and hopes of gaining itt, (which he may bee sure of, soe hee wowld bee as longe againe away if itt were pleasing to him). She cowld well beare itt, yet she lett him see she tooke his fashion ill, and showed rather more scorne thaen sorrow for itt, which brought him the more lowly and humbl[ie] to her. (2: 329)

Since this relationship is never straightforward, such belated tension, apparently brought on by an "inchantment" (2: 329), may simply accord with other oddities associated with this narrative strand. Over the course of the text, for instance, Pamphilia inexplicably marries the king willingly, but with great remorse (2: 274–6); later the Tartartian king appears to die, then reappears alive again almost immediately as the narrative reaches its abrupt conclusion (2: 406). This pattern of irregularities involving Rodomandro notwithstanding, however, it remains unusual to have his character undermined, particularly at this late stage of the story, since his manners and good will earlier have generally been represented as impeccable. When he is introduced, for instance, he is highly praised: "This brave Prince, entering the roome of Presence, came with so brave a countenance and yet soe sivile a demeanor as made all eyes subject to his sweetnes" (2: 42). Prior to the late scene, where his integrity is questioned, Rodomandro is portrayed as a friend of all the main characters, who is happily married to a woman whose heart belongs to someone else. Nonetheless, like Parselius, Rodomandro finishes his role in the narrative with a besmirched reputation. In contrast to Pamphilia's brother's, however, the husband's transgressions remain mysterious, and he continues to travel with his wife and Amphilanthus until the abrupt end of the romance. In both cases, moreover, the romance ends without either estrangement really being resolved, since Parselius and (possibly) Rodomandro die before reconciliation is achieved. These loose ends are particularly striking since the narrative appears to be headed toward a grand triumphant conclusion engineered by the Knight of the Faire Designe when it abruptly ends. No ultimate resolution to the entire story occurs, therefore, just as the mysteriously maligned friends, siblings, and husbands are never exonerated and reinstated into the fold. As MacFaul indicates, such frictions could be conceived as cataclysmic during this time: "even as the order of traditional society was breaking down in the Renaissance, friendship was clung to as one last bastion of wholeness and unity; but for that very reason it was also the subject of particular anxiety, because if friendship failed, there was no unity left" (*Male Friendship* 4). The possible ramifications of these estrangements are never discussed, however.

While Wroth's Sidneian influences clearly contribute to her decision to leave so many components of her tale unresolved, the narrative's consistent relapses into pessimism also appear relevant. A magnificent personal and/or collective grand finale would be contrary to the tenor of the romance, where romantic and monarchical optimism is always tempered by sobering quotidial realities. Just as the hyperbolic rhetoric praising Pamphilia and Amphilanthus remains tinged with irony, so does the possibility of a satisfying ultimate finale. Even in the last full paragraph of the narrative, the grand conclusion is presented in conditional terms, as Andromarko explains to Amphilanthus:

> Sir, your Faire Designe hath now left all things (being certainly informed by severall wizards, especially the sage Melissea), that the great Inchantment will nott bee concluded these many years; nay, nev[er], if you live nott to assiste in the concluding. (2: 418)

However often the narrative might hint at such an outcome, its tentativeness remains. Like many of its literary cohort, the *Urania* is not destined for such closure. These late fissures in the relationships at the center of the text, while relatively modest, reflect the consistent ironic realism that imbues the narrative. Like relationships in real life, even these long-term allegiances are not static. Readers are reminded, therefore, that lives take many turns. Friendship, moreover, remains similarly critical, yet elusive. Characters predominantly find friendship with their peers, lovers, and relatives. They frequently lack the perspicacity necessary to determine which candidates for friendship are most promising, however, and they also regularly fail in their own responsibilities as friends. As the vagaries afflicting relationships in the *Urania* indicate, trust is important but cannot be taken for granted. While the *Urania* predates most realistic fiction, therefore, and often presents fantastical people, events, and circumstances, it continually warns its audience in realistic terms that even the closest ties remain fragile and that faith in similitude can be unwise. However much characters in the text rely upon friends to guide, protect, and support them, Wroth continually introduces complications that impede unduly optimistic views of friendship's reliability in typical human relationships. At the same time, Wroth imagines possibilities for friendship beyond many traditional confines, by representing friendships between men and women who are not married to each other and by emphasizing the importance of friendship between women. Unlike popular sixteenth-century friendship treatises, therefore, such as Edmund Tilney's *The Flower of Friendship* (1568), Wroth envisions a world where men and women can be friends with each other outside the bonds of marriage and where women can create communities of friendship with those of their own sex. Wroth's life was often tumultuous and her characters face innumerable obstacles in their own journeys, but friendship remains one of the ways that this royal coterie contend with their lifelong challenges.

Chapter 9

The Friendship of the Wicked in Novella 12 of Marguerite de Navarre's *Heptaméron*[1]

Marc D. Schachter

Marguerite de Navarre (1492–1549) took friendship as a central concern in her patronage and in her writing. She sponsored a French translation of Plato's *Lysis* by Bonaventure des Périers and wrote a long poem celebrating female friendship entitled *The Coach* (*La Coche* in French). Friendship also plays an important role in her best-known work, the *Heptaméron*, where she offered a particularly grim view of it. In Colette Winn's words, the novella collection shows that "friendship between superiors and inferiors is to be avoided; friendship between men and women is impossible; friendship between men is both fragile and extremely restrictive."[2] In this chapter, I focus on a tale in the *Heptaméron* about a putative friendship between a ruler and a subject. The tale explores how, to borrow an apt formulation from a discussion of the correspondence between Marguerite de Navarre and her sometime spiritual counselor Guillaume Briçonnet, "degenerative motives become hidden behind 'honorable names'" (Vance S186).

Novella 12 of the *Heptaméron* relates a fictionalized account of Lorenzo de' Medici's 1537 assassination of his cousin Alessandro, Duke of Florence. Although Marguerite does not refer to the principal players by name, instead calling them the Gentleman and the Duke, numerous details, including explicit references to the Duke's marriage to Marguerite of Austria and to the location of the tale, establish the novella's historical referent. As scholars have noted, the rhetoric of the classical friendship tradition figures prominently in Marguerite's version of the story. For example, the novella's narrator Dagoucin explains that the Duke loved the Gentleman "like himself" [comme luy-mesme] (90) and suggests that the Gentleman could be called the Duke's "second self" [le second luy-mesmes] (90). The two fictionalized Florentines also evoke the rhetoric of friendship to

---

[1]   Julie Singer first called the homoerotic dimensions of this novella to my attention. I would like to thank the editors for their thoughtful remarks on several drafts of this essay, Lorna Hutson and Carlo Taviani for precious bibliographic suggestions, and Stefano Dall'Aglio for sharing research materials and ideas about Lorenzo de' Medici. Unless otherwise noted, all translations in the essay are mine.

[2]   "[L]'amitié entre supérieurs et inférieurs est à éviter; l'amitié entre homme et femme est une impossibilité; l'amitié entre hommes est à la fois fragile et on ne peut plus contraignante" (9). The focus of Winn's article is not the *Heptaméron* but *La Coche*.

describe their relationship with each other. This relationship is stressed to the breaking point when the Duke makes an importunate request, namely that the Gentleman help procure his own sister for the Duke's pleasure, and subsequently comes to an ignominious end when the Gentleman kills the Duke in a curiously eroticized scene.[3]

I argue below that even before their rupture the men are not meant to be seen as friends in the canonical sense of the term associated with the language used to describe their relationship. Instead, in Novella 12, Marguerite de Navarre portrays an instrumental, self-serving, and perhaps even ultimately self-deceiving deployment of the rhetoric of friendship to disguise a relationship of utilitarian exchange. In the first part of this essay, I read Marguerite's novella alongside period accounts of the assassination of Alessandro. This enables me both to identify how Marguerite might have adapted the historical record for her own purposes and to explore some of the implications of her adaptations.[4] The central role the rhetoric of friendship plays in the relationship between the Duke and the Gentleman is the most striking divergence and thus merits particular attention. I then turn to the discussion about the tale held by the *Heptaméron*'s storytellers. Their conversation quickly evolves into a debate about deception in love but it continues to resonate with the novella that initially inspired it. This allows Marguerite to link her analysis of friendship in Novella 12 to the *Heptaméron*'s broader evangelical critique of faith in human relationships.

Exploiting Friendship

Marguerite de Navarre's representation of the relationship between the Gentleman and the Duke differs significantly from that found in other period sources. According to the historical record, Alessandro and Lorenzo were indeed close,

---

[3]   The transition from friendship to violence and the erotic nature of the assassination have been astutely analyzed by Reeser; Ferguson; Johnson 79–97. By concentrating on the dubious nature of the original friendship between the characters, the present essay offers a complementary account of the novella.

[4]   Rather than presuming that Marguerite would have been familiar with any given account—indeed, some of the historical accounts discussed in this essay were written too late to have influenced the *Heptaméron*—my operating assumption is that on the points where the chronicles all agree, they likely drew on readily available information that would probably also have been accessible to her. The period historical accounts I have considered are Giovio; Nerli; Segni; Varchi. On Renaissance historians of Florence, see Montevecchi as well as the essays collected in Guarini and Angiolini and in Marchand and Zancarini. On the relationship between the *Heptaméron* and the historical record, see Bromfield; Fontaine; Bawcutt. On the historical Lorenzo, see Ferrai; Dall'Aglio. Ferrai has argued that Marguerite heard a version of the story of Alessandro's assassination from Lorenzo himself. For a discussion of history in the *Heptaméron* that works counter to my method in this essay, see Tetel 152.

but their bond was not described in terms drawn from the rhetoric of perfect friendship. Moreover, in the Italian materials I have consulted, the words "amico" and "amicizia" are almost never used to describe the rapport between the two men.[5] Rather, the chronicles emphasize that their intimacy was based on mutual self-interest. For example, Filippo de' Nerli writes of Lorenzo that:

> per acquistare più grazia col Duca ... gli andava mettendo innanzi nuovi modi e nuove imprese di piaceri, massimamente d'amori ... per lo che venne Lorenzo col Duca in tanta domestichezza e in tanto credito, che non era rimaso a Sua Eccellenza né cittadino né servitore, cui egli portasse più fede o con chi più si confidasse.

> [in order to acquire the Duke's good will ... he put before him new forms and new pursuits of pleasure, and above all sexual ones ... . By this means Lorenzo came to be so familiar with the Duke and so prized by him that His Excellency had no citizen or servant in whom he placed more faith or confided more.] (239)

Similarly, after invoking Lorenzo's services as a procurer, Bernardo Segni observes that "For these reasons, Lorenzo had so much credit with the Duke that, if it had been up to the Duke, when he had to select a successor, he would have chosen no one but Lorenzo" [Per questi conti Lorenzo era in sì gran credito col Duca, che quando il Duca di sua voglia avesse avuto ad eleggere un successore, non avrebbe eletto altri fuorché Lorenzo] (199). These two accounts describe the hierarchical association between Lorenzo and Alessandro as highly instrumental. More specifically, they claim that Lorenzo successfully exploited the Duke's rampant pursuit of pleasure in order to insinuate himself into his superior's good graces. By contrast, Dagoucin's characterization of the Duke and the Gentleman shifts the rhetoric used to describe their relationship away from that of servant–master or courtier–prince to that of perfect friendship. But since the association between the men nonetheless remains instrumental, or so I argue, far from offering an accurate representation of their fictional relationship, the shift in linguistic registers instead provides the occasion for an analysis of the strategic deployment of the rhetoric of friendship to disguise something else.[6]

---

[5]   An exception is Bernardo Sanctio's 13 January letter to Marino Caracciolo, the imperial governor of Milan. Dated a week after the death of Alessandro, Sanctio's missive, which offers the most developed epistolary account of the assassination, explains that the Duke was Lorenzo's "cousin and very close friend" [cugino et molto amico strecto] (32r). For discussions of this letter and partial transcriptions, see Jed 111–2 and Ferrai 255–6.

[6]   On the use of the language of friendship to describe patronage relationships and other hierarchical relationships, see Hutson as well as Langer *Perfect Friendship* 199–221. See also Shannon, who addresses the constative or poetic (in the etymological sense of the

The first element I present in my contention that the two men are not represented as ideal friends, despite the language of friendship used by the narrator's exposition and by the men themselves, occurs early in Novella 12 and consists of one of Marguerite de Navarre's most subtle borrowings from the historical record. Dagoucin first explains that about ten years previously in Florence there was a Medici Duke who had married "Madame Marguerite, bastard daughter of the Emperor" [Madame Marguerite, fille bastarde de l'Empereur] (90). This brief contextualization gestures at a complex political situation. In 1527, a revolt in Florence had led to the eviction of the Medici. After a lengthy siege, the imperial armies of Charles V returned the Medici to power in Florence in 1530 with Alessandro as the ruler of the city. The historical Alessandro's marriage to Marguerite of Austria, the natural daughter of Charles V, was one of the Emperor's requirements for supporting the Duke against those who purported to want to return Florence to some sort of popular rule.[7] In the *Heptaméron*, Marguerite has Dagoucin specify about the Duke's wife that:

> pour ce qu'elle estoit si jeune, qu'il ne luy estoit licite de coucher avecq elle, actendant son aage plus meur, la traicta fort doulcement; car pour l'espargner, fut amoureux de quelques autres dames de la ville que la nuict il alloit veoir, tandis que sa femme dormoit.

> [because she was so young that he was not permitted to sleep with her until she had reached a more mature age, he treated her with great tenderness; for in order to spare her, he became the lover of some other ladies of the city whom he would visit during the night while his wife slept.] (90)

This account shares two key elements with the reports found in the Florentine chronicles, which state (1) that Alessandro's wife was too young for the marriage to be consummated and (2) that Alessandro was a debauched pleasure seeker. Concerning this second point, Paolo Giovio writes of Alessandro in his *Istorie del suo Tempo* that:

> l'animo suo per leggierezza giovenile era talmente inclinato ... ne piaceri amorosi, che gli veniva a noia la compagnia della nuova moglie, et perciò si credeva ch'egli havesse posto da parte la cura dell'honore, della sanità, &

---

word) function of the rhetoric of friendship to negotiate relations of hierarchy. For another account of a roughly contemporaneous misleading deployment of the language of perfect friendship, see the discussion of the 1532 *Orlando Furioso* in Schachter 2000.

[7]   On the relevant Florentine history, in addition to the chroniclers identified above, see Stephens; Roth. On Charles V, see Knecht; Blockmans. Salient remarks are also found in Jed.

finalmente della vita; percioche egli … si dilettava sempre & fuor di modo di nuovi stupri e adulterii.

[because of youthful frivolity, his soul was so inclined … towards the pleasures of love, that the company of his new wife bored him, therefore it was thought that he had put aside all care for honor, health, and finally for life, because he … always and beyond all measure took pleasure in new sexual violations and adulterous affairs.] (100v)

Filippo de' Nerli's account adds a particularly damning detail to this picture of a dissolute leader. After his marriage to the Emperor's daughter, "since it seemed to the Duke that he had so well stabilized his state, he turned entirely to pleasures" [parendo al Duca d'aver tanto bene stabilito lo stato suo, si volse tutto a' piaceri] (238). In other words, according to Nerli, having cemented the support of Charles V with his marriage to Marguerite of Austria, Alessandro subsequently felt secure enough in his rule to pursue his sexual predation with abandon. Whereas according to Aristotle "a tyrant studies his own advantage, a king that of his subjects" (*Nic. Eth.* trans. Rackham VIII.x.2), Alessandro so ardently pursued his desires "that he came to acquire many more enemies than he usually had, and furthermore he added greatly to the ill will towards himself in the eyes of the public beyond that which he normally had" [che ne venne a procurarsi molti più nemici, che per ordinario non aveva, e se gli aggiugneva tuttavia maggiormente mala grazia nel cospetto universale oltre a quella che avea … per l'ordinario] (238). In short, Nerli represents Alessandro as a dissolute tyrant exploiting his people. This historical image of Alessandro radically contravenes the ideals established for a Renaissance ruler. Early modern treatises on the education of princes emphasize the need for self-control (Erasmus, Budé). Moreover, scandalous behavior of the sort ascribed to Alessandro was frequently cited in fifteenth- and sixteenth-century Italy to explain and even sometimes to justify tyrannicide (Villard 72–144).

In the *Heptaméron*, Dagoucin seems to offer a more positive view of the Duke's comportment by approving of his treatment of his young wife. The negative dimension found in the historical accounts, however, remains in the *Heptaméron*, albeit more subtly. While male codes of conduct during the period may not have required a husband's fidelity, sleeping with other women could not be considered treating one's wife "doulcement" and adultery was certainly not virtuous, despite what Dagoucin—elsewhere the champion of neo-Platonic love!—seems to imply.[8] Moreover, the Duke doesn't have only one beloved, which would at least correspond to the conventions of courtly love and romance with which Marguerite

---

[8]   For a concise summary of bibliography on Dagoucin, see Reeser. For an argument that adultery is indeed accepted in the world of the *Heptaméron*, see Morrison 63.

is often playing, but "quelques autres dames."[9] The slip from obligation ("he was not permitted to sleep with her") to chivalry ("in order to spare her") as license for the Duke's questionable behavior—a chivalry already belied by his numerous paramours—is but the first of many forms of dubious justification in the novella. Together, these details suggest that the Duke is not a virtuous man, an impression subsequently corroborated by other elements in the novella.

If I am right that the Duke is not meant to be seen as virtuous, then the Gentleman's friendship with him would, according to the letter of the friendship tradition, become suspect. Aristotle emphasizes that "The perfect form of friendship is that between the good, and those who resemble each other in virtue" (VIII.iii.6). In a similar vein, in his *De amicitia*, Cicero insists that friendship can exist only between good men (*Laelius,* eds Gould and Whitely §5). And during a sustained discussion about friendship in Baldassar Castiglione's *Il Cortegiano*, a text written and circulating during Marguerite de Navarre's lifetime, the character Federico observes succinctly that "the friendship of the wicked isn't friendship" [l'amicizia de' mali non è amicizia].[10] Such commonplaces are repeated over and over in friendship literature.

However the relationship between the two men is construed, its original disposition will be stressed to the breaking point when the Duke develops an inopportune—though in a sense also apt—desire for the Gentleman's sister. Directly after the passage recounting the Duke's amorous exploits cited above, Dagoucin expresses the Duke's desire for the sister as follows:

> Entre autres, le fut [=fut amoureux] d'une fort belle, saige et honneste dame, laquelle estoit seur d'un gentil homme que le duc aymoit comme luy-mesme, et auquel il donnoit tant d'autorité en sa maison, que sa parolle estoit obeye et craincte comme celle du duc.

> [He was in love with, among others, a very beautiful, wise and honest lady, who was the sister of a Gentleman loved by the Duke as he loved himself. To this man he had given so much authority in his household that his word was obeyed and feared like that of the Duke.] (90)

Because there is significant debate in the historical record about the identity of the woman Alessandro thought he was to meet on the night of his death, Marguerite's

---

[9]   For a related discussion about courtly love, romance and chastity in *Heptaméron* 10, see Langer, *Perfect Friendship* 120–22.

[10]   I use the *Cortegiano* as a source of standard ideas about friendship and courtiership not because I am arguing for direct influence but because it is a repository of widely available commonplaces. That said, Noakes has made a compelling case for the importance of Castiglione's book for Marguerite's *Heptaméron*. See also Reynolds. On the reception of the *Cortegiano*, see Burke.

focus on the sister to the exclusion of other possibilities is worthy of particular attention.[11] The close proximity of the Duke's expression of love for the Gentleman and his love for the Gentleman's sister suggests that the two loves are not unrelated. Indeed, it is tempting to say that the Duke desires the Gentleman's sister precisely because of whose sister she is.

Desire in the *Heptaméron* is almost always produced by social hierarchy. It reveals class aspiration when a social inferior aggressively pursues or rapes a woman of a higher class or, more infrequently, an abuse of power when a superior violates a social inferior. Not only does love or erotic desire function as the fiction that covers over a will to power; far more provocatively, Marguerite sometimes seems to suggest that terrestrial desire is generated by the will to power.[12] Since women's adultery and sex out of wedlock were generally a matter of great concern to their immediate male relatives, the Duke's desire for the sister and the way in which he wants to act on it would constitute a direct affront to the Gentleman.[13] In the world of the *Heptaméron* it would also offer a way for the Duke to assert his authority over his subordinate. A motivation for this affront can perhaps be found in the very language indicating the extent of the intimacy between the Duke and the Gentleman. When Dagoucin asserts that the Duke loved the Gentleman "as he loved himself" and that "his word was obeyed and feared like that of the Duke," he evokes the commonplace that the friend is another self. Particularly when we recall the conclusion to the novella, however, the indication that the Gentleman's authority extended into the Duke's household and that his commands were fearfully followed already intimates a potential menace to the Duke from his putative friend.[14]

---

[11]   Few sources identify the woman in question as Lorenzo's sister. In Varchi's *Storia Fiorentina* and Segni's *Istorie Fiorentine*, Alessandro desires an aunt of Lorenzo's, while Nerli specifies only that she was "a woman beloved by them whom the Duke greatly desired to have" [una loro inamorata, che il Duca aveva molto desiderato d'avere] (241). Sanctio writes that the Duke used Lorenzo "as a procurer to obtain a certain gentlewoman. Some say a nun, others a widowed sister of the said Lorenzo" [per mezano per ottener' una certa gentildona. Altri dicono una Monicha. Altri una sorella vidua de dicto Lorenzo] (32r).

[12]   For a related discussion, see Hutson 79.

[13]   Vigarello 38–57. For a classic discussion of rape in the medieval period that includes discussions of how rape is a crime against men, see Gravdal. Cholakian offers an influential if contested account of rape in the *Heptaméron*. For a wide-ranging account of the implications of the imperative to police women's bodies in early modern France, see LaGuardia.

[14]   A danger in my analysis here is that it effectively erases women. It is therefore worth recalling that the novella opens with the mention of Marguerite of Austria whereas the Gentleman and the Duke remain nameless. It is through Marguerite de Navarre's designation of a historical woman who is married at a young age for political reasons that she provides the reader the context for the story Dagoucin will recount. This fact may serve to remind us of the costs paid by women exchanged for political reasons within Marguerite's world while the tale the fact serves to anchor depicts more abstractly the

Just as the language of friendship suffuses Dagoucin's initial description of the Duke's desire for the sister, so too it permeates the conversation in which the Duke expresses his longing to the Gentleman. This occurs explicitly at several points, including in the following preamble to the shocking request:

> « S'il y avoit chose en ce monde, mon amy, que je ne voulsisse faire pour vous, je craindrois à vous declarer ma fantaisye, et encore plus à vous prier m'y estre aydant. Mais je vous porte tant d'amour, que, si j'avois femme, mere ou fille qui peust servir à saulver vostre vie, je les y emploirois, plustot que de vous laisser mourir en torment; et j'estime que l'amour que vous me portez est reciproque à la mienne; et que si moy, qui suys vostre maistre, vous portois telle affection, que pour le moins ne le sçauriez porter moindre. »

> [(If there were anything in this world, my friend, that I would not do for you, I would be afraid of declaring my yearning, and even more so of asking you to help me. But I hold for you such love that, if I had wife, mother or daughter who could serve to save your life, I would use them, rather than leaving you to die in torment. And I judge that the love that you hold for me is reciprocal to mine, and that if I, who am your master, hold you in such affection, that at the very least yours could not be lesser.)] (90)

At the outset of Novella 12, the language of friendship is evoked to mask both the instrumental and the hierarchical nature of the relationship between the Duke and the Gentleman. In arguing that the Gentleman should have at least as much affection for the Duke as the Duke has for the Gentleman because the Duke is the Gentleman's superior, the Duke continues to draw on the rhetoric of friendship while dropping the egalitarian facade. When there is a difference in station between friends, Aristotle emphasizes that "The affection rendered in these various unequal friendships should also be proportionate: the better of the two parties, for instance … should receive more affection than he bestows" (VIII.vii.2; see also VIII.xi.6). The Duke evokes a similar logic in his attempt to convince the Gentleman to help him accomplish his desire.

When the Gentleman responds affirmatively to the Duke's entreaties—crucially, before he knows exactly *whom* or *what* his master wants—he also uses the rhetoric of friendship while similarly acknowledging hierarchy:

---

homosocial instrumentalization of the absent sister. On Marguerite de Navarre's implicit meditations in the *Heptaméron* on the political deployment of her own daughter, Jeanne d'Albret, who was married the age of 13 to Guillaume de Clèves, see Freccero "Marguerite de Navarre." For another consideration of how Marguerite de Navarre's engagement with history foregrounds questions of gender, see Freccero "Rewriting the Rhetoric of Desire."

« Monsieur, je suis vostre creature; tout le bien et l'honneur que j'ay en ce monde vient de vous: vous pouvez parler à moy comme à vostre ame, estant seur que ce qui sera en ma puissance est en vos mains. »

["My Lord, I am your creature. All the good and the honor I have in this world come from you. You can speak to me as you speak to your own soul, sure that whatever is within my power to do will be in your hands."] (91)

By specifying that the Duke can speak to him as to his own soul, the Gentleman evokes the commonplace that friends share but one soul between them and his suggestion that "whatever is within my power to do will be in your hands" is reminiscent of the idea that a friend, as another self, can do for his friend something the friend cannot himself accomplish (Aristotle, *Nic. Eth.* trans Rackham IX.ix.1). Thus, we see that the Duke speaks to the Gentleman using the language of friendship, even if it sounds almost contractual, and the Gentleman responds in a similar register. But what has basically been said is "I need you to do something exceptional for me" and "You can ask anything of me and I will do it."

The Gentleman's unconditional offer of assistance is both imprudent and telling. It is imprudent because the Duke next explains that it is the Gentleman's sister whom he desires. Proclaiming that he will die if he does not have her, the Duke asks the Gentleman to help him realize this desire. The Gentleman is shocked and seeks to dissuade the Duke, but without success:

Le frere, qui aymoit sa seur et l'honneur de sa maison plus que le plaisir du duc, luy voulut faire quelque remonstrance, luy suppliant en tous autres endroictz l'employer, hormys en une chose si cruelle à luy. Le duc luy respondit par une grande fureur: « Or bien, puisque je ne treuve en vous nulle amityé, je sçay que j'ay à faire. » Le gentil homme, congnoissant la cruauté de son maitre, eut craincte et luy dist: « Mon seigneur, puis qu'il vous plaist, je parleray à elle et vous diray sa reponse. » Le duc luy respondit, en se departant: « Si vous aymez ma vie, aussi feray-je la vostre. »

[The brother, who loved his sister and the honor of his house more than the pleasure of the Duke, wanted to reproach him, begging him to employ him in any way whatsoever except in a thing that would be so cruel to him. The Duke replied with great rage: "Very well, since I find no friendship in you, I know what I have to do." The Gentleman, knowing the cruelty of his master, was afraid and said to him: "My lord, since it pleases you, I will speak with her and give you her answer." The Duke responded: "If you love my life, I will do the same with yours."] (91)

Despite the Gentleman's promise of assistance in all things, he now balks at the Duke's specific request but still offers to help "in any way whatsoever except in a thing that would be so cruel to him." The Gentleman's willingness to do anything for the Duke except deliver his sister, despite knowing "the cruelty of his master," is particularly telling because cruelty was linked in antiquity and in medieval and early modern Europe with tyranny and the illegitimate exercise of power (Baker 460; Baraz).

The Gentleman's continued willingness to help the Duke should make us reflect on an earlier statement, found at the opening of Dagoucin's tale and cited above, that the Gentleman's word is "obeyed and feared like that of the Duke." The historical record asserts repeatedly that Lorenzo was instrumental—and ruthless—in facilitating his master's sexual exploits. We are not provided with this information in Marguerite's account of the Gentleman, although we might take his willingness to do anything for his master, despite the fact that he knows his master to be a vicious man, as evidence that he is meant to be seen as serving a similar role. Treatises on friendship and on courtiership both emphasize that it is wrong to do a wicked deed, whether for a friend (*Laelius,* eds Gould and Whiteley §37) or for a prince (Castiglione III.xxxiii). Moreover, Cicero insists that a friend shouldn't ask for anything dishonorable to begin with. When first encountered, the phrase underscoring that the Gentleman's word is feared like that of the Duke seems to establish the degree to which they are indeed friends. But, in retrospect, its threatening intimations provide an early hint that neither the Duke nor the Gentleman is virtuous.

Honor, if not virtue, comes to the fore when the Gentleman reflects on the Duke's request, as does his awareness that he has his own interests apart from those of the Duke:

> D'un costé, luy venoit au devant l'obligation qu'il devoit à son maistre, les biens et les honneurs qu'il avoit receuz de luy; de l'autre costé, l'honneur de sa maison, l'honnesteté et chasteté de sa seur, qu'il sçavoit bien jamais ne se consentir à telle meschanceté, si par sa tromperie elle n'estoit prinse ou par force; chose si estrange que à jamays luy et les siens en seroient diffamez.

> [On the one hand, the obligation he owed his master came before him, the goods and the honors that he had received from him. On the other hand, the honor of his house and the honesty and chastity of his sister, who, he knew, would never consent to such wickedness unless she were taken by force. This was a thing so out of the ordinary that he and his family would be forever slandered on account of it.] (91)

A series of lexical slippages in this passage reveals the instrumental logic underlying the mystifying language deployed by the Duke and the Gentleman. Whereas the Gentleman earlier suggested to the Duke that all his *honneur* (in the singular) came from the Duke, here he opposes *honneurs* (in the plural) with *honneur* (in the singular). As with the English cognates, the opposition is between a certain social recognition of virtue linked to a code of behavior (indicated by the singular form *honneur*) and concrete, perhaps even material manifestations of recognition from an official authority (represented by the plural form *honneurs*). Similarly, whereas he had earlier described his *bien* (good) as coming from the Duke, here he invokes *biens* (goods). That he would originally state that his *honneur* and his *bien* came from the Duke, only later to clarify to himself in his own internal deliberations that he had received *honneurs* and *biens* from the Duke, demonstrates how the language of virtue functions in his discourse as a cover for utilitarian exchange.

The passage also suggests that the Gentleman does not respect the "honnesteté et chasteté" of his sister as positive attributes so much as consider them obstacles to be taken into consideration—the problem isn't that the Duke wants to sleep with his sister; it is that the sister is so virtuous she will refuse the Duke. The Gentleman's reasons for not forcing his sister to accept the Duke seem to have nothing to do with his sentiments for her or with any abstract notion of personal duty or honor; rather, his concern is that he and his family would be defamed because of the affair if she were tricked or forced into it against her will. The struggle over the absent sister in the first part of Novella 12 thus reveals the unsavory character of Duke and Gentleman alike while depicting the disintegration of the illusion of perfect friendship when interests are no longer coterminous.

Deceit and Coercion in the Rhetorics of Friendship and Love

Once the Gentleman has decided that it is no longer in his best interest to serve the Duke, he immediately finds a way to glorify his betrayal with further forms of dubious rationalization:

> Si print conclusion de ce different, qu'il aymoit mieulx mourir que faire ung si meschant tour à sa seur, l'une des plus femmes de bien qui fust en toute l'Italie; mais que plustot debvoit delivrer sa patrye d'un tel tyran, qui par force vouloit mettre une telle tache en sa maison; car il tenoit tout asseuré que, sans faire mourir le duc, la vie de luy et des siens n'estoit pas asseurée.

> [So he decided based on this conflict that he preferred to die than to cause harm to his sister, one of the best women to be found in all of Italy, and that he should rather deliver his country from such a tyrant, who by force desired to stain his house. For he was certain that without the death of the Duke, his life and the lives of his family were not safe.] (91–2)

Suddenly, the sister's virtue is paramount, the Duke the Gentleman has so ably served is recognized as a tyrant, and the decision to assassinate him likened to tyrannicide. Although the self-aggrandizing rhetoric about delivering his country from a tyrant might seem to come out of nowhere, an opening has been prepared for it by the earlier invocations of the language of friendship, for, as Ferguson and Reeser both note in their studies of Novella 12, there is a strong classical tradition linking friendship and political freedom.[15]

After murdering the Duke, the Gentleman wants to continue the job of "liberating" Florence by purging the city of those closest to the tyrant:

> Et, quand il se veid victorieux de son grand ennemy, par la mort duquel il pensoit mettre en liberté la chose publicque, se pensa que son euvre seroit imparfaict, s'il n'en faisoit autant à cinq ou six de ceulx qui estoient les prochains au duc.

> [And when he saw himself victorious over his great enemy, by whose death he thought to liberate the republic, he considered that his work would remain unfinished if he did not do the same to five or six of those who were closest to the Duke.] (93)

The Gentleman's purported desire to rescue "la chose publicque" from the man he has only just begun to characterize as a tyrant serves to justify his own strategy for extricating himself from an otherwise untenable situation. Before the request that he furnish the Duke his own sister, the Gentleman had been entirely happy to facilitate his master's depredations and reap the rewards of such services. Indeed, he seems to have forgotten that he himself was the closest of the Duke's servants (Johnson, *Two True Friends* 92). Marguerite has cleverly taken what the historical record depicts as two competing accounts of Lorenzo's motivation for killing Alessandro—a woman's honor and the liberation of Florence—and presented them instead as sequential self-justifications.

When at the end of the novella the storytellers debate the merits of the Gentleman's actions, they express strong differences of opinion along gendered lines. Whereas the women describe the Gentleman as having acted as a virtuous citizen in liberating his *patrie* while rescuing his sister, the men emphasize that he is a disloyal servant (95). In representing this difference, Marguerite again largely follows the historical record. Nerli emphasizes that even if Lorenzo had murdered the Duke in order to rescue the city, "it is not possible to excuse him or exculpate him since he used treachery and was a traitor, being as he was fed by the Duke" [perchè non si potrebbe scusarlo, nè scolparlo dell'avere usato tradimento

---

[15]   On the politics of friendship in Renaissance France, see Macphail. There is an intriguing parallel between Novella 12 and the story of the Athenian tyrannicides Aristogiton and Harmodius. In some accounts, the lovers are depicted as martyrs for freedom; in others, their actions are represented as motivated by personal jealousy and concern about the treatment of Harmodius's sister. See Jed and more generally Schachter *Voluntary Servitude* 32–3.

e dell'essere stato traditore, essendo, com'era, provvisionato dal Duca] (242). Representing the position of those who celebrated Lorenzo's actions, Segni notes that he was called "the FLORENTINE BRUTUS" [il BRUTO FIORENTINO] (227) by Filippo Strozzi. Similar reflections can be found in other historical records from the period.[16]

Is it possible to discern Marguerite's position on this debate from within the notoriously dialogic text of the *Heptaméron*? Several careful readers of the story have suggested that a rare intervention of the narrator of the *Heptaméron* (and not Dagoucin, the narrator of this particular novella) supports the position taken by the men: "les dames, selon leur coustume, parloient autant par passion que par raison" [the ladies, as is their wont, spoke as much from passion as reason] (95) (Ferguson 104; Morrison 62). I submit, however, that this statement is ambivalent, for immediately after the narrator's observation Dagoucin offers a moral for the story that indicates the less-than-rational nature of some men:

« Pour Dieu, mes dames, ne prenez poinct querelle d'une chose desja passée; mais gardez que voz beaultez ne facent poinct faire de plus cruels meurdres que celluy que j'ay compté. »

["For the sake of God, my ladies, do not argue over an event already passed, but take care that your beauty is not the cause of yet more cruel murders than that which I have just recounted."] (95)

Recapitulating in a different register a hotly contested claim he made in Day 1 of the *Heptaméron*, namely that men can die from love, Dagoucin's interruption of the intense disagreement over the merits of the Gentleman's action implies that *women* are to blame when men die because of love. Occurring shortly after the passage proclaiming that women are motivated by passion rather than reason, this claim ironically insinuates that it is *men* who are irrational by calling attention to their potentially overly passionate natures. I would not therefore want to insist that Marguerite supports the Gentleman's actions, but I would like to leave open the possibility that she condemns both men.

According to Morrison, Dagoucin's suggestion that the ladies "take care that [their] beauty is not the cause of yet more cruel murders" flatters them (62); I propose instead that it is part of a more sinister logic of persuasion in the text. Dagoucin's interruption instigates another argument, this one about whether uncooperative women are indeed responsible for the deaths of the men who love them. This dispute quickly segues into yet another debate, now about whether men's proclamations during courtship can be taken at face value or must be seen, like the claim that a man is dying of unrequited love, as a seduction strategy.

---

[16] See also Jed. On the figure of Brutus in humanist thought, see Piccolomini. He addresses Lorenzo de' Medici at some length (79–101).

As Ennasuite observes, men always "'begin with honor and conclude with the opposite'" [« commencent par l'honneur et finissent par le contraire »] (96) and Saffredent remarks that "'we cover our devil with the most handsome angel we can find. And, under that covering, before it can be recognized, we receive a great deal of warm welcome'" [« nous couvrons nostre diable du plus bel ange que nous pouvons trouver. Et, soubz ceste couverture, avant que d'estre congneuz, recepvons beaucoup de bonnes cheres »] (96). In other words, the storytellers' debate about whether men die of love becomes an explicit discussion about the deceptive strategies men use when they seek to seduce women, one of which would be the threat of their death from love.

The discussion seems to have wandered far from the novella that originally instigated it, but I propose that the storytellers' concern with persuasive rhetoric and love actually serves as a commentary on the friendship between the Duke and the Gentleman. Numerous resonances suggest such a link. Most obviously, the Duke employs the very logic invoked by Dagoucin and debated by the storytellers to compel the Gentleman to help him:

> le duc commença à luy declairer l'amour qu'il portoit à sa seur, qui estoit si grande et si forte, que, si par son moyen n'en avoir la jouissance, il ne voyait pas qu'il peust vivre longuement.

> [the Duke began to declare to the Gentleman the love that he had for his sister, which was so great and so strong that, if by means of him the Duke could not take his pleasure with her, he did not see how he could live for long.] (91)

The Duke's insistence that his desire is such that he will die of it if he doesn't have sex with the sister seeks to produce assent in a way analogous to the ploys of lovers discussed by the storytellers, except that the Duke is trying to convince the Gentleman to help him acquire a woman rather than directly cajoling his beloved into sleeping with him.[17] *Mutatis mutandis*, the storytellers' insight into the comportment of men in love—namely that they deceive, that they deploy the trappings of honor in their speech to acquire dishonorable things, and that they disguise their bad intentions under cover of good—is applicable to the tale that initiated the seemingly meandering discussion. Juxtaposing the storytellers' conversation and the tale highlights the extent to which the Duke and the Gentleman deploy rhetorics of persuasion and self-justification to disguise their vicious natures, rhetorics that successfully seduce some of the storytellers but which, I am arguing, are on display for the reader's more critical assessment.

---

[17]   This slippage points to both the homosocial and the ironic dimensions of the story since the Duke will end up in bed with the naked-sword-bearing Gentleman ["une espée toute nue"] (93) rather than the Gentleman's sister and because his desire ultimately does prove fatal, if not for the reason he named.

Conclusion

The discussion of the storytellers also connects the novella's specific concern with male friendship to the preoccupations of the collection as a whole. Elsewhere in the *Heptaméron*, Marguerite rehearses the ability of the rhetoric of love to enable and seemingly to ennoble what will ultimately be revealed as the self-interested pursuit of an inappropriate object. In Novella 10 of the *Heptaméron*, Marguerite depicts the misapplication of the language of classical friendship within the rhetorical confines of a doomed relationship between an ambitious, deceptive gentleman and a naïve, virtuous daughter of a countess (Langer 115–43). In Novella 12, she turns her attention to the abuse of the rhetoric of friendship to facilitate and disguise a utilitarian and hierarchical relationship between two wicked men. We have seen how the Duke and, to a lesser extent, the Gentleman deploy the language of perfect friendship to describe their relationship, and how in the Duke's mouth the very rhetoric of friendship can become not only coercive but even threatening. Furthermore, the Gentleman's self-aggrandizing claim to be saving Florence from a tyrant shows how fickle a "friend" he is while perhaps ironically evoking a long tradition of friends who are also freedom fighters. Cleverly inverting the friendship tradition, Marguerite depicts the Duke and the Gentleman as alike in vice rather than in virtue, thereby condemning both the tyrannical ruler and the treacherous servant and representing the capacity of friendship to mystify, deceive, and coerce.

Chapter 10

"To plainness is honour bound": Deceptive Friendship in *King Lear*

Wendy Olmsted

When Cordelia refuses to flatter King Lear, he makes her "a stranger ... forever" (*King Lear* 1.1.109), as pitied as the "barbarous Scythian, or he that makes his generation messes / To gorge his appetite" (1.1.110–12).[1] "Friend" means in opposition to stranger and enemy. Lear's "friends" fulfill his fantasies of adulation; those who do not are totally Other, as alien as cannibals. The cannibal is most barbaric, because he changes the Other into himself. Ironically, it is Lear who aims to assimilate wholly or reject absolutely. In bifurcating his social world, he destroys the deliberative space and freedom where friendships live.

King Lear dramatizes the costs of losing the space where friends speak freely. Recent scholarship has showed how closely Renaissance friendship depends on honest speech (Shannon 23, 52; Olmsted 14). But when Cordelia uses the frank speech of a friend to reject "that glib and oily art / To speak and purpose not" practiced by her sisters (1.1.219–20), Lear casts her out. And when Kent opposes the exile of Cordelia, claiming "To plainness honour's bound, / When majesty falls to folly" (1.1.142–3), Lear banishes him and with him the principle of speaking truth (see Strier, *Resistant* 182–5; Shannon 205, 209). *King Lear* interrogates the consequences for friendship when social ties are broken and the commonwealth becomes a tyranny. Friendship becomes a risky challenge and plain speech fails or endangers others. Characters must find other resources such as disguise to pursue ethical friendships. And where Cicero insists that friendship should not be founded on advantage, because "friendship springs rather from [virtuous] nature than from need, and from an inclination of the soul ... rather than from calculation of profit" (*De amicitia* trans. Falconer 8.27), *King Lear* explores friendship as a social instrument adaptable to the cultivation of ethical friendships.

The nightmare world that Lear unleashes requires new modes of counsel and new ways to establish friendships, but they are cognitively challenging. Where Cicero points out the need to distinguish "a flatterer". . . from "a true friend," and urges "a watchful care against the deep and crafty one lest he steal upon

---

[1]   Halio, Folio *King Lear*. I also consulted Warren *Parallel*, Bevington, and Halio *Quarto*, and I modernized spellings of proper names. I am grateful to David Bevington, Daniel Lochman, Lorna Hutson, and Maritere Lopez for searching comments on an early draft, but I take responsibility for any mistakes in this one.

us unawares" (26.99), *King Lear* and other later friendship writings articulate a prudential perceptual practice to discern signs and tokens of civil conversation in the "storms" where friendship and enmity live. It makes discriminating the friend from the enemy a perilous enterprise. Even audiences may be misled when evil characters offer "wise" humanist counsel and true friends resort to deception.

The play draws on, extends, and revises ideals expressed in classical and Renaissance friendship writings, especially Cicero's *De amicitia*. Cicero's text decries hypocrisy because "it pollutes truth" (25.92), but later writers struggle with the practice of diagnosing it. Stephano Guazzo's *The Civile Conversation* (1574, Eng. trans. 1581) illuminates the need for prudence when discerning the dangers and uncertainties of friendship. Anniball, the physician and advice-giving friend, likens the knowledge of civil (friendly) conversation and "uncivile" (flattering) conversation to judgment about weather conditions:

> As marriners, before all other thinges, learne to know the signes and tokens of windes and storms ... and al other things any way contrarie or hindersome to navigation, to the ende that foreseeing the imminent dangers, they may know how to avoide them, and to make choice of fit times and places prosperously to sayle in: so we, being desirous to understand thorowly which is the civile conversation, to the intent to follow it, must principally seeke to know which is the uncivile and blameful conversation, to the intent to flee it. (56)

Those seeking friendship need to judge signs and tokens of civil conversation. This search is more a risk-taking adventure that requires foresight than something achieved by a socially instituted rite between virtuous men of high birth (Hutson 12). Detractors and other false friends are as difficult to diagnose as the signs of winds and storms (Hutson 6). For similar reasons, Plutarch's *The philosophie, commonlie called, the morals written by the learned philosopher Plutarch of Chaeronea*, translated by Philemon Holland into English (1603) and brought to critical attention by Laurie Shannon (47–8), stresses the need to recognize the flatterer as a person and not just as a concept. Holland argues that Plutarch paints the deceiver in "his colours, shewing the very draught & lineaments" which may "direct us to the knowledge of him" (83). The metaphor of drawing and painting suggests that the viewer of the portrait comes to see and know the changeable person. The flatterer is hard to see, for he is, above all, changeable, having no anchor in virtue (88).

Thus, Plutarch seeks a remedy for deception. Holland comments, "[Plutarch] describeth with what maner of eie, and eare we ought to see and heare those that procure our good" (84). The *way* we see or hear influences our perceptions and our judgments. Plutarch presents diagnostic signs for recognizing dangers, signs that require perceptive attention over time. The flatterer, for example,

> is so apt to deceive folke, and lieth hidden under the likenesse of a friend; our part it is, by unfolding the differences that are so hidden, to turne him out of

his making habit, and being despoiled of those colours and habilements that he borroweth of others, for want of his owne … to lay him naked and open to the eie. (87)

The word "unfold" means "to disclose or reveal by statement or exposition; to explain or make clear" (*OED* 2). Cordelia uses the word "unfold" in response to Goneril's charge that she has "obedience scanted" (1.1.272): "Time shall unfold what plighted cunning hides; / Who covers faults, at last with shame derides" (1.1.274–5). Cordelia's use of "unfold" suggests a gradual, partial disclosure in which time plays an indispensable role. Contingency, change, and surprise may be involved; *King Lear* unfolds them through time and the action of the play.

The contrast between *King Lear*'s exemplarity and that deployed in the 1606 *King Leir* highlights the former's distinctive creation of a temporal space for the audience's deliberation and judgment. *King Leir* makes Goneril and Regan static *illustrations* of flattery and slander. The characters diagnose their own unacceptable tactics to make the play's didactic message as clear as possible. For example, after Leir has left them to meet the French king, Goneril brags about her slanderous speech: "Well, after him Ile send such thunderclaps, / Of slaunder, scandal, and invented tales, / That all the blame shall be remov'd from me, / And unperceiv'd rebound upon himselfe" (D 3, lines 983–6). She wants others to think she has treated Lear well and that his faults have caused the conflict between them. Statement and implication coincide. But Goneril and Regan's words in *King Lear* sound like a display of good judgment; the implications of their statements unfold through time. The audience's deliberations make the connections between statement, meaning, and moral consequences. For example, Goneril comments, "You see how full of changes his [Lear's] age is; the observation we have made of it hath not been little. He always loved our sister most, and with what poor judgement he hath now cast her off appears too grossly." And Regan answers, "'Tis the infirmity of his age; yet he hath ever but slenderly known himself" (1.1.280–85). In deploring his (alleged) change of character and lack of self-knowledge, Goneril and Regan sound like humanist counselors, and critics have debated whether they are correct about Lear's behavior. But their malicious intentions emerge as their language becomes injurious and bitter. Eventually their use of seemingly wise judgments as grounds for seizing authority from their father becomes clear. It seems frank speech does not guarantee friendship or good counsel.

The discourse of friendship can be as misleading as the discourse of counsel. Consider Gloucester. Grief-stricken and enraged that his eldest son Edgar wishes (as he thinks) to kill him, he confides in Cornwall and Regan. Using the discourse of friendship, Cornwall praises Edmund: "For you, Edmond, / Whose virtue and obedience doth this instant / So much commend itself, you shall be ours; / Natures of such deep trust we shall much need; / You we first seize on" (2.1.111–6). Cornwall's words ("virtue, obedience, and trust") could have been spoken by the good humanist king who seeks a friend's counsel. Regan's words are warmer, more understanding, and more expressive of her wish for an old friend's counsel: "Our good old friend, / Lay comforts to your bosom and bestow / Your needful counsel to our businesses, / Which craves the instant use" (2.1.125–8). Cornwall and Regan sound like friends when they comfort Gloucester's sorrow at his son's betrayal, but soon they brand Gloucester as a traitor. Yet, even when he has been bound, Gloucester addresses the others as "good my friends" and tells them to "consider / You are my guests. Do me no foul play, friends" (3.7.30–31). He assumes that the social relationships of ruler–earl and host–guest will by themselves produce loyal friendship.

King Lear makes friendship a contested category, going beyond Cicero, Plutarch, and Guazzo to produce a searching inquiry into the intersection (or lack of it) between Ciceronian virtuous friendship and social efficacy. It makes the tension between friendship understood as a social instrumentality and as ethical relationship an object of deliberative exploration and judgment. In the Renaissance, family members, dukes and servants, men and women could be political or useful friends, and their relationships did not need to be based primarily in virtue. In one sense, Lawrence Stone argues, "friend" could refer to a loved one: "in 1628 Sir Fulke Greville arranged that the inscription on his tombstone should record that he had been 'friend to Sir Philip Sidney'" (97). The word could also refer to "someone who could help one on in life, with whom one could safely do business, or upon whom one was in some way dependent" (Stone 97; see Davis 19–20 for France). The category of friends included relatives, members of the household "such as a steward, chaplin or tutor, or a neighbour; or a political associate sharing a common party affiliation" (Stone 97).[2]

When adapted to fulfill socially agreed-upon goals, friendship can be efficacious and dependable. *King Lear* emphasizes the usefulness of friendship as a social instrument in its deploying the words "friend" and "friends." When letters damaging to Edmund come into Edgar's hands, he comments, "the letters may be my friends" (4.5.244–6), that is, his allies and helpmates. Gloucester uses the word "friend" in speaking to the Old Man (4.1.15) (whom he doesn't know), Kent (including times when Kent is in disguise) (2.2.135, 3.4.149), and Cornwall (3.7.31). When Gloucester calls Kent in disguise "friend," the word signifies good will but nothing more. The play thus situates friendship as a reciprocal social relationship that includes family members and allies as in Albany's words near the end of the play: "All friends shall taste / The wages of their virtue, and all foes / The cup of their deservings" (5.3.276–8). He believes that good leaders recognize the differences between friends and enemies by rewarding the first and punishing the second. But the ethical validity of rewards and punishments depends on friendship's meaning more than a temporary alliance formed to pursue individualistic self-interested goals.

---

[2]   Lorna Hutson illuminates friendship as a social institution in *King Lear* when she analyzes Cordelia's articulation of the limits of her bond to Lear "as a sign of gift-friendship between the houses of men" (8).

Judgments about friendships depend on the audience's ability to read social discourse as a sign by which to discriminate between purely self-serving friendship, friendship as a socially efficacious instrument, and virtuous friendship. When Regan calls Gloucester their "good old friend" and refers to his "needful counsel" (2.1.125, 127), she sounds just like a humanist ruler seeking advice from a virtuous friend. Regan, Goneril, and Cornwall also rely on Gloucester's friendship as a social instrumentality, and Regan expresses warmth at his help. But, of course, it turns out that he is their friend only when he supports their self-interest; their lack of belief in a shared social good makes friendship a means of exploitation. They use Gloucester rather than allowing him to be of use to them and assimilate him to themselves as an instrument of their desire. Analogously, Goneril's and Regan's praise of Lear at the beginning of the play fulfills his fantasy of adulation, assimilating them to him. But they are clever in using praise to manipulate him, assimilating him to them. Regan's hyperbolic words of love make Lear her ultimate good: "I am alone felicitate / In your dear highness' love" (1.1.70–71). Though her hypocrisy is obvious, the elder sister's use of praise to destroy Lear's identity is subtle.

The elder sister's praise and Lear's narcissism illuminate self-love and its solipsistic consequences. Speaking of their king and father as divine, Goneril and Regan treat him like Domitian in *The Civile Conversation*, who was "blinded" by "folly" and not afraid to be "called God" (Guazzo 81). Lear's expectations and the elder sisters' words create a fairytale fiction whose fragility escapes Lear's understanding. When the sisters raise him up through praise, they make him vulnerable to a fall. Understanding how flattery creates a cocoon of self-regard for Lear helps us grasp later why Caius's counsel fails to bring truth to Lear. Reality itself must penetrate Lear's delusion.

Goneril and Regan use humanist judgments cruelly as weapons to puncture his fantasy of adulation. They also cut the political, social, and familial ties that define his identity. For example, when Lear protests again the diminution of his followers, Goneril's reference to his "insolent retinue" and her insinuation that Lear eggs them on (*King Lear* 1.4.161) shock his belief that she is his daughter. But her formal words out of context might sound like good honest counsel: "I would you would make use of your good wisdom, / Whereof I know you are fraught, and put away / These dispositions, which of late transport you / From what you rightly are" (1.4.179–82). Urging good wisdom seems to be prudent counsel; but in speaking this way to him she reverses the hierarchical relation between them as daughter and father, and she dispenses with the deference due his status as a former king (Colie 197). Regan's words, wise in the abstract, cruel as addressed to King Lear, insult his self-respect and knowledge of himself to the point where Lear asks, "Does any here know me? This is not Lear: / Does Lear walk thus? Speak thus? Where are his eyes? / Either his notion weakens, his discernings / Are lethargied—Ha! Waking? 'Tis not so! / Who is it that can tell me who I am?" (1.4.185–9). Identity depends upon one's place in a social framework and Lear has become aware of the uncertainty of his. He can no longer be sure of his own "discernings." Goneril's speech shatters his identity indirectly so that the problem seems to be his.

Although he gradually becomes aware that his confusion arises partly from flattery, knowledge of the source does not heal his disorientation. Lear diagnoses the consequences of flattery for his sense of self: "They flattered me like a dog and told me I had the white hairs in my beard ere the black ones were there" (4.5.94–6). These words recall Plutarch's comment that a flatterer causes "a man to be … ignorant of the good and evill things that be in him" (Plutarch, *The philosophie* 84). And, reiterating Anniball's maxim that those "who hold up everie ones yeas and nayes … for their [own] advauntage, they are without question flatterers" (Guazzo 84), Lear recognizes what his elder daughters have done to him: "To say 'ay' and 'no' to everything that I said 'ay' and 'no' to was no good divinity" (4.5.96–7). Yet he still unconsciously depends on former social definitions of obligation, so that he is shocked and enraged when his daughters refuse him hospitality. Hospitality in the period was not a personal preference but a sacred obligation; violation of hospitality to one's father or king would have been unthinkable (Heal 2–6; Liebler 33–4). So Lear bleeds from the severing of his bonds; he is lost, not knowing who he is. Diagnosis does not mitigate his solipsism. For alternative remedies, we need to understand the role of Kent's disguise and Lear's feeling in disclosing truth.

But before moving on to the issue of disguise, I wish first to examine how Edmund assimilates Edgar and then Gloucester into a fictional world that almost destroys them. Where Ciceronian and Renaissance ideal friends define themselves by their shared beliefs in virtue, Edmund pretends to share beliefs, shifting his expressed views as he moves from one person to the next. Like the elder sisters, Edmund alters his words to merge with the minds and hearts of others; once he catches them in his imaginative world, he manipulates them and incorporates them into his designs. Whereas Goneril and Regan's distortions of counsel are subtle, Edmund's are overt. He resembles the manipulator of counsel, Andromana, from Sir Philip Sidney's *Arcadia*, whose praise of her stepson before her husband implies the former's threat to her husband's rule. Andromana makes her stepson's every action look treasonous; she translates "all Plangus's actions … into the language of suspicion" (219.32). Shakespeare elaborates and transforms many features of this story (Weiner 250, 256, 258). Whereas Andromana tells the king that Plangus asked her to help him take the king's life, Edmund creates a script that reveals his own character to the audience while he ascribes it to Edgar. Shakespeare "paints" the slanderer who kills with his words, in this instance a letter attributed by Edmund to Edgar but written by Edmund himself. The viciousness of the letter as read by Gloucester has been too little commented upon:

GLOUCESTER   *Reads* '… I begin to find an idle and fond bondage in the oppression of aged tyranny, who sways not as it hath power but as it is suffered. Come to me, that of this I may speak more. If our father would sleep till I waked him, you should enjoy half his revenue forever and live the beloved of your brother. Edgar.' ... My son Edgar, had he a hand to write this a heart and brain to breed it in? (*King Lear* 1.2.47–55)

No father could read the words "the oppression of aged tyranny" with anything but pain.

Edmund voices the noble beliefs of a virtuous friend to Edgar and acts like a wise counselor to Gloucester when the latter refers to the letter:

GLOUCESTER	You know the character to be your brother's?
EDMUND	If the matter were good, my lord, I durst swear it were his; but in respect of that, I would fain think it were not.
GLOUCESTER	It is his.
EDMUND	It is his hand, my lord, but I hope his heart is not in the contents. (1.2.58–63)

With seeming reluctance, Edmund "concedes" that the unworthy sentiments might belong to Edgar and appears to fulfill the Ciceronian ideal according to which a virtuous friend (including, in the Renaissance, a virtuous brother) takes no pleasure in charges brought against a noble friend (*De amicitia* 18.65). And, having written the letter himself, when Gloucester rushes to judgment on its false information, Edmund, like Iago, suggests a test that will clarify matters (see *Othello* 3.3.432ff.). Helping Gloucester reach his own damning conclusions, he manifests "honesty" that bespeaks false friendship. To Edgar he says, "I am no honest man, if there be any good meaning toward you" (1.2.145–6), a true enough speech, when rightly understood. Gloucester mirrors the interpretation that Edmund's story and forged letter invites.

Edmund is the false-tongued forger *par excellence*, an actor/producer who creates deceptive actions to shape the interpretations of others, like the Machiavel astute in managing theatricality. Again following Sidney's Andromana, Shakespeare represents with superior dramatic skill a scenario created by Edmund whereby Edgar arms himself and is "caught." Edmund says: "I hear my father coming. Pardon me, / In cunning, I must draw my sword upon you" (2.1.28–9). This statement expresses apparently noble friendship to Edgar and, at the same time, nearly destroys him and his reputation. Edmund's lines to Gloucester reveal the false friend that speaks true humanist sentences. He says Edgar "fled ... when by no means" could he "persuade me to the murder of your lordship, / But that I told him the revenging gods / 'Gainst parricides did all the thunder bend, / Spoke with how manifold and strong a bond / The child was bound to' th' father" (2.1.41–7). Edmund speaks these lines persuasively even though he intends to violate their precepts. And though King Lear rages at his daughters' insults but repeatedly expresses his disbelief that they can be treating him as they do, Gloucester internalizes Edmund's suggestions, seeks damning information, and takes up Edmund's idea that he obtain "auricular assurance" (1.2.82). He asks that Edmund "wind me into him [Edgar]" (1.2.86). Thus, the gulling of Gloucester is a cooperative effort.

One might search for an antidote to Edmund's assimilations in the ideal Ciceronian truth-speaking friend. After all, Cordelia speaks honestly about the evil of deception in Act 1. And Kent's strong words instruct Lear on the need for political counsel, but once Lear banishes him Caius turns rougher accents and actions against Lear's sons-in-law and daughters and toward the physical defense of Lear. Furthermore, the distorted world of tyranny requires epistemological capacities in friendly helpers that go beyond Ciceronian advice-giving. Friends need to hone their perceptions of others and use imagination; rational counsel is not enough.

Like Plutarch as described by Holland, who improves the reader's perception of the flatterer by bringing him to life as a person, Shakespeare focuses Caius's discernment on the person Oswald. Kent describes this power to Lear just after he has been banished: "See better, Lear, and let me still remain / The true blank of thine eye" (1.1.152–3). "Blank," the Cambridge edition comments, "refers to the white centre of a target, the concentric rings of which resemble the pupil of an eye" (104 n. 152–3). Kent wishes to continue recognizing evil and to let his eye receive truth as the bullseye receives the arrow. But when Lear drives Kent away, Caius serves as an "eye" for the audience. Although Oswald finds him "monstrous … thus to rail on one that is neither known of thee nor knows thee" (2.2.22–3), Kent (Caius) unfolds the diagnostic signs that indicate Oswald's hostility to Lear. He sees Oswald as a known enemy (who comes "with letters against the king" [2.2.31]) and as a person who lacks virtue independent of his current master.

Caius's constant love of his master Lear leads to hatred of his master's enemies, an enmity he expresses roundly. He is angry "That such a slave as this should … smooth every passion / That in the natures of their lords rebel, / Bring oil to fire, snow to colder moods" (2.2.63–8). Caius's words "picture" the activities of the flatterer who manipulates the emotions of others, developing ideas from Plutarch and Guazzo. Flatterers were thought to be like fawning dogs, but Kent fights openly to protect the king. The need for physical intervention on the king's behalf shows how far the world of the play departs from legitimate political rule assumed in *De amicitia*. Kent trips Oswald for ignoring the king's needs and calling him "my lady's father." He shows whose side he supports when doing so works to his disadvantage. He is resourceful in discovering novel ways to reveal his loyalty, when his action speaks louder than others' friendly words to prove his character. It also cements Caius in Lear's good will: "I thank thee fellow. Thou ser'vst me, and I'll love thee" (1.4.75). After being snubbed, Lear appreciates good service. Shortly before he dies, when he barely recognizes or acknowledges Kent or anyone else, Lear remembers Caius with appreciation: "He's a good fellow, I can tell you that; / He'll strike and quickly too" (5.3.258–9). Caius's protective vigor partially succeeded in shielding Lear from the disregard of others, the best a friend can do in this treacherous world.

King Lear also unfolds earlier emphases on plain speech as the mark of a friend to educe a more challenging relation between speech and action than envisioned in friendship writings. When Cornwall tries to undermine plainness as a sign of trustworthiness and says, "These kind of knaves I know, which in this plainness / Harbour more craft and more corrupter ends" than anyone (2.2.91–2), Caius provides a bold counter-argument. Whereas Cornwall blurs the distinction between elaborate rhetorical flattery and plain speech, Kent states baldly, "he that beguiled you in a plain accent was a plain knave" (2.2.100–101). He makes beguilement a moral failing no matter what its linguistic expression.

Though Kent's disguise initially allows him to protect Lear, it raises problems for understanding the nature of friendship in the play. Once Lear cuts the ties that support a commonwealth, Kent and Edgar need to start from scratch to establish new relationships outside the court, even with people they have known well, a situation not envisioned in *De amicitia*. Disguise represents their new roles, but it also raises the question: how can a friend, whose essence is to be open, act in disguise? Renaissance friendship writings agree with Laelius in Cicero's *De amicitia* who asserts that in true friendship "there is nothing false, nothing pretended" (8.26) and "hypocrisy [is] wicked in all circumstances" (25.92). But the disguises of Kent and Edgar signify as tropes for the difficulties of friendship under tyranny. The two characters use disguises to survive and to create a rudimentary community in the storm. While M. C. Bradbrook defines "disguise as a substitution, over-laying or metamorphosis of dramatic identity, whereby one character sustains two roles" (160), Shakespeare uses this doubling to represent the changes of social identity. Edgar articulates his loss of status as son, saying, "Edgar I nothing am" (*King Lear* 2.3.21; Carroll 426, 428–9). In a sense, he really is the beggar he appears to be (Bell 55–6, 64ff.). But Kent both alters and retains his former social identity.

Kent as Caius adapts the skills of the Ciceronian friend to create a link between Lear and his former role as monarch by treating him respectfully. He finds new ways to address Lear outside of his courtly identity (*King Lear* 1.1.174) and changes his appearance to befriend his master (1.4.2–4). At the same time, he maintains his noble status as Earl when he communicates with Cordelia and tries to reinstate the monarchy by working with Cordelia and the King of France. And, in Act 1, he creates a new, miniature society between a rough soldier and his patron by establishing a fresh though imperfect friendship with Lear. Whereas ideal friends may depend on their mutual constancy, persons in a wild world may need to find new grounds for friendship.

Caius reshapes friendship as a social instrument in order to move toward virtuous friendship. He shifts from friendship in an ideal commonwealth to friendship as a resource in adversity. Lear and Caius base their association in shared poverty, not in shared nobility or excellence. When Lear asks the powerful Shakespearean question "What art thou?" Kent answers, "A very honest-hearted fellow, and as poor as the King." Lear responds, "If thou be'st as poor for a subject as he's for a king, thou art poor enough" (1.4.16–17). Caius democratizes the virtues of civility and courage, striving "to love him that is honest, to converse with him that is wise and says little, [and] to fight when I cannot choose," virtues broader than those sought by the nobility (1.4.12–14). His new "civility" is appropriate to what "ordinary men are fit for" in a wild world (1.4.3). Throughout Lear's ordeal, Kent strives to make hospitality available to him at the castle and in the hovel. He attempts to strengthen the fragile ties that connect Lear to a larger social world by continually addressing him as "good my lord" (3.4; see McClean 51; Taylor, *Division* 61). Drawing on a Ciceronian belief in the constancy of the friend in adversity (*De amicitia* 6.22), Shakespeare represents Kent as the stabilizing presence that reduces suffering. In lines that were dropped from the First Folio (1623), Edgar comments philosophically, "Who alone suffers suffers most i' th' mind, / Leaving things and happy shows behind; / But then the mind much sufferance doth o'erskip / When grief hath mates, and bearing fellowship" (Bevington 3.6.102–7; Halio *Quarto* 3.6.93–6). Kent's disguised but faithful presence is unswerving.

Surprisingly, however, the play qualifies the Ciceronian belief that friends should counsel friends who waver from virtue. It represents sorrows that are untouched by comforting discourse. In Act 3, Kent's brief comments, though sensible and realistic, fail to comfort Lear. Instead, they lead to Lear's intense response, his thoughtful, passionate reflections. When Kent comments truly, "The tyranny of the open night's too rough / For nature to endure" (Halio, *Folio* 3.4.2–3), Lear answers with the famous lines: "Thou think'st 'tis much that this contentious storm / Invades us to the skin; so 'tis to thee. / But where the greater malady is fixed, / The lesser is scarce felt" (3.4.6–9). The storm gives Lear matter to express his feeling, and his words initiate a powerful meditation on the circumstantial, subjective conditions of that feeling. Then he reflects on the relative weight of mental and bodily suffering: "the tempest in my mind / Doth from my senses take all feeling else" (3.4.12–13) and "This tempest will not give me leave to ponder / On things would hurt me more" (3.4.24–5). For a moment, he wishes to feel less. But, noticing the Fool, he chooses to go into the hovel with him, directing "pomp" to "Expose thyself to feel what wretches feel" (3.4.33–4). Feeling becomes the touchstone for reality and compassion.

Lear's emphasis on the senses can be understood in light of sixteenth-century beliefs about feeling as a source of truth.[3] Lear finds reality and identity in present pain. The basis of his discovery emerges when we consider Thomas Cranmer's response to the late Bishop of Winchester, Stephen Gardiner. Cranmer asserts that the Catholic fathers asked rhetorically whether Christ's humanity wasn't revealed when "he was heard preach, seene eating, and drincking, labouring and sweating." The hearing and seeing of Christ, not the belief in doctrine, convinced the disciples. Again, Cranmer asks, thinking especially of Thomas, "Do they not also prove his resurrection by seing, hearing and groping of him?" (278). Touch may lead to belief. When Cordelia addresses healing words to Lear, he feels tears that "scald like molten lead" (4.6.43–4). He doesn't know "what to say." "I will not swear these are my hands. Let's see: / I feel this pin prick. Would I were assured / Of my

---

3   Strier stresses the importance of feeling, especially Lear's rage ("Against" 33ff.).

condition" (4.6.51–4). Only flesh senses external reality and its own pain. Lear does not discover his identity as a human being from Kent or even from Cordelia. But Kent befriends Lear by being present to his experience (Egan 152ff.).

Unlike classical and Renaissance representations of noble friendship, which presuppose a shared commonwealth, *King Lear* explores ways to define new social relationships in its absence. Edgar starts afresh to create social ties, the conditions of useful and virtuous friendships, in a wilderness where only fragments of the old order remain. His disguise as the "basest and poorest shape" imaginable expresses his social position after the loss of his former status. Like the contemporary Tom of Bedlam, he deliberately uses dirt, pins, nakedness, and mad rant to save himself and appeal to others (2.3.5–9); his disguise defines him as the "outlaw" or outcast he really is (Carroll 191–5). He "with presented nakedness outface(s) / The winds and persecutions of the sky" (2.3.11–12). Because Edgar as Poor Tom has no social relation to Gloucester or anyone else, he cannot befriend others. Kent, Lear, and the Fool find him in a hovel; he comes forth as a madman, saying, "away, the foul fiend follows me" (3.4.44). Poor Tom becomes an emblem to Lear of his own situation (Levin 93), and, for Lear, the distinction between self and others breaks down when he asks "Didst thou give all to thy daughters? And art thou come to this?" (3.4.47). Though Edgar gives himself a complex history as a former courtier, a servile minister who "served the lust of my mistress' heart," like Oswald or Edmund (3.4.78–9; Halio, *Folio* 186 n. 77), Lear sees a more fundamental truth: "thou art the thing itself. Unaccommodated man is no more but such a poor, bare, forked animal as thou art" (3.4.95–7; see Carroll 435). Whereas Edgar moralizes his assumed identity, Lear recognizes its radical implication. In wishing to "unbutton here," Lear seeks kinship with the naked "thing." They form a bond, affirmed when Lear refuses Gloucester's gesture to lead him into the hovel without Tom: "I will keep still with my philosopher" (3.4.160). Because Lear perceives Edgar as a fellow-sufferer and "entertain[s] him as one of [his] hundred," Poor Tom enters a new social world being constructed on the heath (3.6.35). Hospitality creates a bond between the estranged in ways that had not been envisioned in models of ideal friendship founded on equality of noble status.

Edgar gradually approaches virtuous friendship with his father by using disguise to bridge the break created by Gloucester's rejection of him as a traitor. But the project is difficult and slow. Initially, disguise allows Edgar emotional space to experience his sorrow at Gloucester's blinding and to discover his father's remorse for his anger: "Oh, dear son Edgar, / The food of thy abused father's wrath: / Might I but live to see thee in my touch, / I'd say I had eyes again" (4.1.21–4). Although audiences may wish that Edgar would reveal himself, he is still without resources, naked except for a blanket and without food except for the "frog" and "toad" (3.4.115). We can understand the challenges he undergoes when we consider that the Old Man, a previous tenant of Gloucester's, cannot befriend his former master. They have lost the social relationship that undergirds useful and virtuous friendships. When the Old Man tries to help Gloucester, Gloucester sends him away, just as the Prince of Paphlagonia tries to dismiss his son Leonatus (the precursor to Edgar in Sir Philip Sidney's *Arcadia*, 276). Gloucester and the Prince act benevolently, recognizing that, because of the danger, their helpers should not try to fulfill the obligations of their previous social roles. Gloucester, having absolved his tenant of his "duty," forms a new bond with Mad Tom, asserting, "'Tis the time's plague when madmen lead the blind" (4.1.47). The blind man with money and the madman with sight exchange gifts and become both useful and virtuous friends. In his wretchedness, Gloucester finds meaning and justice by making Tom "happier" out of his own financial abundance: "That I am wretched / Makes thee happier" (4.1.60–61).

This friendship changes over time as each man's beliefs alter in the face of new experiences, unlike the constant Ciceronian friendship. The most dramatic shift occurs when Edgar fashions himself once again, this time as a peasant. Instead of counseling Gloucester as an ideal, equal friend, Edgar stages an elaborate intervention to change Gloucester's mind about despair. In this guise, Edgar engages issues of time, memory, and suffering that overwhelm Gloucester. Shakespeare draws on ideas also present in Plutarch and in Guazzo's characterizations of the search for friendship as a risk-taking adventure in which circumstances can be deceiving and truth can only be discerned gradually through time. Edgar as peasant changes Gloucester's imaginative apprehension of the shape of time by causing him to challenge his own perceptions. But instead of relying on straightforward counsel, Edgar uses a virtuoso creation of Gloucester's imaginative experience at the "cliff" to alter Gloucester's convictions. His discourse comments on the friend's power to counsel the afflicted. *King Lear* suggests that imagination, not rational counsel alone, has a power to illuminate and heal.

Modern audiences may be astonished by or skeptical of Edgar's decision to "describe" imaginary heights upon which he and Gloucester are supposedly poised (Bevington, *Shakespeare* 148–9; Rosenberg 142; see also Carroll 437 n. 26). But Edgar's attempt to "cure … [Gloucester's] despair" (4.5.33–4), draws on memory and imagination in ways illuminated by sixteenth-century writings on rhetoric and counsel (see also Schleiner 274–87). Edgar becomes a poet whose vivid representations of ungraspable vast dimensions changes the bases of Gloucester's perception. His words draw on contemporary writers' views of the deceptiveness of memory and the terror of despair produced by images. Juan Luis Vives, the Spanish rhetorician who wrote *De anima et vita* (1538), tells a story to illuminate the power of frightening memories over people's sense of well-being. Vives remarks that "the horror and dismay that are caused by fear can stretch back into the past as Vergil says: 'It is frightening to remember'" (107, cited in Olmsted 152–3). A similar idea appears in Montaigne's *An Apologie of Raymond Sebond* (315). The story is cited in Robert Burton's *Anatomy of Melancholy* (253) and rewritten in William Perkins's *Works* (284–5, cited in Olmsted 152–3). Vives's story tells how "a man sleeping on his donkey crosses a broken bridge that has only one narrow plank. He is perfectly relaxed at the time and passes over unharmed," but the next day when he finds out about the deep gulf that lay underneath and thinks about "the terrible danger he had been in," he faints (Vives 107, cited in

Olmsted 153). Vives dramatizes how the context of perception (as of the plank) affects the point of view that remembers or perceives it.

Analogously, Edgar's imaginative descriptions before and after Gloucester's "fall" create an experience of the radical danger implicated in falling. They destabilize the framework in which Gloucester perceives his recent past. Shakespeare's probable source, "An Apologie of Raymond Sebond," argues that the sight of intervening objects as Montaigne looks down an infinite precipice, whether it be "but a tree, a shrub, or any out-butting crag of a rock presented itself … doth somewhat ease and assure us from feare" (*Essays* trans. Florio, ed. Rhys 315). But Edgar turns the objects half-way down into additional evidence of terrifying depth: "Half-way down / Hangs one that gathers samphire, dreadful trade! / Methinks he seems no bigger than his head. / The fishermen that walk upon the beach / Appear like mice" (4.5.14–18). Edgar's description dramatizes the relativity of perception to dizzying effect: "I'll look no more, / Lest my brain turn and the deficient sight / Topple down headlong" (4.5.22–4).

Once he leads Gloucester through the defamiliarizing experience of a "fall," Edgar places himself in the here and now of solid sense perception: "Give me your arm. Up; so. How is't? Feel you your legs? You stand" (4.5.64–5). He revises Gloucester's memory of Poor Tom and alters his despair by describing the madman as a devil (see Greenblatt 94–128), commenting, "the clearest gods, who make them honours / Of men's impossibilities, have preserved thee" (4.5.72–4, Halio; see also Bevington, *Shakespeare* 148–9). Gloucester's experience and Edgar's interpretation change Gloucester's attitude; Gloucester says, "I do remember now" and vows to "bear affliction" (4.5.75–6). The realignment of his imagination leads him to fresh belief. By using dramatic and poetic effects that instantiate how change occurs, Edgar becomes a virtuous friend to his wandering father, but in a way suggesting that the Ciceronian emphasis on reasonable counsel is not sufficient in the distorted world of *King Lear*.

Edgar protects Gloucester and diminishes his anguish, but he cannot restore the social and affective relationship of son to father. When he finally reveals himself, his father's "flawed" heart "burst[s] smilingly," caught "'Twixt two extremes of passion, joy and grief" (5.3.187, 190). Similarly, Kent never fully completes the friendship he is developing with Lear. For Lear there is no way to connect the present to his previous Ciceronian friendship with Kent, even though Kent reminds Lear, "I am the very man … that from the first of difference and decay / Have followed your sad steps" (5.3.260–63). Lear cannot believe Caius lives. He is unable to integrate the wilderness world with his old social context. Only Cordelia can reach him, but at the end she is gone. Lear's pain becomes unendurable, and the wise Kent can only comment, "O, let him pass. He hates him / That would upon the rack of this tough world / Stretch him out longer" (5.3.287–9). Kent becomes more a commentator on Lear's suffering than a buffer against it (Egan 146, 151, 152). Neither Gloucester nor Lear can sustain the intensity of contrary passions stirred in those who feel the most. Audiences likewise find the loss of Lear and Cordelia too painful to bear. But works on friendship from Cicero through Guazzo, Sidney, and Shakespeare insist that virtue and virtuous friendship require prudence along with love. Lear's errors of judgment, which permit the ascendancy of Cornwall, Goneril, Regan, and Edmund, break the social ties upon which virtuous friendship depends. Lear's reconciliation with Cordelia and Edgar's exchange of charity with Gloucester and Edmund cannot overcome the nearly pervasive estrangement of all characters from all.

Chapter 11

Politics and Friendship in William Cartwright's *The Lady-Errant*

Christopher Marlow

Despite some valuable recent reinterpretations of the Platonic drama produced at the court of Charles I in the 1630s, it is perhaps still surprising for a play written in this tradition to be called subtle.[1] After all, the disdain with which many critics treat the plays is difficult to ignore. G. Blakemore Evans's early study of William Cartwright's work in the genre, for example, is unstinting in its dispraise. For Blakemore Evans, Cartwright's plays, like all Platonic drama

> reveal all the faults incident to overmuch reliance on the props of rhetoric and argument. Like those of the other dramatists, his characters say too much and do too little; and even the little they do tends to stamp them as lifeless puppets rather than human beings. (24)

Similarly, Graham Parry argues that King Charles's enthusiasm for drama had a detrimental effect upon the work composed under his aegis because,

> too many of the plays written with Court performance in mind strove to please the refined yet artificial and restricted taste of Whitehall, and lost touch with the broad spread of experience that animated so much of Jacobean drama. (*Golden Age* 203)

Even William Cartwright himself, an Oxford scholar later celebrated for his poems, lectures, and sermons and very much aware of the artificiality of the genre in which he was writing, acknowledges in his prologue to *The Lady-Errant* (probably performed 1634–37) that "The Poem's forc'd" (Blakemore Evans 91, l. 22).[2] Although its characters may be lifeless, its appeal restricted, and its style forced, *The Lady-Errant* nevertheless announces its interest in friendship in a remarkably subtle manner. The play is set in a Cyprus populated almost entirely by women whose men have deserted them in order to wage war against Crete. In its third scene, Eumela, an unmarried and intelligent woman, addresses a trio of women described in the *Dramatis Personae* as "busy" and "factious." All four discuss

---

[1]   See, for example, Britland, Tomlinson, and Sharpe.

[2]   All further references are to this edition.

the correct way for a wife to demonstrate grief for the absence of her husband, and Eumela acknowledges the dangers of taking such grief too far. According to Eumela, elaborate displays, including the use of "Ebon Candlesticks" and "black Sarcenet Smocks," are nothing but "vaunting popular sorrow," and her remarks conclude with the following exchange with Pandena, one of the factious women:

Eumela:	This were to grieve to Ostentation,
	Not to a reall friendship.
Pandena:	Is there friendship
	Think you 'twixt man and wife?
Eumela:	You'll say, perhaps,
	You, and your Husband, have not been friends yet. (1.3.238–46)

Eumela's first use of the term "friendship" might sound striking and incongruous to twenty-first century ears attuned to expect "love" instead, but this usage was by no means unprecedented in a culture that was at the time seeking to use the conventions of classical friendship in order to bolster the intellectual weight of the institution of marriage.[3] The usage is also appropriate given the context in which it appears, since one of the chief aims of Platonic drama was to examine the overlapping and often competing demands made by love and friendship upon the early modern subject. Nevertheless, friendship in marriage was considered the exception rather than the rule and, as I will demonstrate below, elsewhere the play largely subscribes to this position.[4] By introducing the concept of friendship in marriage, Cartwright subtly subverts the expectations of the audience and in this small way prompts them to re-examine any preconceptions that they may have about the relationship between wives and husbands. But there is a further effect lying beneath this one. The term "friendship" is appropriate not just because it can be used to challenge seventeenth-century attitudes to marriage. It also works to indicate the play's deep interest in friendship theory and the application of that theory to lived experience, because in this scene Eumela is not just talking about marriage, but about absence, and the mourning of a marriage interrupted. And when absence and mourning are in question, no discourse would spring to the seventeenth-century mind more quickly than that of friendship.[5]

---

[3]   As Luxon notes, the seventeenth century saw the acceleration of a puritan project designed to transfer the attributes of friendship to marriage: "Milton, like many authors of his day, tried to reimagine marriage as friendship, even though this required radical revisions of friendship doctrine" (3 and *passim*).

[4]   See Luxon 7: "Classically speaking, marriage is a less dignified and less specifically human relation than friendship, but some particularly decent spouses might also qualify as friends."

[5]   Both Derrida (290) and Shannon (87) remark that Cicero, Montaigne, and Blanchot offer compelling accounts of the intimate connections between friendship and death.

This episode is a microcosm of Cartwright's practice throughout *The Lady-Errant*. Although there might well be moments when, as Evans has it, the characters say too much and do too little, what they say and do can be understood to comment upon classical and early modern friendship theory. In its subtle and sometimes oblique way, the play examines the Aristotelian notion that "friendship ... seems to be the bond that holds communities together" (*Nic. Eth.* trans. Thomson 201). *The Lady-Errant* seeks to expand the scope of such political friendship so that it might also include women, and in doing so it considers the relative political merits of friendship and love. Cartwright's royalist sympathies notwithstanding, I will suggest that *The Lady-Errant* is more than mere propaganda because it uses friendship as a subtle way of opening up questions of community, government and gender that are not necessarily reactionary.

***

The prominent role allocated to women in Platonic drama is a notable feature of the genre. The popularity of the form at the court of Charles I is inextricably linked with the patronage wielded by Henrietta Maria, and often associated with the pastoral mode, as in the earliest and perhaps most famous example of the genre in English, Thomas Montague's *The Shepherd's Paradise* (1633). Platonic drama was concerned, in the words of Parry, with "honour and duty entangled with love, usually expressed in an elegant, slightly affected language that reflected the Queen's fondness for a preciosity of manner that she had acquired in her youth" (*Golden Age* 203), and with "starry-eyed debate about the refining effects of non-sensual love" (*Seventeenth Century* 29). Because of its female characters and its association with Henrietta Maria, Platonic drama was often seen as a "feminine" genre more at home in Parisian salons than at the English court, and one reason for this was the attempt made by the genre to transform heterosexual desire into a valuable spiritual pursuit rather than an ignoble fleshly one.[6] As such, the drama shares its roots with the Petrarchanism that dominated English verse in the late sixteenth and early seventeenth centuries. However, while lyric poetry—and especially the sonnet—provided Petrarchanism with the ideal formal conditions for literary success, the same cannot be said for drama. Transferred to the stage, it is difficult to distinguish the soul-searching required by neo-Platonism from mere self-indulgence. Indeed, as Karen Britland argues, it may well be the case that even Henrietta Maria enjoyed seeing these impulses satirized.[7] One of the central problems of reading a Platonic play comes in distinguishing what is

---

[6]   Indeed, distaste for "starry-eyed debate" of a French origin is concisely expressed in Evans's lament for the lack of "good Anglo-Saxon attitudes" in Platonic drama (23).

[7]   See Britland 130: "I find it impossible to accept that [Henrietta Maria] could have sponsored two major theatrical productions by two separate authors [Montague's *Shepherd's Paradise* and William Davenant's *The Temple of Love*] in relatively quick succession without being aware of their irreverent stance towards neo-Platonism."

satirical from what is not. Satire is certainly present in *The Lady-Errant*, and it is clearly directed towards what many thought of as the defining characteristic of the plays: the prominence of the female characters. Here, that prominence is exaggerated by the relative scarcity of male characters, and finally ridiculed by what the play represents as a misguided attempt by the women to seize political power in Cyprus. The proposed establishment of a Cypriot female parliament is counterpointed by Machessa, the Lady-Errant herself, who has sworn to glorify her sex by defending men from any danger they may encounter. Machessa is essentially a female *miles gloriosus* figure. The play also offers the familiar pair of male friends, Olyndus, a Cypriot lord too ill to fight in the war, and Charistus, a Cretan prince, who predictably come to blows over the wise and beautiful Cypriot princess, Lucasia. It is difficult to take any of these plot strands entirely seriously, and the tragic element of this tragicomedy is somewhat underdeveloped, to say the least. However, just as it would be a mistake to underestimate the political and philosophical interests of the play simply because of its relative lack of seriousness, it would also be wrong to assume that each of its seemingly positive representations of women is in fact ironic.

Examining what we know about the circumstances of the play's performance can help to clarify the tone of *The Lady-Errant*. Although there is no documented evidence relating to the performance of Cartwright's play, its prologue offers the reader some interesting information. It seems that, as in *The Shepherd's Paradise*, female characters were actually performed by women. This is made clear by the prologue, which tells us that the play will contain no cross-gender casting:

> As then there's no Offence
> Giv'n to the Weak or Stubborn hence,
> Being the Female's Habit is
> Her owne, and the Male's his. (ll.25–8)

Evans notes that the offence that Cartwright refers to may in fact have been caused by *The Shepherd's Paradise*, in which both male and female parts were performed entirely by Henrietta Maria and her ladies-in-waiting, to some consternation (84). Cartwright's aim in *The Lady-Errant* is to confine each sex to what he sees as its appropriate position, and thus avoid the criticism provoked by both male and female cross-dressing. For Jane Farnsworth, this strategy is indicative of *The Lady-Errant* as a whole, which she sees as a play designed to discourage Henrietta Maria from interfering in politics. Farnsworth argues that "in the political context of the play" the lines quoted above "can be seen as well to be a subtle urging of the queen to maintain her place and dignity ... politically as well as sartorially" (384). Sophie Tomlinson suggests that the tone of these lines is less censorious considering the rare presence of women on stage and that in fact the "performative stance [of] *The Lady-Errant* legitimizes the woman-actor *who keeps to her part*"

(107).[8] But perhaps an even more idealistic interpretation is possible. By allowing actors to perform their own biological sex and then presenting a dramatic scenario in which men are largely absent or ridiculous, *The Lady-Errant* offers its women characters a dramatic space within which they can be represented on their own terms. Indeed, this is one of the aims of neo-Platonism, which works to emphasize the spiritual value of women at the expense of the casual misogyny espoused in the period. Crucially, as I will show, the utopian space presented to the women of the play is ordered according to the principles of friendship rather than love.

The utopian possibilities of the play can be clarified by remaining with the prologue for a little longer. With no clear indication of where the play was performed, critics of *The Lady-Errant* make much of the way that the second stanza of the prologue seems to draw a contrast between Charles's court and the place of the play's performance:

> We cannot here complain
> Of want of Presence, or of Train
> For if choice Beauties make the Court
> And their Light guild the Sport
> This honour'd Ring presents us here
> Glories as rich and fresh as there;
> And it may under Question fall
> Which is more Court, This, or White-Hall. (ll.9–16)

Evans hazards that "the play was performed before an aristocratic, if not royal, audience" (84); Tomlinson, more circumspect, suggests only that it received "an elite private staging" (107); Farnsworth confidently asserts that the intended audience was "a courtly and a royal one" (384). While the presence of women on stage almost certainly rules out a private college performance for this, possibly Cartwright's first play, the absence of any mention of royal attendance in the play's prefatory matter, or any direct address to the king or queen in its prologue, is unusual. By contrast, Cartwright's 1636 play *The Royal Slave*, performed at Christ Church, Oxford, with Charles and Henrietta Maria in attendance, trumpets its royal audience on its title page, as does a Cambridge university play of 1631, Peter Hausted's *The Rivall Friends*.[9] If the royal couple was not present, references in the prologue to what Tomlinson calls "an alternative court" take on rather more significance (107). If the arena of performance is not blessed by the attendance of the king or queen, the question "which is more Court, This, or White-Hall" becomes mildly revolutionary, especially if, as it seems to, White-Hall functions

---

[8] Italics in original.

[9] Hausted's play is advertised as "A comoedie, As it was Acted before the King and Queens Maiesties, when out of their princely favour they were pleased to visite their Vniversitie of Cambridge." See Hausted, frontispiece. For a discussion of this play, see Marlow.

as a metonym for royal power. The alternative court proposed by the prologue may well, as Farnsworth suggests, have been constituted to pass judgment upon the queen's political interference as represented by the women who engage in politics in *The Lady-Errant*. However, this would be to ignore the resemblance between the alternative court called into being by the prologue and the alternative parliament constructed by the Cypriot women. If the alternative court is celebrated in the prologue as a rival to the real court, is it possible to celebrate the play's alternative female parliament in a similar way?

***

The place of *The Lady-Errant* in friendship studies has so far been an obscure one. Its main connection to the discipline is via the verse epistles of the seventeenth-century poet Katherine Philips. Philips took Lucasia, her familiar name for Anne Owen—one of her chief correspondents—from Cartwright's play. As Catharine Gray suggests, this borrowing may well point more convincingly to Philips's interest in royalist coterie culture than female empowerment, but it is nevertheless appropriate that *The Lady-Errant* should have influenced the writer of some of the earliest English poems celebrating female friendship ("Katherine Philips" 448–9). Cartwright's was by no means the only Caroline play to present female characters discussing love and friendship in a serious philosophical manner; however, it was the only one to do so against the backdrop of an attempted female uprising. Moreover, and notwithstanding the fact the female parliament of the play is ultimately vanquished, the discussions that Cartwright's Lucasia has with her friend Eumela and her lover Charistus place this parliament in a positive light. Despite the stock ending of the play, which sees the conflict between Cyprus and Crete resolved through the marriage of Lucasia and Charistus, *The Lady-Errant* repeatedly suggests that it is not love that brings conflict to an end, but friendship. Lucasia's encounter with Charistus's friend Olyndus is important to examine in this context.

As in most plays of the Platonic genre, conflict between two supposedly perfect friends is provoked by the interruption of heterosexual desire into the previously exclusive male friendship. The friendship is put in question because the absolute similitude experienced by perfect friends encourages them to believe that the beloved mistress will love each friend just as passionately. This trope was popularized in the English vernacular tradition by Thomas Elyot in *The Book Named the Governor* (1531), an educational manual for aristocrats. Elyot's text includes a brief fictional illustration of perfect friendship in what it calls "the wonderful history of Titus and Gisippus" (135–48), a tale that provides an opportunity for its pair of friends to sacrifice for each other equal romantic interests in a beautiful Athenian gentlewoman. The central question of a friend resigning his interest in his mistress reappears in many early modern texts that post-date Elyot's, including Lyly's *Euphues: The Anatomy of Wit* (1578), and Shakespeare's *The Two Gentlemen of Verona* (c. 1594). By opposing heterosexual desire with homosocial friendship, texts like these bear witness to early modern cultural anxieties about the concept of difference as represented by sexual identity. As Laurie Shannon reminds us, "the pairing of male and female (whether in love or marriage) … reads either as hierarchy or as an endangering mixture in which the self is permeated by an intruding external force" (55). In Platonic drama in general, the fear of love as disease has been replaced by a vision of love as panacea, but the hierarchical nature of desire is still very much present, and the jealousy of the two friends helps to illustrate this in *The Lady-Errant*. Wishing to test the mettle of Charistus, Lucasia asks to meet his friend Olyndus in order to pass on a message. Charistus's jealousy begins before the meeting has even taken place, and only increases when he discovers that, as a token of her admiration for him, Lucasia will transfer her affections to Olyndus while Charistus carries out tasks designed by Lucasia to prove his love for her. Lucasia tells Olyndus:

> To shew that I reject him not, you may
> Tell him, that being he hath such a friend,
> Whiles he is absent I will love *Olyndus*
> Instead of him. (3.1.825–8)

According to the logic of Platonic love, Lucasia acts perfectly reasonably in proposing this substitution. For Platonic lovers, the spiritual experience of being in love is far more significant than the worldly object of that love. Loving is essentially a non-partisan experience and, as Kathleen M. Lynch remarks, "the impersonality of love may even become so accentuated that it is possible for a lady to exchange an accepted lover for his rival … without the slightest qualm" (60). While this aspect of the plot is entirely formulaic, the specific way in which Lucasia requests that Charistus prove himself to her is not. Concerned about Charistus's lack of involvement in the war currently raging between her country and his, Lucasia tells Olyndus that she would rather "court [Charistus's] Valour, than his Love" (3.1.733). To that end, she instructs Olyndus to tell his friend to

> Succour his Country, cheer the Souldier, fight,
> Spend, and disburse the Prince, where e'er he goes,
> Get him a Name, and Title upon *Cyprus*.
> I will not see him 'till he hath Conquer'd, till
> He hath rid high in Triumph, and when this
> Is done, let him consider then, it is
> My Father, & my Subjects, and my Kingdom
> That he hath Conquer'd. (3.1.816–23)

In order to display his "valour," Charistus must do nothing less than defeat Lucasia's father, the king of Cyprus, and play the tyrant over her entire country.

In a play that gives its audience a significant number of female characters who seek seriously to subvert the patriarchy under which they have languished, it is remarkable to find Lucasia so determined to place herself into the hands of another male tyrant. It would be futile to seek any psychological justification for this desire, even within what Evans calls the "warped—if not immoral, at best amoral" value system of Platonic love (27). For Farnsworth, this curious passage is explained by Cartwright having supposedly written the play in order to ridicule what he saw as the dangerous lobbying by the queen and her supporters for entrance into the European war against Spain (391–2). While this may or may not be the case, Lucasia's self-destructive bellicosity emphasizes a remarkable pattern of meanings within the symbolic scheme of the play. By asking Charistus to prove himself in war against Cyprus, Lucasia draws attention to the tyrannical nature of love itself. For her, being conquered by love is a literal, rather than a metaphorical, event, and the supposedly ennobling experience of loving (which I will examine in more detail below) seems to take military submission as its corollary. When he receives her message, Charistus understands immediately that Lucasia's version of love is characterised by an absolute dissimilitude:

> ... If I
> Return, and *Crete* be Conquer'd, then She will
> Count me Spoyl, and Luggage; and my Love
> Only a Slave's Affection. If I Conquer,
> And *Cyprus* follow my Triumphant Chariot,
> My Love will then be Tyranny. (3.2.912–7)

Once recognized, the dissimilitude introduced by the notion of love as tyranny seems to infect the friendship of Charistus and Olyndus, and Lucasia's decision to transfer her affections to Olyndus during Charistus's absence inevitably gives rise to the conventional duel of the friends.

The friends quickly re-establish good relations once their anger has passed, but a rehabilitation of love as anything other than a tyrannical relationship is never convincingly achieved. Although the royal houses eventually resolve their differences through a strategic marriage, the language of tyranny remains active to the end. Remarking upon Charistus's marriage to Lucasia, his father Dinomachus recalls a prophecy that forms the penultimate speech of the play: "*And my* Charistus *doth his Country save / By being thus become his Enemi's Slave*" (5.8.2099–100).[10] Metaphors like these are of course by no means unusual; one need only turn to any sonnet sequence written in England in the 1590s to find numerous examples of similar language. Philip Sidney's Astrophel, for example, declares "like slave-borne *Muscovite*, / I call it praise to suffer Tyrannie" in Sonnet 2 of *Astrophel and Stella* (Evans 4). However, in *The Lady-Errant* the warlike context within which such language is repeatedly situated emphasizes the brutality of the metaphor—most strikingly in Lucasia's request for Charistus literally to conquer her. The figure of lover-as-slave is inappropriate—perhaps we might even

---

[10]   Italics in original.

say in poor taste—because the actual experience of enslaving or of being enslaved has been at stake for every character throughout the play's duration. By setting *The Lady-Errant* in a war-torn state, Cartwright seems determined to draw the attention of his audience to what he sees as the perverse rationale of a love that models itself upon tyranny. While preserving a conventional resolution by uniting its lovers and countries, the play nevertheless signals its distaste for the fashionable understanding of love by pointing out the real implications of the language used so casually to express it.

The play seeks to make a distinction between the tyrannical language of love and the egalitarian language of friendship. The concept of friendship-as-equality pervades the play but is perhaps emphasized most at the moment when Charistus and Olyndus are reconciled after their duel. The stage directions indicate that the two friends should creep towards one another and embrace, and as they do so Charistus says,

> ... The Fates
> Preserve our Friendship, and would have us equall,
> Equall ev'n in our Angers: we shall go
> Down equall to the Shades both, two waies equall,
> As Dead, as Friends. (3.2.1006–10)

Again, none of this is at all revolutionary, as equality has long been the cornerstone of the classical tradition of male friendship.[11] Far more interesting, however, is the way that the discourse of egalitarian friendship finds itself being used in elements of the play that do not involve the classical model of a pair of male friends. We have already seen how Eumela alludes to the discourse of friendship in order to construct a version of marriage that accounts for the sadness some of the Cypriot wives feel for the absence of their husbands. But the play makes it clear that friendship, whose defining characteristic is equality, also exists between all those who experience loving. According to the subtle differentiations made by the play, the experience of being in love—loving—is very different from the tyranny engendered when that love is reciprocated. The latter relationship, according to the play, necessarily leads to inequality; the former emotion has the power to forge equality among all who experience it—even those who belong to widely differing social backgrounds. As Lucasia puts it,

> ... all that do Love,
> In that they love, are equall, and above none,
> None, but those only whom the God denies
> The honour of his Wound. (3.6.1155–8)

---

[11] Aristotle acknowledges that even "qualified and superficial friendships" must be based on equality (trans Thomson *Nic. Eth.* 209–11).

Since classical friendship is grounded upon the principle of equality through similitude, the implication here is that all those that experience loving are made equal and are thus are connected together in bonds of friendship.

The connection between the play's democratization of loving and the discourse of classical friendship is confirmed by Aristotle's *Nichomachean Ethics*. Lucasia's definition of loving echoes one of the key passages in the taxonomy of friendship undertaken by Aristotle in his chapter "The Kinds of Friendship." Aristotle notes that, contrary to received opinion, it is better for the friend to love than to be loved:

> Friendship seems to consist more in giving than in receiving affection. An indication of this is the joy that mothers show in loving their children. Some women give their children to other women to bring up, and although they love them, knowing who they are, do not seek to be loved in return, if it is impossible to have this too; ... they bestow their love upon the children even though the children, through ignorance, make no response such as is due to a mother. So if friendship consists more in loving than in being loved, and if people are commended for loving their friends, it seems that loving is the distinctive virtue of friends. (trans. Thomson 213–4)

This evocative passage is notable for the way that it defines the "distinctive virtue of friends" by referring clearly and exclusively to an experience—motherhood— that only women are capable of having. Aristotle is interested here in valorizing the absence of a relationship between birth mother and child so as to emphasize the selfless love that should obtain in friendship. However, the passage also suggests that another implicit relationship occurs in this situation: what amounts to a clandestine bond between "some women" who give up their children and "other women" who raise those children. Whether or not these women are known to each other, they are united by the love that they bear for their children, irrespective of the reciprocation of that love. These women are, therefore, bound by their experiences into a type of loving community similar to the one invoked by Lucasia, and, despite the unequal return of love they will almost certainly receive from the children, there is no question of a hierarchy of loving.

Thus, while love itself is tyrannical, loving takes on the egalitarian condition shared by friends. And in *The Lady-Errant*, that egalitarianism is expressed in explicitly political terms:

> ... Love's Kingdom is
> Founded upon a Parity; Lord, and Subject,
> Master, and Servant, are Names banish'd thence;
> They wear one Fetter all, or, all one Freedom. (3.6.1150–53)

This statement is particularly striking because it comes soon after Eumela has dared to argue with Lucasia who, as a princess, exceeds her in social rank. In his reading of *The Royal Slave*, Cartwright's most popular play, Martin Butler suggests there are "surprisingly democratic implications in Platonic love, which is free to choose rationally whom it will favour" (47). This is not quite the case in *The Lady-Errant*, where the concluding union of lovers is more explicable in geopolitical terms than emotional ones.[12] However, Butler's "democratic implications" are present in Lucasia's description of loving, which for her inaugurates a collective of individuals united by their equality. While Gray is correct to argue that the democratizing potential of loving in the play "does nothing to alter the material and political differences between the two women," it does seem a little unfair to expect *The Lady-Errant* to carry its theoretical arguments through to the realm of realpolitik, especially given the contemplative bent of Platonic drama as a whole ("Katherine Philips" 449). It is perhaps in keeping with the spirit of the genre to pay more attention to the ways in which the egalitarian community invoked by the play corresponds to the friendship theory with which Cartwright, later appointed university reader in metaphysics, would almost certainly have been familiar (Flynn).

It is of course impossible to establish whether Cartwright is deliberately alluding to Aristotle's conception of the state of loving experienced by women in the debate that occurs between Lucasia and Eumela in act three. But even without this reference, the play's rhetoric of affectionate female equality is analogous to the relationship shared by friends in the classical tradition. Nevertheless, it is interesting that the play's discussion of a state of being that sounds very much like friendship should take place without any mention of the word friendship itself. It is clear that this is not because *The Lady-Errant* refuses the possibility that friendship should exist between women or, if it does, that it should be named as friendship. For, in referring to Charistus's jealousy of her affection for Olyndus later in the play, Lucasia marvels that her lover should suspect her of being "so treacherous unto Friendship, as / To part *Eumela* and my self" (4.6.1600–601). This is a significant and radical moment because it makes clear what elsewhere remains unspoken: contrary to orthodox interpretations of classical friendship theory, these women are explicitly involved in a friendship with one another. This friendship, based in part upon the women's similarity as loving subjects, marks out ground later claimed more forcefully in Katherine Philips's poems of female friendship.[13] Perhaps the refusal in act three to give the name of friendship to a

---

[12]   Both Eumela and Olyndus imply that duty is never disentangled from love in royal marriages (4.6.1699–704).

[13]   Philips's evident fondness for the play might suggest she found its celebration of women's involvement in friendship and politics inspiring. However, her use of the language of tyranny and conquest in her poems on female friendship does not correspond to Cartwright's critique of those terms in *The Lady-Errant*. There is not the space to do justice to this discrepancy here; nevertheless, Philips's use of militaristic discourse may reflect her interest in writing poetry that allowed her to employ "a range of powerful, erotic emotions to [address] female friends without moral censure" (Williamson 73).

relation that perfectly fits that definition should alert the reader to other friendly relations in the play that are not explicitly identified as such.

This is a particularly appropriate way of thinking about the alternative parliament that the play's women attempt to assemble during the men's absence. The set of relationships constructed by this parliament is similarly not referred to as a friendship but, according to both the logic of the play and Aristotelian friendship theory, can be understood as one. The parliament immediately announces its allegiance to friendship rather than to love through the simple fact that it is made up solely by women and thus subscribes to the friendly principle of homogeneity. Since the play makes clear that it associates heterosexual love with tyranny and homosocial friendship with egalitarianism, the female parliament—despite its revolutionary status—can be read as holding a remarkably positive position within the play's philosophical economy. The rhetoric used by Adraste, queen of Cyprus and leader of the female parliament, for example, explicitly locates the political struggle as a throwing-off of the shackles of male tyranny. Employing language elsewhere used to describe love, Adraste asks why the greater bodily strength of some men "should bind us / To be their Slaves" (4.1.1181–2). The opposition of tyranny and amity is a cornerstone of the friendship tradition. As Shannon notes, "the unsubordinating relation of friendly equals represents an alternative to the subordination without limits attempted by the tyrannical ruler and always potential in an ideology of more or less absolute monarchy" (56). In dramatizing the organization undertaken by friendly equals who oppose an absolute monarch, yet gendering these friends female, *The Lady-Errant* is simultaneously faithful and treacherous to the friendship tradition. This curious mixture is maintained in the same speech, when a further reference to the idea that "Nature did mean us Soveraigns" (4.1.1188) accesses the language of friendship understood by Shannon to articulate a sense of self-possession necessary for and inherent in friendship, as well as friendship's capacity to signify as an alternative polity (17–54 and *passim*).[14] Importantly for the egalitarian character of friendship, although Queen Adraste gives the nascent parliament's opening address, it is not clear that she functions as its monarch or leader. Eumela, a mere commoner, takes the role of "Mistres Speaker" and has far more to say about the organization of the state than Adraste. Indeed, the regime change enacted in *The Lady-Errant* is represented from the very beginning of the play as occurring by the mutual will of the current population of Cyprus. This is no political coup enacted by a disgruntled military general or an excitable opposition leader, but a popular uprising that can produce written proof of its widespread approval. This is demonstrated in the first scene

---

[14]   Although, in opposition to Derrida, Shannon argues that "sixteenth-century friendship does not bespeak larger social or national formations in microcosm" (18), her discussion of the similarities between friendship emblems and those in which concord or union is represented by "a multimembered body" (36) displaying three sets of arms suggests that the culture did on occasion demonstrate the capacity to imagine a friendship made up of more than two friends.

of the play, where the women refer to a document that lists all those who support the revolution:

> Eleven Court-Ladies on the Roll already;
> *Hyantha* then sends word, that ten, or twelve
> Very substantiall Countrey-Ladies have
> Subscrib'd …
> The City-wives, swarm in …
> Of Countrey Gentlewomen, and their eldest daughters,
> More than can write their Names. (1.1.30–37)

As Tomlinson acknowledges, "Cartwright's female parliament tackles head-on women's lack of political representation," and just because the political body is eventually undermined by some of its own members does not nullify the rhetorical and philosophical arguments made in its favor while it existed (113–4). Aristotle himself suggests that a community that constitutes itself around a common good "which extends over the whole of life" should not only be considered a "political community," but also a community of friends, albeit a friendship that is inferior to that which arises without any common goal in view (trans. Thomson *Nic. Eth.* 216).

Clearly, *The Lady-Errant* does not present a meticulously argued case in favor of women's involvement in an egalitarian polity that should be structured according to the principles of friendship. However, whether by design or not, the play does contain a number of allusions to such a project. It is curious, for example, that Lucasia's construction of loving-as-friendship should have such a close connection to a passage in Aristotle that offers the example of a mother's love for her son as "the distinctive virtue of friendship." Does the play, perhaps, seek to draw attention to the hidden feminine origins of the supposedly male virtue of friendship?[15] The place of women in the friendship tradition has also exercised Jacques Derrida who, in *Politics of Friendship*, draws attention to the way that friendship has often been understood (or metaphorized) as fraternity. In a reading of Friedrich Nietzsche's "Of the Friend" in *Thus Spoke Zarathustra*, Derrida comments upon Zarathustra's iteration of the misogyny inherent in the Aristotelian friendship tradition. Zarathustra repeatedly claims that women are incapable of friendship because they are ruled by the tyrannical force of love. Derrida describes the position as follows:

> [Woman] is at once tyrant and slave, and that is why she (still) remains incapable of friendship, she knows only love. This thesis concerns not only woman, but the hierarchy between love and friendship. Love is *below* friendship because it is an

---

[15] *The Nicomachean Ethics* otherwise refers to women as individuals generally inferior to men who should have an appropriate sphere of influence in the home, and who bring some virtues to a friendly marriage. See Thomson trans. 211, 218, 222.

above/below relation, one of inferiority and superiority, slavery and tyranny. It is implied, then, that friendship is freedom plus equality. The only thing missing is fraternity, and we are coming to that. (282)

In this essay I have been arguing that *The Lady-Errant*—within its own historical and cultural limitations—attempts to do something subtly different with the tradition of friendship that it inherits from the classical world. Like Nietzsche, the play considers that love and friendship, although superficially similar, are in fact two radically different entities: the former grounded in hierarchy, the latter, equality. However, *The Lady-Errant* departs from Nietzsche and the Aristotelian tradition in three innovative ways. Firstly, it does not explicitly seek to locate the responsibility for the hierarchical nature of love in the figure of the woman but in love itself. Secondly, it acknowledges that women are capable of friendship. Thirdly, and most significantly, it suggests that friendship between women can constitute a political community with an egalitarian impulse, and allows the reader space to understand this as a positive development.

Concluding his discussion of "Of the Friend," Derrida offers a summary and a call to action:

> But as woman has not yet attained to friendship because she remains—and this is love—"slave" or "tyrant", friendship to come continues to mean, for Zarathustra: freedom, equality, fraternity. The fragile, unstable and recent motto … of a republic. Unless it appeals to a friendship capable of *simultaneously* overwhelming philosophical history (Aristotelian, as we have just seen) and Enlightenment fraternity *qua* the sublation [*relève*] … of Christian fraternity: three friendships in one, the same, in sum, with which one must break. (284–5)[16]

Derrida's attack upon fraternity—which he also calls "phratrocentrism"—seems mirrored by *The Lady-Errant*, in its modest way. The play opens up the possibility of a non-phratrocentric political friendship—a friendship that does not just involve brothers but also sisters, and brothers and sisters. By combining the classical philosophical heritage, both Platonic and Aristotelian, with the increased sense of feminine agency felt at the court of Charles I through the influence of Queen Henrietta Maria, *The Lady-Errant* manages to enact a brief break from the tradition of male friendship, and to look forward to a more sustained break to come.

---

[16]   Italics in original.

Chapter 12

Milton against Servitude: Classical Friendship, Tyranny, and the Law of Nature

Gregory Chaplin

In classical literature, the incompatibility of tyranny and friendship is proverbial: tyrants are depicted as fearing true friendship, and, as Aristotle observes, "in a tyranny there is little or no friendship" (*Nic. Eth.* trans. Thomson 278). However much individual authors differ in their definitions of friendship and depictions of tyrants, this commonplace evokes contrasting images of the body politic: one in which a tyrant possesses absolute authority over the state and its subjects, converting it into his private domain, and another—the Greek *polis* or Roman *res publica*—in which freeborn male citizens are endowed with substantial political agency within a clearly established public sphere. For Plato, this opposition exemplifies the broader cultural differences between the Persian Empire and democratic Athens. As he explains in the *Symposium*:

> The reason why such love, together with love of intellectual and physical achievement, is condemned by the Persians is to be found in the absolute nature of their empire; it does not suit the interest of the government that a generous spirit and strong friendships and attachments should spring up among their subjects, and these are effects which love has an especial tendency to produce. The truth of this was actually experienced by our tyrants at Athens; it was the love of Aristogiton and the strong affections of Harmodius which destroyed their power. (48)

To secure its position, the Persian regime promotes a culture of servitude that undermines the personal and interpersonal virtues antithetical to subordination. In Athens, where these virtues have traditionally been cultivated, the social body is inherently hostile to subservience and eventually purges itself of oppressors.

Given these deep-seated associations, we might expect that the humanist revival of classical friendship would have posed a threat to the increasingly absolutist monarchies of the early modern period by intensifying loyalties between subjects, ennobling tyrannicide, and encouraging speculation about non-monarchical forms of government. But while recent scholars have isolated ways in which humanist friendship challenged the existing social order, they have stopped short of making larger political claims. Laurie Shannon, for instance, concludes that "classical *amicitia* served as a vehicle to organize the private subject's sovereign aspirations, a maximization of his autonomy," yet she finds no direct connection between these "sovereign aspirations" and the emergence of alternative political ideologies: "Neither democratic nor republican—and not even directly civic—sixteenth-century friendship does not bespeak larger social or national formations in microcosm" (126, 18). At first glance, this claim seems to hold true for seventeenth-century friendship as well: a poetics of friendship indebted to Horace becomes increasingly linked to political dissent rather than rebellion. Ben Jonson's "Inviting a Friend to Supper," for instance, imagines a space for eating, drinking, and conversation free from censorship and government spies ("we will have no Pooly, or Parrot by" [36]) that will ensure the "liberty" of himself and his guests (42). But Jonson's poetic heirs are decidedly royalist, and the language of friendship and rural retreat associated with the *beatus vir* ("the happy man") tradition expresses their resistance during the English Civil War and interregnum. In "The Grasshopper," Richard Lovelace insists that he and his friend Charles Cotton "will create / A genuine summer in each other's breast" despite the "cold time and frozen fate" of defeat and isolation (21–3), while the extensive friendship poetry of Katherine Philips works to build and maintain a royalist coterie.[1] By the middle of the century, the most conspicuous literary displays of friendship are associated with nostalgia for the old monarchical order.

Milton provides us with a crucial counterexample and evidence that the discourse of friendship could help to legitimate revolution and fashion an alternative to monarchical government. From his initial defense of the execution of Charles I in *The Tenure of Kings and Magistrates* (1649) to his final effort to stave off the restoration of Charles II with *The Ready and Easy Way to Establish a Free Commonwealth* (1660), he devoted himself to "the good Old Cause" of English republicanism.[2] But the sources and nature of his republicanism have been hard to characterize. His political tracts are polemical responses to particular situations rather than theoretical texts outlining the founding principles of a new republic, a fact that has forced scholars to seek more implicit manifestations of his politics. Martin Dzelzainis traces Milton's republicanism to his investment in the classical civic virtues and "the moral economy of the commonwealth" ("Milton's Classical Republicanism" 20), while Thomas Corns finds it expressed in his language: "the cause of English republicanism is a language. It is an idiom in which a value system and an aesthetic are inscribed, and it is an undeferential posture which utterly subverts the assumptions of Stuart monarchism" (42). Thus Milton's dedication to a free commonwealth has less to do with a prior commitment to a particular

---

[1]   For royalist friendship, see Kerrigan, "Transformations of Friendship," and the essays by Penelope Anderson and Christopher Marlow in this volume. For the *beatus vir* tradition, see Røstvig, *The Happy Man.*

[2]   7:462. All references to Milton's prose works are to *The Complete Prose Works of John Milton* (hereafter CPW) and are cited in the text by volume and page number.

constitutional arrangement than it does with his fundamental assumptions about the nature of the political subject, the virtues that this subject should cultivate, and the political environment that best encourages these virtues. Focusing first on his early political tracts, primarily *The Tenure of Kings and Magistrates*, I will argue that Milton draws on the discourse of friendship to fashion his normative political subject—the masculine citizen whose sovereignty over himself and his household is incompatible with absolutism—and the natural laws that govern the relationships among these autonomous subjects. These principles of political agency and interaction, I conclude, remain central to *Paradise Lost* (1667) and testify to the underlying continuity between Milton's radical political prose and his epic.

Shannon rightly observes that the privileged place of Cicero's *De amicitia* and *De officiis* in the early modern curriculum disseminated a Ciceronian–Stoic model of friendship that presupposes the autonomy and self-sufficiency of its constituents (30–31). "[F]riendship springs from nature rather than from need," Cicero has Laelius declare in *De amicitia*, implicitly distinguishing his view of friendship from Platonic and Epicurean relationships (trans. Falconer 139). It is not "the daughter of poverty and want," he insists:

> [T]he truth is far otherwise. For to the extent that a man relies upon himself and is so fortified by virtue and wisdom that he is dependent on no one and considers all his possessions to be within himself, in that degree is he most conspicuous for seeking out and cherishing friendships. (141–3)

Adapting Stoic philosophy, Cicero describes friendship as the natural bond between virtuous and autonomous individuals brought about by their similitude: "Then it surely will be granted as a fact that good men love and join to themselves other good men, in a union which is almost that of relationship and nature. For there is nothing more eager or more greedy than nature for what is like itself" (161). However rare, ideal friendships are not an anomaly for Cicero; they are the ultimate manifestation of the natural laws of amity that unite the human race ("between us all there exists a certain tie which strengthens with our proximity to each other" [129]) and organize the natural universe: "in nature and the entire universe whatever things are at rest and whatever are in motion are united by friendship and scattered by discord" (135).

Written during the death throes of the Roman Republic—at the same time that Cicero was composing his *Philippics* against Antony—*De amicitia* and *De officiis* transmit republican values. Throughout *De amicitia*, Cicero takes care to distinguish between legitimate friendship and conspiracy ("dishonourable it certainly is, and not to be allowed, for anyone to plead in defence of sins in general and especially of those against the State [*contra rem publicam*], that he committed them for the sake of a friend" [151]); to exclude tyrants from participation in *amicitia* ("Such indeed is the life of tyrants—a life, I mean, in which there can be no faith, no affection, no trust in the continuance of goodwill; where every act arouses suspicion and anxiety and where friendship has no place" [163–5]); and to contrast the masculine virtues of true friends ("stability, sincerity, and weight" [201]) with the depravity of flatterers ("fickle and false-hearted men" [199]). Likewise, by focusing on Laelius's relationship with Scipio Africanus, Cicero ties friendship to a Roman hero who exemplified traditional republican values. Milton also saw Scipio as an embodiment of republican virtue: in *Paradise Regained*, he makes the "young African" a positive point of comparison to Jesus.[3] In *De officiis*, Cicero includes friendship and tyrannicide in his discussion of duties. Republican values permeate this influential philosophical work ("And if we will only bear in mind the superiority and dignity of our nature, we shall realize how wrong it is to abandon ourselves to excess and to live in luxury and voluptuousness, and how right it is to live in thrift, self-denial, simplicity, and sobriety" [109]), one which Dzelzainis assigns a crucial role in Milton's political development. "Cicero's analysis of fortitude in *De officiis* served as the blueprint for [Milton's] *Of Education*," he maintains, the pamphlet that "represents something very close to a 'republican moment' for Milton" ("Milton's Classical Republicanism" 13, 14).

Since explicit discussion about alternative political models was so limited prior to the English Civil War, there are no English precedents for a theory of popular sovereignty informed by Ciceronian–Stoic friendship. But a significant sixteenth-century French text, Etienne de La Boétie's *Discours de la servitude volontaire*, also known as *Le Contr'un*, anticipates several key aspects of Milton's *The Tenure of Kings and Magistrates*. For many literary scholars, La Boétie is most famous for his friendship with Michel de Montaigne, who eulogizes their intimacy in "De l'amitié." Indeed, since Montaigne's original plan was to place his friend's political treatise at the center of the first book of his *Essais*, this famous essay was initially envisioned as both a celebration of their relationship and an introduction to *servitude volontaire*. But by the 1570s, the Huguenots were seeking to use the tract against the French monarchy, and Montaigne felt compelled to omit it from his volume—and for good reason: despite his protests, La Boétie's *Discours*, like Milton's *Tenure*, is as dangerous to monarchy in general as it is to tyrants.

In his peroration, La Boétie draws together the separate threads of his argument by asserting the familiar opposition between tyranny and friendship in Ciceronian terms:

> Indeed, it is certain that the tyrant is never loved, nor does he love. Friendship
> is a sacred word: it is a holy thing. It never occurs except between honorable
> people, and it arises only from mutual esteem. It maintains itself not so much by
> means of good turns as by a good life. What renders a friend assured of the other
> is the knowledge he has of his integrity. The guarantees he has from him are
> his good nature, faith in each other, and constancy. There cannot be friendship
> where there is cruelty, where there is disloyalty, where there is injustice. Among

---

[3]   3.101. All references to Milton's poetry are to Hughes's *Complete Poems and Major Prose*.

the wicked when they assemble, there is a plot, not companionship. They do not provide for one another, but fear one another. They are not friends but accomplices. (220)

From the beginning of his essay, La Boétie equates friendship with the fundamental laws of nature and fraternal equality: "Our nature is such that the common duties of friendship take up a good share of the course of our life" (192). If we would recognize "the rights that nature has given us," he insists, "we would be obedient to parents, subject to reason, and slaves to no one" (197). Likewise, he observes "nature, the minister of God, the governess of human beings, has made us all of the same form and as it seems, from the same mold, so that all of us should recognize one another as companions or rather as brothers" (197). Inequalities do not legitimate oppressive hierarchies, but enable "brotherly love to do its work," and the gift of speech that nature has given us allows us "through the common and mutual declaration of our thoughts" to "make a communion of our wills" (197–8). Thus he concludes: "we cannot doubt that we are all naturally free, since we are all companions; and it cannot enter anyone's minds that nature has placed anyone in servitude, having put us all in companionship" (198).

The ideal of friendship that La Boétie sets against the tyrant does not stem primarily from education or other civilizing influences; it is inscribed within the laws of nature. Properly cultivating one's natural impulses leads to friendship and freedom. His emphasis on the "same form" and "same mold" draws on the logic of similitude and identity that Cicero uses to naturalize and connect his theories of friendship and wider human fellowship. "[W]e are born for Justice, and that right is based, not upon men's opinions, but upon Nature," Cicero writes in *De legibus*:

This fact will immediately be plain if you once get a clear conception of man's fellowship and union with his fellow-men. For no single thing is so like another, so exactly its counterpart, as all of us are to one another. Nay, if bad habits and false beliefs did not twist the weaker minds and turn them in whatever direction they are inclined, no one would be so like his own self as all men would be like all others. (329)

La Boétie's argument depends on the same logic ("each one should be able to look into the other as into a mirror and recognize himself" [198]), and this emphasis on similitude as the basis of equality reverberates throughout the friendship tradition, which often stresses the astonishing likeness of close friends. The "mutual declaration" of thoughts and "communion" of wills also has a privileged place in it. Montaigne not only asserts that "friendship feeds on communication," but he describes his relationship with La Boétie as a complete blending of their wills (*Complete Essays* 136). For La Boétie, as for Cicero, the organizational principles of human society are the basic premises of friendship writ large.

The equation that La Boétie makes between nature, reason, and friendship frames his investigation into the origin of voluntary servitude. Despite the dictates of nature and reason, he finds that whole nations of men have lost their innate love of freedom and voluntarily subjugate themselves to tyrants. He seeks to understand the forces that have made this possible: "what unfortunate accident is it that has so denatured man—the only being truly born to live freely—as to make him lose the remembrance of his original state and the desire to regain it?" (199). He discerns that custom can distort even the strongest natural predispositions and traces the subsequent elements of servitude to its influence. People born into servitude "easily become cowardly and effeminate," and tyrants establish social practices that cultivate these tendencies (207). Tyrants also suppress learning and "liberty of action and of speech," so that those "better born than the others" who have "polished their heads through study and knowledge" will not recognize each other and will have to live "completely alone in their imaginings" (205–6). Finally, he finds that "the spring and secret of domination, the support and foundation of tyranny" is the corrupt system of patronage that it establishes (215). Every tyrant has minions, flatterers, and sycophants, who are "the accomplices of his cruelties, the companions of his pleasures, the pimps of his lust, and who share in the loot of his pillages" (215). Each of his favorites has his own accomplices, generating a system of patronage and dependence that stratifies the social order and props up the tyrant's regime. Friendship has no place within such a society. In contrast to the fraternal society grounded in nature and reason, La Boétie describes every element of a tyrannical society as denatured and effeminate—the tyrant, his flatterers, and the populace subordinated to his will.

Although we cannot confirm that Milton was familiar with the *Discours* of La Boétie, their writings demonstrate a common debt to Cicero and analogous applications of humanist principles. They both see custom as the primary force that encourages servitude—a parallel that Merritt Hughes notes in his introduction to *The Tenure* (CPW 3:109). They stress that the law of nature and the law of reason conform to one another and correspond to divine law. In addition, they often draw on similar texts and examples: both use the anointment of Saul to undermine monarchy (1 Samuel 9–10); both allude to the example of Harmodius and Aristogiton; both echo classical commonplaces to describe a tyrant's crimes and maintain that a tyrant's power destroys the notion of a public sphere; and both embrace the orientalist politics of their classical sources. But the parallels between La Boétie's *Discours* and Milton's *Tenure* should not obscure their differences. La Boétie's essay is a general and primarily secular inquiry into the origin and continuing causes of servitude, whereas *The Tenure* responds to a very specific political situation and defends tyrannicide with a specific monarch in mind.

Published two weeks after the execution of Charles I, *The Tenure of Kings and Magistrates* offers a theory of popular sovereignty that goes well beyond the needs of the moment. As Dzelzainis observes, Milton proposes "not a theory of resistance so much as a theory of revolution" (Introduction xvii). This theory is rooted in the absolute right to personal sovereignty guaranteed by the law of nature. Milton begins his narrative of the origin of political communities with this assertion: "No man who knows ought, can be so stupid to deny that all men naturally were born free, being the image and resemblance of God himself, and were by privilege above all creatures, born to command and not obey: and that they liv'd so" (CPW 3:198–9). He bases natural equality on the claim, as La Boétie phrases it, that "nature ... has made us all of the same form, and as it seems from the same mold." The controversial nature of this declaration becomes clear when it is compared with the basic assumptions of royalist political theory. In *Patriarcha*, for instance, Sir Robert Filmer labels "the natural liberty of mankind new, plausible and dangerous" and dismisses it as "contradict[ing] the doctrine and history of the Holy Scriptures, the constant practice of all ancient monarchies, and the very principles of the law of nature" (1, 3).

Royalists such as Filmer assert that the authority that God invested in Adam as father becomes the basis for all future political authority: "For as Adam was lord of his children, so his children under him had a command and a power over their own children, but still with subordination to the first parent, who is lord paramount over his children's children to all generation, as being the grandfather of his people" (6–7). The absolute power of monarchs, then, stems from their status as "first parent," or rather, as the legitimate heirs to the power of the first parent. Of course, the genealogical problems with this theory were quite apparent to its critics, as Milton declares: "Kings in these dayes ... boast the justness of thir title, by holding it immediately of God, yet cannot show the time when God ever set on the throne them or thir forefathers" (CPW 3:211). The power of the royalist position, however, stems not from history but from the emotional power and compelling if logically suspect analogy between king and father—an analogy that Milton disputes in his first *Defense of the English People*. It assimilates the principles of patriarchy, patrilineal descent, and primogeniture so widely accepted in early modern England into the fundamental laws of nature. Political authority and power pass from God to Adam to the Stuart monarchs like a patrimony transmitted through an imaginary line of first-born sons of first-born sons. Since the king possesses the authority of the first parent, his subjects are forever minor children subordinate to his command.

Milton's claim that all men are "born free, being the image and resemblance of God himself" undermines the basic premises of the royalist position. Like Cicero and La Boétie, he employs the logic of similitude and identity to establish natural liberty and political equality. Because all men are born in the image of God, they are all facsimiles of the same original, and since all of them are cast from the "same mold," all have equal right "to command and not obey." Authority is not a singular property passed from father to eldest son; it is embodied equally in everyone who shares in the image of God. And the multiplication of authority through similitude, as recent studies of Renaissance friendship stress, undermines the dynamics of hierarchical authority.[4] Rather than envisioning the entire state as a household with a single patriarch, Milton makes the patriarch of every household a sovereign. To be under "tyranny and servitude," he argues, is to be deprived of "that power, which is the root and sourse of all liberty, to dispose and *oeconomize* in the Land which God hath giv'n them, as Maisters of Family in thir own house and free inheritance" (CPW 3:236–7). Thus Milton's republicanism limits full political agency to men. As Adam acknowledges to Raphael in *Paradise Lost*, Eve "resembl[es] less / His Image who Made both" and therefore "less express[es] / The character of that Dominion giv'n / O're other Creatures" (8.542–6). The ambiguities generated by this position haunt Adam and Eve's relationship throughout the epic, but Milton never addresses them in his political tracts. When references to women appear in *The Tenure* and first *Defense*, they either confirm the sovereignty of the male subject by presenting women as part of a household that needs to be protected or undermine that sovereignty by depicting women who have seized control of the household.

By beginning his political narrative with Genesis 1:26 ("Let us make man in our image, after our likeness") rather than the Fall, Milton follows the humanist practice of reviving "the classical ideal of the *vir humanus* by subsuming it under the biblical ideal of Man as the *imago Dei*," which foregrounds "Man's unique dignity" and "capacity for self-perfection" (Bradshaw 103, 115). This classical–biblical synthesis ties upholding the divine image—which is the basis of masculine sovereignty—to the cultivation of the classical political virtues. For Milton, then, political virtue becomes synonymous with a properly realized masculinity. This connection drives the rhetorical patterns of his political tracts, which consistently align legitimate political agency with masculine self-mastery and its absence with male effeminacy. He opens *The Tenure* by framing political allegiance in terms of a disciplined adherence to reason:

> If men within themselves would be govern'd by reason, and not generally give up thir understanding to a double tyrannie, of Custom from without, and blind affections within, they would discern better, what it is to favour and uphold the Tyrant of a Nation. But being slaves within doors, no wonder that they strive so much to have the public State conformably govern'd to the inward vitious rule, by which they govern themselves. For indeed none can love freedom heartilie, but good men; the rest love not freedom, but licence; which never hath more scope or more indulgence then under Tyrants. (CPW 3:190)

Disputing the legitimacy of Charles's execution, like Milton's Presbyterian opponents, indicates that one has given up mastery over oneself by failing to follow

---

4   Shannon writes: "friendship arrived from classical models ... [and] offered Renaissance readers a world in which there are, so to speak, *two sovereigns*" (7). Also see Masten 12–27.

the dictates of reason. Like La Boétie, Milton sees a fundamental connection between internal and external servitude: giving in to the tyranny of inner passions predisposes one to tyrannical regimes. In addition to preparing men for political servitude, "being slaves within doors" carries with it the insinuation of domestic servitude. The triumph of passion over reason within the male subject parallels the failure of masculine authority within a household.

This image of a domestic world-turned-upside-down helps organize the opposition between good men, who love freedom and are naturally feared by tyrants, and bad men, who are servile and allied with tyrants, that structures Milton's political tracts. In the *Defense*, Charles I is described as an unstable tyrant whose ungoverned lust leads to a shifting theatrical self and to his criminal transgressions. His inability to govern himself and his state are tied to his inability to manage his household: "It was then within his own household that he began to be a bad king" (CPW 4:521). Salmasius, the author of *Defensio Regia*, is ridiculed as a paid performer, whose attempt to produce sympathy for the dead king "resembles nothing so much as the senseless wailing of women hired to mourn at funerals" (310). Milton savages Salmasius's masculinity, declaring him a "eunuch" and then transforming him into the nymph Salmacis, whose "false tears" are intended "to draw the strength from manly hearts" (309, 312). He insists that Salmasius's politics stem from his own domestic servitude: "so naturally you want to force royal tyranny on others after being used to suffer so slavishly a woman's tyranny at home" (380). In *The Tenure*, Milton characterizes the Presbyterians as "old gray headed Flatterers" who seek to use "unmaskuline Rhetorick" to soften the "mild and tender dispositions" of the men who still adhere to their duty (CPW 3:209, 195). They would rather restore tyranny, Milton stresses in the *Defense*, than "allo[w] their brothers and friends a position of just equality with themselves" (CPW 4.511).

The heroes of Milton's political tracts maintain their masculinity and proper political agency—and thus the *imago Dei* in which they were created—by cultivating the classical virtues. They are "sincere and real men" who have "swett and labour'd out amidst the throng and noises of Vulgar and irrational men" (CPW 3:191–2). Cromwell, in particular, exemplifies the masculine self-mastery that the defenders of the Stuart monarchy lack:

> Nor was this remarkable, for he was a soldier well-versed in self-knowledge, and whatever enemy lay within—vain hopes, fears, desires—he had either previously destroyed within himself or had long since reduced to subjection. Commander first over himself, victor over himself, he had learned to achieve over himself the most effective triumph. (CPW 4:667–8)

In defense of his own character, Milton calls attention to his own republican virtues: his steadfastness ("I stand unmoved and steady in my resolution"); his "good repute among good men"; and his disdain of luxury: "I maintain my frugal way of life" (589, 627). And since ennobling friendships presuppose virtue and self-mastery, Milton cites the continued loyalty of his friends ("some with whom I might as with true friends exchange the conversation of Pylades [with Orestes] and Theseus [with Heracles]" [590]) as evidence that his blindness is a sign of divine favor, confirming his status as a good man. In essence, Milton presents the same opposition as La Boétie: a fraternal society that stems from the first laws of creation and nature—a natural republic that can be regained through the exercise of discipline and virtue—versus an effeminate, denatured social order that embraces tyranny and servitude.

In *The Tenure*, Milton emphasizes that the need for centralized government stems from the effects of the Fall, which prompts the larger social group to invest the "authority and power of self-defence and preservation … originally and naturally in every one of them" in either a single individual or a select group (CPW 3:199). But by defining the transference of authority from sovereign subjects to kings and magistrates as a trust rather than as a contract, he maintains that the people have the right to resume authority and change monarchs or forms of government whenever they see fit.[5] At first, the implications of these claims—individuals invested with an unprecedented degree of personal sovereignty that they can reassert whenever they please—seem to flirt with anarchy. Milton avoids this problem by appealing to another principle drawn from the Ciceronian–Stoic theory of friendship.

Although he claims that a king may be deposed "merely by the liberty and right of free born Men, to be govern'd as seems to them best" (CPW 3:206), Milton goes on to attack the distinction between tyrants-by-practice and tyrants-by-usurpation—and thus the Presbyterian claim that subjects are not allowed to take action against a legitimate king who has degenerated into a tyrant. Having defined a tyrant in conventional terms ("his will [is] boundless and exorbitant, and the fulfilling whereof is for the best part accompanied with innumerable wrongs and oppressions of the people, murders[,] massachers, rapes, adulteries, desolation, and subversion of Cities and whole Provinces"), Milton claims that the actions that can be taken against him are self-evident: "Against whom what the people lawfully may doe, as against a common pest, and destroyer of mankind, I suppose no man of clear judgment need go further to be guided then by the very principles of nature in him" (212). These principles render the subtle distinctions of the Presbyterians superfluous, as Milton makes clear: "For look how much right the King of Spain hath to govern us at all, so much hath the King of England to govern us tyrannically" (213–4). An English king has no more right to govern as a tyrant than a foreign monarch has to impose his rule on the nation through conquest. Milton then declares the natural principle behind this claim: "who knows not that there is a mutual bond of amity and brotherhood between man and man over all the world, neither is it the English Sea that can sever us from the duty and relation: a straiter bond yet there is between fellow-subjects, neighbors, and friends" (214). Milton takes this "bond of amity" directly from Cicero who, in *De officiis*, *De*

---

⁵   On the difference between a contract and a trust, see Dzelzainis, Introduction xvii–xviii.

amicitia, and other works, cites it as the foundation of human society and the guiding principle of political organization and law.

This bond of amity, which underwrites and links Cicero's theories of friendship and politics, is derived from Stoic thought, as he acknowledges in *De officiis*:

> Since, as the Stoics hold, everything that the earth produces is created for man's use; and as men, too, are born for the sake of men, that they may be able mutually to help one another; in this direction we ought to follow Nature as our guide, to contribute to the general good by an interchange of acts of kindness, by giving and receiving, and thus by our skill, our industry, and our talents to cement human society more closely together, man to man. (23–5)

Cicero observes that the most perfect realization of this natural fellowship is the bond of friendship: "But of all the bonds of fellowship, there is none more noble, none more powerful than when good men of congenial character are joined in intimate friendship" (59). Milton's debt is quite clear, just as his assertion that "a straiter bond yet there is between fellow-subjects, neighbors, and friends" is a close paraphrase of Cicero: "there is the closer [bond] of belonging to the same people, tribe, and tongue ... a still closer relation to be citizens of the same city-state ... But a still closer social union exists between kindred" (57). Within this framework of universal amity, those who seek to "destroy the universal brotherhood of mankind" are acting contrary to the laws of nature and are the common enemy of humankind (295). On this basis, Cicero insists that "we have no ties of fellowship with a tyrant ... So those fierce and savage monsters in human form should be cut off from what may be called the common body of humanity" (299). These are the "very principles of nature" that Milton assumes should be apparent to everyone "of clear judgment."

Although Milton is certainly indebted to "the newly available theories ... of non-authoritarian agency and organization" of the 1640s and 1650s, as John Rogers has argued, he derives the conceptual framework for these new patterns of republican agency from the discourse of friendship (27). Milton disperses authority and establishes the sovereignty of individuals by invoking the logic of similitude and identity: "all men naturally were born free, being the image and resemblance of God himself." The harmonious interaction between these sovereign individuals stems from the universal laws of amity that govern or should govern human interaction. These two premises—similitude and amity—allow Milton to postulate an ideal political order that frees virtuous and rational individuals from the constraints of centralized authority. Thus he establishes an open-ended theory of popular sovereignty that avoids anarchy and the state of nature that Hobbes describes as a "miserable condition of War" (225–6).

Both premises remain crucial in *Paradise Lost*. The poem repeatedly stresses that Adam—and to a lesser and thus problematic extent, Eve—is created in the image of God and that this divine similitude gives Adam and his offspring dominion over the beasts: "Let us make now Man in our image, Man / In our similitude, and let them rule" (7.519–20; also see 4.288–94 and 8.437–44). The language comes directly from Genesis 1:26, of course, and the subject of Milton's epic forces him to address the moment when God creates Adam. Nonetheless, Adam's reaction to Nimrod's tyranny in Book 12 indicates that Milton continues to see the dissemination of God's image as the basis of individual sovereignty and human freedom:

> O execrable Son so to aspire
> Above his Brethren, to himself assuming
> Authority usurpt, from God not giv'n:
> He gave us only over Beast, Fish, Fowl
> Dominion absolute; that right we hold
> By his donation; but Man over men
> He made not Lord; such title to himself
> Reserving, human left from human free. (12.64–71)

Adam's words echo Milton's repeated insistence that kings and tyrants have no basis for setting themselves above their peers: "God's own law has taught us that a king should obey the laws and not exalt himself above the rest who are also his brethren" (CPW 4:345). Michael describes Nimrod as displeased "With fair equality, [and] fraternal state" and thus banishing "concord and [the] law of nature" (26, 29). As a would-be tyrant, he excludes himself from the "mutual bond of amity" that unites humanity in brotherhood and fraternal equality. "A mighty Hunter" who hunts "Men not Beasts," Nimrod is Cicero's "beast … in human form" (33, 30).

But amity is not a new principle unveiled in the post-lapsarian world of Book 12: it is central to God's plan and final glory. In Book 8, God, who is "alone / From all Eternity," asks Adam why he needs a companion, when God himself does not. Adam has two responses. The first is that God is perfect, whereas Man needs "conversation with his like to help / Or solace his defects" (418–9). This need for conversation echoes Milton's divorce tracts and reveals the debt that Adam and Eve's relationship owes to another mode of friendship, an emotional and intellectual union that is at odds with Ciceronian friendship's investment in masculine sovereignty.[6] Adam's second response is more difficult:

> No need that thou
> Shouldst propagate, already infinite;
> And through all numbers absolute, though One;

---

[6] In "'One Flesh, One Heart, One Soul': Renaissance Friendship and Miltonic Marriage," which traces Milton's marital ideal to his Platonically inspired friendship with Charles Diodati, I suggest that the conflict between egalitarian impulses and hierarchical imperatives impels Adam and Eve toward the Fall. For a different view, see Luxon, *Single Imperfection: Milton, Marriage and Friendship.*

But Man by number is to manifest
His single imperfection, and beget
Like of his like, his image multipli'd,
In unity defective, which requires
Collateral love, and dearest amity. (8.419–26)

God is both infinite and singular; he fills the infinite cosmos—he is everything—and yet he is still one entity. Man is finite, and his singularity is a sign of his imperfection. He can only approach God's perfection by multiplying his image through reproduction. But because each image is a separate entity, there is no guarantee that it will interact in harmony with others. Although this potential defect in unity has ominous implications, especially after the Fall when the image of God in Man is defaced and disorder infiltrates the natural world, it also creates the need for "collateral love and dearest amity." This need, I would argue, is an opportunity: the experience of love and amity through "[s]ocial communication" makes Man more like Milton's materialist God, for whom chaos is an occasion to fashion concord out of discord.

Indeed, God creates by instilling amity into the primal matter of chaos, "a dark / Illimitable Ocean" composed of "endless wars" between the elements: "hot, cold, moist, and dry, four Champions fierce / Strive here for Maistry, and to Battle bring their embryon Atoms" (2.891–2, 898–900). The Son of God initiates the process of creation by command: "Silence, ye troubl'd waves, and thou Deep, peace, / Said then th' Omnific Word, your discord end" (7.216–7). On the now "wat'ry calm" of chaos, the "Spirit of God" continues:

And vital virtue infus'd, and vital warmth
Throughout the fluid Mass, but downward purg'd
The black tartareous cold infernal dregs
Adverse to life; then founded, then conglob'd
Like things to like, the rest to several place
Disparted, and between spun out the Air,
And Earth self-balanc't on her Centre hung. (234–42)

Together, these two gestures—the words of the Son and the vital heat of the Spirit—alter the harmonics of matter, transforming chaos into a created universe organized by the guiding and unifying principle of amity ("Like things to like"). The images of discord, misrule, and civil war are displaced by the natural forces of concord and sympathy that guarantee peaceful interaction among all levels of the natural and human world. The Fall impairs these forces, prompting the return of violent disorder:

Thus began
Outrage from lifeless things; but Discord first
Daughter of Sin, among th'irrational,

> Death introduc'd through fierce antipathy:
> Beast now with Beast gan war, and Fowl with Fowl,
> And Fish with Fish. (10.706–11)

This "war" extends to Adam and Eve and their offspring. So instead of a proliferating society of humans who share the image of God and are bound together by love and amity, we are presented with Cain's murder of Abel (11.429–49) and Nimrod's war on "his brethren" (12.24–63).

But a perfect creation undermined by sin and degenerating into various kinds of chaos is only half of the overarching narrative. The other half records how God employs his Son to expel the elements of discord and enact a new creation that restores the faithful and incorporates them into a renewed and perfect order. This "return to pristine beginnings," as David Norbrook has demonstrated, is characteristic of republican ideology, which tends to view history "as a series of restorations or reductions" (474). Milton's epic provides us with several intimations of the final apocalyptic restoration. The war between the angels threatens to destroy Heaven ("horrid confusion heapt / Upon confusion rose: and now all Heav'n / Had gone to wrack" [6.668–70]) before the intervention of the Son takes charge of the unfallen angels ("Under thir Head imbodied all in one" [779]), restores Heaven ("At his command the uprooted Hills retir'd / Each to his place ... / ... Heav'n his wonted face renew'd" [781–3]), and purges this renewed world of the rebel angels. The Flood is another instance of "the world destroy'd and world restor'd" (12.3). For a time, "Concord and law of Nature" are re-established: men "spend thir days in joy unblam'd, and dwell / Long time in peace by Families and Tribes / Under paternal rule" (22–4). This is the period of "fair equality, fraternal state" that Nimrod will bring to an end—just as Satan's rebellion shattered concord in Heaven.

These proleptic moments suggest what will happen after the Son finally "dissolve[s] / Satan with his perverted World" and "raise[s] / From the conflagrant mass, purg'd and refin'd, / New Heav'ns, new Earth" (12.546–9). In this new world "wherein the just shall dwell / And after all thir tribulations long / See golden days, fruitful of golden deeds," the redeemed will have recovered the *imago Dei* in which they were created (335–7). The Son will no longer need to reign as "universal King" (317); he his "regal Sceptre shalt lay by, / For regal Sceptre then no more shall need, / God shall be All in All" (339–41). The kingship of the Son, which Norbrook identifies as "a temporary expedient" (475), will no longer be necessary because "the just" will once again be linked by divine similitude and "dearest amity." The repetition of "golden" suggests alchemical perfection as well as the classical golden age described by Hesiod and Ovid. Human society after the apocalypse becomes what it would have been before the Fall: a world of distinct, sovereign subjects governed by the natural law of friendship. At the same time, this future represents the culmination of God's glory as he disseminates his goodness and image throughout his creation ("All in All"). This harmonious, self-governing world echoes God's earlier creation of a perfect world out of chaos, but rather than "embryon Atoms," it is fashioned from rational creatures who have demonstrated their virtue and chosen to participate out of their own free will. For Milton, then, the "good Old Cause" of English republicanism is tied by the laws of nature and reason to the final cause of creation: God's glory.

Taken as a whole, the revival of classical friendship may be too widespread and diverse a phenomenon to be associated with any particular political ideology or social formation. Some expressions of Renaissance friendship were distinctly apolitical, while others became a vehicle for conservative nostalgia. But Milton demonstrates that the Ciceronian–Stoic model of friendship could be invoked to articulate a masculine political subject whose dignity and autonomy are antithetical to absolutism and subordination. As developed by Cicero, this model presupposes a theory of natural law that renders the excessive centralization of political power and authority unnecessary, intolerable, and unnatural. Ciceronian friendship is not simply a relationship; it is a world-view. As such, it provides Milton with a republican ethos and an implicit theory of personal sovereignty and decentralized organization that remains constant from *The Tenure of Kings and Magistrates* to *Paradise Lost*. At the same time, Milton provides us with some insight into the fate of Renaissance friendship and the "sovereign aspirations" that it expressed. In the turbulent years of the mid-seventeenth century, this discourse helps give birth to the ideal of an autonomous political subject—the self-possessed individual of the liberal tradition—endowed with an inalienable freedom.

Chapter 13

From Civic Friendship to Communities of Believers: Anabaptist Challenges to Lutheran and Calvinist Discourses

Thomas Heilke

The sixteenth-century Protestant Reformation introduced to Renaissance Europe new patterns of relationships between religious faith and political life that were not merely side effects or unintended consequences; they were often at the core of the Reformers' efforts to re-envision Christendom or, sometimes, to dismantle it. Friendship in the public realm was one aspect of human life dramatically affected by these efforts.

Friendship has a rich tradition of existence not only in the private sphere—an emphasis we see developing in the early modern period as exemplified in Montaigne's essay on friendship ("Of Friendship")—but especially in the public sphere. This emphasis leads Horst Hutter to propose that the Greek understanding of politics inherited by the West did not *engender* ideas of friendship, but itself *emerged* from primary experiences of friendship, so that the "idea of friendship" was prior to the activities, understanding, and analysis of politics (2). Politics does not "enable" friendship, as we might imagine in a post-Hobbesian conception of politics; rather, friendship *begets* politics.

Luther, Calvin, and the Absence of Friendship[1]

Such a conception of friendship and politics seems remote to the ears of the two central magisterial reformers. Martin Luther and John Calvin had friends, and friendship was part of their lived experience; yet neither provided a theological or political account of human life that could make sense of friendship beyond a strictly utilitarian level. Neither their ecclesiology nor their political theology had a place for non-utilitarian friendship. This absence functions nihistically, where nihilism is the claim not that nothing exists, but that we cannot give an accounting of what is (Nietzsche §3, §11, §13) We find in Calvin and Luther an inability to account for what continues to be—human friendship.

---

[1]   The following several pages are a summary of my argument in "Friendship in the Civic Order: A Reformation Absence."

Two forces anterior to an ecclesiology seem to exclude a serious consideration of friendship from Luther's conception of church or civil society. The first is simplification itself as a primary theoretical drive for Luther. Reducing the complexities of social, political, and religious life to simple relations and simple formulae, Luther flattened class distinctions, hierarchies, and familial relations to every extent possible (Wolin 143). He fit them all into one category: the useful (*das Nützliche*). Where Aristotle had understood friendship as a genus of human activity with at least three discrete yet interrelated species, and where other classical and medieval writers had expanded on the virtue and pleasure species of friendship, Luther discussed friendship solely and purely as a relationship of utility, as one among many utilitarian goods that humans need and enjoy. Friendship plays no discernible constituting or sustaining role in civil or church life. Civil and ecclesiastical institutions and processes exist to restrain evil, but they cannot accomplish more than this negative (Luther, *Catechismus* 22, 70, 76).

Theologically, neither friendship nor any of the other relations of everyday life such as family, kinship, or political hierarchies are properly understood for Luther as aids to moral excellence. For example, he gives no explication of the Christian problem that bearing love for all and having select friends contradict one another ("Appeal" 471; cf. Cassidy 45–67). Doing good only to friends, Luther asserts, is a "heathen virtue." Christians know that every "neighbor [*Nächsten*] deserves material and spiritual support, regardless be he friend or foe." All such acts of support toward the neighbor are acts done out of "friendship" (Luther, *Catechismus* 72). All human relations not between kinfolk or with duly constituted authorities appear to be friendships,[2] and all friendships appear to be of one category—the useful. Friends, like most other external goods, provide material or social support and stability; in a negative mode, they—like other human relations—may keep us from spiritual loss or a fall from grace (*Luther Says* xxx; he is lecturing on Genesis 13:5–7). Friendship is not a mutual aid to virtue or a relationship in such virtue, since no such end seems possible for Luther.

Second, Luther's simplifying trend continues in his flattening of all philosophical–anthropological considerations into one question: how can I be justified before God? The question and answer alike are forensic and openly hostile to further philosophical or ethical exploration. The conception of friendship that results from this forensic philosophical anthropology has a reciprocal effect on and with Luther's ecclesiology. As it works its power in the life of individual believers, the Holy Spirit gathers them into a church amongst whom God's word is proclaimed and the faith of the individual instilled and nourished. Collective nouns describe the believers: church, assembly, "holy congregation," and called-together flock. But Luther does not generally consider this assembled flock from the perspective of friendship and the mutual support such assembled friends might provide (*Catechismus* 98, 104). Having reduced all social and kinship relations to

---

2   This, too, is a departure from Aristotle, who counts such relationships among the kinds of friendship (*Nic. Eth.* trans. Irwin 1161b11–1162a35).

relations of utility, and having reduced the political sphere to a realm of "repressive power" that is little more than "law backed by coercion," with the God-given role of suppressing evil in society, Luther reduces the morally and spiritually formative role of the church to an assembly of hearers of the Word with the underspecified role of forgiving, carrying, and helping one another (*Catechismus* 161). Luther thereby notes the simple, basic tasks of Christian friendship, but—except as a guardian against evil—he does not tell us what it means. An impressive drive to simplify, coupled with a substitution of a teleological philosophical anthropology for a forensic account of human salvation, lead Luther to a remarkably thin account of life together in either a church or a political community. There are friends, but, beyond utilitarian reasoning, we cannot say why or for what.

Calvin, strikingly, offers even less on friendship than does Luther. He uses "friend" or "friends" in a casual associational mode, employing no careful parsing, analysis, or commentary when the term arises. Friendship has no significant role in any of his behavioral or ethical prescriptions. Friendship serves an instrumental role in the provision of social cohesion, but how or why it does so is left aside. He makes no special distinction between friends outside or inside a community of Christian believers, and he treats the proper conduct between friends as a prescription of duty. Like Luther, Calvin makes no moves either to resolve, address, or analyze the tension between particular friendship and love of all that emerges in Christian doctrine. He, too, tends to treat all relationships as the same, leading one sympathetic scholar to comment that "friendships with Calvin were concentrated love of neighbor" [Freundschaften mit Calvin waren konzentrierte Nächstenliebe] (Büsser 76).

Calvin restores to Christian thought a political vocabulary that Luther had cast off, but without restoring a notion of friendship that is more than utilitarian or that makes any significant distinction between the various (Aristotelian) species of companionable relations. There is no sense of any special relationship amongst or between believers, and he offers a minimalist account of the church, reducing it in various exegetical passages to a set of patterned relationships between a divine sovereign and elect individuals who are gathered together primarily to receive an assurance of grace. In his authoritarian model, compliant believers imbibe sound doctrine from authoritative preachers of the word, thereby receiving that assurance of grace (IV.i.5). There is no substantive role for friendship in this conception, but only individual obedience to divine commands; that obedience—and neither virtue nor some common quest—binds the individuals together (IV.i.3). Like Luther, Calvin does not conceive of friendship as anything more than a relation of pleasure or utility in the course of a life in which we move not toward moral excellence and maturity in that excellence, but toward the overwhelming experience of the grace and election of God that descends upon the solitary individual.[3] Whatever

---

[3] Even Calvin's most sympathetic commentators do not move beyond this boundary. See, for example, Stauffer 47–51 and again Büsser 76.

the influences of Stoicism on Calvin's thought, we hear the voice of neither Seneca nor Cicero here.

Politically, friendship played a similarly negligible role in Calvin's thinking. When Luther thought about government, he had in mind some kind of strong monarchy or a territorially centralized authority that did not exclude what an Athenian Greek might have called tyranny. Authoritarian rulers and tyrants are unlikely to have friends, and, in either case, friendship is an important category for understanding such rule only negatively (Plato, *Republic* trans. Bloom 567a–569c; Xenephon VI.1–16). Unsurprisingly, then, Luther did not see friendship as a useful category of human activity for thinking about government. Calvin, however, saw a republican form of government as a viable and perhaps even preferable political possibility. But his imagined republic was founded in laws, rules, and decrees, not the give and take of deliberation in political association (Höpfl 152ff.). More disconcerting still is the absence of friendship in thinking about ecclesiastical polity. The authority of divine grace (Luther) or divine command quickened by divine grace (Calvin) seems to have overtaken any consideration of even a God-centered and God-directed polity as being informed by friendship.

Luther and Calvin were both closely acquainted with the classical tradition in which friendship was an aspect of human life that evoked extensive poetic and philosophical reflection.[4] Even setting aside these classical sources—Luther's assessment of Aristotle, after all, is hardly complimentary—the medieval inheritance passed to both Luther and Calvin included deep traditions of friendship, friendship language, and reflection on friendship. Finally, the New Testament itself—ostensibly the baseline for the *sola scriptura* theological methodology of both Luther and Calvin—contains both friendship language and the topos of friendship (Mitchell *passim*).

Anabaptists and Friendship: Context

In popular scholarly prejudice, Anabaptists were generally simple-minded folk with little appreciation for complex theological or philosophical problems. Nevertheless, many of the original Anabaptist leaders were well-educated in Roman Catholic theology, biblical and classical languages, and the literature of antiquity. Many were in correspondence with and even friends of such luminaries of the early sixteenth century as Erasmus, Zwingli, Johann Kessler, or Luther himself (cf. Harder 28–9, 50ff, 342, 709 n. 34; Friesen 20–42; Littell 12, 13; Snyder 276–87).

Swiss Anabaptism began in early 1525. Within a decade, Anabaptism had spread throughout Austrian, Swiss, and southern German territories, and most of

---

[4]   Luther, "Appeal" 470–71; Luther, "Disputation" 9–16, esp. §34, §41–53. Calvin's early work on Stoicism would have familiarized him with both Seneca's and Cicero's writings on friendship.

the original leaders were dead at the hands of the political authorities. Intense persecution ensured that few of the movement's educated leaders were able to focus on articulating broad theological themes, let alone philosophically refined topics such as friendship. Most sixteenth-century Anabaptist writings are more nearly *pièces de circonstance*, written in response to specific problems. Even the relatively prolific second generation Dutch Anabaptist leader, Menno Simons, found that the constant threat to his life and the cares and concerns associated with keeping together a fledgling, persecuted movement of disparate believers prevented him from much systematic reflection.[5]

One pressing "*circonstance*" of nearly all of these early Anabaptist congregations is the need for establishing a stable community. A majority of the surviving documents from the formative years of the Anabaptist movements are occupied with developing a doctrinal basis for such establishment. We might therefore expect friendship language to appear there with a greater than normal probability (which we might also have expected from the magisterial reformers); the fragility of establishing and maintaining communities has, since antiquity, tended to evoke friendship language.[6] To ask the question of friendship about an episode in the sixteenth century is to be consistent with the experience of antiquity and the medieval European period in which the bonds of friendship were a prevailing and seemingly natural response to the exigencies of political instability. A classical conception of friendship "embodies a shared recognition of and pursuit of a good," and "this sharing ... is essential and primary to the constitution of any form of community, whether that of a household or that of a city" (MacIntyre 155). If this claim is not merely historical but anthropological, then similar circumstances should, or at least could, evoke similar responses. If they do not, it is reasonable to examine the precise terms in which such recognition, pursuit, and constitution do or do not take place.

Space constraints lead me to select two early documents from the wide variety of available sixteenth-century Anabaptists sources: the so-called "Schleitheim Confession" and the well-known "Admonition" of 1533/1542 written by Bernard Rothmann in 1533 and reworked with extensive additions (and without attribution to the disgraced Rothman) by Pilgram Marpeck or the group associated with him in 1542. The "Admonition" therefore has roots in two separate Anabaptist traditions. The "Schleitheim Confession" or "Brotherly Union of a Number of Children of God Concerning Seven Articles" is an early, standard text of the Swiss Anabaptist movement that receives regular reference in recent scholarship.

---

[5]   Horst 203–13; Bender 18, 19ff.; see also the editors' remarks concerning Dirk Philips's writings in Dyck 32 and 51.

[6]   See, for example, the politically pregnant moments of friendship in the *Epic of Gilgamesh* (Sandars).

Schleitheim and "Brotherly Union"

The philology of Schleitheim is "treacherous and contested" historiographical terrain (Biesecker-Mast 97). There exists no scholarly consensus concerning the meaning, genesis, authorship, or even subsequent importance to Anabaptists of these Articles (Biesecker-Mast 97–8). Along with most other early Anabaptist texts, the Schleitheim articles are not immediately amenable to a search for systematic "doctrinal unities and themes"; they articulate "a situational and controversial faithfulness through ad-hoc reason-giving" (Biesecker-Mast 101). While we are therefore less likely to find a systematic treatment of, say, friendship, we may well expect to find practical implications for friendship emerging from the instructions for good communal practice.

The prevailing language of Schleitheim concerns unity (*Vereinigung*[7]). The unity foreseen by the Schleitheim authors is based on common practice, named as "obedience" (Sattler, "Union" 35), and secured by separation from the surrounding society. This separation has monastic qualities; it does not imply emigration, but a separateness of behavior, of communal worship, communal economic sharing and support, and communal discipline. A variety of relations with the surrounding society—including its religious, political, economic, and social functions and institutions—will continue to exist for this community and for its members. As Article VI on the use of violence, Article VII on promising, and scattered comments throughout on public morality make clear, these relationships will be carefully defined and regulated. To speak in terms of separation from "the world" (Sattler, "Union" 35) and to carefully delineate the terms of that relationship of separation is, it seems to me, to conceive of a communal order that embodies some notion of "a shared recognition and pursuit of a good," however conceived and described. That would imply the sharing of friendship.

The unity of the community is signified by the language of sibling bonds ("brothers and sisters," "children of God," "sons and daughters" of God) or by the metaphor of the physical members (*Glieder*) of a physical body, and occasionally the metaphor of a flock (Sattler, "Union" 35, 36, 39, 45, 50 n. 41). Maintenance of that unity requires specific ceremonies, and specific practices, and it entails specific governing rules and structures, all outlined in the Articles. The *purpose* of the unity is to fulfill "the will of God as revealed through us [the writers of the Confession] at this time … persistently and unswervingly" (Sattler, "Union" 42–3). The recipients are admonished to maintain a purity of moral practice, which implies, or even demands, a close community discipline.

Hints of friendship may be found in this account of church community, but by inference and indirection, not directly articulated. In contrast to Luther and Calvin, who note friendship as a utilitarian category of human activity, but without further comment, the Schleitheim authors do not name friendship, but the specific qualities

---

[7]   See especially the editor's note 45 (Sattler, "Union" 50) for the rhetorical and substantial importance of this term.

of the community articulated in the Confession imply friendship's unexplored possibility. Its members choose the community freely, they maintain it through acts of mutual material and spiritual support, and they have in mind specific common ends (of behavior and spiritual formation) that identify a commonly articulated good. All of these factors are necessary conditions for the friendship of moral excellence to flourish (Aristotle, *Nic. Eth.* trans. Irwin 1155b21–6; 1156a5; 1157b25–1158a2).

In Aristotle's analysis, "complete friendship" is a friendship that is neither an association of mere utility or usefulness nor a relationship based simply on the pleasure people find in the company of one another by reason of wittiness, beauty, physical or even intellectual attraction. Instead, it is "the friendship of good people similar in virtue; for they wish goods in the same way to each other insofar as they are good, and they are good in their own right" (Aristotle 1156b7–9). But this description of friendship requires a language of virtue, which is absent from the vocabulary of Schleitheim. Aristotle's language of the "good and the pleasant" (Aristotle 1175b27) is not present here, and his language of the "lovable and choiceworthy" that unites friends would require—at a minimum—a careful and extensive reworking to make sense in reference to these articles. Consider, for example, the following passage:

> Baptism shall be given to all those who have been taught repentance and the amendment of life and [who] believe truly that their sins are taken away through Christ, and to all those who desire to walk in the resurrection of Jesus Christ and be buried with Him in death, so that they might rise with Him; to all those who with such an understanding themselves desire and request it from us. (Sattler, "Union" 36)

Can we distill the language of "lovable and choiceworthy" from this practice? Perhaps; if so, can we extrapolate to a friendship amongst those who are gathered under the practices of walking in the resurrection and being buried in death and rising? Perhaps. In fairness to my earlier analysis of Luther and Calvin and its summary in this essay, however, these are implications that the Schleitheim authors do not themselves draw from their community-preserving work. Nor do they attend to the problem Aristotle identifies that even good people who lack nothing require the pleasure of friendship and cannot live on the basis of contemplating the good alone (Aristotle 1158a24–6). If, instead, we are to serve God alone, that might include the possibility of virtue friendship; where Luther and Calvin disregarded such a possibility, the Schleitheim Anabaptists do not have space to consider it. The authors are aware, in a non-Aristotelian manner, that the specific order of a regime enables or disables certain sorts of activities and therefore certain sorts of associations between people (Aristotle 1159b25ff). Hence their desire for separation from the world. The presence of command and rule language in the absence of virtue language, however, attenuates friendship language (esp. Sattler, "Union" 35–6).

The implications for an understanding of friendship are at times more clearly given in the responses of the *opponents* to the Anabaptist authors of Schleitheim than in the Confession itself. For example, the cover letter to the Articles "refer[s] not simply to a common determination to be faithful to the Lord, but much more specifically to the actual Schleitheim experience and the sense of unity (*Vereinigung*) which the members had come to in the course of the meeting" (Sattler, "Union" 49 n. 37). In response to the Confession, of which he had a copy, Ulrich Zwingli "considered the very report that 'we have come together' to be the proof of the culpable, sectarian, conspiratorial character of Anabaptism" (Sattler, "Union" 49 n. 37). Similarly, Johann Bullinger criticized the Anabaptists for their unwillingness to live "in concord and friendship"—understood here in a civic mode—with unbelievers (Sattler [Yoder], "Union" 52 n. 64).

The Schleitheim Confession is an early, abbreviated articulation of Anabaptist principles, *not* the culmination of long practice and careful deliberation. Its language of community expresses unity and outlines practices that may identify friendship. So two of its opponents seemed to think. The explicit vocabulary of friendship itself, however, is absent. Yet, in contrast to the carefully articulated ecclesiology of the two leading magisterial reformers who are chronological bookends to Schleitheim, this document at least holds open the possibility of developing a notion of the "other self" set in the church (Aristotle 1166a30–34). Bullinger's criticism recognizes that the Schleitheim call to separation does exclude some kinds of friendship, with the implication that other kinds, of which he might disapprove, may be included. The practical concerns of Schleitheim do better at making practical, necessary distinctions between kinds of friends and not-friends (church and world) than the problematic bifurcation of the magisterial reformers and their involuntary, civically controlled churches.

In a letter and an outline for basic congregational procedures written in the same year as the Confession, Michael Sattler offered practical advice on what the love of a "Christian congregation" should look like when actualized. His advice included practical procedures for good congregational practice (Sattler "Horb" and Sattler "Order"). Aristotle argued that the form of a regime determines the forms of friendship that are available to its inhabitants; so Sattler, having been trained in a Benedictine tradition that acknowledges this claim indirectly (cf. MacIntyre 263), continues it with a new regime that enables and fosters "love and unity." Is friendship really included here? A common quest does arise in this community, even though its source is—in part—a divine command.[8] Moreover, while love is the only virtue explicitly named (but as a commandment), benevolence and alms-giving are both described and advocated without being specifically identified, and the vice of gluttony is named and criticized, and practical advice for avoiding it given. The mutual exhortation that is part of the community practice Sattler

---

[8]   "When a brother sees his brother erring, he shall warn him according to the command of Christ, and shall admonish him in a Christian and brotherly way, as everyone is bound and obliged to do out of love" (Sattler, "Order" 44).

enjoins is not so far from the "complete friendship" of Aristotle, in which friends "wish goods in the same way to each other insofar as they are good" (Aristotle 1156b7).

Anabaptists tended for the most part toward separation after initial efforts at conversation with religious and political authorities ended in persecution,[9] but we have at least one case in which an Anabaptist writer recognized the implications of the Anabaptist ecclesial order for a political regime: "such a community of the children of God has ordinances here in their pilgrimage. These should constitute the polity for the whole world. But the wickedness of men has spoiled everything" (Stadler 278). The author of this plaint offers an explicit critique of legal regimes, suggesting that practicing good morals cannot take place under the legal structures of the society from which he and his companions (friends?) seek to separate themselves while continuing to witness to it. Talk of friends is implied, but the comparison of regimes is explicit.

The 1542 "Admonition" and Friendship

The "Admonition" (*Vermanung*) of 1542 dates to what one might call the "second generation" of the Anabaptist movement. It is specifically concerned with baptism and the Lord's Supper, and it is the longest and most detailed such treatment available from an Anabaptist pen. It is attributed to Pilgram Marpeck and his group, who defended their work in a series of exchanges with Caspar Schwenkfeld. About two thirds of this work originated with a 1533 work by Bernard Rothmann, a central figure in the infamous Münster revolution that ended in 1535.[10] The Marpeck document was, therefore, supported by a tradition that had become more deeply rooted than the Schleitheim beginnings, but its major content reached back to the first decade of Anabaptism. As with the Schleitheim Articles, its authors were not theological "beginners." Rothmann was theologically well-educated (de Bakker 191–2), and Marpeck was a supremely gifted engineer who had received a classical education.

In contrast to the Schleitheim Articles, the "Admonition" contains a substantial language of friendship, and it directly and explicitly links the practices of the church with friendship. These links occur most especially in those portions of the text (about one third of the total) that the Marpeck circle added to Rothmann's original.

Within the first ten pages of the original folio print, we find this passage treating the meaning of the "holy" aspect of sacrament:

---

[9]   See, for example, Harder 25–32. We should recall that most Anabaptists were executed for treason, not heresy.

[10]   See de Bakker 191–202. For a precise and readable historical account of this episode, see Arthur 1999. The philological information is from Klassen and Klaassen 159–60.

[W]hen friends shake hands and receive a guest with gifts and presents, all that is done thereby is to indicate the friendliness, love, and faithfulness of those who give them toward those who receive them. In the same way, love and faithfulness are not the gifts themselves but are, rather, the heart which the gifts indicate. Unity and trust are indicated to the receiver of the gifts, and all goodness, love, friendliness, and faithfulness to the one who gives it. Similarly, the word sacrament has no other meaning, sense, or interpretation. He who receives that for which it was given: sanctification. The reason for the gift is recognized when one demonstrates help, advice, faithfulness, and love. The gift must come spontaneously as an act of love and an inclined will, and it must come from one who could very well neglect it without any shame or disrespect. Even if he were not to do it at all, he would not be punished for it. It is also done without hope for reward. To recognize in the gift the faithfulness of the person from whom it was given is to have all these things demonstrated. He who receives the gift reciprocates in turn with his whole heart and being, and that is called sanctification. God has also commanded that we should be holy just as He is holy, and this, in brief, is what it means to be holy. Thus people often act because of obligation. Such actions may be called sacraments in their natural sense.[11]

This passage contains the gist of what the "Admonition" explicates in more detail. The document makes at least four substantive arguments involving Christian friendship.

First, the sacramental practice of the church—in this case the memorial service of the Lord's Supper—cannot be understood apart from an *imitatio Christi* that reflects the love that Jesus modeled in his actions during and around his final meal which the Church celebrates in the Lord's Supper. Thus: "Let us remember that the Lord's communion can rightly be seen as a physical meeting. When Christians assemble, they are to be girded with love for one another, in the same way as Christ loved them, in order that they might thereby confirm and reveal the love of believers in Christ" (Marpeck 264). The Lord's Supper, ever repeated amongst the believers, requires that those believers "follow Him in constant and sincere love, practicing and proving it to one another in order to achieve a true union and remembrance ... ." This practice the writers set in sharp contrast to mere religious ceremonies that lack "spirit, love, and truth" (Marpeck 265).

Second, the friendship of the table necessarily includes and excludes. Because this "communion is a physical gathering of those who believe in Christ" and whose activities toward one another should manifest this belief, "all those who lack faith and love do not belong at the Lord's table" (Marpeck 264). The Christian requirement to love all is not, as it was for Luther and Calvin, elided into friendship. Those who celebrate the Lord's Supper together "submit to one another and serve

---

[11]   Marpeck 169–70. The editors indicate by means of italicization (here excised) which portions of the text stem from Rothmann and which from Marpeck. Nearly the entire text cited here is a Marpeck addition.

one another in patience, and not in conflict of the sword of steel; rather, they are willing and ready to do good to friends and enemies" (Marpeck 267). While eating and drinking the Lord's Supper "represents a lasting bond of love among Christians" (Marpeck 266) and though this bond may serve to separate friends from not-friends, such outsiders deserve consideration, but that is not the same as friendship.

Third, the document connects the friendship of the Lord's Supper with the discipline of the church. "We all eat of one bread and drink of one cup, witnessing that we are at one with each other through Christian love"; those, however, "who take part without having rebuked, according to the order of the Spirit, any sins or vices dealing with a brother are also unworthy to eat and drink communion, because the body of Christ is not differentiated from the hatred and scorn of the devil, and the innocent participated in others' sins" (Marpeck 275). Friendship, or Christian love, is chosen in freedom and freely, which "cause[s] the community to be of one heart and soul." Such unity cannot derive from "coercion or commandment," even though it is manifested in discernible, practical acts of sharing (Marpeck 278–9). This unity requires an ecclesiastical regime that opens up a space for its practice, even as it defines (ultimately with the ban) what is and is not such practice. The writers suggest that without institutions, freedom—including the freedom of friendship—is not possible. Here we see a continuation of the unity theme of Schleitheim, which the writers articulate toward the theme of friendship, finding textual support from Protestant reformers, early church theologians, and canonical scriptures (Marpeck 279–80).

Fourth, this question of church discipline, raised in the Schleitheim Confession and extended in remarkably harsh ways in some of the Dutch Anabaptist traditions, receives a gentler face at the hands of Marpeck and his group. That gentleness has as its context the recognition of friendship. Community discipline, Marpeck reminds his readers, is to be a punishment not of enemies but of friends, for a variety of vices, "but only for their improvement and maintenance" (Marpeck 278). His readers "are not to be like those who maintain the ban, banning people from the face of the earth, seizing life and land, forbidding place and people." "Such a ban," he continues, "does not belong to the Christian church, nor may such a ban ever be permitted in the kingdom of Christ, according to the words of the Lord and Paul" (Marpeck 275–6). Using the religious terms of sanctification and sacrament, but also the non-religious terms of "love," "faithfulness," "gifts," "goodness," and "freedom," the "Admonition" identifies the practice of friendship. Locating the practice in a broader set of developing Anabaptist practices, it formulates doctrine around the identification of the practice.

The additions and insertions of the Marpeck circle to the document are especially valuable to the extensions of the friendship theme, amplifying that theme, its meaning, and its implications. Not only does the introductory passage that explicitly names friendship come from the pen(s) of that group, so too do the explicit identifications of friendship and its activities at several other places in the text, including insertions such as "patience," the addition of admonitions to love the enemy, and the insertion of strong distinctions between a language of "command and function" (277) and a view beyond command to a "freedom of love" (278–9; cf. 267, 270, 275). These insertions indicate a development toward friendship themes in the context of articulating communal Anabaptist practices that the writers of Schleitheim did not have the luxury to develop, and some of which escaped Rothmann's sensibilities.

Conclusions

The Anabaptist texts considered here make a distinction between the community of believers, in which a practice of true friendship in all its dimensions is possible, and the world outside that community, where the right practice of moral excellence and obedience to divine command is neglected. That neglect makes friendship—properly understood—with its inhabitants (but not good behavior toward them) difficult or impossible. Both Zwingli and Bullinger understood the civic implications of these separationist arguments and criticized them for their challenge to civic harmony. To repeat: treason, not heresy, was the usual charge under which Anabaptists were capitally punished.

These writings contain a developing understanding of friendship that is not the rarified and legalized "love of neighbor" of Calvin or the utilitarian partnership of Luther, but an association in virtue, as Marpeck says explicitly on at least one occasion. The Anabaptists were determined to recover the "life and virtue of the Early Church." Part of this recovery "presupposed a freely acting congregation which did not depend upon any worldly power but upon its own spirit of fellowship." Establishing such churches clearly raises the question of what government *within* the church must look like, but it also implies questions about secular government and natural right (Littell 79, 87). Except in rare episodes such as Stadler's cosmic claim, where the church serves as a model for the world (cf. Schiemer 104–5), Anabaptists generally left such questions aside.

A complete treatment of the conception of friendship among the Anabaptists would require us to consider the Anabaptist understanding of the relationship between church and saeculum, but space prohibits. Aristotle supplies a summary of what we might need to consider. Civic friendship may be a utilitarian association. Friendship "based on the recognition of moral goodness" may require mutual concern in virtue and therefore a community in virtue, but other kinds of friendship do not. On one reading of Aristotle, some kinds of friendship require no polis for their maintenance. As the Anabaptists seemed to understand in unknowing agreement with Aristotle, some kinds of friendship *do* require a community to flourish, and, in order themselves to flourish, some kinds of communities require certain kinds of friendship. Perhaps everyday political associations are friendships of utility, not friendships in virtue, and perhaps "lesser," non-virtuous regimes that populate the world do not require friendships in virtue but only associations of utility to sustain themselves.[12] In a common Anabaptist view, secular rule is a divinely ordained means of dealing with human error. It cannot, in and of itself, foster human virtue:

> ... the government is a picture, sign and reminder of man's departure from God, and ought well to be to all men an urge to retire within themselves and to consider to what they have come and to what they have fallen, that they might with all the more haste turn back to God to receive again the grace they had lost. ... Over and above all this, because governmental authority is a servant of God's anger and vengeance, as long as it has being it indicates that God's anger and wrath is still over sinners and is not at an end. (Riedeman 259–60)

In this typical Anabaptist view of government, "the power of the sword has passed to the heathen, that they may therewith punish their evildoers," and the faithful are to separate themselves from this enterprise. "The way of life" is open to all, but not on the terms offered outside the community of believers (Riedeman 261–2).

This Anabaptist view is consistent with Aristotelian sensibilities. If a regime lacks the "decent attention" that "works through excellent laws" to train its citizens and especially the young in virtue, then "it seems fitting for each individual to promote the virtue of his children and his friends—to be able to do it, or at least to decide to do it" (Aristotle 1180a31–3). Having arrived at a negative conclusion concerning the society into which they had been born and raised, the Anabaptists turned to the circle of like-minded friends—the church—mutually to promote virtue. For the results of this effort—moral purity and the sharing of goods, for example—they were widely praised, even while their insistence on civic separation and certain theological doctrines led to intense and extensive persecution. Unlike the magisterial reformers, the Anabaptist paid attention to the qualities of community beyond constraint and command, moving in some cases to a vocabulary that included friendship and not merely the force of discipline, where it largely remained for Luther and Calvin.

The textual exemplars examined here show that the Anabaptists retained and developed a conception and practice of friendship that could address secular, ecclesial, and private realms alike. While persecution may have diminished their voice concerning friendship and most other matters of community to near silence in the modern European tradition of thought, this diminution was not the theological disregard for friendship that equally silenced the two principle magisterial reformers. It was, most importantly, a loss to the Western tradition of friendship.

---

[12]   See Clayton 1997 (cited with the kind permission of the author).

Afterword

Lorna Hutson

So polyvalent and associative is the term "friend" in early modern English that its most fleeting literary use is analytically rich. To open with an example: in the final act of Shakespeare's *Macbeth*, the warrior king drops, for a moment, his mask of cruel determination before the impending battle and confides to an attendant that he has begun to loathe what is left of his life:

> Seyton!—I am sick at heart
> …
> I have lived long enough. My way of life
> Is fall'n into the sere, the yellow leaf,
> And that which should accompany old age,
> As honour, love, obedience, *troops of friends*,
> I must not look to have …[1]

In the movement of this painfully self-knowing speech, the phrase "troops of friends" requires a pause as the emotive accumulation and embodiment of the abstractions that precede it. Macbeth's longing for honour, love, and obedience—the moral, psychic, and material well-being or "wealth" of a ruler's good government—is expressed as a recognition of profound loneliness, of having sacrificed, for ever, the hope of a beloved, befriended old age.

This is a single, fairly random instance of a "representation" of friendship in early modern European literature that also invokes a larger hinterland of classical "discourse." And as such it both exemplifies the subject of this collection of essays and typifies the brilliantly original absorption and remaking of an earlier complex discourse—the tradition of Greek and Roman moral philosophy—into the iconic literature of nationhood and identity in the modern, developed Western world. For, on the one hand, Macbeth's prediction of his friendless old age instances a commonplace of ancient republican political philosophy. In Plato's *Republic* and Cicero's *De officiis*, tyranny is the antithesis of the *koinonia* or *societas* (partnership) bound by *philia* or *amicitia* (friendship) that characterizes the ideal polity (*Republic* 576A; *De officiis* I.xvii.53–8; Konstan, *Friendship* 105–15). The tyrant is, then, quintessentially the man without friends. Macbeth, by these words, identifies himself a tyrant in the Greco-Roman and Christian–humanist tradition.

---

[1]   Shakespeare, *Macbeth*, ed. A.R. Braunmuller (Cambridge: Cambridge UP, 2008) 5.3.19–25 (added emphasis). Further references to this edition will appear in the text.

On the other hand, the commonplace is no inert illustration of a political theory. We *feel* Macbeth's loneliness and abjection, as Shakespeare's use of hyperbaton first evokes throngs of people and then subsequently banishes them ("troop of friends / I must not look to have"), making it seem as if the speaker's heart were an empty hearth, destined to expect the guests that would never arrive.

Nor do these two aspects of the representation—its location within the classical tradition, its deployment as a profoundly subjective emotional effect—exhaust the possible analyses of the discourse of friendship here. For the collective noun "troops," of course, usually qualifies soldiers, not friends. Macbeth's "troops of friends" thus seems to build on a prevailing notion of friendship (within the highly stylized eleventh-century "Scotland" depicted in the play) as the ruler's economic and military *strength*. Hints of such a conception go back to the opening scenes of Act 1, when the "bloody" soldier who reports Macbeth's defeat of the rebel Macdonald is addressed as "brave friend" by Malcolm and when Duncan, arriving at Glamis, announces the royal investiture of his son to "Sons, kinsmen, thanes / And you whose places are the nearest" (1.4.35–6). Qualification for nearness of place, as critics have noticed, thus depends on blood and willingness to do violence against "traitors" (disturbingly defined as whoever happen to be the king's enemies) (Berger 1–31; Sinfield 95–108). Shakespeare depicts a Scotland of underdeveloped institutional infrastructure in which "friendship," understood as propinquity of blood and shared enmity, is the radically unstable ground of politics and government. While there is some support for such an image from Scotsmen writing at this time of debate over the union (Robert Pont observed that Scottish lords so "pester and throng the places of judgement with their clients, followers and friends" that "they prove terrible even to the judges themselves"), the point to be made here is less the hyperbolic travesty of this English portrayal than what it reveals about Shakespeare's skill in deploying the various "discourses of friendship" available to him (Pont 22). In this one instance we have seen how Macbeth's words on friendship first locate him within a classical republican tradition of the portrayal of tyranny; second, evoke in us, through rhetorically patterned language, feelings correspondent to those aroused by friendship; and, third, deftly and almost imperceptibly define Scotland's bewitched abjection as a longing for political alliance or friendship with England.

In Macbeth's figuring of his life's futility as the absence of true friends, Shakespeare offers us a way into three topics that weave through the essays in this collection on the discourses and representations of friendship in early modern Europe. An afterword is not the place in which to embark on a full commentary either on the contents of a book or on the disciplinary history of its subject: having used this example from *Macbeth* to indicate something of the range of topics broached by the terms "friend" and "friendship" in early modern English, I will limit myself from henceforward to opening up these topics a little further in relation to the preceding essays.

The first topic, inevitably, concerns the early modern appropriation and transformation, via sixteenth-century humanist philology, of an extensive Greek and Roman literature on friendship as a political and moral virtue. The second concerns the rhetorical mode and print media of that humanist transformation, and the way in which the thematics of friendship, as an emotionally intense relationship, were associated with the capacity of heightened literary language and rhetorical patterning to awake understanding and evoke feeling in others. The third involves representations which create the sense of there being a historical transition from one model of friendship to another—from an older "kin and alliance" model of friendship to a newer individualistic model of intimacy and personal choice.

In fact, though distinct, all these topics are closely interrelated. To begin with the third, for example, it is often said that society in the early modern period in Europe was characterized by a cultural shift from the predominance of kin-friendship to that of individual, private intimacy. As Keith Thomas has recently put it: "The novelty of the early modern period is that it witnessed the emergence into public view of a type of relationship which differed from these older kinds of alliance in purporting to be based wholly on mutual sympathy, and cherished for its own sake rather than for its practical advantages" (193). But of course, as Thomas also goes on to say, there is in a sense nothing really *novel* about this novelty, since nearly all the early modern writing witnessing friendship as an intimate union of souls consciously draws on the literary language of Plato, Aristotle, and Cicero. So what turns out to be really new, in the first age of the printing press, is not the prevalence of a different model of friendship (one based on exclusive mutual sympathy rather than the collective strength associated with kinship) but rather the extraordinarily various literary deployments and transformations of friendship as a topic. To quote Thomas again, "There was a torrent of printed literature—sermons, essays, poems, plays and novels—celebrating the value of 'perfect' friendship" while "[a] modern bibliography of Elizabethan verse reveals that, of all moral topics, friendship was the one most frequently treated" (193). The example given from *Macbeth* proves this contention with peculiar clarity. For while the model of friendship invoked by Shakespeare in this example is that of "older kinds of alliance," the deployment itself serves to hint that this model is part of Scotland's problem: that governing through amassing "troops of friends" perpetually tips Scotland into what the English would understand as tyranny. Thus it is not only Macbeth's own way of life but that of the whole hag-ridden Scottish warrior society that seems, by the end of the play, to have fallen into the yellow leaf. At the same time, however, the powerful emotional effect of Macbeth's eloquent words have for centuries created in audiences and readers a feeling of sympathy for Shakespeare's creation—a feeling akin to the affection and compassion reserved for those whom we love, our friends. In this way, we see that what is new in early modern Europe is the variety and versatility with which the topic of friendship, associated as it is with the affective power of figurative language, is deployed. And it is this newfound protean variety in the discourse and representation of friendship in the vernacular literature of early modern Europe that the present collection of essays takes as its unifying theme.

A number of the essays in this collection—those by Sheila Cavanagh, Donald Gilbert-Santamaría, Daniel Lochman, Wendy Olmsted, and Allison Johnson—touch on either the complementarity of or the tension between ideas of instrumentality and commonplaces of mutual likeness/liking as the bases of friendship. The consensus among social historians that the early modern period sees an older kin-alliance model of friendship giving way, as social, economic, and political institutions become more differentiated, to a newer model of intimacy based on choice and liking "for its own sake," while clearly accurate in a sense, can also be misleading to the extent that it gives the impression of an absolute demarcation between instrumentality and affection in the early modern concept of friendship. In fact, early modern uses of the word "friend" tend to denote *both* a relation of affection and the understanding that one is able to do good on behalf of another, and there is rarely a sense that the latter assumption alone renders the former insincere. Such an understanding of friendship is characteristic of this historical period; by the nineteenth century, it seems to have largely disappeared. In the Victorian women's diaries, correspondence and biographies examined by Sharon Marcus, for example, friendship is a "pervasive" topic, because "middle-class Victorians treated friendship and family life as complementary," but a material or moral ability to help is no longer explicitly identified, alongside mutual sympathy, as a criterion of the relationship (32–43).

At the end of the spectrum of meanings covered by the seventeenth-century use of the word "friend" was the sense of assistance that could be relied on, a store of help more reliable than money. Thus, in Rowley, Dekker and Ford's *The Witch of Edmonton*, for example, Frank Thorney, a gentleman in service to Sir Arthur Clarington, reminds the latter that he promised to help him and his young bride when they were to marry. Sir Arthur prevaricates about the sum of money promised, but asks Frank, "What thinkest thou of two hundred pound, and a continual friend?" and then continues: "Frank, I will be thy friend, and such a friend" (1.1.103–4, 129). In Shakespeare's *Measure for Measure* (1606), Claudio confesses to Lucio that his secret marriage to Juliet has not been made public because of friends withholding their consent and their material support. The public solemnization, he confides,

we came not to
Only for propagation of a dower
Remaining in the coffer of her friends. (1.2.139–40)

In the context of Shakespeare's larger topic—the vexed relation between sexual desire, procreation, and civic order—this metaphor of friendship's withholding as a failure to propagate hints at classical theories of the founding of the polity on kinship, affinity, and friendship (Cicero, *De officiis* I.xvii.55–6). This in turn reminds us that the definition of friendship as an ability and desire to do good to one's friend belongs not only to an essentially non-literary kin-alliance model (such as social historians might argue was superseded by an intimacy based on similarity of literary taste) but to the very literary tradition of ethical and political friendship itself. Eoin G. Cassidy observes that, while Aristotelian friendship, founded on *eunoia* or benevolence, is "both pleasant and useful," it is not motivated by pleasure or utility. However, "the difference between friendship based on virtue and that based on pleasure or utility cannot simply be conceived as that between a disinterested love and one founded on pragmatic or utilitarian concerns because benevolence is present in both the latter type of friendship and the former" (45–67, 49). In 1657, the Anglican divine, Jeremy Taylor, wrote:

> although I love my friend because he is worthy, yet he is not worthy if he can do no good ... He is only fit to be chosen for a friend who can give me counsel, or defend my cause, or guide me right, or relieve my need, or can and will, when I need it, do me good ... therefore those friendships must needs be most perfect, where the friends can be most useful. (25–7)

For Taylor, it was a relative lack of ability to do good that rendered women less capable of ideal friendship than men:

> I cannot say that Women are capable of all those excellencies by which men can oblige the world; and therefore a female friend in some cases is not so good a counsellor as a wise man, and cannot so well defend my honour, nor dispose of reliefs and assistances if she be under the power of another. (88–9)

In this collection, Sheila Cavanagh's essay on Lady Mary Wroth's *Urania* shows that friendship is still largely understood, in the aristocratic world of Wroth's romance, as assistance-providing allies, but that there is also witty play with the humanist idea of the friend as another self. Donald Gilbert Santamaria reads picaresque narrative as a limit case for the credibility of the Christian–humanist discourse of friendship. In picaresque, where self-interest dominates interpersonal relations, moments of sympathetic identification generative of friendship are rare and have little to do with the mutual striving for moral excellence typical of the discourse in more aristocratic genres. Daniel Lochman, drawing on Wendy Olmsted's work, finds in Sidney's revised *Arcadia* a reworking of his first depiction of the princes' morally and materially aspirant friendship into something more receptive to the positive qualities of passion: something like the "love-fellowship" figured by the shepherd pair, Strephon and Claius. On the other hand, in contradistinction to Jeremy Taylor's relative exclusion of women from friendship on the grounds of their lack of the public agency that would define them as useful to their friends, Allison Johnson finds in Isabella Whitney's *Sweet Nosgay* (1573) a printed anthology of versified aphorisms paired with "familiar Epistles and friendly Letters by the Auctour," an attempt to claim the position of the humanist friend–counsellor to a wider affinity both within and outside London. In one such letter, "To my friend, Master T.L., whose good nature I see abusde," Whitney even assumes the voice of the friend who persuades a bachelor to marry to increase his standing and ensure a more loyal and reliable set of kin-friends: "But this I wish," she urges, "that you my frind / go chuse some vertues wife / ... For whylst you are in single state, / none hath that right regard: / They all think well that they can win, / and compt it their reward" (sig. Dviii^v). Though what Whitney counsels Master T.L. to embrace is the long-term security and social credibility of belonging to a wider set of "friends" as kinsfolk and allies, her own strategy as an author is clearly imitative of the Erasmian humanist model of the friend as author addressing a circle of "friends," whose fame in the wider world rests on the print dissemination of the familiar epistles that evoke and characterize them in such vivid and intimate terms.

Other essays in the collection—those by Thomas Heilke, Greg Chaplin, Penelope Anderson, Marc Schachter, and Christopher Marlow—focus on the centrality of friendship to political theory and vice versa. For, in addition to never quite losing its connections with benevolence, utility, and property, early modern friendship is strongly associated, in humanist writing, with the communication of a literary tradition and with philosophizing about the ideal polity. Connections between friendship and pleasure in the literary tradition are not simply, as in later periods, a matter of intimate friends sharing tastes. Rather, as Kathy Eden has shown, friendship (*philia* or *amicitia*) is the conceptual model chosen by the greatest sixteenth-century humanist, Erasmus, to express a radically new conception of *tradition* itself: that is, the legal title and transfer of pagan literature and philosophy to the modern Christian world. Where the Church Fathers had conceptualized the Christian right to pagan literature on the model of spoils of war—a hostile appropriation—Erasmus transformed their metaphors into a sharing between friends, epitomized in the opening Pythagorean adage of the 4,000 proverbs collected in his *Adagiorum Chiliades*, "koina ta tōn philōn" or *amicorum communia omnia*: "between friends all is common" (Eden, *Friends* 8–32, especially 25). Erasmus's reading of the Pythagorean elements of the Platonic, Aristotelian, and Ciceronian writings on friendship and the polity supported his own advocacy of the adage and the commonplace as the discursive forms most suited to the storing and conveying of literary and philosophical riches. As Eden reconstructs an Erasmian reading of Plato's *Phaedrus*, friendship and *eros* become associated with the philosophical search for commonalities or qualities in common within the disparity of lived experience: "For, like friends after the Pythagorean fashion, discourse in the form of speaking, writing and even thinking assumes not only as its own standard of excellence the criterion of unity or wholeness (246C), but also in relation to its subject matter, the task of apprehending what seemingly disparate things *have in common*" (*Friends* 72). This perception of the affinity between friendship and the conveying or enabling of a philosophical apprehension of likenesses and differences through the rhetorical use of proverbial language has a profound effect on humanist political theory. While Platonic writings apply the Pythagorean adage to communality of material property (More's *Utopia* following in this tradition), Cicero, whose influence on sixteenth-century thinkers was more pervasive, founds the state on the inviolability of private property while at the same time safeguarding, in the name of friendship, the commonality of intellectual property (Eden, *Friends* 100). Sixteenth-century English humanists developed the Ciceronian model: Thomas Starkey's *Dialogue between Pole and Lupset* opens with Lupset's professing "the frenchyp and famylyaryte ... of yowth growying betwyx us" and the "sure band & knot" of "true love & amyte" that prompts him to persuade Pole to "commyn" or communicate his intellectual travail, for "vertue & lernyng not communyd to other is like riches hepyd in cornerys never applyd to the use of other" (1, 4).

It is surprising, then, to learn from Thomas Heilke's chapter that Luther and Calvin so neglected considerations of friendship in their writings on the organization of church and civil society. By contrast, the Anabaptists, to whose writings scholars have rarely ascribed theological or philosophical complexity or classical knowledge, begin, in the second generation of their movement, to develop a conception of friendship as the freedom made possible by the institution of an ecclesiastical regime. The persecution that reduced the Anabaptist voice to near-inaudibility resulted, concludes Heilke, in a loss to the Western tradition of friendship. In contrast to Heilke's focus on the centrality of friendship to a communistic theological movement, Greg Chaplin's interest is in the sources of Milton's republican ideas in a Ciceronian language of friendship that founds masculine political equality in the sovereignty of the masculine self as householder, enjoying the freedom "to dispose and *oeconomize* in the Land which God hath giv'n them, as Maisters of Family in their own house and free inheritance." As Chaplin elsewhere argues, Milton's simultaneous founding of the oeconomic order of the household on the model of spiritual friendship between husband and wife, however, renders his depiction of prelapsarian marriage uncertain: "among unequals what society / Can sort ...?" This same instability, the product of using friendship discourse to elevate the moral status of matrimony, while at the same time denying women the equality on which philosophical friendship is based, is exploited fruitfully by Katherine Philips, the subject of Penelope Anderson's chapter. Philips was poetically concerned with the question of "friendship multiplied"— indeed this question seems to have been at the heart of her correspondence with Jeremy Taylor, to which his *Discourse on ... Friendship* was the reply. Anderson interprets Philips' allusion to Sidney's *Arcadia* in her poetry on this subject as a royalist revision of the republican politics of the trial scene. Philips's poetry of multiple friendships, and of the betrayal of exclusive friendship, advocates, she argues, a feminine politics of remembered and forgiven shifts of allegiance rather than acts of oblivion. Katherine Philips, of course, was also a great admirer of the playwright William Cartwright, and Christopher Marlow's chapter on Cartwright's *The Lady Errant* (c. 1634–37) helps us understand why. Marlow explains that "*The Lady-Errant* seeks to expand the scope of ... political friendship so that it might also include women," but he argues that in so doing the play also forces an ironic awareness of the incompatibility of the mixture of political models (equal friendship *versus* the tyranny and slavery of love) from which the metaphors of ideal marital relations are drawn. Finally, Marc Schachter examines Marguerite de Navarre's subtle critique of her narrator's perspective in the twelfth novella of the *Heptaméron*, a reworking of various historical accounts of the assassination of Alessandro de' Medici in 1537. As Schachter's tracing of minute shifts of terminology and phraseology shows, Marguerite's decision to have her narrator, Dagoucin, present the mutually exploitative relationship between Alessandro and his assassin in the language of an ideal friendship ironically exposes both the demeaning treatment of women that could make such a rhetorical trick even superficially persuasive and the emptiness of the assassin's implicit claim to have modelled himself on the Athenian tyrannicides Aristogiton and Harmodius (Schachter, *Voluntary Servitude* 31–8).

I have touched on the diverse ways in which essays in this collection engage with key aspects of the early modern discourse of friendship: with the ethics of the moral and material usefulness of friends, and with the centrality of friendship to political philosophy. How, in conclusion, does this collection treat that elusive but pervasive aspect of early modern friendship, its association with *eloquentia*, and especially with the persuasive and instructive uses of the commonplace and the proverb? Most of the essays here are written by literary scholars on literary texts, and even those that derive from political and religious studies are immersed in the commonplaces of the Platonic, Aristotelian, and Ciceronian texts on friendship: *amicitia aequalitas* ("friendship is equality"), *amicus alter ipse* ("a friend is another self"), and so forth. The proverb, as Kathy Eden says, "complements its antiquity with its adaptability"; Erasmus explains "how the proverb takes now one shape, now another, and how the rhetorician in control of his proverb 'fits the same wording with multiple meanings' … or, through irony, with contrary meanings … or again, by changing a single word, with different meanings" (Eden, "'Between Friends'" 405–19, 409). Constance Furey's chapter examines humanist meditations on the likeness and disparity between the adage *amicus alter ipse* and the biblical injunction that husband and wife become "one flesh." Hannah Chapelle Wojciehowski revisits the debate over the meaning of Quentin Matsys' double portrait of Erasmus and Pieter Giles and its relation to More's *Utopia* by glossing David Wootton's remark: "For More, and the men of his day, it was a friend, not a wife, who was 'another self'" (Wootton 28–47, 43). But the great virtue of the Erasmian project of making the classical literary wisdom on friendship available in the authoritative yet flexible form of adages was, of course, that those traditionally excluded from the discourse might be able, through irony, or change of words, to invest its forms with different meanings. So it seems appropriate to close with a short poem by Katherine Philips, in which she addresses Lady Elizabeth Boyle (whom she calls "Celimena"), positioning herself as Boyle's abject, unrequited lover:

> Forbear, fond heart (say I), torment no more
> That Celimena whom thou dost adore;
> For since so many of her Chains are proud,
> How can thou be distinguish'd in the crowd?

But say, bold trifler, what dost thou pretend?
Wouldst thou depose thy saint into thy Friend?
Equality in friendship is requir'd,
Which here were criminal to be desir'd. (*Collected Works* I.227)

In Philips's witty self-laceration, the lover berates herself for desiring to be "distinguish'd" from among the crowds of Elizabeth Boyle's many proud "Chains" or admiring hangers-on. For such a desire would be, she pretends to recognize, a desire to be Boyle's "friend," and thus a claim to be her equal. The renunciation of that claim as a criminal act of "deposition," however, not only pays a tactful social compliment to Boyle, but clearly implies by its renunciation the relevance of discourse of *amicitia perfecta* to women, a claim that was in itself highly controversial (as Taylor's *Discourse* shows). Cleverer than that, though, is the way that the apparent modesty of Philips's denial to be so bold as to claim friendship with Boyle smuggles in the much more audacious conclusion that the highly charged language of erotic subjection—the swooning adoration of Celimena as a "saint"— is in fact a *more* decorous and appropriate way of expressing their relationship than friendship could be. Though not something Erasmus would have envisaged or approved, Philips's adapting of the adage *amicitia aequalitas* is undoubtedly a product of the humanist tradition and fittingly concludes a collection of essays devoted to early modernity's rich variety of adaptations and transformations of the discourses of friendship.

Works Cited

Ackroyd, Peter. *The Life of Thomas More.* New York: Nan A. Talese, Doubleday, 1998. Print.

Aelred of Rievaulx. "Spiritual Friendship, Book 1." Trans. Eugenia Laker. *Other Selves: Philosophers on Friendship.* Ed. Michael Pakaluk. Indianapolis, IN: Hackett, 1991. 129–45. Print.

Agrippa von Nettesheim, Heinrich Cornelius. *Commendation of Matrimony.* Trans. David Clapham. London, 1545. *EEBO.* Web. 20 July 2009.

Alberti, Leon Battista. *The Family in Renaissance Florence.* Books One–Four. Long Grove, IL: Waveland, 2004. Print.

Alemán, Mateo. *Guzmán de Alfarache.* Vol. II. Ed. José María Micó. Madrid: Cátedra, 1987, 2005. Print.

Allen, Peter. "*Utopia* and European Humanism: the Function of the Prefatory Letters and Verses." *Studies in the Renaissance* 10 (1963): 91–107. Print.

Alpers, Paul. *What is Pastoral?* Chicago: U of Chicago P, 1996. Print.

Andreadis, Harriette. "Reconfiguring Early Modern Friendship: Katherine Philips and Homoerotic Desire." *SEL* 46.3 (2006): 523–42. Print.

Andresen, Martha. "'Ripeness is All': Sententiae and Commonplaces in *King Lear.*" *Some Facets of King Lear: Essays in Prismatic Criticism.* Eds Rosalie L. Colie and F.T. Flahiff. Toronto: U of Toronto P, 1974. 145–68. Print.

Aquinas. *Summa Contra Gentiles.* Trans. J. Bourke. *On the Truth of the Catholic Faith.* New York: Doubleday, 1956. Print.

Aretino, Pietro. *La cortigiana.* Milan: Rizzoli, 1988. Print.

——. *Lettere.* Ed. Francesco Erspamer. 2 vols. Parma: Ugo Guanda, 1995. Print.

Aristotle. *The Nichomachean Ethics.* In *The Works of Aristotle.* Vol. 2. Ed. W.D. Ross. New York: Encyclopedia Britannica, 1952. 334–436. Print.

——. *Nichomachean Ethics.* Trans. Terence Irwin. Indianapolis, IN: Hackett, 1985. Print.

——. *Nichomachean Ethics.* Trans. H. Rackham. Loeb Classical Library. Cambridge, MA: Harvard UP, 1962. Print.

——. *The Nichomachean Ethics.* Trans. J.A.K. Thomson; rev. Hugh Tredennick. London: Penguin, 2004. Print.

——. *The Rhetoric and The Poetics.* Ed. Edward P.J. Corbett. New York: Modern Library, 1984. Print.

Arthur, Anthony. *The Tailer-King: The Rise and Fall of the Anabaptist Kingdom of Münster.* New York: St. Martin's, 1999. Print.

Aubrey, John. *Brief Lives, Chiefly of Contemporaries.* Ed. Andrew Clark. Oxford: Clarendon, 1898. Print .

Augustine. *De bono coniugali*; *De sancta uirginitate.* Oxford Early Christian Texts. Trans. P.G. Walsh. Oxford: Clarendon, 2001. Print.

——. *De civitate Dei.* Trans. Henry Bettenson. Harmandsworth, Middlesex: Penguin, 1984. Print.

Bacon, Francis. *The Essays or Counsels, Civill and Morall.* Ed. Michael Kiernan. Oxford: Clarendon, 2000. Print.

——. "Of Followers and Friends." *Francis Bacon: A Critical Edition of the Major Works.* Ed. Brian Vickers. Oxford: Oxford UP, 1996. 83–4. Print.

Baker, Nicholas Scott. "For Reasons of State: Political Executions, Republicanism, and the Medici in Florence, 1480–1560." *Renaissance Quarterly* 62 (2009): 444–78. Print.

Avalle-Arce, Juan Bautista. *Deslindes Cervantinos.* Madrid: Edhiger, 1961. Print.

Bakhtin, M.M. "Discourse in the Novel." *The Dialogic Imagination.* Trans. Caryl Emerson and Michael Holquist. Austin: U of Texas P, 1981. 259–422. Print.

de Bakker, Willem. "Bernhard Rothmann: The Dialectics of Radicalization in Münster." *Profiles of Radical Reformers: Biographical Sketches from Thomas Müntzer to Paracelsus.* Eds Hans-Jürgen Goertz and Walter Klaassen. Kitchener and Scottdale: Herald Press, 1982, 191–202. Print.

Barash, Carol. *English Women's Poetry, 1649–1714: Politics, Community, and Linguistic Authority.* Oxford: Clarendon, 1996. Print.

Barish, Jonas A., and Marshall Waingrow. "'Service' in King Lear." *Shakespeare Quarterly* 9.3 (Summer 1958): 347–55. Print.

Baraz, Daniel. "Violence or Cruelty? An Intercultural Perspective." *"A Great Effusion of Blood"? Interpreting Medieval Violence.* Eds Mark Meyerson, Daniel Thiery, and Owen Falk. Toronto: Toronto UP, 2004. 164–89. Print.

Basanesse, Fiora. "Selling the Self; or, the Epistolary Production of Renaissance Courtesans." *Italian Women Writers from the Renaissance to the Present: Revising the Canon.* Ed. Maria Ornella Marotti. Philadelphia: Pennsylvania State UP, 1996. 69–82. Print.

Basset, Bernard, S.J. *Born for Friendship: The Spirit of Sir Thomas More.* London: Burns & Oates, 1965. Print.

Bausi, Francesco. "'Con agra zampogna': Tullia d'Aragona a Firenze (1545–48)." *Schede Umanistiche* 2 (1993): 61–91. Print.

Bawcutt, N.W. "The Assassination of Alessandro de' Medici in Early Seventeenth-Century English Drama." *The Review of English Studies* 56.225 (2005): 412–23. Print.

Beilin, Elaine V. "Writing Public Poetry: Humanism and the Woman Writer." *Modern Language Quarterly: A Journal of Literary History* 51.2 (1990): 249–71. Print.

Bek, Lise. "Thomas More on the Double Portrait of Erasmus and Pierre Gillis: Humanist Rhetoric or Renaissance Art Theory?" *Acta Conventus Neo-Latini Guelpherbytani.* Eds Stella P. Revard, Fidel Rädle, and Mario A. Di Cesare. Binghamton, New York: Medieval & Renaissance Texts and Studies, 1988. 469–79. Print.

Bell, Millicent. "Naked Lear." *Raritan* 23.4 (Spring 2004): 55–70. Print.

Bender, Harold Stauffer. "A Brief Biography of Menno Simons." *The Complete Writings of Menno Simons*. Ed. J.C. Wenger. Trans. Leonard Verduin. Scottdale, PA: Herald Press, 1956. 3–29. Print.

Berger, Harry, Jr. "The Early Scenes of *Macbeth*: A New Interpretation." *ELH* 47 (1980): 1–31. Print.

Bevington, David. *Shakespeare: The Seven Ages of Human Experience*. Oxford: Blackwell Publishing, 2002, 2005. Print.

Bevington, David, and David Scott Kastan, eds. *King Lear*. By William Shakespeare. New York: Bantam Dell, 2005. Print.

Biagi, Guido. "Un'etera romana, Tullia d'Aragona." *Nouva Antologia, Serie III* 4.6 (1886): 655–711. Print.

Biesecker-Mast, Gerald. *Separation and the Sword in Anabaptist Persuasion*. Telford: Cascadia Publishing House, 2006. Print.

Blanchot, Maurice. *Friendship*. Trans. Elizabeth Rottenburg. Stanford: Stanford UP, 1997. Print.

Bleiler, E.F. "Pieter Gillis and Thomas More's *Utopia*." *Extrapolation* 27.4 (1986): 304–19. Print.

Blockmans, Wim. *Emperor Charles V, 1500–1558*. Trans. Isola van den Hoven-Vardon. Oxford: Oxford UP, 2002. Print.

Boccaccio, Giovanni. *The Decameron*. Trans. G.H. McWilliam. London: Penguin, 1995. Print.

Bongi, Salvatore. "Il velo giallo di Tullia d'Aragona." *Rivista Critica della Letteratura Italiana* 3.3 (1986): 86–95. Print.

Bradbrook, M.C. "Shakespeare and the Use of Disguise in Elizabethan Drama." *Essays in Criticism* 2 (1952): 159–68. Print.

Bradshaw, Brendan. "Transalpine Humanism." *The Cambridge History of Political Thought 1450–1700*. Ed. J.H. Burns. Cambridge: Cambridge UP, 1991. 95–131. Print.

Brancaforte, Benito. *Guzmán: ¿Conversión o degradación?* Madison, WI: Hispanic Seminary of Medieval Studies, 1980. Print.

Brashear, Lucy. "The Forgotten Legacy of the 'Matchless Orinda'." *The Anglo-Welsh Review* 65 (1979): 68–79. Print.

Bray, Alan. *The Friend*. Chicago: U of Chicago P, 2003. Print.

——. *Homosexuality in Renaissance England*. Second ed. New York: Columbia UP, 1996. Print.

Bridgett, T.E. *Life and Writings of Sir Thomas More, Lord Chancellor of England and Martyr under Henry VIII*. New York: Catholic Publication Society, 1891. Print.

Britland, Karen. *Drama at the Court of Queen Henrietta Maria*. Cambridge: Cambridge UP, 2006. Print.

Bromfield, Joyce G. *De Lorenzino de Médicis à Lorenzaccio: Étude d'un thème historique*. Études de Littérature Étrangère et Comparée. Paris: Marcel Didier, 1972. Print.

Budé, Guillaume. *De Linstitution du Prince: Liure contenant plusieurs histoires, enseignements, & saiges dicts des anciens tant Grecs que Latins.* Paris: Maistre Nicole, 1547. Farnborough, England: Gregg Press Ltd, 1966. Print.

Bullard, Melissa M. *Filippo Strozzi and the Medici: Favor and Finance in Sixteenth-Century Florence and Rome.* Cambridge: Cambridge UP, 1980. Print.

Bullinger, Heinrich. *The Christen State of Matrimonye.* Trans. Miles Coverdale. Antwerp, 1541. *EEBO.* Web. 20 July 2009.

Burke, Peter. *The Fortunes of the Courtier: The European Reception of Castiglione's "Cortegiano."* University Park: Pennsylvania State UP, 1995. Print.

Büsser, Fritz. *Calvins Urteil über sich selbst.* Zürich: Zwingli-Verlag, 1950. Print.

Butler, Martin. *Theatre and Crisis, 1632–1642.* Cambridge: Cambridge UP, 1984. Print.

Calvin, John. *Institutes of Christian Religion.* Trans. Henry Beveridge. Grand Rapids: William B. Eerdmans Publishing Company, 1983 [1945]. Print.

Campbell, Lorne, Margaret Mann Phillips, Hubertus Schulte Herbrüggen, and J.B. Trapp. "Quentin Matsys, Desiderius, Erasmus, Pieter Gillis and Thomas More." *The Burlington Magazine* 120.908 (1978): 716–25. Print.

Carrell, Jennifer Lee. "A Pack of Lies in a Looking Glass: Lady Mary Wroth's *Urania* and the Magic Mirror of Romance." *SEL* 34 (1994): 79–107. Print.

Carroll, William C. *Fat King, Lean Beggar: Representations of Poverty in the Age of Shakespeare.* Ithaca: Cornell UP, 1996. Print.

Carson, Anne. *Eros: The Bittersweet.* N.p.: Dalkey Archive P, 1998. Print.

Cartwright, William. *Comedies, Tragi-comedies, With other Poems.* London: Humphrey Moseley, 1651. Print.

Casagrande di Villaviera, Rita. *Le cortigiane veneziane nel cinquecento.* Milan: Longanesi, 1968. Print.

Cassidy, Eoin C. "'He Who Has Friends Can Have No Friend': Classical and Christian Perspectives on the Limits to Friendship." *Friendship in Medieval Europe.* Ed. Julian Haseldine. Stroud: Sutton Publishing, 1999. 45–67. Print.

Castiglione, Baldassar. *Il Libro del Cortegiano.* 1981. Ed. Nicola Longo. Milan: Garzanti, 1991. Print.

Cavanagh, Sheila T. "Endless Love: Narrative Technique in the *Urania*." *Sidney Journal* 26.2 (2008): 83–100. Print.

——. "Romancing the Epic: Lady Mary Wroth's *Urania* and Literary Traditions." *Approaches to the Anglo and American Female Epic, 1621–1982.* Ed. Bernard Schweizer. Burlington, VT: Ashgate, 2006. 19–36. Print.

Cavillac, Michel. *Pícaros y mercaderes en el* Guzmán de Alfarache. Granada: Universidad de Granada, 1994. Print.

Cellini, Benvenuto. *The Autobiography of Benvenuto Cellini.* Trans. Addington Symonds. Whitefish, MT: Kessinger Publishing, 2005. Print.

Certaine sermons or Homilies, appointed to be read in churches, in the time of Queen Elizabeth I, 1547–1571. London, 1623. Facsimile ed. Gainesville: Scholars' Facsimiles & Reprints, 1968. Print.

Chalmers, Hero. *Royalist Women Writers 1650–1689.* Oxford: Clarendon, 2004. Print.

Chaplin, Gregory. "'One Flesh, One Heart, One Soul': Renaissance Friendship and Miltonic Marriage." *Modern Philology* 99.2 (2001): 266–92. Print.

——, ed. *The Culture of Early Modern Friendship.* Special issue of *Texas Studies in Language and Literature*, 47.4 (2005). Print.

Chernaik, Warren. "Katherine Philips (1632–1664)." *Oxford Dictionary of National Biography.* Oxford: Oxford UP, 2004. Web. 25 July 2007.

Cholakian, Patricia Francis. *Rape and Writing in the Heptaméron of Marguerite de Navarre.* Carbondale: Southern Illinois UP, 1991. Print.

Cicero, Marcus Tullius. *De amicitia.* Loeb Classical Library. Vol. 20. Ed. Jeffery Henderson. Trans. William Armistead Falconer. Cambridge, MA: Harvard UP, 1923. 2. Print.

——. *"Laelius, On Friendship" and "The Dream of Scipio."* Ed. and trans. J.G.F. Powell. Warminster: Aris and Phillips, 1990. Print.

——. *Laelius sive de amicitia dialogus.* 1941. Eds H.E. Gould and J.L. Whiteley. Bristol: Classical Press, 1983. Print.

——. *Letters.* Trans. E.S. Shuckburgh. New York: P.F. Collier & Son, 1909. Print.

——. *De officiis.* Trans. Walter Miller. Loeb Classical Library. Cambridge, MA: Harvard UP, 1968. Print.

——. *De Republica, De legibus.* Trans. Clinton Walker Keyes. Loeb Classical Library. Cambridge, MA: Harvard UP, 1928. Print.

——. *De senectute, De amicitia, De divinatione.* Trans. William Armistead Falconer. Loeb Classical Library. Cambridge, MA: Harvard UP, 1923. Print.

Clayton, Edward W. "Aristotle and Political Friendship." Unpublished Manuscript, 1997.

Cohen, Elizabeth S. "'Courtesans' and 'Whores': Words and Behavior in Roman Streets." *Women Studies.* Special Issue: *Women in the Renaissance: An Interdisciplinary Forum. MLA (1989).* Eds Ann Rosalind Jones and Betty Travitsky. 19.1 (1991): 201–8. Print.

Colie, Rosalie L. "Reason and Need: *King Lear* and the 'Crisis' of the Aristocracy." *Some Facets of King Lear: Essays in Prismatic Criticism.* Eds Rosalie L. Colie and F.T. Flahiff. Toronto: U of Toronto P, 1974. 184–220. Print.

Corns, Thomas N. "Milton and the Characteristics of a Free Commonwealth." *Milton and Republicanism.* Eds David Armitage, Armand Himy, and Quentin Skinner. Cambridge: Cambridge UP, 1995. 25–42. Print.

Craig, Martha. "Negotiating Sex: The Poetics of Feminization in Sidney's *Arcadia*." *Explorations in Renaissance Culture* 31.1 (Summer 2005): 89–106. Print.

Cranmer, Thomas. *An aunsvvere by the Reuerend Father in God Thomas Archbyshop of Canterbury.* N.p.,1580. Print.

Cros, Edmond. *Protée et le gueux: Recherches sur les origins et la nature du récit picaresque dans Guzmán de Alfarache.* Paris: Didier, 1967. Print.

Dall'Aglio, Stefano. *Il Filosofo Tirannicida: Esilio e morte di Lorenzino de' Medici, 1537–1548.* Florence: Leo S. Olschki, forthcoming.

D'Aragona, Tullia. *Dialogue on the Infinity of Love*. Eds and trans. Rinaldina Russell and Bruce Merry. Chicago: U of Chicago P, 1997. Print.

——. *Lettere al Varchi*. Autografi Palatini, I: 10–17. Biblioteca Nazionale Centrale di Firenze. Transcribed in Guido Biagi. "Un'etera romana, Tullia d'Aragona." *Nouva Antologia, Serie III* 4.6 (1886): 655–711. Print.

——. *Rime di Tullia d'Aragona Cortigiana del Secolo XVI*. 1891. Ed. Enrico Celani. Bologna: Romagnoli, 1968. Print.

Davis, Natalie Zemon. *The Gift in Sixteenth-Century France*. Madison, WI: U of Wisconsin P, 2000. Print.

Derrida, Jacques. *Politics of Friendship*. Trans. George Collins. London: Verso, 1997. Print.

Descartes, René. *Treatise of Man: French Text with Translation and Commentary*. Trans. Thomas Steele Hall. Cambridge, MA: Harvard UP, 1972. Print.

Dolan, Frances. *Marriage and Violence: The Early Modern Legacy*. Philadelphia: U of Pennsylvania P, 2008. Print.

Donne, John. "To Sir Henry Wotton." *John Donne's Poetry: A Norton Critical Edition*. Ed. Donald R. Dickson. New York: Norton, 2007. 54. Print.

Doyle, Charles Clay. "The Mysterious Malady of Pieter Gillis." *Moreana* XXIX, 110 (1992): 35–7. Print.

Duncan-Jones, Katherine. *Sir Philip Sidney: Courtier Poet*. New Haven, CT: Yale UP, 1991. Print.

Dunn, E. Catherine. *The Concept of Ingratitude in Renaissance English Moral Philosophy*. Washington, DC: Catholic University of America P, 1946. Print.

Dunn, Peter N. *Spanish Picaresque Fiction: A New Literary History*. Ithaca: Cornell UP, 1993. Print.

Dyck, Cornelius, William E. Keeney, and Alvin J. Beachy, eds and trans. *The Writings of Dirk Philips: 1504–1568*. Scottdale, PA: Herald Press, 1992. Print.

Dzelzainis, Martin. Introduction. *Political Writings*. By John Milton. Cambridge: Cambridge UP, 1991. ix–xxv. Print.

——. "Milton's Classical Republicanism." *Milton and Republicanism*. Eds David Armitage, Armand Himy, and Quentin Skinner. Cambridge: Cambridge UP, 1995. 3–24. Print.

Eckerle, Julie A. "Urania's Example: The Female Storyteller in Early Modern English Romance." *Oral Traditions and Gender in Early Modern Literary Texts*. Eds Mary Ellen Lamb and Karen Bamford. Burlington, VT: Ashgate. 25–40. Print.

——. "'With a tale forsooth he cometh unto you': Sidney and the Storytelling Poet." *Sidney Journal* 21.1 (2003): 41–65. Print.

Eden, Kathy. "Between Friends All is Common." *Journal of the History of Ideas* 59.3 (1998): 405–19. Print.

——. *Friends Hold All Things in Common: Tradition, Intellectual Property, and the Adages of Erasmus*. New Haven: Yale UP, 2001. Print.

Egan, Robert. "Kent and the Audience: The Character as Spectator." *Shakespeare Quarterly* 32.2 (1981): 146–54. Print.

Ellinghausen, Laurie. "Literary Property and the Single Woman in Isabella Whitney's 'A Sweet Nosegay.'" *SEL* 45.1 (2005): 1–22. Print.

Elliott, Dyan. *Spiritual Marriage: Sexual Abstinence in Medieval Wedlock.* Princeton: Princeton UP 1993. Print.

Elyot, Thomas. *The Boke Named the Governour.* London: Thomas Berthelet, 1531. *EEBO.* Web. 22 August 2006.

——. *The Book Named The Governor.* Ed. S.E. Lehmberg. London: Dent, 1962. Print.

——. *The Castel of Helthe.* London: Thomas Berthelet, 1539. *EEBO.* Web. 11 March 2009.

Erasmus, Desiderius. *The Correspondence of Erasmus.* 12 vols. Trans. R.A.B. Mynors and D.F.S. Thompson; annot. J.K. McConica (Vols. 3–4). Trans. R.A.B. Mynors and D.F.S. Thompson; annot. P.G. Bietenholz (Vols. 5–7). Toronto: U of Toronto P, 1974. Print.

——. *The Education of a Christian Prince, Translated by Neil M. Cheshire and Michael J. Heath with the Panegyric for Archduke Philip of Austria, Translated by Lisa Jardine.* Cambridge: Cambridge UP, 1997. Print.

——. *Institutio christiani matrimonii. Spiritualia* 3. Eds John W. O'Malley and Louis A. Parraud. *The Collected Works of Erasmus,* Vol. 69. Toronto: U of Toronto P, 1988. 203–438. Print.

——. *Opus epistolarum Des. Erasmi Roterodami.* 12 vols. Ed. P.S. Allen (Vols. 1–2). Eds P.S. Allen and H.M. Allen (Vols. 3–8). Eds H.M. Allen and H.W. Garrod (Vols. 9–12). Oxford: Clarendon, 1906–1958. Print.

Evans, Blakemore G., ed. *The Plays and Poems of William Cartwright.* Madison: U of Wisconsin P, 1951. Print.

Evans, Maurice, ed. *Elizabethan Sonnets.* London: Everyman, 1994. Print.

Farnsworth, Jane. "Defending the King in Cartwright's *The Lady-Errant* (1636–37)." *SEL* 42.2 (2002): 381–98. Print.

Ferguson, Gary. "History or Her Story? (Homo)sociality/sexuality in Marguerite de Navarre's *Heptaméron* 12." *Narrative Worlds: Essays on the Nouvelle in 15th and 16th Century France.* Eds David Laguardia and Gary Ferguson. Medieval and Renaissance Texts and Studies. Phoenix, AZ: Arizona State UP, 2005. 97–122. Print.

Ferrai, L.A. *Lorenzino de' Medici e la Società Cortigiana del Cinquecento.* Milano: Ulrico Hoepli, 1891. Print.

Ficino, Marsilio. *The Philebus Commentary: A Critical Edition and Translation.* Ed. Michael J.B. Allen. Berkeley, CA: U of California P, 1975. Print.

Filmer, Sir Robert. *Patriarcha and Other Political Writings.* Ed. Johann P. Sommerville. Cambridge: Cambridge UP, 1991. Print.

Finch, Francis. *Friendship.* N.p.: N.p., 1654. Print.

Fiore, Benjamin, S.J. "The Theory and Practice of Friendship in Cicero." *Greco-Roman Perspectives on Friendship*. Ed. John T. Fitzgerald. Atlanta: Scholars Press, 1997. 59–76. Print.

Fischel, Oskar. *Raphael*. Trans. Bernard Rackham. London: Spring Books, 1964. Print.

Flossi, Justin. "On Locating the Courtesan in Italian Lyric: Distance and the Madrigal Texts of Costanzo Festa." *The Courtesan's Art: Cross-Cultural Perspectives*. Eds Martha Feldman and Bonnie Gordon. Oxford: Oxford UP, 2006. 133–43. Print.

Floyd-Wilson, Mary. "English Mettle." *Reading the Early Modern Passions: Essays in the Early Modern History of Emotion*. Eds Gail Kern Paster, Katherine Rowe, and Mary Floyd-Wilson. Philadelphia: U of Pennsylvania P, 2004. 130–46. Print.

Flynn, Dennis. "Cartwright, William (1611–1643)." *Oxford Dictionary of National Biography*. Oxford: Oxford UP, 2004. Web. 19 April 2007.

Fontaine, Marie-Madeleine. "Les Enjeux de pouvoir dans l'*Heptaméron*." *Marguerite de Navarre: Actes de la journée d'étude Marguerite de Navarre, 19 octobre 1991*. Ed. Simone Perrier. Paris: U.F.R., 1991. 133–49, 55–60. Print.

Freccero, Carla. "Marguerite de Navarre and the Politics of Maternal Sovereignty." *Women and Sovereignty*. Ed. Louise Olga Fradenburg. Edinburgh: U of Edinburgh P, 1991. 133–49. Print.

——. "Rewriting the Rhetoric of Desire in the *Heptaméron*." *Contending Kingdoms: Historical, Psychological, and Feminist Approaches to the Literature of Sixteenth-Century France and England*. Eds Marie-Rose Logan and Peter L. Rudnytsky. Detroit: Wayne State UP, 1991. 298–312. Print.

Freeman, John. "Utopia, Incorporated: Reassessing Intellectual Property Rights to 'the Island.'" *English Literary Renaissance* 37.1 (2007): 3–33. Print.

Friedman, Edward. "Insincere Flattery: Imitation and the Growth of the Novel." *Cervantes: Bulletin of the Cervantes Society of America* 20.1 (2000): 99–114. Print.

Friesen, Abraham. *Erasmus, the Anabaptists, and the Great Commission*. Grand Rapids: William B. Eerdmans Publishing Company. Print.

Galen. *On the Natural Faculties*. Trans. Arthur John Brock. Loeb Classical Library. Cambridge, MA: Harvard UP, 1916. Print.

——. *On the Passions and Errors of the Soul*. Trans. Paul Harkins. Columbus, OH: Ohio State UP, 1963. Print.

Gerló, Alois. *Erasme et ses portraitistes*. Nieuwkoop: B. de Graaf, 1969. Print.

Gil, Daniel Juan. *Before Intimacy: Asocial Sexuality in Early Modern England*. Minneapolis: U of Minnesota P, 2006. Print.

Gilbert-Santamaría, Donald. *Writers on the Market: Consuming Literature in Early Seventeenth-Century Spain*. Lewisburg: Bucknell UP, 2005. Print.

Giovio, Paolo. *Il Rimanente della Seconda Parte dell'Historie del suo Tempo*. Trans. Lodovico DomeNici. Venice: Comin da Trino, 1557. Print.

Goldie, Mark. "James Tyrrell." *Oxford Dictionary of National Biography.* Web. 30 May 2007.

Gowing, Laura, Michael Hunter, and Miri Rubin, eds. *Love, Friendship and Faith in Europe, 1300–1800.* New York: Palgrave, 2005. Print.

Graf, Arturo. *Attraverso il Cinquecento.* Turin: Chiantore, 1888. Print.

Gravdal, Kathryn. *Ravishing Maidens: Writing Rape in Medieval French Literature and Law.* Philadelphia: U of Pennsylvania P, 1991. Print.

Gray, Catharine. "Katherine Philips and the Post-Courtly Coterie." *English Literary Renaissance* 32.3 (2002): 426–51. Print.

——. *Women Writers and Public Debate in Seventeenth-Century Britain.* New York: Palgrave, 2007. Print.

Greenblatt, Stephen Jay. *Shakespearean Negotiations.* Berkeley: U of California P, 1988. Print.

Greenhalgh, Darlene C. "Love, Chastity and Women's Erotic Power: Greek Romance in Elizabethan and Jacobean Contexts." *Prose Fiction and Early Modern Sexualities in England, 1570–1640.* Eds Constance C. Relihan and Goran V. Stanivukovic. London: Palgrave, 2003. 15–42. Print.

Grossberg, Benjamin Scott. "Politics and Shifting Desire in Sidney's *New Arcadia.*" *SEL* 42.1 (2002): 63–83. Print.

Guarini, Elena Fasano, and Franco Angiolini, eds. *La Pratica della Storia in Toscana: Continuità e mutamenti tra la fine del '400 et la fine del '700.* Milano: FrancoAngeli, 2009. Print.

Guazzo, M. Steeven (Stephano). *The Civile Conversation of M. Steeven Guazzo, the first three books translated by George Pettie (1581) and the fourth by Bartholomew Young (1586).* Ed. Charles Whibley. New York: Knopf, 1925. Vol. 1. Print.

Hairston, Julia L. "Bradamante, 'Vergine Saggia': Maternity and the Arts of Negotiation." *Exemplaria* 12.2 (2000): 476–9. Print.

Halio, Jay L., ed. *The First Quarto of King Lear.* By William Shakespeare. Cambridge: Cambridge UP, 1996. Print.

——. *The Tragedy of King Lear.* By William Shakespeare. Cambridge: Cambridge UP, 1992. Print.

Harder, Leland, ed. *The Sources of Swiss Anabaptism: The Grebel Letters and Related Documents.* Scottdale: Herald Press, 1985. Print.

Hausted, Peter. *The Rivall Friends: A Facsimile of the 1632 Edition.* Amsterdam: Theatrum Orbis Terrarum, 1973. Print.

Heal, Felicity. *Hospitality in Early Modern England.* Oxford: Clarendon, 1990. Print.

Heilke, Thomas. "Friendship in the Civic Order: A Reformation Absence." *Friendship and Politics: Essays in Political Thought.* Eds John von Heyking and Richard G. Avramenko. Notre Dame: Notre Dame UP, 2007. Print.

Hexter, J.H. Appendix A, "More's Visit to Antwerp in 1515." *Utopia. Complete Works of St. Thomas More.* Vol. 4. Eds Edward Surtz, S.J., and J.H. Hexter. New Haven: Yale UP, 1965. 573–6. Print.

The History of King Leir (1605). Malone Society Reprints. Oxford: Oxford UP, 1907. Print.

Hobbes, Thomas. *Leviathan*. Ed. Richard Tuck. Cambridge: Cambridge UP, 1991. Print.

Hock, Ronald F. "An Extraordinary Friend in Chariton's *Callirhoe*: The Importance of Friendship in the Greek Romances." *Greco-Roman Perspectives on Friendship*. Ed. John T. Fitzgerald. Atlanta, GA: Scholars Press, 1997. 145–62. Print.

Höpfl, Harro. *The Christian Polity of John Calvin*. Cambridge: Cambridge UP, 1982. Print.

Hopkins, Lisa. "Reason and Passion in Sidney's *Arcadia*." *Prose Fiction and Early Modern Sexualities in England, 1570–1640*. Eds Constance C. Rehihan and Goran V. Stanivukovic. New York: Palgrave, 2003. 61–75. Print.

Horst, Irvin B. "Menno Simons: The New Man in Community." *Profiles of Radical Reformers: Biographical Sketches from Thomas Müntzer to Paracelsus*. Eds Hans-Jürgen Goertz and Walter Klassen. Kitchener and Scottdale: Herald Press, 1982. 203–13. Print.

Hutson, Lorna. *The Usurer's Daughter: Male Friendship and Fiction of Women in Sixteenth Century England*. New York: Routledge, 1994. Print.

Hutter, Horst. *Politics as Friendship: The Origins of Classical Notions of Politics in the Theory and Practice of Friendship*. Waterloo: Wilfrid Laurier UP, 1978. Print.

Hyatte, Reginald. *The Arts of Friendship: The Idealization of Friendship in Medieval and Early Renaissance Literature*. Leiden: Brill, 1994. Print.

Il Dialogo dello Zoppino de la vita e genealogia di tutte le cortigiane di Roma. Ed. Gino Lanfranchi. Milan: L'Editrice del Libro Raro, 1922. Print.

Irigaray, Luce. *This Sex Which Is Not One*. Trans. Catherine Porter. Ithaca: Cornell UP, 1985. Print.

Jankowski, Theodora. *Pure Resistance: Queer Virginity in Early Modern English Drama*. Philadelphia, PA: U of Pennsylvania P, 2000. Print.

Jardine, Lisa. *Erasmus, Man of Letters: The Construction of Charisma in Print*. Princeton: Princeton UP, 1993. Print.

Javitch, Daniel. "Rival Arts of Conduct in Elizabethan England: Guazzo's *Civile Conversation* and Castiglione's *Courtier*." *Yearbook of Italian Studies*. Firenze, Italy: 1971. 178–98. Print.

Jed, Stephanie. "Making History Straight: Collecting and Recording in Sixteenth Century Italy." *The Bucknell Review* 35.2 (1992): 104–20. Print.

Johnson, Carroll. "Defining the Picaresque: Authority and the Subject in *Guzmán de Alfarache*." *The Picaresque: Tradition and Displacement*. Ed. Giancarlo Maiorino. Minneapolis: U of Minnesota P, 1996. 159–82. Print.

——. *Inside Guzmán de Alfarache*. Berkeley: U of California P, 1978. Print.

Johnson, E. Joe. *Once There Were Two True Friends, or Idealized Male Friendship in French Narrative from the Middle Ages through the Enlightenment*. Birmingham: Summa Publications, 2003. Print.

Jones, Ann Rosalind. "The Poetics of Group Identity: Self-Commemoration through Dialogue in Pernette du Guillet and Tullia D'Aragona." *The Currency of Eros: Women's Love Lyric in Europe, 1540–1620.* Bloomington, IN: Indiana UP, 1990. 79–117. Print.

——. "Writing to Live: Pedagogical Practices in Isabella Whitney and Catherine des Roches." *The Currency of Eros: Women's Love Lyric in Europe, 1540–1620.* Bloomington, IN: Indiana UP, 1990. 36–78. Print.

Jones, Roger, and Nicholas Penny. *Raphael.* New Haven: Yale UP, 1983. Print.

Jonson, Ben. "Inviting a Friend to Supper." *Seventeenth-Century British Poetry: 1603–1660.* Eds John Rumrich and Gregory Chaplin. New York: Norton, 2006. 89–90. Print.

Jordan, Constance. *Renaissance Feminism: Literary Texts and Political Models.* Ithaca: Cornell UP, 1990. Print.

Kartchner, Eric J. "Playing Doubles: Another Look at Alemán's Vengeance on Martí." *Cincinnati Romance Review* 16 (1997): 16–23. Print.

Keller, Eve. *Generating Bodies and Gendered Selves: The Rhetoric of Reproduction in Early Modern England.* Seattle, WA: U of Washington P, 2007. Print.

Kent, Dale. *Friendship, Love, and Trust in Renaissance Florence.* Cambridge, MA: Harvard UP, 2009. Print.

Kerrigan, William. "Transformations of Friendship in the Work of Katherine Philips." *Seventeenth-Century British Poetry: 1603–1660.* Eds John Rumrich and Gregory Chaplin. New York: Norton, 2006. 955–70. Print.

Klassen, William, and Walter Klaassen, eds. *The Writings of Pilgram Marpeck.* Kitchener and Scottdale: Herald Press, 1978. Print.

Knecht, Robert J. *Renaissance Warrior and Patron: The Reign of Francis I.* Cambridge: Cambridge UP, 1994. Print.

Konstan, David. *Friendship in the Classical World.* Cambridge: Cambridge UP, 1997. Print.

——. *Sexual Symmetry: Love in the Ancient Novel and Related Genres.* Princeton: Princeton UP, 1994. Print.

La Boétie, Etienne de. *Discours de la servitude volontaire. Freedom Over Servitude: Montaigne, La Boétie, and* On Voluntary Servitude. Ed. and trans. David Lewis Schaefer. Westport, CT: Greenwood Press, 1998. 191–222. Print.

LaGuardia. David P. *Intertextual Masculinity in French Renaissance Culture: Rabelais, Brantôme, and the* Cent nouvelles nouvelles. Burlington and Aldershot: Ashgate Publishing, 2008. Print.

Langer, Ullrich. *Perfect Friendship: Studies in Literature and Moral Philosophy from Boccaccio to Corneille.* Geneva: Droz, 1994. Print.

——. "Théorie et representation de l'amitié à la Renaissance." *L'amitié.* Eds Jean-Christophe Merle and Bernard N. Schumacher. Paris: Presses Universitaires de France, 2005. 47–62. Print.

La tariffa della puttane. Ed. Antonio Barzaghi. *Donne o cortigiane? La prostituzione a Venezia: Documenti di costume dal XVI al XVIII secolo.* Verona: Bertani, 1980. Print.

Lawner, Lynn. *Lives of the Courtesans: Portraits of the Renaissance*. New York: Rizzoli, 1987. Print.

Lee, Egmont, ed. *Descriptio Urbis: The Roman Census of 1527*. Rome: Bulzoni, 1985. Print.

Lemnius, Levinus. *The Touchstone of Complexions*. Trans. Thomas Newton. London: Thomas Marsh, 1576. *EEBO*. Web. 12 March 2009.

Levin, Harry. "The Heights and the Depths: A Scene from 'King Lear.'" *More Talking of Shakespeare*. Ed. John Garrett. London: Longmans, Green, 1959. 87–103. Print.

Liebler, Naomi Conn. *Shakespeare's Festive Tragedy: The Ritual Foundations of Genre*. New York: Routledge, 1995. Print.

Lilley, Kate. "'Dear Object': Katherine Philips's Love Elegies and Their Readers." *Women Writing, 1550–1750*. Eds Jo Wallwork and Paul Salzman. Bundoora, Australia: Meridian, 2001. 163–78. Print.

Limbert, Claudia. "Katherine Philips: Controlling a Life and Reputation." *South Atlantic Review* 56.2 (1991): 27–42. Print.

Lipton, Emma. *Affections of the Mind: The Politics of Sacramental Marriage in Late Medieval English Literature*. Notre Dame, IN: U of Notre Dame P, 2007. Print.

Littell, Franklin Hamlin. *The Anabaptist View of the Church: A Study in the Origins of Sectarian Protestantism*. Second ed. Boston: Starr King Press, 1958. Print.

Locke, John. Commonplace book. ms. MS Locke e. 17. Bodleian Library, Oxford.

López, Maritere. *Writing a Letter, Writing the Self: Courtesans of the Italian Renaissance and their Epistolary Writings*. Diss: State U of NY at Buffalo, 2003. Ann Arbor: UMI, 2003. ATT 3089168. Print.

Lo Re, Salvatore. *La Crisi della Libertà Fiorentina: Alle Origini della Formazione Politica e Intellettuale di Benedetto Varchi et Piero Vettori*. Rome: Edizioni de Storia e Letteratura, 2006. Print.

Luján de Sayavedra, Mateo (Juan Martí). "Vida del pícaro Guzmán de Alfarache." *Novelistas anteriores a Cervantes: Autores españoles, desde la formación del lenguaje hasta nuestros días*. Madrid: M. Rivadeneyra, 1876. 363–420. Print.

Luther, Martin. "An Appeal to the Ruling Class of German Nationality as to the Amelioration of the State of Christendom." *Martin Luther: Selections from his writings edited and with an introduction*. Ed. John Dillenberger. Garden City, NY: Doubleday, 1961. 403–85. Print.

——. "Disputation Against Scholastic Theology, 1517." *Career of the Reformer: I*. Ed. Harold J. Grimm. *Luther's Works*. Vol. 3. Ed. Helmut T. Lehman. Philadelphia: Muhlenberg Press, 1955. Print.

——. *Der Grosse Catechismus*. München and Hamburg: Siebenstern Taschenbuch Verlag, 1964. Print.

——. *What Luther Says*. Vol. 1. Ed. Ewald Plass. St. Louis, MO: Concordia Publishing House, 1986. Print.

Luxon, Thomas H. *Single Imperfection: Milton, Marriage and Friendship*. Pittsburgh: Duquesne UP, 2005. Print.

Lynch, Kathleen M. *The Social Mode of Restoration Comedy*. New York: Macmillan, 1926. Print.

Lytle, Guy Fitch. "Friendship and Patronage in Renaissance Europe." *Patronage, Art, and Society in Renaissance Italy*. Eds F.W. Kent and Patricia Simmons. Oxford: Clarendon, 1987. 47–61. Print.

McClean, Hugh. "Disguise in *King Lear*: Kent and Edgar." *Shakespeare Quarterly* 11.1 (Winter 1960): 49–54. Print.

McCutcheon, Elizabeth. *My Dear Peter: The* Ars Poetica *and Hermeneutics for More's* Utopia. Angers: Moreana, 1983. Print.

MacFaul, Tom. "Friendship in Sidney's *Arcadias*." *SEL* 49.1 (2009): 17–33. Print.

——. *Male Friendship in Shakespeare and His Contemporaries*. Cambridge: Cambridge UP, 2007. Print.

McGrady, Donald. *Mateo Alemán*. New York: Twayne Publishers, 1968. Print.

McGrath, Lynette. "Isabella Whitney. The Printed Subject: Print, Power and Abjection in *The Copy of a Letter* and *A Sweet Nosgay*." *Subjectivity and Women's Poetry in Early Modern England*. Burlington: Ashgate, 2002. 123–63. Print.

MacIntyre, Alasdair. *After Virtue: A Study in Moral Theory*. Second ed. Notre Dame: U of Notre Dame P, 1984. Print.

Mack, Maynard. *King Lear in Our Time*. Berkeley: U of California P, 1965. Print.

Macphail, Eric. "Friendship as a Political Ideal." *Montaigne Studies* 1 (1989): 177–87. Print.

Mann-Phillips, Margaret. "The Correspondence of Erasmus and More." *Thomas More 1477–1977: Colloque international tenu en novembre 1977*. Brussels: Editions de l'Université de Bruxelles, 1980. 27–37. Print.

Maravall, José Antonio. *La literature picaresca desde la historia social*. Madrid: Taurus Ediciones, 1986. Print.

Marc'hadour, Germain. "Thomas More in Emulation and Defense of Erasmus." *Erasmus of Rotterdam: The Man and the Scholar*. Eds J. Sperna Weiland and W.Th.M. Frijhoff. Leiden: E.J. Brill, 1988. 203–14. Print.

Marchand, Jean-Jacques, and Jean-Claude Zancarini, eds. *Storiografia Repubblicana Fiorentina (1494–1570)*. Firenze: Franco Cesati Editore, 2003. Print.

Marcus, Sharon. *Between Women: Friendship, Desire and Marriage in Victorian England*. Princeton, NJ: Princeton UP, 2007. Print.

Mariscal, George. *Contradictory Subjects: Quevedo, Cervantes, and Seventeenth-Century Spanish Culture*. Ithaca: Cornell UP, 1993. Print.

Marius, Richard. *Thomas More: A Biography*. New York: Alfred A. Knopf, 1984. Print.

Marlow, Christopher. "Friendship, Misogyny and Antitheatrical Prejudice: A Reading of *The Rivall Friends*." *Peer English* 1 (2006): 25–33. Print.

Marpeck, Pilgram. "The Admonition of 1542." *The Writings of Pilgram Marpeck.* Trans. and eds William Klassen and Walter Klaassen. Scottdale: Herald Press, 1978. 159–302. Print.

Marquis, Paul A. "Oppositional Ideologies of Gender in Isabella Whitney's 'Copy of a Letter.'" *Modern Language Review* 90.2 (1995): 314–24. Print.

Masten, Jeffrey. *Textual Intercourse: Collaboration, Authorship, and Sexualities in Renaissance Drama.* Cambridge: Cambridge UP, 1997. Print.

Mentz, Steve. *Romance for Sale in Early Modern England.* Aldershot: Ashgate, 2006. Print.

Mieli, Mario. *Elementi di Critica Omosessuale.* Torino: Giulio Einaudi, 1977. Print.

Miller, Jacqueline T. "Ladies of the Oddest Passion: Early Modern Women and the Arts of Discretion." *Modern Philology* 103.4 (2006): 453–73. Print.

——. "The Passion Signified: Imitation and the Construction of Emotions in Sidney and Wroth." *Criticism* 43.4 (2001): 407–21. Print.

Mills, Laurens J. *One Soul in Bodies Twain: Friendship in Tudor Literature and Stuart Drama.* Bloomington, IN: Principia Press, 1937. Print.

Milton, John. *Complete Poems and Major Prose.* Ed. Merritt Y. Hughes. New York: Odyssey, 1957. Print.

——. *The Complete Prose Works of John Milton.* Eds Don M. Wolfe et al. 8 vols. New Haven: Yale UP, 1953–82. Print.

Mitchell, Alan C. "'Greet the Friends by Name': New Testament Evidence for the Greco-Roman Topos on Friendship." *Greco-Roman Perspectives on Friendship.* Ed. John T. Fitzgerald. Atlanta, GA: Scholars Press, 1997. 225–62. Print.

Montaigne, Michel de. *The Complete Essays of Montaigne.* Trans. Donald M. Frame. Stanford: Stanford UP, 1958. Print.

——. *Essayes.* Trans. John Florio, ed. Desmond McCarthy. London: J.M. Dent and Sons, 1928. Print.

——. *The Essayes of Michael Lord of Montaigne.* Trans. John Florio. London: Routledge, 1894. Print.

——. "Of Friendship." Trans. Donald M. Frame. *Other Selves: Philosophers on Friendship.* Ed. Michael Pakaluk. Indianapolis, IN: Hackett, 1991. 185–99. Print.

Montevecchi, Alessandro. *Storici di Firenze: Studi su Nardi, Nerli e Varchi.* Bologna: Pàtron, 1989. Print.

More, Thomas. *Latin Poems. The Complete Works of St. Thomas More.* Vol. 3, Part II. Eds Clarence H. Miller, Leicester Bradner, Charles A. Lynch, and Revilo P. Oliver. New Haven: Yale UP, 1984. Print.

——. *St. Thomas More: Selected Letters.* Ed. Elizabeth Frances Rogers. New Haven: Yale UP, 1961. Print.

——. *Utopia. Complete Works of St. Thomas More.* Vol. 4. Eds Edward Surtz, S.J., and J.H. Hexter. New Haven: Yale UP, 1965. Print.

——. *Utopia: Latin Text and Translation*. Eds George M. Logan, Robert M. Adams, and Clarence H. Miller. Cambridge: Cambridge UP, 1995. Print.

Morrison, Ian R. "La nouvelle 12 de l'*Heptaméron* de Marguerite de Navarre." *Studia Neophilologica* 67 (1995): 61–6. Print.

Navarre, Marguerite de. *L'Heptaméron*. 1991. Ed. Michel François. Paris: Dunod, 1996. Print.

Nerli, Filippo de'. *Commentarj dei Fatti Civili Occorsi dentro la Città di Firenze dall'anno 1215 al 1537*. Vol. 1. 2 vols. Trieste: Colombo Coen, 1859. Print.

Nietzsche, Friedrich. *The Will to Power*. Trans. Walter Kaufmann and R.J. Hollingdale. Ed. Walter Kaufmann. New York: Vintage Books, 1967. Print.

Noakes, Susan. "The *Heptaméron* Prologue and the Anxiety of Influence." *Studi sul Boccaccio* 20 (1991–92): 267–77. Print.

Norbrook, David. *Writing the English Republic: Poetry, Rhetoric and Politics, 1627–1660*. Cambridge: Cambridge UP, 1999. Print.

Noreña, Carlos G. *Juan Luis Vives and the Emotions*. Carbondale, IL: Southern Illinois UP, 1989. Print.

Oberhuber, Konrad. *Raphael: The Paintings*. Munich: Prestel Verlag, 1999. Print.

Olmsted, Wendy. *The Imperfect Friend: Emotion and Rhetoric in Sidney, Milton and Their Contexts*. Toronto: U of Toronto P, 2008. Print.

O'Neil, Edward N. "Plutarch on Friendship." *Greco-Roman Perspectives on Friendship*. Ed. John T. Fitzgerald. Atlanta, GA: Scholars Press, 1997. 105–22. Print.

Pakaluk, Michael, ed. *Other Selves: Philosophers on Friendship*. Indianapolis, IN: Hackett, 1991.

Pangle, Lorraine Smith. *Aristotle and the Philosophy of Friendship*. Cambridge: Cambridge UP, 2003. Print.

Parry, Graham. *The Golden Age Restor'd: The Culture of the Stuart Court, 1603–42*. Manchester: Manchester UP, 1981. Print.

——. *The Seventeenth Century: The Intellectual and Cultural Context of English Literature, 1603–1700*. London: Longman, 1989. Print.

Paster, Gail Kern, Katherine Rowe, and Mary Floyd-Wilson, eds. *Reading the Early Modern Passions: Essays in the Early Modern History of Emotion*. Philadelphia: U of Pennsylvania P, 2004. Print.

Pateman, Carole. *The Sexual Contract*. Stanford, CA: Stanford UP, 1988. Print.

Peck, Russell A. "Edgar's Pilgrimage: High Comedy in *King Lear*." *SEL* 7.2 (1967): 219–37. Print.

Pesuit, Margaret. *Representations of the Courtesan in Sixteenth-Century Venice: Sex, Class, and Power*. MA Thesis, McGill University, 1997. Ann Arbor: UMI, 2003. ATT MQ37227. Print.

Philips, Katherine. *The Collected Works of Katherine Philips*. Vol 1: *The Matchless Orinda*. Ed. Patrick Thomas. Stump Cross: Stump Cross Books, 1990. Print.

——. *Poems*. London: Printed by J.M. for H. Herringman, 1667. Print.

Phillippy, Patricia. "The Maid's Lawful Liberty: Service, the Household, and 'Mother B' in Isabella Whitney's 'A Sweet Nosegay.'" *Modern Philology* 95.4 (1998): 439–62. Print.

Piccolomini, Manfredi. *The Brutus Revival: Parricide and Tyrannicide During the Renaissance*. Carbondale and Edwardsville: Southern Illinois UP, 1991. Print.

Pirotti, Umberto. *Benedetto Varchi e la cultura del su tempo*. Florence: Olschki, 1971. Print.

Pisana, Camilla. *Lettere di cortigiane del Rinascimento*. Ed. Angelo Romano. Rome: Salerno Editrice, 1990. Print.

Plat, Hugh. *The Floures of Philosophie, With the Pleasures of Poetrie annexed to them, as wel plesant to be read as profitable to be folowed of all men*. London: Henrie Bynneman and Frauncis Coldocke, 1592. Print.

Plato. "Le Discours de la queste d'amytié, dict, Lysis de Platon." Trans. Bonaventure des Periers. *Recueil des œuvres de feu Bonaventure des Periers*. Lyon: Jean de Tournes, 1544. 1–44. Print.

——. *Republic*. Trans. and ed. Allan Bloom. New York: Basic, 1968. Print.

——. *Republic*. Trans. Desmond Lee. Harmondsworth: Penguin, 1955. Print.

——. *The Symposium*. Trans. Walter Hamilton. Harmondsworth: Penguin, 1951. Print.

Plutarch. *Moralia*. Trans. Frank Cole Babbitt. Loeb Classical Library. London: Heinemann, 1926. Print.

——. *The philosophie, commonlie called, the morals, written by the learned philosopher Plutarch of Chaeronea. Translated out of Greeke into English, and conferred with the Latin translations and the French*. Trans. Philemon Holland. London: Arnold Hatfield, 1603. Print.

Pont, Robert. "Of the Union of Britayne." *The Jacobean Union: Six Tracts of 1604*. Eds Bruce Galloway and Brian P. Levack. Edinburgh: Scottish History Society, 1985. Print.

Pratt, Kathryn. "'Wounds still cureless': Estates of Loss in Mary Wroth's *Urania*." *Privacy, Domesticity, and Women in Early Modern England*. Ed. Corinne S. Abate. Burlington, VT: Ashgate, 2003. 45–64. Print.

Prisco, Michele. *Raphael*. New York: Rizzoli, 2005. Print.

Reeser, Todd W. "Fracturing the Male Androgyne in the *Heptaméron*." *Romance Quarterly* 51.1 (2004): 15–28. Print.

Reiss, Timothy. *Mirages of the Self: Patterns of Personhood in Ancient and Early Modern Europe*. Stanford: Stanford UP, 2003. Print.

Reynolds, Régine. "*L'Heptaméron* de Marguerite de Navarre: Influence de Castiglione." *Studi di Letteratura francese* 5 (1979): 25–39. Print.

Riedeman, Peter. "Account of our Religion, Doctrine, and Faith" [1542]. *Anabaptism in Outline*. Ed. Walter Klaassen. Scottdale: Herald Press, 1981. 259–60. Print.

Roberts, Sasha. *Reading Shakespeare's Poems in Early Modern England*. New York: Palgrave Macmillan, 2003. Print.

Robin, Diana. "Courtesans, Celebrity, and Print Culture in Renaissance Venice: Tullia d'Aragona, Gaspara Stampa, and Veronica Franco." *Italian Women and the City: Essays*. Eds Janet Levarie Smarr and Daria Valentini. Madison, NJ: Fairleigh Dickinson UP, 2003. Print.

Rogers, John. *The Matter of Revolution: Science, Poetry, and Politics in the Age of Milton*. Ithaca: Cornell UP, 1996. Print.

Rosenberg, John D. "King Lear and His Comforters." *Essays in Criticism* 16.2 (April 1966): 135–46. Print.

Rosenthal, Margaret F. *The Honest Courtesan: Veronica Franco, Citizen and Writer in Sixteenth-Century Venice*. Chicago: U of Chicago P, 1992. Print.

Røstvig, Maren-Sophie. *The Happy Man: Studies in the Metamorphosis of a Classical Ideal*. 2 vols. Second ed. Norway: Norwegian Universities Press, 1962. Print.

Roth, Cecil. *The Last Florentine Republic*. London: Methuen, 1925. Print.

Routh, E.M.G. *Sir Thomas More and His Friends, 1477–1535*. London: Oxford UP, 1934. Print.

Rowley, William, Thomas Dekker, and John Ford. *The Witch of Edmonton* in *Three Jacobean Witchcraft Plays*. Eds Peter Corbin and Douglas Sedge. Manchester: Manchester UP, 1989. Print.

Rubin, Gayle. "The Traffic in Women: Notes on the 'Political Economy' of Sex." *Towards an Anthropology of Women*. Ed. Rayna R. Reiter. New York: Monthly Review Press, 1975. 157–210. Print.

Rudolph, Julia. *Revolution by Degrees: James Tyrrell and Whig Political Thought in the Late Seventeenth Century*. New York: Palgrave Macmillan, 2002. Print.

Ruggiero, Guido. "Who's Afraid of Giuliana Napolitana: Pleasure, Fear and Imagining the Courtesan at the End of the Renaissance." *The Courtesan's Art: Cross-Cultural Perspectives*. Eds Martha Feldman and Bonnie Gordon. Oxford: Oxford UP, 2006. 280–92. Print.

Sanchez, Melissa E. "The Politics of Masochism in Mary Wroth's *Urania*." *ELH* 74.2 (2007): 449–78. Print.

Sanctio, Bernardo. Jan. 13, 1537. "Letter to Marino Caracciolo." CSM 12bis. Archivio di Stato, Milan. Fols 32r–33v.

Sandars, N.K., ed. *The Epic of Gilgamesh: An English Version with an Introduction*. London: Penguin Books, 1972. Print.

Sattler, Michael, et al. "Congregational Order." *The Legacy of Michael Sattler*. Ed. John Howard Yoder. Scottdale: Herald Press, 1973. 44–5. Print.

——. "Letter to the Church at Horb." *The Legacy of Michael Sattler*. Ed. John Howard Yoder. Scottdale: Herald Press, 1973. 55–65. Print.

——. "The Schleitheim Brotherly Union." *The Legacy of Michael Sattler*. Ed. John Howard Yoder. Scottdale: Herald Press, 1973. 28–43. Print.

Scarry, Elaine. *On Beauty and Being Just*. Princeton: Princeton UP, 1999. Print.

Schachter, Marc. "'Egli s'innamorò del suo valore': Leone, Bradamante and Ruggiero in the 1532 *Orlando Furioso*." *Modern Language Notes* 115 (2000): 64–79. Print.

——. *Voluntary Servitude and the Erotics of Friendship: From Classical Antiquity to Early Modern France*. Burlington, VT: Ashgate, 2008. Print.

Schiemer, Leonhard. "A Letter to the Church at Rattenberg." *Anabaptism in Outline*. Ed. Walter Klaassen. Scottdale: Herald Press, 1981. 104–5. Print.

Schleiner, Winfried. *Cure by Imagination: Melancholy Genius and Utopia in the Renaissance*. Wiesbaden: Renaissance Forschung, 1991. Vol. 10. Print.

Schoeck, R.J. "Telling More from Erasmus: An *Essai* in Renaissance Humanism." *Moreana* XIII, 91–2 (1986): 11–19. Print.

Schoenfeldt, Michael C. *Bodies and Selves in Early Modern England: Physiology and Inwardness in Spenser, Herbert, and Milton*. Cambridge: Cambridge UP, 1999. Print.

Schroeder, Frederic M. "Friendship in Aristotle and Peripatetic Philosophers." *Greco-Roman Perspectives on Friendship*. Ed. John T. Fitzgerald. Atlanta, GA: Scholars Press, 1997. 35–57. Print.

Segni, Bernardo. *Istorie Fiorentine dall'Anno MDXXVII al MDLV*. Ed. G. Gargani. Florence: Barbèra, Bianchi e Comp., 1857. Print.

Seneca. *Epistulae Morales ad Lucilium*. Trans. Richard M. Gummere. Cambridge, MA: Harvard UP, 1917.

Shakespeare, William. *Macbeth*. Ed. A.R. Braunmuller. Cambridge: Cambridge UP, 2008. Print.

Shanley, Mary Lyndon. "Marriage Contract and Social Contract in Seventeenth Century English Political Thought." *Western Political Quarterly* 32.1 (1979): 79–91. Print.

Shannon, Laurie. *Sovereign Amity: Figures of Friendship in Shakespearean Contexts*. Chicago: Chicago UP, 2002. Print.

Sharpe, Kevin. *Criticism and Compliment: The Politics of Literature in the England of Charles I*. Cambridge: Cambridge UP, 1987. Print.

Shepard, Alexandra. *Meanings of Manhood in Early Modern England*. Oxford: Oxford UP, 2003. Print.

Shifflett, Andrew. "Kings, Poets, and the Power of Forgiveness, 1642–1660." *English Literary Renaissance* (2003): 88–109. Print.

Shuger, Debora. "Castigating Livy: The Rape of Lucretia and *The Old Arcadia*." *Renaissance Quarterly* 51 (1998): 526–48. Print.

Sidney, Philip. *"An Apology for Poetry" and "Astrophil and Stella": Texts and Contexts*. Ed. Peter C. Herman. Glen Allen, VA: College Publishing, 2001. Print.

——. *The Countesse of Pembrokes Arcadia*. London: William Ponsonbie, 1590. Facsimile ed. Kent, OH: Kent State UP, 1970. Print.

——. *The Countess of Pembroke's Arcadia*. Ed. Maurice Evans. Harmondsworth: Penguin, 1977. Print.

——. *The Old Arcadia*. Ed. Katherine Duncan-Jones. Oxford: Oxford UP, 1983. Print.

Sinfield, Alan. "*Macbeth*: History, Ideology and Intellectuals." *Faultlines: Cultural Materialism and the Politics of Dissident Reading*. Oxford: Clarendon, 1992. 95–108. Print.

Siraisi, Nancy G. *Medieval and Early Renaissance Medicine: An Introduction to Knowledge and Practice*. Chicago: U of Chicago P, 1990. Print.

Smith, Vanessa, and Richard Yeo, eds. *Friendship in Early Modern Philosophy and Science*. Special issue of *Parergon* 26.2 (2009). Online.

Snyder, C. Arnold. "Revolution and the Swiss Brethren: The Case of Michael Sattler." *Church History* 50.3 (September 1981): 276–87. Print.

Souers, Philip Webster. *The Matchless Orinda*. Cambridge, MA: Harvard UP, 1931. Print.

Speroni, Sperone. *Dialogo d'amore*. *Trattatisti del Cinquecento*, Vol. 1. Ed. M. Pozzi. Milan and Naples: Riccardo Ricciardi Editore, 1978. 511–63. Print.

Stadler, Ulrich. "Cherished Instructions on Sin, Excommunication, and the Community of Goods" [c. 1537]. *Spiritual and Anabaptist Writers*. Eds George Williams and A.M. Mergal. Philadelphia: Westminster Press, 1957. 274–84. Print.

Stanivukovic, Goran V. "'Knights in Armes': The Homoerotics of the English Renaissance Prose Romances." *Prose Fiction and Early Modern Sexualities in England, 1570–1640*. Eds Constance C. Relihan and Goran V. Stanivukovic. London: Palgrave, 2003. 171–92. Print.

Starkey, Thomas. *A Dialogue between Pole and Lupset*. Ed. T.F. Mayer. London: Royal Historical Society, 1989. Print.

Stauffer, Richard. *The Humanness of John Calvin*. Trans. George H. Shriver. Nashville: Abingdon Press, 1971. Print.

Stephens, J.N. *The Fall of the Florentine Republic: 1512–1530*. Oxford: Clarendon, 1983. Print.

Stern-Gillet, Suzanne. *Aristotle's Philosophy of Friendship*. Albany: SUNY UP, 1995. Print.

Stillman, Robert E. "The Truths of a Slippery World: Poetry and Tyranny in Sidney's *Defence*." *Renaissance Quarterly* 55 (2002): 1287–319. Print.

Stone, Lawrence. *The Family, Sex and Marriage in England 1500–1800*. New York: Harper & Row, 1977. Print.

Stretter, Robert. "Cicero on Stage: Damon and Phithias and the Fate of Classical Friendship in English Renaissance Drama." *Texas Studies in Literature and Language* 47.4 (2005): 345–65. Print.

——. "Rewriting Perfect Friendship in Chaucer's *Knight's Tale* and Lydgete's *Fabula Duorum Mercatotum*." *The Chaucer Review* 37.3 (2003): 234–52. Print.

Strier, Richard. "Against the Rule of Reason: Praise of Passion from Petrarch to Luther to Shakespeare to Herbert." *Reading the Early Modern Passions: Essays in the Cultural History of Emotion*. Eds Gail Kern Paster, Karen Rowe, and Mary Floyd-Wilson. Philadelphia: U of Pennsylvania P, 2004. 23–42. Print.

——. *Resistant Structures: Particularity, Radicalism, and Renaissance Texts.* Berkeley, CA: U of California P, 1995. Print.

Surtz, Edward. "More's *Apologia Pro Utopia Sua.*" *MLQ* 19 (1958): 319–24. Print.

Taylor, Jeremy. *A Discourse on the Nature, Offices and Measures of Friendship.* London, 1657. Print.

Tetel, Marcel. *L'Heptaméron de Marguerite de Navarre: Thèmes, language et structure.* Paris: Klincksieck, 1991. Print.

Thom, Johan C. "'Harmonious Equality': The *Topos* of Friendship in Neo-pythagorean Writings." *Greco-Roman Perspectives on Friendship.* Ed. John T. Fitzgerald. Atlanta: Scholars Press, 1997. 77–103. Print.

Thomas, Keith. *The Ends of Life: Roads to Fulfilment in Early Modern England.* Oxford: Oxford UP, 2009. Print.

Thomas, Patrick. "Introduction." *The Collected Works of Katherine Philips, the Matchless Orinda.* Vol. I. Stump Cross: Stump Cross Books, 1990. Print.

Tilney, Edmund. *The Flower of Friendship: A Renaissance Dialogue Contesting Marriage.* Ed. Valerie Wayne. Ithaca: Cornell UP, 1992. Print.

Tomlinson, Sophie. *Women on Stage in Stuart Drama.* Cambridge: Cambridge UP, 2005. Print.

Tournon, André. "Rules of the Game." *Critical Tales: New Studies of the Heptaméron and Early Modern Culture.* Eds John D. Lyons and Mary B. McKinley. Philadelphia: U of Philadelphia P, 1993. 188–99. Print.

Traub, Valerie. "Friendship's Loss: Alan Bray's Making of History." *Love, Friendship and Faith in Europe, 1300–1800.* Eds Laura Gowing, Michael Hunter, and Miri Rubin. New York: Palgrave Macmillan, 2005. 15–42. Print.

Trexler, Richard. "The Friendship of Citizens." *Dependence in Context in Renaissance Florence.* Binghamton, NY: Centre for Medieval & Renaissance Studies, 1994. Print.

Trull, Mary. "'Philargus' House Is Not in All Places': Marriage, Privacy, and the Overheard Lament in Mary Wroth's *Urania.*" *ELR* 35.3 (2005): 459–89. Print.

Tully, James. "Locke." *The Cambridge History of Political Thought 1450–1700.* Ed. J.H. Burns. Cambridge: Cambridge UP, 1991. 615–52. Print.

Turner, James Grantham. *One Flesh: Paradisal Marriage and Sexual Relations in the Age of Milton.* Oxford: Oxford UP. 1987. Print.

Tyrrell, James. *Bibliotheca politica.* London: Printed for Richard Baldwin, 1691/2. *EEBO.* Web. 22 August 2006.

——. *A brief disquisition of the law of nature ... as also his confutations of Mr. Hobb's principles put into another method.* London: Printed by Richard Baldwin, 1692. *EEBO.* Web. 22 August 2006.

——. *Patriarcha non monarcha.* London: Printed for Richard Janeway, 1681. *EEBO.* Web. 22 August 2006.

——. "To the memory of the Excellent *Orinda.*" *Poems.* By Katherine Philips. London: Printed by J.M. for H. Herringman, 1667. e1–e1^v. Print.

Vance, Jacob. "Humanist Polemics, Christian Morals: A Hypothesis on Marguerite de Navarre's *Heptaméron* and the Problem of Self-Love." *Modern Language Notes* 120 Supplement (2005): S181–S195. Print.

Varchi, Benedetto. *Storia Fiorentina*. Ed. Lelio Arbib. 3 vols. Florence: Società Editrice delle Storie del Nardi et del Varchi, 1838–41. Print.

Venier, Lorenzo. *La Zaffetta*. Catania: Libreria Tirelli di F. Guaitolini, 1929. Print.

Venier, Maffio. *Il Libro Chiuso di Matlio Venier*. Ed. Manlio Dazzi. Venice: Neri Pozza, 1956. Print.

Vigarello, Georges. *A History of Rape: Sexual Violence in France from the 16th to the 20th Century*. 1998. Trans. Jean Birrell. Cambridge: Polity, 2001. Print.

Villard, Renaud. *Du Bien commun au mal nécessaire: tyrannies, assassinats politiques et souveraineté en Italie, vers 1470–vers 1600*. Rome: École française de Rome, 2008. Print.

Vives, Juan Luis. "De coniugio." *De institutione foeminae christianae*. Trans. and ed. Charles Fantazzi and Constant Matheeussen. 2 vols. Leiden: Brill, 1996–98. Print.

——. *De institutione foeminae christianae*. Trans. and ed. Charles Fantazzi and Constant Matheeussen. 2 vols. Leiden: Brill, 1996–98. The translation is reprinted in *The Education of a Christian Woman: A Sixteenth-Century Manual*. Chicago: U of Chicago P, 2000. Print.

——. *The Instruction of a Christen Woman* (1531). Ed. Virginia Walcott Beauchamp. Urbana: U of Illinois P, 2002. Print.

——. *The Office and Duetie of an Husband*. Trans. Thomas Paynell. (London, 1555?). *EEBO*. 30 June 2009. Web. 1 June 2009.

Wagner, Geraldine. "Contesting Love's Tyranny: Socially Outcast Women and the Marginalized Female Body in Lady Mary Wroth's *Urania*." *English Studies* 87.5 (2006): 577–601. Print.

Wall, Wendy. "Isabella Whitney and the Female Legacy." *ELH* 58.1 (1991): 35–62. Print.

Wall-Randell, Sarah. "Reading the Book of the Self in Shakespeare's *Cymbeline* and Wroth's *Urania*." *Staging Early Modern Romance: Prose Fiction, Dramatic Romance, and Shakespeare*. Eds Mary Ellen Lamb and Valerie Wayne. New York: Routledge, 2009. 107–21. Print.

Warren, Michael. "The Diminution of Kent." *The Division of the Kingdoms: Shakespeare's Two Versions of King Lear*. Eds Gary Taylor and Michael Warren. Oxford: Clarendon, 1983. 59–73. Print.

——, ed. *The Parallel King Lear, 1608–1623*. By William Shakespeare. Berkeley, CA: U of California P, 1989. Print.

Weiner, Andrew D. "Sidney/Spenser/Shakespeare: Influence/Intertextuality/Invention." *Influence and Intertextuality in Literary History*. Eds Jay Clayton and Eric Rothstein. Wisconsin: U of Wisconsin P, 1991. 245–68. Print.

White, Thomas I. "Legend and Reality: The Friendship Between More and Erasmus." *Supplementum festivum: Studies in Honor of Paul Oskar Kristeller.*

Eds James Hankins, John Monfasani, and Frederick Purnell, Jr. Binghamton, New York: Medieval & Renaissance Texts & Studies, 1987. 489–504. Print.

Whitney, Isabella. *The copy of a letter, lately written in meeter, by a yonge gentilwoman: to her vnconstant louer: With an admonitio[n] to al yong gentilwomen, and to all other mayds in general to beware of mennes flattery. By Is. VV. Newly ioyned to a loueletter sent by a bachelor, (a most faithful louer) to an vnconstant and faithles mayden.* London: Richard Jones, 1567. *EEBO*. Web. 2 July 2009.

——. *A Sweet Nosgay, or Pleasant Posy.* London: Richard Jones, 1573. Providence, RI: Brown University Women Writers Project, 1999. Print.

Williamson, Marilyn L. *Raising Their Voices: British Women Writers, 1650–1750.* Detroit: Wayne State UP, 1990. Print.

Winn, Colette H. "Aux origins du discourse feminine sur l'amitié. Marguerite de Navarre, *La Coche* (1541)." *Women in French Studies* 7 (1999): 9–24. Print.

Woods-Marsden, Joanna. "One Artist, Two Sitters, One Role: Raphael's Papal Portraits." *The Cambridge Companion to Raphael.* Ed. Marcia B. Hall. Cambridge: Cambridge UP, 2005. 120–40. Print.

Wolin, Sheldon. *Politics and Vision: Continuity and Innovation in Western Political Thought.* Second ed. Princeton: Princeton UP, 2004. Print.

Wootton, David. "Friendship Portrayed: A New Account of *Utopia.*" *History Workshop Journal* 45 (1998): 28–47. Print.

——. "Friendship Portrayed: A New Account of *Utopia.*" *The Renaissance: Italy and Abroad.* Ed. John Jeffries Martin. London: Routledge, 2003. 253–75. Print.

Wright, Thomas. *The Passions of the Minde in Generall.* London: Valentine Simmes for Walter Burre, 1604. *EEBO*. Web. 12 March 2009.

Wroth, Mary. *The first part of The Countess of Montgomery's Urania.* Ed. Josephine A. Roberts. *Medieval & Renaissance Texts & Studies.* Vol. 140. Binghamton, NY: Center for Medieval and Early Renaissance Studies, 1995. Print.

——. *The second part of the Countess of Montgomery's Urania.* Ed. Josephine A. Roberts; completed by Suzanne Gossett and Janel Mueller. *Medieval and Renaissance Texts & Studies.* Vol. 211. Tempe, AZ: Arizona Center for Medieval and Renaissance Studies, 1999. Print.

Wynne-Davies, Marion. "'For *Worth*, Not Weakness, Makes in Use but One': Literary Dialogues in an English Renaissance Family." *"The Double Voice": Gendered Writing in Early Modern England.* Eds Danielle Clark and Elizabeth Clarke. New York: St. Martin's Press, 2000. 164–84. Print.

Xenephon. *Hiero or Tyrannicus. On Tyranny.* Ed. Leo Strauss. Ithaca: Cornell UP, 1968. 1–20. Print.

Index